Outlook Annoyances

Outlook Annoyances

Woody Leonhard, Lee Hudspeth,
and T.J. Lee

O'REILLY™

Cambridge · Köln · Paris · Sebastopol · Tokyo

Outlook Annoyances, First Edition
by Woody Leonhard, Lee Hudspeth & T.J. Lee

Published by O'Reilly & Associates, Inc., 101 Morris Street, Sebastopol, CA 95472.

Editor: Ron Petrusha

Technical Editor: Frederic Gordon

Production Editor: John Files

Editorial and Production Services: *TIPS* Technical Publishing

Printing History:

June 1998: First Edition.

This book is printed on acid-free paper with 85% recycled content, 15% post-consumer waste. O'Reilly & Associates is committed to using paper with the highest recycled content available consistent with high quality.

ISBN: 1-56592-384-7   [7/98]

Four years ago, Linda and I started a non-profit organization called the Tibetan Children's Fund. As of this writing TCF sponsors more than 150 refugee children in northern India and Nepal. These children are chosen on the basis of financial need and scholastic performance—particularly in English, math, and science. Most of them come from families that can only be described as destitute; many have been orphaned. Few of the refugee families have more than one room to call their own, many live in shanties, and none can afford medical care on even the most basic level.

TCF exists because of people like you. A significant portion of the proceeds from the sale of this book go to the TCF. Donations from people like you make TCF possible. Yes, computer geeks *do* care. And the donations are deductible.

The Tibetan Children's Fund is a unique organization. Nobody draws a salary. There's no "overhead." Volunteers who travel to India pay their own way. They don't solicit donations by phone, or hire companies to mount advertising campaigns. When they need to put something together—say, a new brochure, or a newsletter, or a web page—volunteers do the work, and companies donate the supplies. The net result: every single penny donated by individuals goes directly to the children. I know. I keep a close eye on it. My money's in there, too.

TCF isn't a religious organization. It isn't a political organization. It isn't a welfare organization, either. Sponsored kids must maintain good grades or they're put on probation. If they still can't keep their grades up, we remove them, to make way for kids who can. TCF has no particular axe to grind or point of view to impose: they just want to give the kids a chance to succeed in the world at large. Heaven knows the Tibetans have had a terrible time just surviving.

I could write about TCF's successes, and its failures, but the tales would fill a book. Suffice it to say that TCF has been very fortunate to find and support a handful of really brilliant refugee kids—and it's been unfortunate enough to see more than a few children die, when good medical care at the right time would've made all the difference.

If you would like to know more about TCF, please write to:

Tibetan's Children Fund
Post Office Box 473
Pinecliffe, Colorado USA 80471
Phone: (303) 642-0492
Email: *woody@wopr.com*

Thanks for your help.

— Woody Leonhard
Coal Creek Canyon, Colorado

Table of Contents

Preface

Hmmm, let's see, just where was that setting? Oh yeah, it's the Tools menu, then click on Options—so far so good—now, was it Preferences? No, I think it was on the Other tab—yeah, that's it—now click on the Advanced Options button and I should be able to...oh, another dialog box. Wait, now, I think it's the Custom Forms button that takes me to the Options dialog. Okay, now a final click on the Manage Forms button and that should let me...WHAT! Where's the Manage Forms button? Arrrrrrgh!

Outlook *is* annoying.

Outlook is great, too, and we use it to do real work every day. It manages our contacts' names, addresses, phone numbers, and email addresses; it tracks our appointments; it lets us assign tasks to each other; it does meeting requests. Heck, Outlook holds our collective email lives in its sometimes shaky cyberhands. It has an incredible depth of useful features. Even after working with test versions for many months, the product continues to take our collective breaths away. *If only it wasn't so annoying!*

At best, Outlook 97 is still in its beta cycle and Outlook 98 is a 1.0 release camouflaged with an 8.5 version number. Remember when the first release was "1" and the next release was "2"? Ah, the good ol' days before the Microsoft marketeers took over. But we digress. Mixed in with the many outstanding features that Outlook sports, you'll find a number of very annoying gotchas, hiccups, and pitfalls. So, what's not to like? One of Woody's favorite, ahem, annoyances (to coin a phrase) crops up when you reply to a formatted message: heaven only knows what format your reply will be in. Outlook also lacks many features most Office 97 aficionados take for granted; VBA stands at the top of that list.

The good news is that a little knowledge can go a long way in helping you cope with Outlook's annoying eccentricities, and you're holding that knowledge in your hands right now. From checklists for troubleshooting email problems to configuration and interface optimizing tips, we'll walk you through the landmines right to the productivity gold.

And by the way, that Manage Forms button won't appear on the Options dialog if you're running Outlook 98's Internet Only mode. It's a bug. Annoying, huh?

The Book's Audience

If you've tried Outlook only to be left feeling frustrated, dazed, and confused, we sympathize. The program is on the obtuse side, its myriad features are buried beneath a labyrinthine interface, the Help won't help; it's enough to peg your annoyance meter. All you want to do is be more productive with your computer's software.

Whether you're a novice or a seasoned pro, we don't think you need more marketing hype. You don't need to be told you're the dummy, nor do you need a rehash of the...well, we were going to say "User's Manual," but they don't have user manuals anymore. Instead, you get beeping icons that won't tell you what you need or want to know. *What you need is some help!* Someone with useful advice so you can harness the substantial horsepower that hums under the Outlook hood.

That's where this book comes in. Trying to make Outlook do email distribution lists? Problems when searching, sorting, entering, or converting data? Not clear on the differences between Internet Only versus Corporate/Workgroup modes, or how to force Outlook to let you install the mode you want instead of the mode it mandates you need? If you've ever found yourself annoyed with Outlook, this is the book for you.

Also, if you're thinking about migrating from another personal information manager (PIM) product and would like that process to be as painless as possible, then this is the book for you.

Organization of This Book

The book contains nine chapters.

Chapter 1, *It's a Bit Like Whacking Your TV Set,* discusses the causes, nature, and most annoying annoyances to be found in Outlook 97 and 98. An insightful journey through a full-blown Outlook crisis and some of the voodoo "fix-it" techniques that we've discovered but that you won't read about anywhere else. Of course, we also describe the new and improved features that make working with Outlook 98 worthwhile.

Chapter 2, *Vital Changes, Settings, and Customizations,* shows you how to figure out the numerous versions of Outlook floating around in general circulation. Find out the best way to upgrade to Outlook 98 so you can choose which of its three modes to install. Get the lay of the Outlook land from Personal Folders, and learn how to fix a plethora of annoyances with add-ins and some hard-won know-how. Learn how to optimize Outlook's many configuration settings and create your own custom toolbars.

Chapter 3, *Outlook Repair Tactics,* shows you how to troubleshoot and deal with the most common email problems you are likely to run into using Outlook. This chapter covers creating new Personal Store files in Outlook 97 and in Outlook 98's Internet Only and Corporate/Workgroup modes, as well as how to avoid difficulties when setting up various information services.

Chapter 4, *Enigmatic Journal,* takes you on a thorough tour of this potentially intrusive and poorly understood facility. Find out just what the Journal does and how you can use it for tracking email, meetings, and task items. From manually creating Journal items, to letting the Auto-Recording feature book activity work for you in the background, to using the Journal to tame your telephone call tracking, we take the mystery out of this amazing facility.

Chapter 5, *Outlook's Key Ingredients,* covers how best to enter and use information in each of Outlook's various facilities. We share many tips, tricks, and pitfall avoidance techniques for working with the Calendar, Contact, Task, Note, and Mail facilities. Learn what email nicknames are all about and how to attach flags and alerts to outgoing messages. We cover everything from assigning and monitoring tasks to the difference between appointments and meetings.

Chapter 6, *A Cookbook for Conversion,* focuses on importing data into Outlook from various sources with a minimum of fuss. You'll learn how to walk through the data mapping minefield and convert Personal Address Book (PAB) entries to Contacts. Then shift productivity into high gear by using AutoCreate to transfer Outlook entries from one facility to another. Finally, find out what Outlook offers by way of backup and archiving features and how best to utilize them.

Chapter 7, *Beyond the Basics*, shows you how to utilize some of Outlook's most useful features step by step. View and filter like a pro with user interface tips that can save you time and make Outlook easier to use. Learn to categorize your data and to create and maintain your categories. Set reminders on tasks and calendar items, set recurring reminders that don't clutter up your calendar, flag and set reminders on incoming emails, build Outlook email distribution lists, and integrate Outlook with Word's impressive mail merge feature.

Chapter 8, *Introduction to VBScript, the Outlook Object Model, and Custom Forms*, is a tutorial on Outlook's macro language, VBScript, and how to use it with custom forms. This chapter also covers Visual Basic for Applications (VBA), the common macro programming language found in Outlook's Office siblings, which you can use to control events and processes in Outlook from other applications. We discuss working within the Script Editor and walk you through creating several VBScript programs, as well as provide examples of Excel controlling Outlook and Outlook controlling Word. Find out just what the heck an object model is and what it means to you.

Chapter 9, *Where and How to Get Help*, is a discussion of your best sources for additional help and information on Outlook. Books, magazines, newsletters, listservers, and Web sites—we point you in the right direction for the latest and greatest sources of news and knowledge on Outlook.

Conventions in This Book

Throughout this book we've used the following typographic conventions:

`Constant width`
indicates a language construct such as that used in VBA. Code fragments and code examples appear exclusively in constant width text. In syntax statements, text in constant width indicates such language elements as the function's or procedure's name and any invariable elements required by the syntax. Key combinations are also shown in constant width, as are VBA language statements (like `FOR...NEXT`) and constants.

Italic

in command syntax indicates parameter names. Italicized words in the text also represent the names of procedures and functions, as well as variable and parameter names. System elements like filenames and pathnames also are italicized.

→

is used to indicate a drop-down or pop-up menu command. For example, the View menu pops down revealing Current View, which in turn shows another submenu. To indicate the selection Messages from this submenu, we would write View → Current View → Messages.

How to Contact Us

We have tested and verified all the information in this book to the best of our ability, but you may find that features have changed (or even that we have made mistakes!). Please let us know about any errors you find, as well as your suggestions for future editions, by writing to:

O'Reilly & Associates, Inc.
101 Morris Street
Sebastopol, CA 95472
(800) 998-9938 (in the U.S. or Canada)
(707) 829-0515 (international/local)
(707) 829-0104 (FAX)

You can also send messages electronically. To be put on our mailing list or to request a catalog, send email to:

nuts@oreilly.com

To ask technical questions or comment on the book, send email to:

bookquestions@oreilly.com

Obtaining Updated Information

The VBScript and VBA code listings in *Outlook Annoyances* can be found on our FTP site at *ftp://ftp.ora.com/published/oreilly/windows/outlook.annoy*. These code listings, updates to the material contained in this book, plus information on the other books in the Annoyances series are also available on our Web site at *http://www.primeconsulting.com/annoyances*.

Acknowledgments

Our heartfelt thanks to Ron Petrusha, without whose help and guidance this book in the Annoyances series would not exist. Troy Mott and Katie Gardner also played an important part in getting this book in print, and thanks to Sara Winge and John Dockery, who keep the sales machine running. Claudette Moore was the lynchpin that held everything together. Many thanks to Helen Feddema, Darrique Barton, Dan Butler, as well as the entire Microsoft design team that created this amazing application.

Special thanks go to Frederic Gordon, our daring technical editor, who is always willing to risk his data and his hard disk while testing one hare-brained Outlook scheme after another. And for keeping us forever on course with frequent reality checks.

Helen Feddema did an outstanding job on her technical review of Chapter 8. She submitted excellent code samples as well (see the chapter for the citations).

Thanks to David Karp, who penned *Windows Annoyances,* the book that started the series. Be sure to visit David's Windows Annoyances site at *http://www.annoyances.org.*

Thanks to everyone who worked on the production of this book. Rachel Pearce Anderson (Archer Editorial Services) was the copy editor, Sarah O'Keefe (Scriptorium Publishing Services, Inc.) was the compositor and indexer, and Jennifer Huntley Mario was the proofreader.

Woody would like to personally thank his loving wife Linda, who's been putting up with him for 20 years, and his nine-year-old son Justin, who already describes himself as a computer nerd. Their considerable accomplishments have made him very proud.

T.J. not only thanks Loretta (who as a Daisy Troop leader, cub scout Den leader, wife, and mother works much harder than he does), but is extremely grateful she married him in the first place. Thanks also to his four kids, Andreana, Jason, Vicky, and Lillian, who are pretty much perfect, ah, most of the time. And thanks to M. David Stone for his help and counsel over the years.

From Lee Hudspeth, heartfelt thanks all around to his endearing wife Liz, his sons Aaron and Tate, his parents Eloise and George, and to Gloria, his second mom.

And from the three of us to all of you out there in the trenches just trying to make Outlook and Microsoft Office do useful work—fighting annoyances day in and day out while trying to retain your sanity. Keep 'em flying!

1

It's a Bit Like Whacking Your TV Set

Picture this. You run email for the last time one evening, your outbound mail is sent, some stuff pours in that you defer reading until the next day—after all, you've been hard at it for 12 hours already. Enough's enough.

The next day you start by typing up three new ideas for your partner to comment on, fire each one off as a separate email, head for the coffee room for a fresh libation, and upon returning discover the three emails weren't sent. They're sitting in your Outbox, motionless. And over the course of the next two days they—and any other outbound messages—prove immutable. What's up?

Tracking down the cause—and cure—of such a seemingly innocuous little mishap is par for the course for the Outlook aficionado. It's awfully bloody out on the bleeding edge. That's what this book is all about. It's your comfort, your succor, your safety net, your Reference of First Resort. Because if you use Outlook, you're going to get hurt, and hurt bad, over and over again. (We have, and lived to tell the tale.) After all, in spite of its numerous compelling features, Outlook 97 was really a version 1.0 product still in its beta cycle. Look at the various versions—8.0, 8.01, the three different flavors of 8.02, 8.03, and so on—as different beta builds, and you'll understand where Outlook is coming from and where it's headed. With the advent of Outlook 98, you can expect greater stability than its predecessor, with some interesting new features to boot. Nonetheless, the vast majority of annoying bugs and inconsistencies remain unsquashed in Outlook 98, so read on.

Consider the following anecdote straight from our own Outlook X-files. The events you are about to read are from a real Outlook 97 problem report; not even the names were changed to protect the guilty. (Well, maybe some minor editorial polishing and major excision of well-justified profanity.) If you're using Outlook 98, the problems you experience may be just as severe, but the details will most certainly change.

Tuesday

It's the kind of day on the coast that makes you want to shoot off an email to someone back east so you can casually mention the glorious outside temperature.

I'm running Outlook 97 (pre SR1-EU) with the latest IMEP update and no add-ins (I'm a no-frills kinda guy). Feeling inspired, I knock out a handful of outgoing messages in nothing flat.

NOTE   What's SR1-EU? What's IMEP? Good questions. These are
              the latest versions of Office 97 (Service Release 1-Enter-
              prise Update) and Outlook's Internet Mail Enhancement
              Patch, respectively. We cover that labyrinthine story and
              the straight scoop on how to get the latest version of Of-
              fice 97 and Outlook in Chapter 2, *Vital Changes, Settings,*
              and Customizations.

I had gotten fed up with the Microsoft Network's inconsistent mail delivery performance and the service's unannounced and disruptive use of a prefix for all my mail (*yourid@classic.msn.com* instead of *yourid@msn.com*), so a week ago my partner and I added a new ISP (GTE). Everything was running fine.

NOTE   See "Problems with Your Email Provider (ISP or Online Ser-
              vice)" in Chapter 3, *Outlook Repair Tactics*, for the straight
              scoop on troubleshooting ISP problems.

Or so I thought. I checked for new mail, and as suddenly as a slammed door, I'm in the email twilight zone. Internet email in my Outlook Outbox doesn't get sent: the traditional Delivering Messages dialog appears for a few seconds then goes away; there's no error, but queued mail is not going out. I'm receiving mail fine through this service. (Let's refer to this "Outlook Internet mail service with original profile" as "OIMS-original" from here on.)

I've been using Microsoft software since I traded in my slide rule, so I'm intimately familiar with the Microsoft KnowledgeBase (MSKB). I check out article Q162343, *How to Troubleshoot Mail Stuck in the Outbox,* among others. First, I took all the traditional, simple, precursor steps. After having done so, I conferred at length with my partner and our associate, Frederic Gordon. Frederic's an Outlook bug sleuth extraordinaire and all-around good guy. We decided to round up all the usual suspects:

NOTE   Some of these quick-fix steps are from the aforementioned MSKB article; however, most are from our own email troubleshooting cookbook, provided in full in Chapter 3.

See Chapter 9, *Where and How to Get Help*, to learn more about the Microsoft KnowledgeBase and how to access it.

— **Verify the message hasn't been opened before being sent.** If you've edited a message after pressing Send but before Outlook attempts to deliver your email, it'll appear as normal text (not italics) in the Outbox queue. *Result: the stuck messages weren't in edit mode.*

— **Verify all critical profile and connectoid (the dial-up networking or DUN item for the service) settings.** A setting might have gotten knocked loose or changed somehow. *Result: no effect.*

— **Try a different POP*** (ISP dial-up number). If another POP works alright, then it's time to call your ISP's technical support folks to report a problem on their end. *Result: no effect.*

— **Send a few test messages with literal email addresses in the To field instead of using address book data.** Outlook/Exchange replies to the address stored in the Personal Address Book (PAB) or Contact record for received messages, so if the stuck mail is a reply to someone already in your address book *and* that stored address (unlike the address to which you think that you're replying) is a mail address type other than SMTP† (CompuServe or MSNINET, for example), that would explain the bottleneck. *Result: no effect.*

---

* Point Of Presence.

† Simple Mail Transport Protocol.

NOTE   The indefatigable Frederic Gordon originally brought this Outlook/Exchange "Reply to illogic" bug to our attention. For more details about the tactics you need to thwart it, see Chapter 2.

— **Try a mail session with my MSN service.** Trying another service (if you have one set up) may determine if the problem is specific to a service or the whole profile. *Result: no effect (this might indicate a problem with the whole profile).*

— **Cold boot.** Hitting the Big Red Button is always a good idea at a time like this, and if you have an external modem, power it down too. *Result: no effect.*

— **Empty the Inbox and Deleted Items folders** (don't forget to archive messages first). Occasionally a corrupt message in another mail folder can wreak havoc on other mail-related folders and activity. *Result: no effect.*

NOTE   The typical size for a Personal Folders (PST) file is double-digit megabytes; that's right, we said *megabytes*. Comprised of 22 Inbox items, 601 Sent Items, 20 Calendar items, 270 Contacts (filled out in minimalist fashion), 54 Tasks, 78 Notes, and no Journal items, one author's *Mailbox.pst* weighs in at 18 MB. With so much critical data stored in a single, proprietary format repository, you need a rigorous cleanup and archival strategy. Turn to Chapter 5, *Outlook's Key Ingredients*, for just such detailed advice.

— **Run the Inbox Repair Tool** *Scanpst.exe.* You can run *Scanpst.exe*, then empty the Inbox, or vice versa, depending on personal preference. *Result: no effect.*

— **Compact the Personal Folders file** *Mailbox.pst.* It's best to do this after running *Scanpst.exe. Result: no effect.*

It was no dice. With all the easy solutions out of the way, and no beneficial effect, it's looking like this could be a tough case. On to the profile....

The current profile has the following services defined: CompuServe, Internet, Outlook Address Book, PAB, Personal Folders, and MSN. I created a new profile with just an Internet service. (Let's call this "Outlook Internet mail service with new profile" or OIMS-new from here on.) Using OIMS-new, Outlook sends mail (after an odd almost-precisely 30-second delay before there's any modem send activity), but it's immediately bounced back from the System Administrator as Undeliverable with the message "No transport provider was available for delivery to this recipient." Inbound mail is still coming in unimpeded. But a guy in my line of work can't get by on just incoming mail. I was being made into a patsy and didn't like it. Time to get tough.

I used Microsoft Internet Mail and News (IMN)—it comes free with Internet Explorer 3.01 and higher—to send and receive some test messages with no problems (although again, there's an odd almost-precisely 30-second delay before there's any modem send activity). At the very least, I'll be able to use IMN for day-to-day work while tracking down the culprit. Oh yeah, starting with Internet Explorer 4.0, some wise guy at Microsoft changed the name of IMN to *Outlook Express* even though it has nothing to do with Outlook. It occurred to me that the next time I work a crossword puzzle and am asked for an 11-letter word describing Microsoft's product-naming practices, I'd be ready with the answer: obfuscation. But I digress.

NOTE   Interested in a practically bomb-proof, simple, yet elegant Internet mail program? Hey, it's free! IMN/Outlook Express isn't Outlook, it's just an email client, and so it lacks Outlook's other compelling features (although as a mail application it does have several features that Outlook doesn't). For more information about obtaining and using this free email client, see Chapter 2.

With the heat off for the moment, I decided to do a little snooping. I looked over my notes for the past week and noticed I got general protection faults (GPFs) twice when the Internet service disconnected from the GTE connectoid. Both times Explorer had an illegal op in *Kernel32.dll* at 0137:bff9a28c, and I warm-booted with no apparent consequences. However, these GPFs did not occur right before Outlook stopped sending Internet mail; there was approximately a one-day lag.

I was no stranger to GPFs—for the last six months when using the CompuServe service with Outlook, it routinely GPFed when the service disconnected from the host. Sometimes the GPF was Explorer in *Comctl32.dll* at 0137:bfc10e64, sometimes it was Explorer in *Kernel32.dll* at 0137:bff798e9, sometimes it was Explorer illegal page fault in *Kernel32.dll* at 0137:bff9a28c. I always warm-booted with no apparent consequences (no lost or corrupted mail that I'm aware of). Go figure. Microsoft blames CompuServe (who wrote the driver), CompuServe points the finger at Microsoft—stop me if you've heard this before—and I'm caught in a pickle like a runner stuck between first and second.

Now it's getting late. Not willing to go down the rocky and time-consuming road of rebuilding a new profile just yet, I decided to call in some hired muscle. I rang up Microsoft's pay-per-incident technical support at (800) 936-5700. It would cost me $35, but at least they didn't ask for car fare.

NOTE   When I gave the customer service representative my Out-
            look product ID number, she said, "That's odd. Oh, this is
            a not-for-resale number so we can't support you." I was
            seeing red and ready to start tossing furniture, but took a
            deep breath and told her the truth, "I got this CD from the
            Microsoft Office 97 beta team, it's a 'gold code' CD, I got it
            for participating in the beta program. Surely you support
            the 'ship to manufacturing' product you sent to your own
            beta testers?" A few minutes later she came back and told
            me to write down a new product ID number, then patched
            me through to an Outlook technical support engineer, no
            charge. True story.

Microsoft Engineer #1 had me do the following:

a. Clear the IPX/SPX and NetBEUI protocols for the Dial-Up Adapter network component's Bindings tab: right-click Network Neighborhood, choose Properties, click the Configuration tab, select Dial-Up Adapter, click Properties, and click the Bindings tab. I had all three protocols active: IPX/SPX, NetBEUI, and TCP/IP, so I unchecked IPX/SPX and NetBEUI, then restarted my system. *Result: no effect.*

b. Use Ping from the MS-DOS command prompt to ping GTE's SMTP server. *Result: the server is up and active.*

c. Temporarily try the "I connect manually" setting in the Connection tab of the Internet service's Properties dialog. *Result: no effect.* (This was clearly a rabbit trail, but short of risking outright data loss, you typically do what the engineer says just to stay on her or his good side.)

NOTE   At this point I had to ring off. Engineer #1 recommended the following course of action, and said another engineer would call back within 72 hours to follow up.

---

   d. Run **setup.exe** **/y** **/r** against the Office 97 CD-ROM to auto-re-register Office with the Registry (**/y** for Registry, **/r** for a re-install with no dialogs displayed). This is to clear out any IMEP-related Registry corruption.

NOTE   Occasionally Office 97 gets so goofed up on your system that you're better off blowing the blasted beast right off your hard disk and re-installing from scratch. But don't just do an Office, Setup, Remove All. No siree, don't do that. First you need to back up critical files, take notes about your application configuration preferences and custom tool-bars you may have to rebuild (or not, if you use our tricks), then uninstall, defrag your hard disk, reinstall, and so on. We show you how to run this gauntlet in "The Ultimate Scorched Earth Solution" section of Chapter 3.

---

   e. Reinstall IMEP.

   f. Create a completely new profile, add only the Internet service, and see if mail goes out.

NOTE   Creating a new profile to match the settings of one that's headed south is easy. Just take our prescription for it in Chapter 3's "Problems with Profiles."

I didn't undertake any of the engineer's parting suggestions. It all seemed too drastic and I needed a day to recover. After all, what if it's something simple I overlooked, or an intermittent problem with GTE's SMTP servers? I posted a message summarizing my experience to Microsoft's Outlook newsgroup.

Wednesday

Today I mostly avoided looking at the problem; instead, I just used IMN for all mail. On reviewing these facts and re-testing once more using the OIMS-original profile, the MSN service successfully sends SMTP mail and receives incoming test mail to my MSN ID. Remember that the MSN service wouldn't send any mail yesterday. I'm beginning to think Outlook is as fickle as Becky Clarke, my old high-school sweetheart (but that's another story). What a world, but at least I can both send and receive with IMN.

Thursday

At 2:06 P.M., Microsoft Engineer #2 called. Nice guy; knew his stuff. I gave him an update. Here's what he says he would have recommended if he had been Engineer #1:

   a. Ctrl+Alt+Del and close everything except Explorer and Point32* (including PowerToys, etc.—in other words, close literally everything except Explorer and Point32).

   b. Rename *Mapisp32.exe, Mapi32.dll,* and *Minet32.dll* to *Mapisp32.1, Mapi32.2,* and *Minet32.3,* respectively. It was amusing to see that even Microsoft's own engineers were still living in an eight-dot-three filename world. Our standard method when renaming files is to change the name to something like *Mapisp32.exe.old,* which makes it easier to restore since it preserves the original filename intact.

   c. Reinstall IMEP, configure the Internet service as appropriate, then cold-boot.

   d. Restart the PC, then close all applications except Explorer and Point32 again and see if mail gets sent. If not, it's time to build a new profile from scratch. If mail does get sent, restart the machine and *without* closing applications see if mail gets sent. If mail does not get sent, there's a possible conflict with one of these applications (the implication being the unsupported PowerToys, but he didn't explicitly say so); if the mail does get sent, then it's smooth sailing.

His most poignant comment was, "It's a bit like whacking your TV set." Indeed. He also claimed that Outlook messages use a "big, honking MAPI 1.0 footprint" whereas IMN uses a vastly simpler message-packaging technology, so it is possible that an ISP's SMTP server might choke on an Outlook message but not the same message sent via IMN. It sounded fishy, but I took no action, just notes. I was beginning to think someone was being taken for a ride. I hoped it wasn't me.

After hanging up I checked the newsgroup, and Vince Averello—an outstanding Outlook MVP†—had replied. (Actually, he had replied

---

* The IntelliMouse driver.

† MVP is an acronym for Most Valuable Professional, a distinction Microsoft bestows on folks that—for no pay—roam the newsgroups and answer questions intelligently.

within 10 minutes of my posting yesterday. Wow.) Vince suggested moving the Internet service to the top of the delivery stack and this did the trick, temporarily. For about the next five hours I could send mail using OIMS-original. Then without warning, Outlook's Outbox mail got stuck again.

I immediately called GTE, and the technician said, "Newer email clients like Outlook and Communicator do occasionally cause our servers some grief and we're working to rectify this, but as of right now the SMTP servers are at 100 percent. There were some minor server problems last night, all resolved."

The Bleeding-edge Time Sink, Ours and Yours

Here's a synopsis of how much time we've spent on this problem since Tuesday morning: 13 hours. This takes the adjective "annoyed" to new heights. It's our fervent belief that this type of problem occurs every day and afflicts hundreds of thousands if not millions of people—both in business and personal affairs—simply trying to use electronic mail as a communications medium. The popularity and saturation in this field are growing exponentially, but the tools for diagnosing problems (either with user intervention or without) are sadly, criminally lacking. It's no longer sufficient for software manufacturers or help desks to defend themselves by saying, "This is bleeding-edge stuff, so you have to expect problems like this." Wrong. The entire technology industry has a very long way to go before email is as reliable as the dial-tone we've all come to believe in as a fundamental indicator of our progress as a civilization. Improvements in the national telecommunications infrastructure (including ISPs) can't come too quickly for all of us.

We are writing this book to reduce your burn time over catastrophes like these—cataclysms that afflict not just your email but your appointments, notes, addresses, and other personal information. With this problem log we want you to know you're not alone when it comes to Outlook. This nonsense happens to us all the time, too.

Epilogue

My partner got a hot tip from a guy in Redmond that these types of Internet mail problems are fundamental to Outlook prior to the 8.02 SR-1 Enterprise Update version (even with the latest IMEP). So we made some calls to our Microsoft pals and reeled in some favors; we were assured we'd have the update CD in a few days.

SR-1 Enterprise arrives, but before I can install it, email starts working again. Pure voodoo effect. It's a bit like whacking your TV set, indeed. I thought of the grief Outlook had caused me. I thought of the bucks flowing into Redmond for software that's supposed to make our lives easier. I thought of reprogramming Outlook right then and there with a large caliber handgun. Sometimes computer software brings out the extrovert in me.

The problems of a guy trying to use a piece of computer software may not amount to a hill of beans in this crazy mixed-up world, but I know one thing. It's annoying as hell, and someone should write a book about it....

The Annoyances Troika

If, like us, you're not satisfied with the "it's just like whacking your TV set" approach to recognizing and solving problems, then the remaining chapters are for you. Annoyances, like bugs, are in the eye of the beholder: if you find something that doesn't work the way you think it should, it's a bug. If you find that you can fix or work around the bug, it's downgraded to an annoyance. From our point of view, annoyances with fairly easy workarounds are simply galling.

You're almost sure to consider at least a handful of the annoyances discussed here of no consequence to you, and that's fair. Your work style may never take you into a particular realm of Outlook, even if this is a place where other readers tread frequently. But despite the room for disagreement, you're sure to find a long list of features that you consider annoying, even though the individual items in the list may vary.

We arrange Outlook annoyances into three different categories.

- Annoyances that are manifestly stupid. Outlook's rife with 'em, more so than any other Office application.

- Annoyances that stem from the complexity of using a single container to manage all your diverse personal information. Outlook adds Calendar (Appointment, Meeting, and Event), Contact, Journal, Note, and Task data types, plus forms and a development language in the form of VBScript to Exchange's PST file format. Some data types can even be transmuted—drag an email message onto the Task icon and it gets added as a Task. Getting this mix of data types to reside together harmoniously and share a common interface is a daunting challenge. Sometimes the challenge yields outright bugs, other times Outlook resonates mellifluously, and there are times when you'd best have a road map handy just to navigate down the Outlook block (thus this book).

- Annoyances that relate directly to design decisions made by Microsoft. Outlook sports a new interface and several new data categories, that's undeniable. But many of Outlook's quirky annoyances could have been eliminated entirely if Redmond had been willing to close the door on the antiquated, unenlightened way Exchange does things. Since that door didn't always get closed, you're stuck between Exchange's outmoded ways and a new variation on that technology embedded in Outlook. The ultimate solution to an annoyance in this category is typically a detailed, dog-eared checklist of action verifications, workarounds, and even software patches—and we provide these by the score in this book. Remember, "it's a bit like whacking your TV set." (We'd laugh if it didn't hurt so much.)

Each type of annoyance warrants its own approach. However, to solve any type of annoyance, you first need a modicum of enlightenment, a tiny sliver—well, sometimes a truckload—of the gleaming, merciless truth about Outlook. That's where we come in. Rather than wallow in an Outlook-bashing denigration funk, we're going to consistently and persistently remind you about the benefits—tremendous, mind you—to being an Outlook lover. In that positive context, where we all agree that we gain something valuable by using Outlook, understanding its quirks, pitfalls, and limitations will be a far more pleasant process. So relax, take a deep breath, and repeat our Outlook mantra, "Lord give me patience...and hurry!"*

A Bug Fête

Outlook 97 is a version 1.0 product (maybe a "released beta" would be a better description). It's clear that the product was rushed to meet the Office 97 manufacturing deadline. The giant flashing yellow neon arrow attesting to this is Outlook's use of VBScript as a development language and what amounts effectively to Notepad as a development environment. Appalling. Early rumors had it that Outlook 98 would replace VBScript with Visual Basic for Applications (VBA) and the quintessential Visual Basic Editor (VBE), which are consistently supported in Outlook's siblings—Access (sort of),† Excel, PowerPoint, and Word. Too bad

---

* George Robinson Ragsdale.

† If you plan on working in several of the Office applications that host VBA, keep in mind that although Access 97 *includes the VBA language*, it definitely *does not include VBA's integrated development environment (IDE)*. Oh, it has some of the VBA IDE's nice IntelliSense features and an Object Browser, but that's about it.

Microsoft couldn't get all the products to converge on VBA simultaneously. But that hasn't happened, and Outlook 98 is still saddled with VBScript.

Outlook 97 SR-1 Enterprise Update offers enough incremental stability and bug fixes that we consider it a true version 1.0.

Outlook 98 takes another small step forward, and we consider it to be version 1.1. So don't be surprised by the number of rough edges and gotchas still present in Outlook 98. Yet we find this PIM—even in its earliest buggy incarnations—to be a marvelous combination of email and personal-data tracking capabilities with numerous compelling—even astounding—features.

Of Outlook 97's three most egregious bugs, the most galling is that Outlook 97 has no customizable toolbars. In fact, Outlook 97 doesn't use the Office-wide Command Bars object model. So if you want to customize Outlook 97's user interface to suit your style, forget it. One could argue that the Outlook Bar feature with its editable groups and Shortcuts represents a pseudo-toolbar (we wouldn't, but some might). It just ain't so. Sure, you can rename, add, delete, and rearrange groups and Shortcuts, but these are simply storage locations for Outlook data. You can't customize the way Outlook 97 presents its feature set to you with its toolbars, menu bar, or shortcut menus. Outlook (both 97 and 98) even takes a powder on standard keyboard shortcuts that you'll find in other Office applications. Press `Ctrl+F` in Word or Excel and you'll get the Find dialog box. Press it in Outlook and you invoke "forward message." And that's a crying shame.

If you use Outlook 97 for mail sessions that last more than a few minutes each day, this next quirk will jack your blood pressure into the ultra-red. Outlook 97 is application-modal when it is reading and delivering messages. Which means you can't interact with Outlook 97's interface at all until the current mail session is completed—so you can't read the first few messages while more are coming in, you can't create an outgoing message, or you can't interact with Outlook 97 in any way whatsoever until the mail session is done. The Exchange email client was not like this when connected, so why is Outlook 97? With this bizarre annoyance, Outlook 97 actually disinherits a nice feature in Exchange.

OUTLOOK 98 You can continue working in Outlook 98 while downloading email in the background. However, this is still not true for Remote Mail.

As mentioned earlier, Outlook doesn't support VBA and doesn't include its integrated development environment, VBE. Instead, Outlook supports VBScript, a diluted subset of the Visual Basic language, and a development environment that suspiciously resembles Notepad (see Figure 1-1). If you've bought into the colossal benefits of an Office-wide programming language and development environment—and you should—then you'll be very frustrated when working with VBScript to control Outlook. Keep in mind that VBScript isn't crippled capriciously. Microsoft purposefully designed it to be small, lightweight, and Internet-safe (meaning no direct access to file operations or the operating system); thus, the missing features. That's fine for Internet Explorer, which also hosts VBScript, but it's completely unacceptable for Microsoft's inaugural PIM.

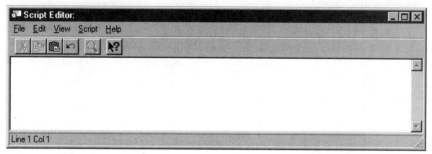

Figure 1-1: This isn't a development environment; it's Notepad with a toolbar!

Another annoying aspect of Outlook 98 is the program's updated user interface. (For those of you upgrading from Outlook 97, you'll probably get used to the shuffled commands fairly quickly, but initially it's different and therefore potentially annoying.) Although overall the user interface is an improvement over the Outlook 97 labyrinth, some unusual command arrangements persist, and these are conspicuously inconsistent with Outlook's Office siblings. For example, in every Office application except Outlook, working with add-ins is a simple two-step process: Tools → Add-Ins (in Word it's worded a tad differently: Tools → Templates and Add-Ins). In Outlook 98, it's a five-step process: Tools → Options → Other → Advanced Options → Add-In Manager; and in Outlook 97, it's four steps: Tools → Options → General → Add-In Manager. In every other Office application except Access, the Customize command is on the Tools menu. In Outlook 98 (this feature doesn't even exist in Outlook 97) it's not there; you have to go the long way around the barn: View → Toolbars → Customize. We're hard-pressed to see the point in these inconsistent arrangements.

Finally, although Outlook 98 is an important upgrade—one that you should make unhesitatingly if you're still using Outlook 97—the net on bugs is that far too many remain uncorrected.

The Kitchen Sink

Many Outlook neophytes trying to add a new piece of information are quickly disoriented by Outlook's interface (see Figure 1-2). "Let's see, do I go to the folder through the Outlook Bar, the Go command, the Folder List (oh, but first I have to turn it on)...now do I use a menu bar command or click a button, hmmm, which one, is it File then New then...*Uncle!*"

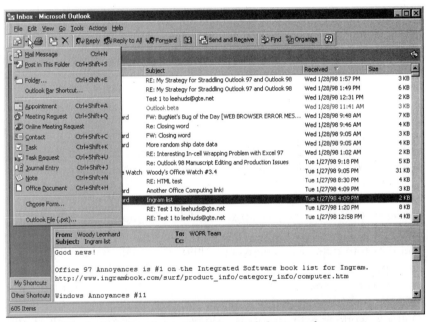

Figure 1-2: The Outlook interface—it's a bit overwhelming at first

And what about Outlook's three different types of calendar activities (Appointment, Meeting, Event)? An Appointment can easily be rendered into a Meeting, which can easily be rendered into an Event, *ad infinitum*. But you'd never get this big picture perspective by reading the help file.

Here's a good test: how do you change the order in which your various address books appear when searching for a contact? How do you change the priority delivery order of email and related services for the current profile? Where do you go to tell Outlook which profile to use at startup? How do you rebuild a profile from scratch? If you can answer these questions cold, without hunting and pecking around the Outlook and

Windows interface, then you've achieved Outlook guruhood and you should call our Human Resources department to set up a job interview. More likely, these questions—and numerous others like them—rub you and your colleagues raw day in and day out. We provide clear-cut procedures for these types of common data management and configuration annoyances throughout this book.

That's the Way It's Always Been Done

Outlook confusingly offers a variety of different ways to get to contact information that is stored somewhere other than the Contacts folder, depending on what services you have currently installed. From Outlook, you could have access to the rickety, vestigial Exchange Personal Address Book (PAB), Outlook's Contacts folder (part of the PST file), a CompuServe address book, the MSN address database, and so on, all depending on your configuration. Why the archaic PAB is still around is a mystery. Microsoft squandered an opportunity to provide a central "contacts" repository with the release of Outlook. And why no connection to Access? Access is vastly superior to Outlook as a storage database for contact information. If you don't have a flavor of Office that comes with Access, then Outlook should store contact information in its own *.mdb* file (a relational, table-driven data storage format). If Access is detected during Outlook setup, the installation program should ask whether you want to store contact data directly in Access, and offer to fire up a Contacts Wizard to create the appropriate links from an existing Access address information database to the Outlook Contacts module. Such a dynamic interface to the data in the user's existing Access tables would be fabulous. Maybe next time.

On the "one step forward, two steps backward" front, what were they thinking when they designed Outlook's "Delivering Messages" dialog, which is shown in Figure 1-3, with no count like "Message 1 of 3" and no status bar? Heck, CompuServe's been doing this for years, and so does Microsoft's own IMN product (see Figures 1-4 and 1-5). Oy vey.

Figure 1-3: This is the brain-dead way Exchange and Outlook report on message delivery status

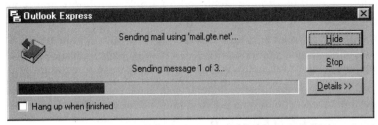

Figure 1-4: Here's how the humble little Outlook Express 98 does it

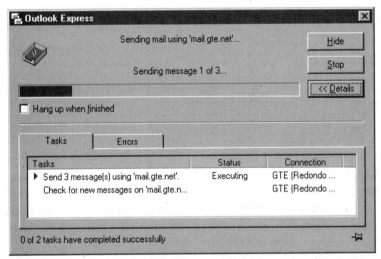

Figure 1-5: Outlook Express 98's delivery status dialog in Details mode

A New and Improved Outlook 98

Outlook is a work in progress. But Microsoft is dedicated to fixing bugs and tweaking features, as evidenced by a steady flow of updates, patches, and—most recently—a new version. The most recent incarnation is Outlook 98, which includes a number of very slick enhancements over the earlier 97 flavors, along with the standard number of over-hyped features.

If you have not yet decided to upgrade to Outlook 98, consider the following:

• As mentioned earlier, you can continue working in Outlook 98 while downloading email in the background. See Chapter 3.

• Outlook now provides a MAPI-less mode called Internet Only for users who only deal with email via the Internet. This mode makes creating an email distribution list a snap, and easily supports multiple accounts. Internet Only mode also supports IMAP.* Both modes support Internet directory (LDAP) servers. See Chapters 2 and 3.

- A much-welcomed new Send command *sends* mail without receiving any new messages. See Chapter 2.

- You can quickly set up rules to automatically format items that meet certain conditions (for example, you can display any incoming message from Bill Gates in red). And you can drill deeper for even more control by customizing the current view's Automatic Formatting preferences. See Chapter 2.

- There is now a no-email option when installing Outlook 98. You can use another software package for email and use Outlook for all your other information management needs. See Chapters 2 and 3.

- Outlook 98 now supports an HTML email editor, so you can add background and animated graphics to your email messages. Hmmm, we're not really sure if the world needs more blinking icons. See Chapter 2.

- At last, multiple signatures. You can create more than one boilerplate text block as a closing signature to your email messages. See Chapter 2.

- Customizable command bars. Now you can modify toolbars and menus to adapt Outlook to the way you want to work, not the other way around. See Chapter 2.

- Outlook Today, a new frame-like tool that displays the number of unread messages in your Inbox, your appointments over the next few days, and your task list. Although it's nice, it's also slow to load (even on snappy systems), and we find the Calendar provides more useful information overall. Strictly a subjective call. See Chapter 2.

- You can flag contacts for follow-up just like email messages. Set a reminder that will pop up at a specified date and time. This is a much-needed feature for staying current with your contacts. See Chapter 2.

- A Preview Pane is now built right into Outlook (it was an add-in in Outlook 97). Alas, the one place we'd like to have the Preview Pane available is the Outbox folder, but it's not available there. See Chapter 2.

---

* Internet Mail Access Protocol is a method of accessing email or BBS messages stored on a mail server. IMAP allows a client email program to access remote messages as if they were on the user's local machine.

- Incoming email messages now default to read-only to prevent unwanted changes. Makes sense, but we would also like a way to change this default setting. You have to open the message, then choose Edit → Edit Message to make changes. See Chapter 2.

- Outlook 98 provides junk email filters to automatically prune spam from your Inbox. This is a great feature as long as you understand how it works. See Chapter 2.

- Outlook 98 attempts to make its frequently used features more accessible via the new web-like Organize and Find tools. To a large degree it works. However, mixing these new and very different web-style components with a majority of pre-Internet-style interface components (traditional dialog boxes, toolbars, shortcut menus, etc.) may confuse more than enlighten.

These are the new features in Outlook 98 that impressed us the most. We cover other new features along the way throughout this book. This inspiring list in and of itself should make you seriously consider upgrading to Outlook 98. Keep in mind that there are still annoyances aplenty in Outlook 98—enough to raise your blood pressure to the red line. We'll take 'em all on and show you the workarounds.

In the meantime, remember that many Outlook annoyances are due in part to the nature of PIMs—they track large amounts of radically different information that has to be presented in very different ways, all within a single container program. Corralling this quivering data miasma into a consistent, cohesive whole is a daunting task. Our hats are off to the Outlook developers for a remarkable achievement.

Just Where Do You Want to Go Today?

Microsoft has missed the simple fact that people want to go home at the end of the work day, and that in order to do so they—at least 80% or more of them, according to market researchers—use Office to get their work done. To that end, Outlook has become their PIM of choice. If you feel Outlook's more part of the problem than part of the solution, take a few deep breaths and realize that Outlook's annoyances aren't imaginary. In fact, Outlook contains hundreds of annoying idiosyncrasies such as the ones mentioned earlier, but you *can* eliminate or work around the vast majority of them. That's what the rest of this book is all about. We'll help you strike up that beautiful friendship with Outlook.

Of course, the Augean Stables* weren't cleaned in a day—well, okay, they *were* cleaned in a day, but Hercules had the advantage of being the son of Zeus, and as far as we know he didn't have to contend with General Protection Faults, corrupt profiles, and mail stubbornly stuck in his Outbox. For mere mortals like us, you need to keep your perspective and realize you aren't going to conquer Outlook's manifest shortcomings in a day or even a week, for that matter. But if you hang in there, your efforts to understand and coerce Outlook so it works with you instead of against you will be repaid many times. We honestly believe you'll pay for this book (and the time you took to read it) by simply following the steps in the next chapter, which covers the simple but important changes every Outlook user should make or at the least be aware of. Beyond that, your efforts with this book are money in the bank.

We'll cover topics such as troubleshooting problems that you are likely to run into, from the minor annoyance category to the catastrophic gotchas that bring Outlook to a screeching halt. Moving data into and out of Outlook is covered, along with the care and feeding of the Personal Folders file, and we'll actually explain what the Journal facility is all about and what it can do for you. The mysteries of auto-archives will be revealed, and in Chapter 8, *Introduction to VBScript, the Outlook Object Model, and Custom Forms*, we introduce you to the world of macros, the Outlook object model, VBScript, VBA, and forms—the basic set of tools that you can use to cure many otherwise difficult-to-get-at annoyances.

It's not entirely clear if Outlook 99 (or 2000, or whatever Microsoft crowns the next version) will include VBA, but it's only a matter of time before all Office applications support VBA. With that in mind we'll take the approach of developing forms and procedures that work in VBScript but that can be quickly and easily ported to Outlook/VBA. Just because Outlook's own development environment leaves much to be desired, by learning the object model you'll be ready for the full implementation of VBA, and in the meantime be able to use Visual Basic 5 or VBA in other Office applications to control Outlook with OLE Automation—we'll show you how, of course.

All of the programs you'll find listed here are available for download at the O'Reilly & Associates Web site, *www.ora.com*, and mirrored at the authors' sites, *www.primeconsulting.com* and *www.wopr.com*. There's no charge, and you may distribute the programs freely, anywhere you like, any way you like. In return, we only ask that you encourage folks to get

---

* One of the Twelve Labors of Hercules.

this book, so they can follow along and make Outlook work right for them too.

If you have a question, tip, or observation, the best way to reach us is by sending email to *ask.woody@wopr.com* or *info@primeconsulting.com*. If we can figure out an answer to your question, or if your tip really hits the spot, we'll publish it in our free email newsletter called WOW—"Woody's Office Watch." No promises, of course, as the volume of mail sometimes gets overwhelming. And no, Microsoft doesn't pay us a penny for our technical support services. But thanks for asking.

NOTE   You can subscribe to Woody's Office Watch, our *free* elec-
            tronic weekly newsletter, by simply sending email to
            ohwow@wopr.com. We think you'll find WOW an excellent
            source of up-to-the-nanosecond news on Microsoft Out-
            look. And the price sure is right.

And now, if you're ready to whack your TV set, er, get started taming Outlook...

2

Vital Changes, Settings, and Customizations

While many people think of Outlook as primarily an email package, it is really a comprehensive personal information manager, or PIM. Microsoft tries to set Outlook in a category by itself by referring to it as a *desktop information manager*, or a DIM, which is how we think of Outlook when it doesn't behave properly—and misbehave it can, as we'll discuss at length in Chapter 3, *Outlook Repair Tactics*.

In any event, the market for information managers is a mature one, PIMs have been around for ages, and users are quite passionate about their favorite PIM (with "their favorite" usually being the first one they actually managed to get all their information stuffed into). Indeed, the prospect of migrating all the telephone, address, email, and other related information from their present PIM to a different software package is enough to make most users break out in a cold sweat.

In this already crowded software category, Microsoft had its work cut out to achieve any significant market penetration. Stealing a page from Internet Explorer's marketing plan, they included Outlook in the Office 97 package, essentially making it a freebie in the most popular office suite software package. It's tough to compete with *free*, and more and more users are trying Outlook with varying results. But as we pointed out in Chapter 1, *It's a Bit Like Whacking Your TV Set*, the path to Outlook nirvana is an arduous one, mainly because Outlook is still a bit of a work in progress. In this chapter, we'll tackle the initial setup and tweaking that Outlook needs "out of the box" so that it's, well, *less annoying*.

NOTE   In addition to being bundled with Microsoft Office 97, Outlook is available as a standalone package running under Windows 95 (part number 92236) and does not require that Microsoft Office be installed. Oops, unless you want to use spell checking in Outlook. Seems that while other Office 97 applications can use the Office 95 spelling files, and Office 95 applications can use the Office 97 spelling files, Outlook can only use Office 97 spelling files. This means if you're going to run Outlook without Office 97, don't make any spelling errors.

Version Vertigo

The first hurdle is figuring out what version of Outlook you have. We don't know for a fact that Outlook 97 (8.0) was rushed out the door, but since it's been released there has been a steady number of updates and patches. This is not entirely without rational reason, as certain changes in the computer world have complicated the lives of PIM developers in general. Consider that only recently has email become a core component of the PIM feature set, having heretofore been a separate software category altogether. Next, factor in that traditionally, email has been of a very network-centric design, working primarily with proprietary backends running on network servers. The unbridled success and popularity of the Internet took everyone totally by surprise (including the seers at Microsoft); adding support for messaging over the Internet turned out to be harder than it looked.

In a hurry to get to market, Outlook appears to have been thrust into production a bit precipitously, and some of the kinks have not been entirely worked out yet. Don't get us wrong though, we use Outlook on our production machines, warts and all.

Outlook Patched and Updated

Already there have been three versions of Outlook 97: 8.0, 8.01, and 8.02. Then there is something called Outlook Express. Oh, and the 8.02 version comes in three different flavors (or *configurations*, as Microsoft calls them) just to make things really interesting. Then there is also 8.03, which takes advantage of features in Microsoft Exchange Server 5.5. And now we have Outlook 98, which Microsoft has designated version 8.5, discussed in the next section.

Here's the lowdown on the various versions in chronological order by release date for those of you still running a version of Outlook 97. To see the version stamp, just click on the Help menu option and then on About Microsoft Outlook.

Version 8.0

Version 8.0 (officially known as Release 3511) is the first version released with Office 97 (and subsequently available as a standalone product, as we've mentioned), although this release number is not shown in the Help → About Outlook dialog box (see Figure 2-1). If you have one of the subsequent flavors of Outlook 97, the detailed version release number is shown in parentheses, as in Figure 2-2.

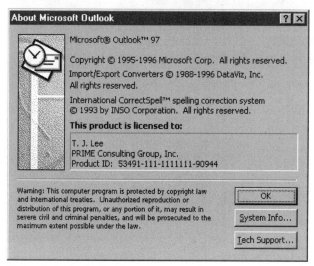

Figure 2-1: Outlook Version 8.0

NOTE   The characters "8.0" are strangely missing from Outlook 8.0's About dialog box. This strangeness is characteristic of Microsoft's recent initial Office product releases: the marketers call it 95 and then 97, the version number is called 7 and then 8 and then 8.01 and...you get the idea. With Outlook, if the About dialog reads as shown in Figure 2-1, bingo, it's 8.0. (You can also right-click on *Outlook.exe*, choose Properties, click the Version tab, and examine the file version shown there.)

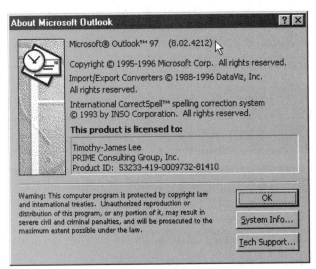

Figure 2-2: Outlook Version 8.02, Release 4212

Version 8.01

The first update to Outlook, Release 3817, came with Microsoft Exchange Server 5.0, and to get this version you had to purchase or upgrade to Exchange Server 5.0. There was some confusion about precisely what client features were in Outlook 8.01. Microsoft said that 8.01 was *not a maintenance release* and *does not contain new Outlook client features*. On the other hand, 8.01 substantially increases the number of fields and actions that can be stored in a custom form.

Internet Mail and News, a.k.a. Outlook Express

Make no mistake, Microsoft Internet Mail and News (IMN, now called Outlook Express) is not in any way, shape, or form Outlook. But Microsoft seems intent on confusing the heck out of everyone in this regard. After the 8.01 update, Internet Explorer 4.0 came out as an open beta—ahem, excuse us...*a platform preview* release (to use the correct Microspeak term)—and it contained an upgraded version of the Internet Mail and News client that originally shipped with Internet Explorer 3.x.

Instead of calling it Internet Mail and News, Microsoft decided to call it Outlook Express, implying that it was a scaled-down version of Outlook. To make things even more annoying, Outlook Express incorporated a number of very nifty mail features not available in Outlook at the time. Outlook Express lets you have more than one email account (set up for different users if you want), connects to multiple news servers, provides email searching with services like Four-11 and Bigfoot, supports creating messages in HTML* format, and lets you customize its toolbar (all features that wound up in Outlook 98, we might add).

On the other hand, Outlook Express does not have any of Outlook's PIM capabilities. Two different products with some overlap in the email arena have been made massively confusing by Microsoft's choice of product names. Very annoying.

Internet Mail and News comes with the full download of Internet Explorer 3.x or later. It can also be downloaded separately (*www.microsoft.com/ie/download/*†). You can install it when you install Internet Explorer, install it separately by rerunning the Internet Explorer install, or if you've downloaded *Mailnews.exe* separately, just double-click on this executable file.

Installation is straightforward, although if you are dialing into the Internet you'll have to provide your email account information the first time you run the application. You fill in the install Wizard panels with your name, your email address, the POP3‡ and SMTP§ server names for your ISP,** and finally your logon settings—account name and password. When installed, all these settings appear in the Mail → Options → Server tab of the Options dialog box. See Figure 2-3.

While it's not a PIM (despite the Outlook Express moniker), it is a very credible email client, and if Outlook starts behaving, er, eccentrically, Internet Mail and News makes a great contingency email program. Of course, once again Microsoft has introduced a new, separate, and completely unintegrated address book! The "Windows Address Book" is completely separate from the Outlook Contact List and the Personal Address Book (PAB) and requires you to import—that's right, *import*— your address book information from the PAB, Eudora, or even Netscape's address book before you can use it with Internet Mail and News. Can you import from Outlook? Sure you can, as long as you export all your Contact List data to a PAB or comma-separated-value (CSV) file first. This is annoying to the point of tears. You'd think that with the database technologies of both FoxPro and Access in-house, Microsoft could come up

---

* Hypertext Markup Language.

† Between the way Microsoft moves things around on their Web site and their predilection for encouraging users to upgrade, you might have to spend some time hunting down anything but the latest and greatest versions of their software on the Web.

‡ Post Office Protocol—The protocol used by mail clients to retrieve messages from a mail server, currently up to version 3.

§ Simple Mail Transport Protocol—This is the protocol used on TCP/IP networks to exchange mail on the Internet between SMTP servers.

** Internet Service Provider—a company that provides access to the Internet.

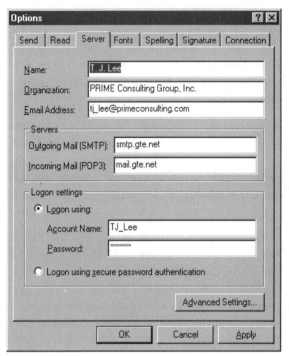

Figure 2-3: Internet Mail settings

with one, count 'em, one address book that could be built into Windows and that every application could query for name, address, email, phone, and fax information. Oy!

Version 8.02

Outlook 8.02 comes in three, count 'em, three different flavors—er, configurations—and they are all different, of course!

First is the version that ships with Microsoft Exchange Server, version 5.0 Service Pack 1, known as SP1. The only way we know of to get this patch is through the Exchange Server 5.0 Service Pack 1.

Next is the Outlook update that you get if you install the Microsoft Office 97 Service Release 1 Patch. When you install this patch, Outlook's files are updated to version 8.02. This "patch" for Office is available on the Microsoft Web site at *www.microsoft.com/Office/Office97/ServiceRelease/*.

NOTE   A "patch" is very different from a new version of your software application. With a patch you typically get an executable file that—when run—actually modifies certain files that belong to your already installed software package. Patching involves changing your existing application by performing the cybernetic equivalent of open-heart surgery on your files.

Microsoft had some trouble with the first release of the SR1 patch and had to recall it shortly after it was posted on their Web site. SR1 updated several Office 97 applications, and it seems it introduced a bug into Word that could cause you to lose data when you saved files under certain circumstances. But the currently available patch corrects this bug.

If you installed the first version of the SR1 Patch, you need to get the "patch update" (same Web address as in the preceding paragraph) to patch the patch, as it were. Your only other recourse is to uninstall all of Office 97 and reinstall it from your original CD. Patches can rarely be "rolled back," so be cautious when patching your software. Make sure you have the original CD (or diskettes <groan>) handy so you can do a full reinstall of the original software if things go awry.

Then there is the Microsoft Office 97 Service Release 1 Enterprise Update (SR1 EU—possibly pronounced Ess-Arr-One-Ewwww). Now, as confusing as it may seem, the SR1 Patch does not include all the fixes, updates, and corrections that are in the SR1 Enterprise Update. Confused yet? Well, join the club. The SR1 Enterprise Update is really just a new, updated version of Office 97 that incorporates all the latest bug fixes (all as in more fixes than the SR1 Patch addresses). To be sure you have the latest and greatest, you have to have the Enterprise Update to Office 97. Just to keep things interesting, the Enterprise Update comes in several flavors, as does Office. You have the Standard, Professional, Small Business, and Developer Editions. Since the Update suggests you *completely uninstall Office 97* prior to installing the Enterprise Update, you need to make sure you have the Update for the version of Office you are uninstalling. If you uninstall the Professional Edition and then install the Standard flavor of the Enterprise Update, you'll lose Access in the process. Be aware or be annoyed!

Both SR1s include the Internet Mail Enhancement patch (IMEP), but SP1—that's right, SP1—does not. SR1 EU and SP1 include some improvements for dealing with cc:Mail, but the SR1 Patch does not. The Patch does not include the Rules Wizard add-in for Outlook 97, but SR1 EU and SP1 both do (although the Rules Wizard is available separately as a standalone enhancement which we'll discuss further in a moment). The potential for having your annoyance level spike the meter here is enormous! You'd think that as long as all three versions are pegged as 8.02 Release 4212, they'd all have the same bloody fixes, wouldn't you? Sheesh. See the Microsoft KnowledgeBase article *OL97: Outlook 8.02 Distribution Information* (Q166024) for a full list of which update has what fix at *http:// support.microsoft.com/support/kb/articles/Q166/0/24.asp.*

NOTE   If you don't have the full version of Office 97 (say you pur-
                chased Excel 97 or Outlook 97 as a standalone product),
                rest assured that you can get an SR1 EU update (essentially
                a new version of the single application you have) for each
                of the individual Office 97 components. To get the SR1 En-
                terprise Update, just call Microsoft at (800) 370-9272 and or-
                der it for the version of Office 97 you have or for whatever
                individual Office 97 application you need to upgrade (as-
                suming you don't have the Office 97 suite).

Version 8.03

Outlook version 8.03 is another Exchange release like version 8.01 or the SP1 release that came with the Exchange Server 5.0 maintenance release. Microsoft does not like the general computing public to think of an Outlook upgrade specific to a new release of Microsoft Exchange Server as an upgrade to Outlook *per se*. They usually downplay any feature enhancements and assert the party line that unless you are upgrading to the new version of Microsoft Exchange Server, you don't need the new release of Outlook. This leads to statements from Redmond about how a new Outlook release is *not* a maintenance release and does not contain new Outlook client features *even though it really is and usually does.*

Since Outlook is Microsoft's email client for its "backend" enterprise mail server software, Microsoft Exchange, it makes sense for Microsoft to provide enhancements in Outlook that can only be taken advantage of if Exchange is running on one of your network servers, handling email for your entire company. Outlook is a "toss-in" that comes with Office. Exchange Server requires you to fork over some serious bucks.

The Inbox Assistant is an example of this type of enhancement. Origi-nally, in order to get rules-based filtering of your email, you had to have Exchange on the backend. If you did, then the Inbox Assistant feature would become available on Outlook's Tools menu. Users who did not have access to Exchange Server felt decidedly left out in the cybercold, and so Microsoft eventually came up with the Rules Wizard to provide similar functionality for those using Outlook 97 without Exchange.

Outlook version 8.03 ships with the new Microsoft Exchange Server 5.5, and again Redmond says that unless you are upgrading to this new release of Exchange, you don't need to worry about getting Outlook 8.03.

Outlook 98 Comes Free with a Split Personality

Outlook 98's new features were covered in Chapter 1, and hopefully you have upgraded and don't have to contend with Outlook 97's version madness. With Outlook 98, you only have to deal with three different *modes* that the program can manifest. Annoying? Only if it catches you unaware.

When you install Outlook 98, it does a reasonably good job of analyzing your system's current email configuration and determining (sometimes without asking you—more on this in a moment) which mode to configure: "Internet Only" or "Corporate or Workgroup" (which from here on we'll refer to as "Corporate/Workgroup"). There's also a third mode: no email components whatsoever; its official moniker is "No E-mail." See Figure 2-4.

Figure 2-4: Outlook 98 has two distinct email personalities (three if you count "No E-mail")

Take a moment to study this dialog box. The text Microsoft has chosen to describe each mode is extremely well crafted, speaking volumes in just a few words:

- Internet Only—Optimize Outlook to connect only to one or more Internet Service Providers or E-mail Servers using Internet standards for e-mail delivery (POP3, SMTP, or IMAP).

- Corporate or Workgroup—Configure Outlook to connect to Microsoft Exchange, Microsoft Mail 3.x, 3rd-party e-mail services, or any combinations of the above plus Internet e-mail.

- No E-mail—Do not setup Outlook to read e-mail; I do not use e-mail or I use another program to read e-mail.

The annoyance lurking here is that you may not see this dialog box when you install Outlook 98. So you could end up with an Internet Only mode when you would have preferred Corporate/Workgroup or vice versa. Before we discuss what you can do to coerce Outlook 98's installer to use a particular mode (or even better, to let you choose during setup), let's discuss the pros and cons of these two modes.

NOTE   If Outlook 98's already on your system, here's how you can tell what mode it's in. Select Help → About; the second line of text, immediately below the "Microsoft® Outlook 98..." line, will say either "Corporate or Workgroup" or "Internet Mail Only."

Earlier Microsoft messaging products were based on MAPI*—products (services) like Exchange Server, Microsoft Fax, and Microsoft Mail. Since Internet Only mode does not use MAPI, it's faster to start and close than the MAPI-based Corporate/Workgroup mode. Also, *theoretically*, you get faster email send/receive and fewer problems with messages once they reach a mail server. (We have not seen any significant improvement with Internet Only versus either Outlook 97 or Outlook 98 Corporate/Workgroup, but your mileage may vary.) You're not stuck with the entrenched MAPI user interface, one example of which is the annoyingly uninformative "Delivering messages..." dialog. Since Internet Only mode has no profiles, the overall complexity of setting your preferences and diagnosing problems is reduced. This mode also requires less disk space (1.8 MB vs. 4.6 MB for Corporate/Workgroup).

---

* Messaging Application Program Interface is an open API and messaging subsystem developed by Microsoft.

However, not being MAPI could also be a negative, since the Internet Only mode's mail engine is new and proprietary; new is not always better, and proprietary is not necessarily good in this context (although technologies that start out as proprietary to Microsoft have a way of becoming industry standards). Without MAPI, you don't get Remote Mail, a feature some of us find indispensable.

On the other hand, with Internet Only you can easily create distribution lists for emailing messages to a group of people in your Contact facility (Tools → Address Book → File → New Group). In Corporate/Workgroup mode you have to jump through hoops to accomplish the same thing (the process is detailed in Chapter 7, *Beyond the Basics*). Internet Only also has a much better connecting dialog when dialing into the Internet; it includes nice statistics, and if there's an error, you get a complete description of what happened should you want to know. *What a concept!*

Which mode is right for you? In a nutshell, if you don't need MAPI services (Microsoft or third-party), go with Internet Only mode. Otherwise, Corporate/Workgroup mode is the ticket (note that Corporate/Workgroup doesn't support IMAP or automatic dial-up of mail accounts). If you are using another software package for email, go with the No E-Mail option and use Outlook just for its PIM features.

Switching Outlook 98's Personality

NOTE   We're purposefully writing about changing Outlook 98's personality before we describe what it's like to actually upgrade to it. We want you to be informed about these two personalities in a strategic way. Then you'll be able to read the tactical details and our tips for a successful setup experience.

Switching between modes requires some advance planning. If you're in Corporate/Workgroup mode and want to step down to Internet Only, be prepared for a complete uninstall and reinstall of Outlook 98. We tried dynamically stepping down by running setup, simultaneously removing the Corporate/Workgroup component, and selecting Internet Only. Although the installer let us do this, when the dust settled, Outlook 98 was highly unstable; it hung the system repeatedly, and the only fix was a complete uninstall and reinstall. You've been warned.

If you're in Internet Only mode and want to step up to Corporate/Workgroup, this is easy to do. You simply run setup again and check the

"Corporate or Workgroup E-mail Service" line item (more on this shortly). And if you want the flexibility of Corporate/Workgroup mode without the big ol' MAPI footprint, forget it. The two email engines are incompatible.

Upgrading to Outlook 98

A little advance planning goes a long way here. Whether you're running Exchange, Outlook 97, or some other email client, be sure to back up your system before upgrading. If you're running Exchange or Outlook 97, we suggest you configure your client to automatically use your preferred profile (Tools → Options → General, pick the appropriate profile in the "Always use this profile" list, then click on OK). This gives Outlook 98's installer the best odds of determining which mode is best for you. The best way we've found to *guarantee* that you see the E-mail Service Options dialog (shown back in Figure 2-4) is discussed next.

Guaranteeing you get to choose a mode during setup

Here's one sure-fire way to guarantee that setup displays the E-mail Services Option panel that allows you to choose among email modes.

1. We said it before, we'll say it again: back up your entire system.

2. Delete all existing profiles. That's right, all of 'em.*

3. Temporarily archive (with WinZip, PKZip, or a similar utility) all PST and PAB files. There should be no free-standing PST or PAB files on any drive on your system.

4. Run Outlook 98 setup, and after selecting the type of installation, always select Yes in response to the Outlook Mail Usage's panel when it asks, "Do you currently use the version of Outlook installed on this computer to read electronic mail?"

NOTE   Outlook's default installation choices are Minimal, Standard, and Full. If you want the maximum amount of control over what Outlook 98 component does or does not get installed, choose the Standard or Minimal installation option. After the install is complete, rerun the setup and the Maintenance Wizard will appear. Choose Add New Components and you can pick and choose what you want added.

---

* If you're using WinFax Pro on your system: before you delete your existing profiles, go into the WinFax setup menu and turn off the "use Exchange in WinFax" option, or WinFax will keep searching for and creating Exchange profiles.

5. The next panel you see will be E-mail Service Options, as shown in Figure 2-4. Make whatever choice is appropriate for you, as we discussed earlier.

6. If you choose Internet Only mode, Setup will walk you through the Internet Setup Wizard, for which you need to know your logon ID and password, the precise names of your ISP's mail servers, and how you plan to connect to the Internet. Then you'll see the Symantec WinFax Starter Edition Setup Wizard, which asks some more easy questions (name, fax number, voice number, etc.). After a Windows Restart and some more configuration churning, Outlook 98 will be displayed on your system, along with the usual Office Assistant greeting.

7. Outlook will have created a new Personal Folders file for you. (To see this file's path, right-click on Outlook Today in the Outlook Bar, choose Properties, then click the Advanced button.)

The Outlook 97 to 98 upgrade continuum

Although it's not possible to list all conceivable Outlook 97 profile permutations, in Table 2-1 we endeavor to cover the broad spectrum so you can see what's likely to happen when you upgrade. As you read in the previous section, the sure-fire lowest-common-denominator approach—a "scorched earth" strategy, if you will—is to strip your system of all profiles, Personal Folder files (PSTs), and Personal Address Books (PABs), then set up Outlook 98. This gives you absolutely clean, empty, Outlook 98–spawned services and files into which you can safely copy or import data from your archived data sources.

Table 2-1: What Outlook 98 setup does when upgrading from various Outlook 97 configurations

Outlook 97 Profile Services	What Outlook 98 Setup Does
No profiles and no PST or PAB files on system	Displays E-mail Service Options panel allowing you to choose an email mode
Internet E-mail (Internet) + Personal Folders (PST) + Outlook Address Book (OAB)	No E-mail Service Options panel; Outlook imposes Internet Only mode
Includes *any* MAPI service (CompuServe Mail or MS Fax, for example)	No E-mail Service Options panel; Outlook imposes Corporate/Workgroup mode

Stepping up from Internet Only to Corporate/Workgroup mode

You can easily step up from Internet Only to Corporate/Workgroup mode. Here's how:

1. Run Outlook 98 setup again. Check "Corporate or Workgroup E-mail Service" which automatically checks (then disables, so you can't uncheck it) "Fax Update for Corporate or Workgroup E-mail Service."

2. Click the Next button and then click on the Install Now button.

3. Outlook warns, "Switching from Internet Only E-mail Service to Corporate or Workgroup E-mail Service may be incompatible with existing applications!" No problem, click on OK.

4. When setup is done, start Outlook and choose Tools → Services. You now have a profile called Microsoft Outlook Internet Settings that includes these four services: Internet E-mail, Internet E-mail—Symantec WinFax Starter Edition, Outlook Address Book, and Personal Folders.

Installation Odds and Ends

Besides having to deal with Outlook 98's three installation modes, there are some more general installation issues that you need to be aware of in order to keep the annoyance level at ebb tide.

Record Your CD-ROM Key

Chances are better than even that you installed Outlook 97 from a CD-ROM, most likely as part of your Office 97 install. Outlook 98 is a long and dreary Internet download/installation, but it's also a fair bet that a number of you opted to pay the shipping and handling charges to get Outlook 98 on a CD-ROM. Here's a hot tip that can cut down your annoyance potential should you ever need to reinstall Outlook from a CD.

Microsoft CDs require you to enter a "key" number when you install the software they contain. This key is an 11-digit number (4 numbers and a dash followed by 7 numbers) that you'll find on a bright orange sticker on the back of the CD-ROM plastic case. If you're like us, you probably get the cases and the CDs mixed up on a regular basis, so we recommend you write the number on the front of the CD itself. Yep, right across the printed side of the disk, using a permanent marker. It won't hurt the CD—unless you write it on the wrong, non-printed side—and now you always have the disk and the number in the same place.

You can also pop open the Help → About dialog in Outlook to see the product ID number (see Figure 2-1). The middle two groups of numbers are the same as your key number. So if you've already misplaced your key number, you can read it in the Help About box and get it recorded on your CD disk. Consider doing this right now, as in, right this very minute. You may not have a chance to read the ID number from Help → About when you need it most because a frequent reason for re-installing Outlook or any Office 97 component (and thus the need for the number) is that your system has gotten trashed and you ain't gonna be opening the Help → About dialog.

Get the Latest and Greatest

You need to keep current and get the latest version or update for Outlook, since they are coming fast and furious, as discussed in the previous section. Check the Microsoft Web site at *www.microsoft.com/ Office/Office97/ServiceRelease/* or call Microsoft at (800) 370-9272 and find out what the latest and greatest version for Outlook is. Be aware though, if you call the 800 number you may not get the straight scoop. Microsoft is not known for disseminating upgrade information in a coherent, logical, or timely manner even to their own minions, and the poor folks answering the phone may genuinely not know there is a new update, patch, or release available. Double-check at the Microsoft Web site and consider signing up for WOW, the free weekly email newsletter *Woody's Office Watch*, where we try to keep you up to date on all things Office. You can subscribe from the *www.wopr.com* site.

If you're installing a patch or upgrade, carefully read any and all accompanying notes, instructions, or readme files. We really can't stress this part enough. When the SR1 EU version was first made available, Microsoft mistakenly shipped the Standard version to folks who had ordered the Professional version. The instructions recommended uninstalling Office 97 completely and then reinstalling from the new CD. Blindly following this procedure removes Access from your system under these circumstances.

NOTE   For a comprehensive, soup-to-nuts checklist of how to go about uninstalling and reinstalling Office (whether the reinstall is the original version or an update) and live to tell the tale, see Chapter 3.

The Outlook Personal Folders File

Outlook stores everything—every bit of your personal information—in a single file. Your names and addresses, appointments, to-do list items, notes, email (we'll assume that you're using Outlook and are dialing into the Internet or some online service for email as opposed to having Microsoft Exchange Server on the backend); we mean everything! This file, *mailbox.pst,** is created when you install Outlook (or, if you've been using Exchange, the existing Personal Folders file is used) and is typically found in the *C:\Exchange* folder.†

Needless to say, with all your informational eggs in one cyberbasket, you need to take good care of your Personal Folders file, also known as the PST (Personal STore) file.

This file gets BIG! As tiny Elvis would say, "Huge, man, really huge." A hundred or so contacts, a besieged calendar full of entries, a few months worth of email important enough to keep around, and you could easily find yourself with a Personal Folders file in the 30–50 MB range, or more. Ouch! Makes keeping multiple backups of this file a bit awkward. But a backup you should have, as it's not unheard of for this file to become corrupted.

NOTE   Okay, okay, so you've heard this one before—always make a backup and/or archive of your Personal Folders file. Please. Make it—and your PAB—one of the files you back up incrementally every single day. We do. We're not kidding. You'll be glad you did.

In Chapter 3 we go into detail about troubleshooting the Personal Folders file, but there are a few things you should be aware of regarding its care and maintenance (even when it's behaving nicely) as you install Outlook and get it set up.

---

* It's possible, depending on how Outlook is installed (upgrading when you may or may not have an existing *.pst,* for example), that you'll have an *outlook.pst* file instead of a *mailbox.pst.* Same thing, different name. We'll use the *mailbox.pst* name for the Personal Folders file throughout the book.

† Some of you running in a networked environment may have a file named *mailbox.ost,* not *mailbox.pst.* That's okay. Wherever we say *mailbox.pst,* just substitute *mailbox.ost.* Your OST file (OST stands for Offline Store) is only different from a PST file in that items in the OST can also reside in your Mailbox on the server.

The Journal: eating up your free disk space

Outlook has a kind of built-in "Dear Diary" feature called the Journal. While the Journal is very handy in some respects (it's the only way to create a phone log, for example), not everyone needs to record every email message, meeting request, task request, task response, or document they create in Word, Excel, Access, PowerPoint, or the Binder. No matter what the Microsoft marketeers say in their press releases.

By default, when Outlook is installed it starts creating Journal entries every time you do practically anything. These items push the size of your Personal Folders file in a big, annoying way. If you don't need everything tracked in the Journal timeline, you can turn off this auto-record feature on an item-by-item or filetype basis. In Outlook 98, select Tools → Options, select the Preferences tab, then click on the Journal Options button. See Figure 2-5.

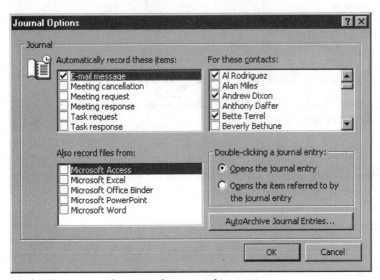

Figure 2-5: Setting the Journal auto-tracking options

The more boxes you uncheck, the fewer things are automatically tracked. Chapter 4, *Enigmatic Journal*, tackles the journal facility and gives you the foundation you'll need to rationally decide which of these automatic tracking features you need and which you can do without. In addition to determining what is tracked, you can also set the response you want when you double-click a Journal entry (open the entry or open the item referred to by the entry). By clicking on the AutoArchive Journal Entries button, you access the Journal properties dialog box, where you can set its AutoArchive settings. We'll discuss the best ways to utilize AutoArchive in Chapter 6, *A Cookbook for Conversion*.

Even with archiving and cutting back on the Journal, you'll be surprised at how fast your Personal Folders file grows. To see what's causing your *.pst* file to swell in Outlook 98, right-click on the Outlook Today – [Personal Folders] folder (either in the Folder List or in the Outlook Bar) and click Properties. Then click on the Folder Size button. See Figure 2-6.

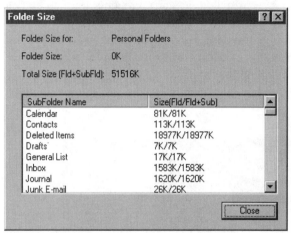

Figure 2-6: Tracking runaway folder growth

Compacting the Personal Folders file

The *mailbox.pst* file needs to be compressed from time to time to recover the space used to store deleted items. After carefully making a backup copy of your *mailbox.pst* file in a nice safe place, compress the file using the following steps:

1. Close all of your other running applications. (You really can't be too careful when it comes to the Personal Folders file.)

2. In Outlook, click on Tools → Services to display the installed services.

3. Select the Personal Folders item in the Services tab, as shown in Figure 2-7.

4. Click on the Properties button to open the Personal Folders dialog, shown in Figure 2-8.

5. Click on the Compact Now button.

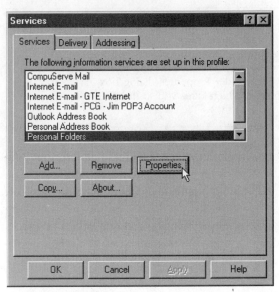

Figure 2-7: Outlook's Services dialog box

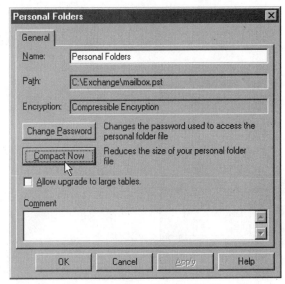

Figure 2-8: Compacting the Personal Folders file

OUTLOOK 98 If you're running Outlook 98 in Internet Only mode, you'll have to jump through some hoops to do this. Right-click on the Outlook Today – [Personal Folders] folder (either in the Folder List or in the Outlook Bar) and choose Properties. In the Personal Folder Properties dialog box, click on the Advanced button, which takes you to the dialog shown in Figure 2-8.

Once the compacting is done, click on OK to close the dialogs. How long this process takes depends on how much compacting is necessary. The more often you compact, the less time it should take. Too bad Microsoft didn't provide any progress indicator so you'd have an idea of how long the process would run. The worst news is that compacting does not seem to squish the Personal Folder's file size down as much as you might hope.

Using the Inbox Repair Tool

Office 97 has a handy utility called the Inbox Repair Tool (*Scanpst.exe*), also included in the standalone version of Outlook that scans a Personal Folders file and, according to its help file, offers to "repair the errors and inconsistencies" that may be present. See Figure 2-9. You'll find this utility on the Start → Programs → Accessories → System Tools menu.

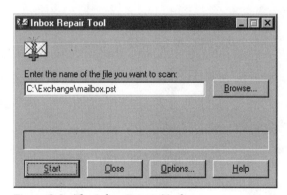

Figure 2-9: The Inbox Repair Tool

This is a dynamite little utility that thoughtfully creates a backup of your Personal Folders file before attempting to correct anything. In Chapter 3, we discuss troubleshooting problems in Outlook and how to use the Inbox Repair Tool.

Relocating the Personal Folders file

Outlook's Personal Folders file can get very large, and you might wind up in a situation where it begins to outgrow the free space on the disk where it was first created. If you have your *mailbox.pst* on *C:\Exchange*, you could, for example, start running low of free space on the C: drive. But your new 8 GB F: drive has loads of space, and you start thinking how nice it would be to just relocate the Personal Folders file.

First, find out where your *mailbox.pst* file is residing at present. If Outlook is not running, fire up Control Panel and double-click on the Mail* icon. Select Personal Folders in the list and click on the Properties button. This displays the same dialog box you saw in Figure 2-8 and shows you where the Personal Folders file is located. If Outlook is running, you can just follow the steps in the "Compacting the Personal Folders File" section shown earlier to see where your Personal Folders file is located.

NOTE   Note how the path to the Personal Folders file is displayed in Figure 2-8 but the text box is not editable, nor is there a Browse button for it. Services like the Personal Address Book can be dynamically relocated through their properties dialog box, but not the Personal Folders file.

Close Outlook if it is running and use Windows Explorer to move the Personal Folders file to its new home. When you restart Outlook, you'll see the dialog box shown in Figure 2-10.

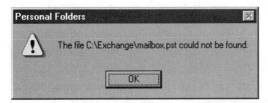

Figure 2-10: Outlook can't find the moved Personal Folders file

Click on OK and you can then browse the new drive/folder where you have transplanted your Personal Folders file. Drill down to the appropriate folder and select the file, then click on Open. See Figure 2-11.

---

* In Outlook 98 the applet's name and title bar read "Mail," but in Outlook 97 they read "Mail and Fax."

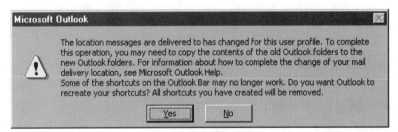

Figure 2-11: Choose the relocated Personal Folders file and click on Open

In theory that should do it; fire up Outlook and things should be peachy. Back when we ran the Microsoft Exchange client (pre-Outlook), this procedure worked dandy and it works great with Outlook 98. But if you are using any flavor of Outlook 97, things can get very annoying. This may be the single best reason to upgrade to 98. When you move the Personal Folders file as we've described in the preceding steps and point Outlook 97 to the new location, you'll get the dialog box shown in Figure 2-12. If you're lucky.

Figure 2-12: Outlook 97, dazed and confused

Here you have two choices, both of them annoying as all get out. Click on Yes and you'll lose your Outlook Bar customizations. You get the factory default Outlook bar. Click on No and you get your Outlook Bar unchanged, but try clicking on *anything* on it and you'll get the message shown in Figure 2-13.

Figure 2-13: Outlook 97 is now totally lost

The folder does not exist? Outlook is not complaining that the folder containing the Personal Folders file does not exist; it thinks the folders within the Personal Folders file don't exist. Of course they exist—they're in the Personal Folders file, and you just copied it from one place to another. Sheesh! Outlook 97 gets gonzo confused, and once you are in this position the only way out is to delete all the items from your Outlook Bar and recreate them all manually. Are we having fun yet or what?

Obviously, you're better off answering Yes to the dialog shown in Figure 2-12 and dealing with the loss of any customizations. At least you get the default Outlook Bar set up. The real gotcha here is that you don't always get the chance to click Yes or No. Sometimes the dialog box in Figure 2-12 simply doesn't pop up. Outlook 97 fires up as if nothing is wrong and then starts giving you the error message shown in Figure 2-13 whenever you click on items on the Outlook Bar. If this happens to you, try starting Outlook from the Start → Run dialog box with the following switch:

```
Outlook.exe /resetoutlookbar
```

This causes Outlook to regenerate a default Outlook Bar. You'll find all the command switches (those listed in the help file and this one, which is undocumented) later in this chapter.

Fixing Annoyances with Add-ins and Know-how

There are a number of Outlook 97 add-ins that address several of Outlook's initial shortcomings (to a greater or lesser extent). Microsoft has either incorporated Outlook 97 add-in features into Outlook 98 itself or provided and installed the add-ins as part of the Outlook 98 installation process.

You can get Microsoft add-ins from their Web site, which is easiest to reach by going into Outlook, pulling down the Help menu → Microsoft on the Web → Free Stuff. This will kick off your browser and take you to the right area on the Microsoft site. Be forewarned, though: Microsoft seems to revamp and reorganize their site with annoying regularity, moving things around and rendering your bookmarks useless. Last time we checked for Outlook add-ins (accessing the Microsoft Web site through Outlook 98's Help menu as described) we wound up on the Microsoft Office Update page. From there we had to click on Product Enhancements and then jump to Outlook in order to find the right page. Be prepared to search around.

When last there, we found add-ins for Outlook, Exchange, and Schedule+; additional converters; the Internet Mail Enhancement Patch; and even additional Help material.

NOTE   If you want to see what add-ins you have installed in Outlook, click the Tools menu, then Options → Other → Advanced Options. On the Advanced Options dialog, click on the Add-In Manager button (see Figure 2-14). (In Outlook 97 the steps are Tools → Options → General → Add-In Manager.) This lists the currently installed add-ins and shows you which add-ins are presently active (a checked box indicates an active add-in). To remove an add-in, select it from this list and click on Remove.

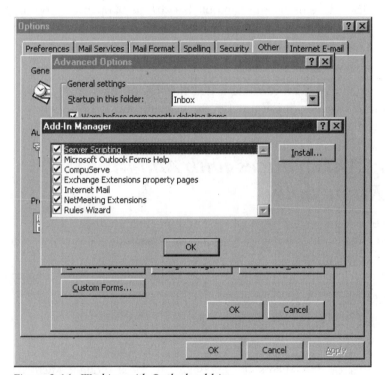

Figure 2-14: Working with Outlook add-ins

Rules Wizard

The Rules Wizard lets you trigger an action automatically when email meeting some preset criteria is received or sent. This replicates the features of the Inbox Assistant (if you use Outlook with Microsoft Exchange Server as your email backend). The Rules Wizard is included with Outlook 98 and can be installed as part of the Outlook installation routine, but you have to install it yourself manually if you are still running Outlook 97. You can download *Ruleswiz.exe* from the Microsoft Web site, as discussed earlier.

NOTE   You can also find *Ruleswiz.exe* in the *Valupack\Ruleswiz* folder of your Office 97 CD (the SR1 EU version).

Once installed, you create rules by selecting Rules Wizard from the Tools menu.

With Rules you can:

- Move messages to a folder when sent or when they arrive.

- Automatically assign categories to messages.

- Have yourself notified when a message of a given priority (High, Normal, or Low) arrives.

For example, say you want all email related to a particular project you are corresponding about with your workgroup filed in a folder when it comes in so you can see just those messages without having to wade through all the items that collect in your Inbox folder. You create a special folder (File → New → Folder) to hold these messages, then create a rule to move the messages when they arrive to the proper folder. Click on Tools → Rules Wizard and follow the simple prompts to create a rule that automatically moves mail as it comes in or is sent out. See Figure 2-15.

The Rules Wizard is very handy and works pretty much as advertised, although it does get confused at times. Occasionally, we've experienced rules being ignored when dialing in for mail on the Internet. It's sporadic, and just opening the Rules Wizard dialog or closing and restarting Outlook seems to fix it. Very annoying, but still worth the hassle to have your email presorted for you.

NOTE   There is an outstanding FAQ on the Rules Wizard available online. Point your browser at *www.slipstick.com/exchange/ rwizfaq.htm* for helpful information on working with the Rules Wizard.

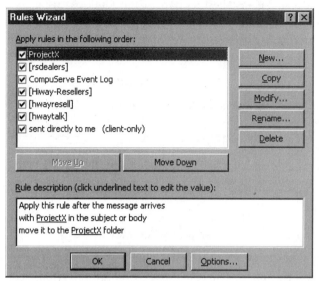

Figure 2-15: Outlook's Rules Wizard

Eliminating Junk Email

Outlook 98 has a new feature that builds on the idea of *rules* for automatically handling junk email (more commonly referred to as spam*) based on certain conditions being met. When the junk email feature has been activated and configured, you can highlight any email message you receive and designate its sender as either an "Adult Content Sender" or "Junk Sender" and cause any future messages received from that source to be flagged or moved to a specified folder, among other possible actions. In a nutshell, you can establish rules that inspect almost any message characteristic (sender, content, size, flags, importance, categories, attachments, sent only to you, where your name is not in the To box, and so on); and the actions rules take can be as aggressive or permissive as you want.

First let's cover the "out of the box" junk email filters provided by the Organize tool:

1. Select the Inbox facility and choose Organize from the Tools menu. In the pane that appears, click on the Junk E-Mail button.

2. From the drop-down lists, pick the actions you want taken for messages that meet the criteria for Junk and/or Adult Content messages. See Figure 2-16.

---

* Spam is a catch-all term used for almost any unsolicited email you receive, usually from someone trying to sell you something. Much like the junk mail that inundates the postal system.

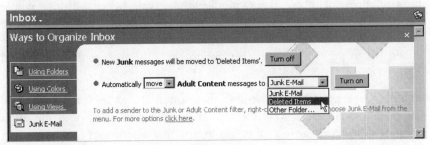

Figure 2-16: Turning on the junk email features

3. Click on the "Turn on" button(s) to activate the junk email feature in Outlook 98.

NOTE The Organize tool's Junk E-mail options represent a friendly interface on top of two separate features: (1) a new rule-based automatic formatting feature that changes *only* a message's font and color, and (2) rules stored in the Rules Wizard that act on messages by moving them, deleting them, or taking some action. You can lift the hood on the automatic formatting feature like this: View → Current View → Customize Current View, then click on the Automatic Formatting button. Here in the Automatic Formatting dialog you can turn junk email formatting on or off by checking or clearing the two built-in rules "Adult Content" and "Commercial e-mail." You can also customize the font and color for these rules, refine their conditions, or create your own formatting rules.

On the action side of the coin, there's the Rules Wizard. If you've already activated the "move" features of Organize's Junk E-Mail then you'll see an Adult Content Rule and a Junk E-mail Rule checked in the list. Unlike rules you create yourself, these built-in rules can't be modified, although they can be disabled.

Once you have activated junk mail formatting/handling rules using whichever interface you prefer, you can designate a sender whose address you want blackballed. Just right-click on a spam message, and from the pop-up menu you can click on the Junk E-mail option and designate the message as having come from a Junk Sender or an Adult Content Sender. Outlook will then perform whatever action you have defined on any new messages from that sender.

You could mimic this behavior in Outlook 97 by installing the Rules Wizard add-in and creating a rule to cover each junk address that found its way into your inbox. But Outlook 98 goes one better with this whole concept by actually filtering your incoming messages (assuming you've activated the junk email features) against the text strings listed in a file called *filters.txt* which can be found in *C:\Program Files\Microsoft Office\Office.*

Filters.txt contains the text strings most often found in spam messages. There are separate sections for general, commercial spam and the adult X-rated stuff. You can edit this file in any text editor and add your own spam traps if you are so inclined. A portion of a *filters.txt* file is shown in Figure 2-17.

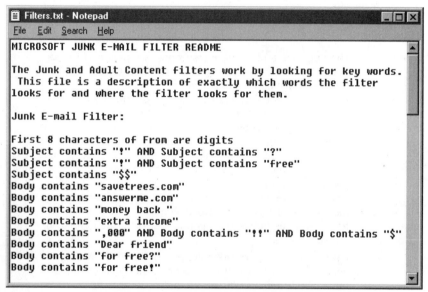

Figure 2-17: Outlook 98's filters.txt *file*

If you're a cautious soul, set up your junk filters to move messages to a custom folder so you can look over the types of messages Outlook deems spam before you delete them. That way you can fine-tune *filters.txt* if you find it is declaring some messages as junk that you don't want arbitrarily deleted. Nor is moving messages to the Deleted Items folders or a custom folder your only option. You can change the color of the message instead of moving it, as we explained earlier in the discussion of automatic formatting.

To tweak your junk options after they've been set up, open the Organize pane and click on the underlined "click here" part of the sentence "For more options click here." (Seems that this Web interface is one we'd all better get used to.) This gives you access to a number of options: you can manually edit the names you've added as junk or adult senders, or even access updated filters made available on the Microsoft Web site. See Figure 2-18. For the former option, you can alternately use the Rules Wizard interface to the same effect.

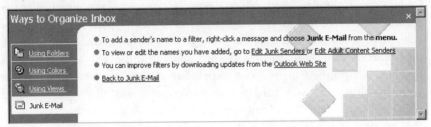

Figure 2-18: Outlook 98's junk messages options in the Organize pane

Preview Pane

Outlook 97 offered only the AutoPreview feature for displaying email message information without having to actually open a given message. AutoPreview is shown in Figure 2-19.

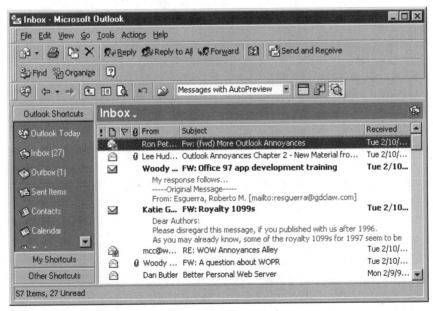

Figure 2-19: Outlook 97's messages in AutoPreview view

The AutoPreview view shows you the first three lines of each unread email message in your Inbox. This was okay, but Outlook users really wanted to be able to view messages in a separate pane as they scrolled through items in their Inbox. Microsoft came up with the 3-Pane add-in, which adds a window pane to Outlook that shows you the selected email message in a scrollable window.

To set up the 3-Pane Viewer in Outlook 97, just download *Ol3pane.exe* from the Microsoft Web site. Annoyingly, if you are in a non-email folder—say Calendar—and select Tools → Options, you won't see the 3-Pane Viewer's Preview tab where you can set the pane's options. *You can only see the add-in's Preview tab if you are in an email folder.* This is a completely non-standard design—just imagine if the Tools → Options → Spelling tab popped in and out depending on what type of folder you were in—and can easily lead you to think the viewer didn't get installed or is malfunctioning. We're very glad that Microsoft moved the location of the preview pane options controls in Outlook 98, and that now the controls don't disappear unexpectedly.

NOTE   The Microsoft 3-Pane Viewer add-in for Outlook 97 shows up in Control Panel's Add/Remove Programs utility, so you can both remove it as an add-in from Outlook (Tools → Options → General → Add-In Manager) and physically remove it from your computer via the Control Panel. The Rules Wizard does *not* show up in the Add/Remove utility.

Outlook 98 has a preview pane built-in, shown in Figure 2-20. Outlook 98's preview pane is more stable than the 97 add-in, and you can set options for the preview pane by right-clicking on the header area of the pane and clicking on Preview Pane Options in the pop-up menu. Or you can click Tools → Options → Other → Preview Pane. As you select each message shown in the list, the selected message is displayed in the preview pane (which is a resizable window, so you control how much display real estate you're willing to give to the pane). This makes more of the message visible, and you can scroll this window to read the entire message.

By default, every message in the list that you click on to preview is marked as "read" (unread messages are displayed in bold; they also display the closed envelope icon, and in AutoPreview view they show you the first three lines of the message in blue). While this may not be annoying to everyone, we like to be able to preview a message and still have it show up as unread in the Inbox. As we deal with messages by replying, printing, filing, and so on, we mark them as read, so we know they've been dealt with. Having the message so marked just because we clicked on it is a bit draconian to our way of thinking. Fortunately, this annoyance can be dealt with easily.

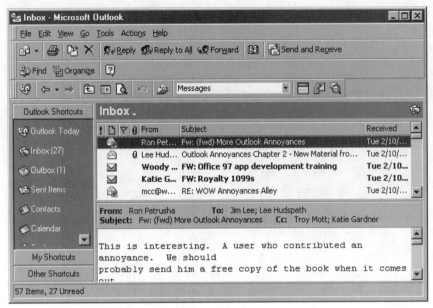

Figure 2-20: Outlook 98's preview pane

From the Tools menu, click on Options and then select the Other tab. Click on the Preview Pane button. See Figure 2-21. Uncheck the "Mark messages as read in preview window" checkbox, and then you can preview messages without having them marked as read. If you like the idea of having the messages marked as read for you automatically, you can opt for the "Wait *x* seconds before marking item as read" setting. Having the pane viewer mark your messages as read won't turn off the envelope icon in the tray, a minor annoyance if you get the mail waiting envelope icon in your system tray and you *don't* click on the icon to switch to Outlook. You'll have to actually open a message in Outlook to switch off the tray icon.

Where to Find Third-party Add-ins

The architecture of Office 97 applications provides for building add-ins that add features or functionality not found in the original. As an Office component, Outlook 98 (and 97) provides for add-ins, as we discussed in the previous section. Some, such as the Rules Wizard and the 3-Pane Viewer, are available directly from Microsoft. Others are available from third parties and in some cases directly address limitations in Microsoft's add-ins. For example, a Microsoft KnowledgeBase article (Q173101) actually notes the limitations of the 3-Pane Viewer and recommends that the

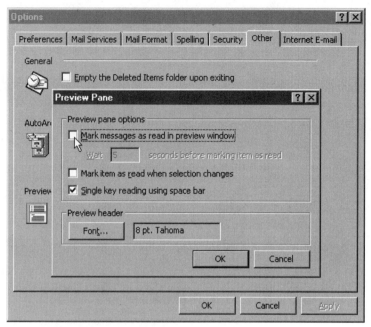

Figure 2-21: Configuring the Preview Pane

user download a third-party add-in, Chilton Preview, if the user still uses Outlook 97.

You can find the Chilton Preview add-in along with dozens of other Outlook and Exchange add-ins at SlipStick Systems' Web site (*www.slip-stick.com*, a site put together and managed by Sue Mosher). Some are freeware, others shareware, and all are pretty much "use at your own risk." The site is tricky to navigate, having several pages where you'll find downloadable add-ins with some overlap between the pages. Check out both of these pages at Sue's site:

- *http://www.slipstick.com/exchange/gallery.htm*
- *http://www.slipstick.com/exchange/add-ins.htm*

You'll also want to check out the following pages on the Microsoft site (assuming Microsoft does not reorganize their Web site again, breaking links throughout all of cyberspace) which contain some vertical market and special use add-ins for Outlook:

- *www.microsoft.com/Outlook/documents/thirdparty_addons.htm*
- *www.microsoft.com/Outlook/Optimize/*

Annoying Details and Customizations

Outlook is a complex piece of software, no doubt about it. Much of its interface is different from its Office siblings (although we suspect Microsoft will be spreading the "make it work like a Web browser" philosophy across the other Office applications as time goes on). On top of everything else, Outlook has a bewildering array of customization options, leaving you to fathom where to go to change what. In this section, we point out some of the more common customization options available and some of the more confusing problems you're likely to run into.

Profile Profundities

Profiles are something you'll have to understand if you're going to get along with Outlook. If you're running Outlook 97 or Outlook 98 in Corporate/Workgroup mode and you click on Tools → Services (see Figure 2-22), what you're looking at are all the services currently in your active *profile*. A profile is a collection of services. The Services, Delivery, and Addressing tabs show you all the settings contained within a given profile. Note that Windows 95 and Outlook treat things such as your Outlook Personal Services folder or Exchange address book as a "service."

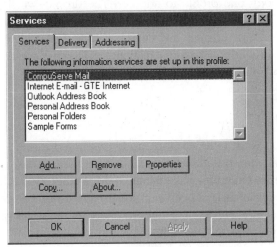

Figure 2-22: A profile is a collection of services

You might want to create multiple profiles, since some services are not compatible with others (for example, Microsoft Fax and Internet Mail in the same profile give many users fits) or you might share a computer with someone else and you both want to keep separate profiles. To get a list of the profiles you currently have set up, start the Control Panel (Start → Settings → Control Panel) and double-click on the Mail icon. Click on the Show Profiles button and you'll see the dialog shown in Figure 2-23.

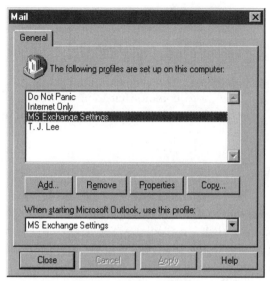

Figure 2-23: Current profiles

From this dialog box you can Add, Remove, view the Properties of the individual services, and Copy one profile to another. The drop-down list box lets you choose the default profile that is used when you first start Outlook or Exchange. You can change the default profile from within Outlook, but changing it in Outlook changes it globally; in other words, change it in Outlook, and the Mail dialog box will reflect that change, and vice versa.

Internet Only mode

If you are running Outlook 98 in Internet Only mode (discussed earlier in this chapter), you have only one pseudo-profile. Since a profile is a collection of services, and Internet Only mode is a single service (the Internet), it's not really a profile at all in that respect, but you'll have a number of what Outlook calls "Directory Services" grouped under a category of "Internet Accounts." Yes, we think this is confusing too.

In Internet Only mode, click Tools → Accounts (there is no Services option, as in Corporate/Workgroup mode). See Figure 2-24.

You can have multiple Internet accounts, and Outlook automatically provides access to a number of directory services. See Figure 2-25.

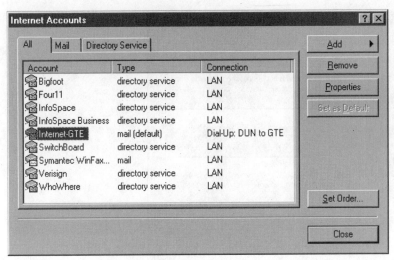

Figure 2-24: Internet accounts (Outlook 98 in Internet Only mode)

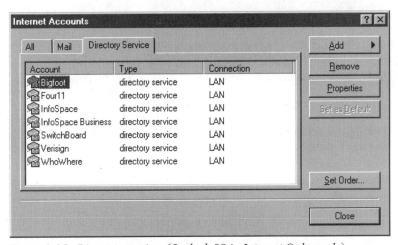

Figure 2-25: Directory services (Outlook 98 in Internet Only mode)

A directory service can be configured so that when you're composing email, names entered as Internet addresses are checked against various Internet service providers' servers (such as the Bigfoot or Four11 servers, so if you want to send email to 'John Doe' but don't have his email address, you would enter 'John Doe' in the "To" field, and the directory services will search for Doe's actual email address). Configure services by selecting them in the Directory Services tab in the Internet Accounts dialog box. Then click on the Properties button (see Figure 2-26).

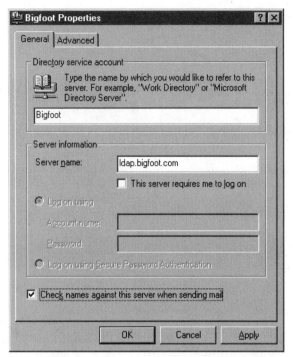

Figure 2-26: Tweaking a directory service (Outlook 98 in Internet Only mode)

Multiple profiles in Corporate or Workgroup mode

Click on Tools → Options, and on the Mail Services tab there's a section called Startup settings, shown in Figure 2-27. If you have multiple profiles you can set Outlook to always start with a particular profile or you can have it prompt you for the profile to use each time Outlook is started (see Figure 2-28).

NOTE   If you set the "Always use this profile" value and then click on the "Prompt for a profile to be used" option button, you'll be prompted to pick a profile, but the default choice in the prompt dialog will be the setting from the "Always use this profile" value list.

Most people just pick the profile they want when prompted, hit OK, and never look back. But from the Choose Profile dialog, you can fire off a wizard that walks you through creating a new profile by clicking on the New button, or you can set your selected profile as the default by checking the "Set as default profile" checkbox. In case you're keeping

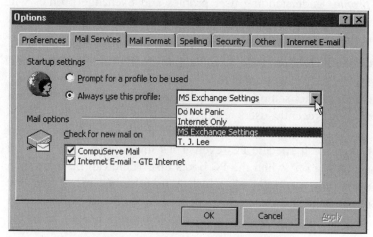

Figure 2-27: Controlling the default profile from within Outlook

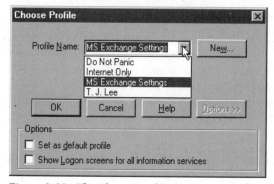

Figure 2-28: The Choose Profile dialog with Options displayed

count, this is the third way to change the default profile that we've discussed so far.

The "Show Logon screens for all information services" checkbox causes each service's Properties dialog to be displayed (same as doing Tools → Services, selecting each service in turn, and clicking the Properties button). This gives you all the details on the profile you're about to use. Unfortunately, if you've picked the wrong profile, you have to slog through each service's properties screen and wait for Outlook to load before you can shut Outlook down and start again.

Profile mechanics

As you've seen in the previous sections, *profile* is a term you'll hear and use a lot when dealing with Outlook. But you'll also hear it used in conjunction with Windows, as in *user profile*, and with Exchange, as in

Exchange profile. Understanding user profiles and Exchange profiles will help you understand the convoluted path you must so often tread when customizing or troubleshooting Outlook.

First, what's a *user profile?* A user profile governs the user interface and operating system behavior settings for a specific user (usually, that's you), including Control Panel settings, desktop appearance, the Start menu, and information about recently used resources such as documents, searches with Find, setup activity, printer ports, and so on. There is always at least one user profile for a specific PC, even if it's invisible to you (i.e., you never explicitly "log on" when the PC boots up). There can be more than one user profile for a specific PC, which is useful when more than one person uses the same PC or when users roam from PC to PC. From the operating system's perspective, a user profile's main residence is the registry.

NOTE   If you really look under the hood, a user profile is spread across several different storage locations: data is in the HKEY_CURRENT_USER branch of your registry as well as in numerous folders like *Desktop, Recent,* and so on (the folders themselves are also part of the profile). So you can't actually "see" a user profile sitting in a single storage location. For more information on user profiles, see the *Microsoft Windows 95 Resource Kit.*

Next let's consider what an *Exchange profile* is. An Exchange profile is the part of a user profile that defines all the Exchange settings for that user profile. Thus an Exchange profile lives where the user profile lives (primarily in the registry, and also in the loose association of files that comprise the various services installed for a particular Exchange profile).

Two other aspects of Outlook that affect how it presents itself to you are related to this issue of profiles: Outlook Bar settings and Outlook view customizations. Outlook Bar customization data lives in a *<profile_name> .fav* file in your *C:\Windows* folder. Outlook folders include unique signatures tied specifically to the user's configuration, and since Outlook Bar shortcuts point to these folders, one user's *.fav* files won't work on another user's computer. Outlook view customizations live in the Personal Folders file.

Deleting Items

Outlook is unique in that it maintains its own version of the Windows Recycle Bin. When you delete items or folders in Outlook, they go to the

Deleted Items folder, which is maintained within the Personal Folders file, *not the Windows Recycle Bin*. From the Deleted Items folder in Outlook, you can move deleted items back to other folders if you find that you (or a rule you set up, or the junk email feature) deleted something hastily; this is a good thing. On the other hand, things tend to pile up rather quickly, so the Deleted Items folder requires regular housekeeping. In Outlook 98, on the Tools → Options → Other tab you can check the "Empty the Deleted Items folder upon exiting" checkbox and have this folder emptied whenever you exit Outlook (in Outlook 97, it's Tools → Options → General). Of course, if you opt for deleting on exit, you have a safety net only as long as the current Outlook session lasts, since once the Deleted Items folder is dumped, there's no going back; items deleted from the Deleted Items folder bypass the Recycle Bin and go directly to the cyberbit bucket.

NOTE   Outlook's Deleted Items folder deserves a special note as it relates to the Rules Wizard discussed earlier in this chapter. Say you create a Rule that moves all incoming email messages with "ProjectX" in the subject to a folder you create named "Deal." Later you delete the Deal folder, but don't empty the Deleted Items folder or delete or change the Rule. All incoming messages are still subject to the Rule and any message with "ProjectX" in the subject winds up in the deleted Deal folder, which is now a sub-folder of the Deleted Items folder. If you delete a folder that is needed by a rule, even from the Deleted Items folder, you'll get a warning message that the rule cannot find the missing folder and that Rule is then disabled.

The alternative is to either manually clean up the Deleted Items folder from time to time, or to archive its contents. Archiving is discussed at length in Chapter 6.

How Will that Email Be Sent?

In Outlook 98 if you click on Tools → Options → Mail Format, you can specify the email editor you want when creating new email messages (see Figure 2-29). You can play it safe and go with Plain Text; use Microsoft's Rich Text format, commonly referred to as RTF; dabble with HTML, which lets you have background images and animated graphics just like a Web page (is this necessarily a good thing?); or even use Microsoft Word (as discussed in the next section) to create your messages.

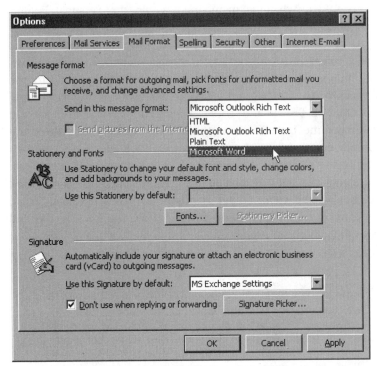

Figure 2-29: Choosing your email editor

So far so good. The problems start when you realize that despite Redmond fantasies to the contrary, not everyone in cyberspace uses Outlook for email. Lots of folks use email readers that have no format in common with Outlook except Plain Text (making Plain Text the most conservative choice for a mail format). You can easily wind up sending email to someone in a format that they can't read. Getting a phone call from someone asking you to read him or her the email message you sent them sort of defeats the purpose, wouldn't you agree?

You pick an email format that you think will work for everyone you correspond with electronically and hope for the best. But it's even more complicated than that. When you reply to an email, Outlook 98 looks at the format of the received message and tries to format the outgoing message accordingly. On the contrary, new messages you create from scratch—not in response to an incoming message—are controlled by the setting in Tools → Options → Mail Format (TOMF). At least that's how it's supposed to work.

If you send a message to a group of people, then the TOMF setting is used for all the recipients. This is true even if you are using Internet Only mode, which has an override setting on each Contact record (see Figure 2-30).

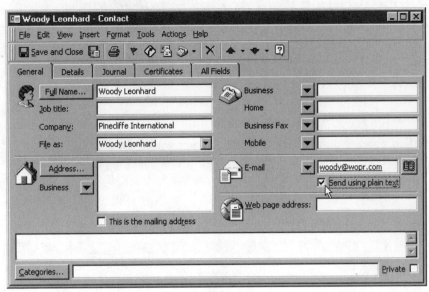

Figure 2-30: Outlook 98 Internet Only mode Contact set for Plain Text

You get the TOMF setting unless you're replying to a message received in a different format or if you're in Internet Only mode and have checked the "Send using plain text" checkbox, unless you're sending to a group of recipients, in which case you're back to the TOMF. At least in theory. In testing the various email settings between multiple people all running Outlook 98, we ran into a number of problems with messages sent across the Internet, and these problems occurred often enough to warrant this simple global recommendation: *switch everything to Plain Text until Microsoft works out all the kinks*. The problems included the following:

- Messages were often received as Plain Text no matter how they were formatted when sent.

- Occasionally, an HTML background wallpaper was received as a file attachment.

- Messages formatted with Microsoft Word were received as attachments (Word needs to be the default mail format on both the sender and recipient's systems to avoid this).

Pretty annoying. Unless you know in advance that your recipients can handle RTF, HTML, or Word, just stick with Plain Text and avoid the headaches.

Using Microsoft Word as Your Email Editor

As we just discussed, Outlook provides for using Microsoft Word as your email editor, thereby giving you access to all of Word's features (like the Thesaurus and Word's amazing AutoText/AutoCorrect features, for example) when creating your messages. In Tools → Options → Mail Format, select Microsoft Word in the "Send in this message format" drop-down list, as shown back in Figure 2-29.

When you create messages, Word appears within the message dialog. In Figure 2-31, you can see that below the Outlook toolbar is the familiar Word Annoyances Standard and Formatting toolbars. (Familiar, that is, if you've read *Word 97 Annoyances*, by Woody Leonhard, Lee Hudspeth, and T.J. Lee; ISBN 1-56592-308-1.)

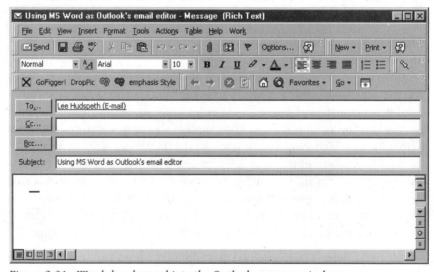

Figure 2-31: Word shoe-horned into the Outlook message window

When you have this option checked and you start Outlook, Word runs in a hidden window (assuming it is not already running) so its features can be whistled up when you create a new mail message. We bring this up for several reasons. First, Word offers you the most formatting options of all Outlook's available choices. Second, you're probably already familiar with it as your word processor. Still, this is a massive program to keep idling in the background on the off chance you might want to send some email (rather like swatting a fly with a sledgehammer), and many of us have opted to not use Word as our email editor, given some of the odd instabilities it causes. But if you really need full word processing power and access to Word's advanced functionality when you are writing your email correspondence, then this is the way to go.

Services—Processing in Order

If you have multiple services installed—say, CompuServe and an Internet provider—you can click Tools → Send and Receive → All Accounts to check all your email accounts (or just click the Send and Receive button on the Standard toolbar). The services are processed in the order in which the accounts are shown on the Send and Receive cascading menu. You'll see the same order on the Tools → Options → Mail Services tab (see Figure 2-32).

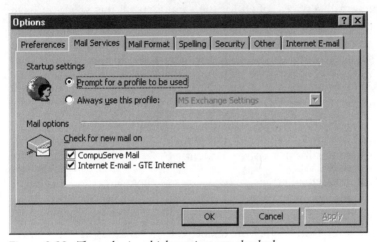

Figure 2-32: The order in which services are checked

Outlook cycles through all the services, from the top of the list to the bottom, processing each service (dialing if necessary, connecting, checking for mail, sending faxes, etc.) in turn.

The order of these services is determined by the order in which you originally installed your services, but in reverse; the first service you installed is at the bottom of the list and gets processed last. This is really annoying because if you want to control the order in which services are accessed, *the only way to change the order is to uninstall and reinstall each service in the reverse order of how you want them processed.*

OUTLOOK 98   If you're running Outlook 98 in Internet Only mode, you can dynamically reorder multiple Internet accounts (Tools → Accounts → Set Order).

The PAB's "Reply To" Bug

Lots of people, tired of the endless stream of address books coming out of Redmond, have settled into keeping address information in the Personal Address Book (PAB). The PAB was first used with the original Exchange email client that shipped with Windows 95. The PAB is popular especially given the lack of a straightforward way to create distribution lists in Outlook Contact folders (notwithstanding Outlook 98's Internet Only mode, which *does* let you create distribution lists). If you use the PAB in this fashion then beware of the bug we are about to describe.

A common PAB aggravation is discovering that a message you intended for one service went out instead over a different service. You probably use multiple email services, often for the same person; this way you have a better chance of being able to get your email through despite a particular mail provider's ups and downs. But the potential for trouble compounds as you add email addresses to your PAB.

Unlike a Contact record, which supports three separate email addresses per person, the PAB creates a separate record for each of the possible ways to send email to the same person. If someone you correspond with is on CompuServe and also has an Internet address, you would have two separate PAB entries for that correspondent.

Outlook, like most email applications, has a "display name" and an underlying email address for messages. But unlike many Internet email applications, the display name is what counts to the PAB. Let's say the ever-popular John Doe sends you email with "John Doe" as the display name. The underlying email address could be his CompuServe address or his ISP account. PAB would store both addresses as "John Doe." In replying, Outlook will *ignore the underlying email address* in a message's From field in favor of whatever PAB listing corresponds to the display name. This means if he sent you a message from his ISP account, but you have him in your PAB under his CompuServe account, when you reply, Outlook will send it to him over—you guessed it—CompuServe.

If you launch a Check for New Mail On session for Internet Mail only by unchecking the other services in the Check for New Mail On list box, thinking that will process the reply to Mr. Doe, it won't. This affects incoming mail only. Since the listing in your PAB is for his CompuServe address, Outlook treats your reply—*regardless of how the incoming message had been sent*—as a CompuServe message. So, the reply will sit in the Outbox until you connect to CompuServe.

What if some other John Doe (let's call him #1) is already in your PAB, you get a message from a different John Doe (let's call him #2) but you don't add John Doe #2 to your PAB, and instead you simply reply to his message? *The wrong John Doe gets the reply.* Specifically, John Doe #1 gets the reply instead of John Doe #2, who actually sent you the message. There's more...

Outlook is unpredictable in handling mail if there's more than one PAB entry under the same name. If you have two John Doe listings in your PAB, one for his ISP and one for CompuServe, there's no way to know what Outlook will do with a reply message. The mail may just sit in your Outbox forever, or Outlook may use one of the John Doe entries at random. So what do you do about this? Sadly, your choices are few. You can fill in a message's To field with the recipient's literal email address. Outlook won't override that.

You can also manually update your PAB as follows: open the PAB, find any duplicate listings, and make each one unique. Outlook doesn't make this easy. You can't simply change a listing's type. Oh no, you have to delete the old listing and create a new one. Blecch. You can add a refer-ence to each listing to indicate what service is involved—for example, "John Doe (Internet)" and "John Doe (CIS)." Use whatever system works for you, just remember: no duplicate names, and try to set up each listing so it's unlikely to conflict with anyone's email return address.

Or better yet, drop the PAB and switch over to the Contact list. We cover converting and importing information into Outlook's Contact list in Chapter 6.

A Spell Checking Bug-a-boo

A number of users we know (including ourselves) have run into the problem of Outlook suddenly refusing to spell check messages. You go to spell check a message and suddenly you're staring at a message box that tells you to reinstall the shared spelling component of Office (see Figure 2-33).

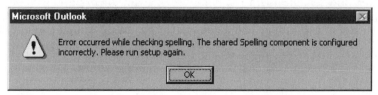

Figure 2-33: Outlook loses track of the common spell check files

Mind you, all your other Office applications keep spell checking just fine, but Outlook acts like it's never heard of spell checking. Turns out that of all the Office applications, Outlook is "spell sensitive." It's prone to thinking some files are corrupt when all the other applications are using the same files with nary a complaint. Then again, Outlook cannot use any of the spell check files found in Office 95, although all the other Office 97 applications can, so go figure. Maybe Outlook just gets cranky.

The good news is that this annoyance can be remedied. Oddly enough, you just follow the advice in the message box and reinstall the Office spell check feature. Pop in your Office CD and run Setup. Click on Add/Remove and then select the Office Tools entry. Click on the Change Option button. Uncheck the box for Spelling Checker (see Figure 2-34).

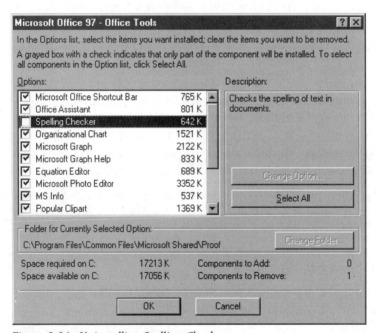

Figure 2-34: Uninstalling Spelling Checker

Next use Windows Explorer to search your disk for *Mssp232.dll* and *Mssp2_en.lex* and rename them temporarily by giving them an extension of *.old*. Then run Office Setup again, only this time *check* the Spelling Checker option under Office Tools and reinstall it. Finally, rename *Mssp232.old* and *Mssp2_en.old* back to their original names.

Handy Outlook Command Line Switches

Outlook has a number of command line switches you can use to control what Outlook does on startup or to pop up a module within Outlook (although Outlook itself does not appear). While these switches are best used with Windows shortcuts, you can also use the Start → Run dialog and type outlook.exe /*switch* to trigger an action.

Table 2-2 lists the switches you can use with Outlook.

Table 2-2: Outlook startup switches

Switch	Function
/resetoutlookbar	Causes Outlook to start and regenerates the default Outlook Bar shortcuts (the icons that appear in the Outlook Bar itself).[1]
/cleanfreebusy	Causes Outlook to start and regenerates any free/busy information for calendar items. (Useful should your Exchange Server primary calendar folder be deleted, leaving you with bolded days in the mini-calendar that do not have appointments.)[1]
/cleanreminders	Causes Outlook to start and regenerates any reminders. (Useful should scheduled reminders stop appearing.)[1]
/cleanviews	Causes Outlook to start and restores all default views.[1]
/resetfolders	Causes Outlook to start and restores any missing default folders.[1]
/cleanschedplus	Causes Outlook to start and deletes all Schedule+ data from the Exchange Server and allows Outlook's free/busy information to be accessible to Schedule+ users. (Useful for those who have upgraded from Schedule+ to Outlook but need to still share information with Schedule+ users.)[1]
/select "d:\path\folder name"[2]	Opens a particular folder (such as My Documents) when Outlook starts.
/folder	Causes Outlook to start with the Outlook Bar hidden.
/profiles	Forces Outlook 98 in Corporate/Workgroup mode to display the Choose Profiles dialog box on startup no matter what the Tools → Options → Mail Services setting is.

Table 2-2: Outlook startup switches (continued)

Switch	Function
/c ipm.note	Automatically creates an email message. Outlook starts in a hidden window if it is not already running.
/c ipm.post	Automatically creates a post item in the default Outlook folder. Outlook starts in a hidden window if it is not already running.
/c ipm.appointment	Automatically creates an appointment item. Outlook starts in a hidden window if it is not already running.
/c ipm.activity	Automatically creates an activity item. Outlook starts in a hidden window if it is not already running.
/c ipm.task	Automatically creates a task item. Outlook starts in a hidden window if it is not already running.
/c ipm.contact	Automatically creates a contact item. Outlook starts in a hidden window if it is not already running.
/c ipm.stickynote	Automatically creates a note item. Outlook starts in a hidden window if it is not already running.
/a "*path/file name*"	Creates an item with the specified file as an attachment. (If no item type is specified with the /c switch, ipm.note is used.) Outlook starts in a hidden window if it is not already running.

[1] These switches are not documented in Outlook's help file but they are mentioned in KnowledgeBase Article Q156982. These switches carry the warning from Microsoft that you use them "at your own risk."

[2] If your switch includes a path that has spaces, you must enclose the string with quotation marks. For a path to a folder within Outlook, precede the path with "Outlook:\\".

NOTE   If you don't already have a shortcut for Outlook on your desktop, you can easily create one by copying the Outlook shortcut in your *C:\Windows\Start menu\Programs* folder. Right-click on the shortcut file and choose Copy from the pop-up menu. Then right-click on your desktop and choose Paste Shortcut. To edit the shortcut and add startup switches, right-click on the icon and choose Properties from the pop-up menu. Click on the Shortcut tab and edit the Target line (see Figure 2-35).

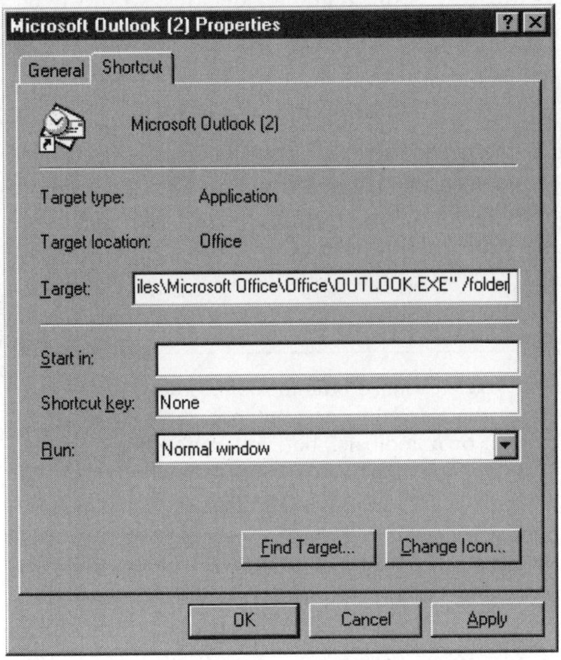

Figure 2-35: Outlook shortcut using the /folder switch

The switches that "automatically" create some item in Outlook do just that—create some item in Outlook. They'll start Outlook itself in a hidden window if it's not running, but once you've created the item, Outlook is closed again. These switches are used extensively on the OSB (Office Shortcut Bar). Call up the OSB for Office and find the button that has the tooltip New Message. Right-click on that button and select properties. Click on the Shortcut tab and study the text in the Target text box. You should see something like `C:\Program Files\Microsoft Office\` `Office\OUTLOOK.EXE /c IPM.Note`.

Clicking on this OSB button fires off a shortcut and all you see is a new message form pop up. No magic here, just startup switches. For all the switches available, Outlook lacks one you'd think would be basic: a way to start it up minimized. Oh, you can create a shortcut for Outlook and choose the "run/minimized" option in the shortcut properties in Outlook 98. But there's a bug in Outlook 97 and this trick won't work in that version.

Customizing Outlook 98 Toolbars

If you've read our other books in this series, you know that we're big on customization. Anytime you can make an Office application work more the way you work and less the way some marketer decided would make a good software demo, you're increasing your productivity.

One of the most annoyance-reducing, productivity-enhancing things you can do with Outlook 98 or any Office application is to customize its toolbars. Okay, if you're going *tsk tsk* and shake your head at our use of terminology, we'll agree that *technically* it's not a toolbar, it's a command bar* of the toolbar variety. Toolbar, menu bar, command bar, what the heck, as long as you know you can—and should—customize the thing, that's what counts.

OUTLOOK 98   Outlook 98 will let you customize built-in toolbars and the Outlook menu bar—there's only one—but not shortcuts. You can create your own toolbars, but you can't create new menu bars or shortcuts. Sadly, you cannot do *any* of this in Outlook 97.

We'll show you how you might customize Outlook 98's toolbars, but keep in mind that this example is intended to show you how to mechanically modify your toolbars and why it's such a great thing to do. You should modify *your* version of Outlook to work *your* way. Customization is a very individual thing.

Creating a custom toolbar in Outlook 98

If you click on View → Toolbars, you'll see that Outlook comes with three built-in toolbars: Standard, Advanced, and (possibly) Remote. While you can modify these existing toolbars, we suggest you create your own custom toolbars. That way you can just turn off the default toolbars and use your custom bars in their place. The original toolbars are only a click away, and you can reconfigure Outlook with the defaults should you need to.

NOTE   It's annoying that Office is inconsistent in where to go to customize toolbars. In Word, PowerPoint, and Excel, you'll find Customize on the Tools menu. In Outlook 98 and Access, you start on the View menu, and drill down to Toolbars → Customize.

---

* A command bar is a toolbar, menu bar, or shortcut.

(Note: Please make sure the Inbox is the active facility; this will make the upcoming steps flow more smoothly.) Click on View → Toolbars → Customize, click on New, type in **OutlookAnnoy Standard** (this replaces the default custom toolbar name, which is "Custom 1"), then press Enter. The Customize dialog remains on screen and you should also have a fledgling custom toolbar that is somewhat nondescript (see Figure 2-36).

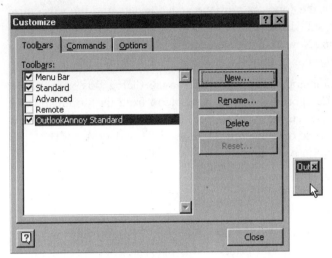

Figure 2-36: Creating a custom toolbar

We like some of the buttons provided on the default Standard toolbar and some of those on the Advanced toolbar. There are also some buttons available in Outlook 98 we think you might find handy that aren't offered on any default toolbar. You can combine all three categories of buttons on your custom toolbar.

Outlook is really a collection of separate modules—Calendar, Contact, Message, Task, and Notes—each of which do very different things. Outlook is unique among Office applications in that its toolbars change dynamically depending on which facility is active at the moment. This makes customizing a bit more difficult, since you have to create your custom toolbar in one facility, get the buttons you want just right, then switch to each other facility in turn. Some buttons do not exist in that context so they disappear, and you'll want to add others that only make sense to display when in that facility.

Let's start by copying the New button from the Standard toolbar to your new custom toolbar and then building from there. Now, this New button is not our favorite due to the odd context quirks it displays. Clicking on the button gets you a new item form depending on the active facility at the time. But if you click on the down-pointing triangle to the right of the icon, you get a menu from which you can choose the type of item you want to create. (We recommend you memorize the keyboard shortcuts for creating the items you create most often, and we have included a nifty table for this purpose in Chapter 5, *Outlook's Key Ingredients*.) In any case, we can begin to populate our custom toolbar as follows:

1. Make sure that the Inbox is now the active facility and the Customize dialog box is still displayed. Hold down the Ctrl key and then drag the first button (New Mail Message) from the Standard toolbar to your new custom toolbar (OutlookAnnoy Standard).

2. Select the Commands tab in the Customize dialog box, select New Menu in the Categories list, drag New Menu from the Commands list over to your new custom toolbar, and place it to the right of the New button. Right-click on this New Menu button, and in the Name field type &Print, then press Enter.

3. This next step only sounds tricky: left-click on this new Print button to unveil an empty gray square dangling off the lower left corner of the Print button.

4. Select File in the Categories list, and drag Print Preview from the Commands list to this gray square. This puts the Print Preview button on the Print drop-down menu.

5. (If, during this drag-and-drop frenzy, you find the Print drop-down menu has collapsed, just left-click the Print button to expand it so you can keep adding items to it.) Again from File in the Categories list, drag the Print icon from the Commands list to just below the Print Preview button on the Print drop-down menu.

6. Right-click on the Print button on your custom toolbar—the main Print button on the toolbar itself, not the "Print...(Ctrl+P)" button on the drop-down menu—and choose Begin a Group. This puts a vertical separator between the Print button and the New button you added in step 1. We'll have you add other separators *en masse* at the end of the next section.

When you've finished with this step, your toolbar should resemble the one shown in Figure 2-37.

Fleshing out the toolbar for email facilities

Since they appear on all the toolbars in Office, we've gotten used to using the Cut, Copy, and Paste buttons from the toolbar. So for consistency's sake, add these three buttons to your OutlookAnnoy Standard

Figure 2-37: OutlookAnnoy Standard under construction—the New and Print controls

toolbar. The procedure is the same: select Edit in the Categories list, and drag the Cut, Copy, and Paste items from the Commands list. Then right-click on the Cut button and choose Begin a Group to add a separator to its left.

Select View in the Categories list and drag the Folder List and Preview Pane items to the right of the Paste button. This gives you a one-click toggle to display or hide the Folder List or to turn on or off the Preview Pane. You can utilize your available display space more efficiently if you only display the pane you need at the moment.

Now switch to the Edit category and drag the Delete item to the right of the Preview Pane button. From the Go category, drag the Back and Forward items to your custom toolbar. Then drag the Reply, Reply to All, and Forward items from the Actions category. Finally, from the Tools category, add the Send and Receive menu item, and then the Find and Advanced Find buttons.

As marginally helpful as the Office Assistant is in Outlook (just try asking the OA about "junk" or "spam" to discover the junk mail features in Outlook—ha!), we do consult it on occasion. But we also like to look things up in the help index when the OA falls on its face. So from the Help category, drag the Contents and Index item and the Office Assistant item to complete your custom OutlookAnnoy Standard toolbar. Add separators as shown in Figure 2-38, then click on Close in the Customize dialog box.

Figure 2-38: OutlookAnnoy Standard complete—for the Inbox facility, that is

This toolbar configuration will appear when you are in any email-type facility (Inbox, Sent Items, and the Outbox).

Fine-tuning for each facility

Now, click on the Contacts icon in the Outlook bar to make Contacts the active facility. Your custom toolbar changes instantly. The Reply, Reply to

All, Forward, and Send and Receive buttons don't apply to the Contacts facility, so Outlook dynamically removes them.

You have to add any menu items you want in the Contacts context—like the Flag for Follow Up, New Message to Contact, and New Call buttons— to the custom OutlookAnnoy Standard toolbar. Work your way through each facility, adding the buttons you want when in that facility, and you'll not only have a customized toolbar, it'll change in accordance with the current facility.

Once you're finished adding buttons to your custom OutlookAnnoy Standard toolbar, you can uncheck the box for the Standard toolbar on the Toolbars tab of the Customize dialog and position your custom toolbar to be docked at the top of Outlook just below the menu bar. You're all set! Look carefully through all the buttons and menus you can add to your toolbars in the various command categories and you'll undoubtedly find some buttons that can make it even easier to use Outlook.

To Organize or Not To Organize

While building the OutlookAnnoy Standard custom toolbar, you probably noticed that we do not recommend keeping the Organize button. Under pressure to make some of Outlook's features more accessible and easier to use, the Redmond Rangers came up with this Web browser-like tool. You may like it, but we find that it's typically easier to right-click on an item to produce the desired effect (or right-drag the item to another folder, with all the neat shortcut extras that come by right-dragging instead of left-dragging).

If you haven't already given it the deep-six, click on the Organize button (or, if you have gotten rid of the Organize button already, choose Tools → Organize from the menus) and a new pane opens at the top of the facility area to help you organize your data (see Figure 2-39).

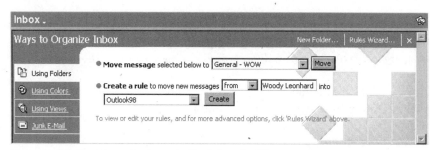

Figure 2-39: The Organize pane in the Inbox facility

You click on the horizontal tab-like buttons on the left-hand side of the Organize pane to change functions. We've found this pane useful only when in an email-type folder like the Inbox. Here you can move the selected message in the folder to another folder (something done faster by right-clicking on the message and selecting Move to Folder) or, if you're in the Inbox folder, quickly create a rule for messages from this message's author. In a display of righteous IntelliNonsense, the Organize tool stubbornly ignores which particular email folder you're in. From the Inbox, its "Create a rule..." option dynamically puts the message author name's in the right place, but switch to Sent Items and this same option offers to create a rule to put email from you—that's right, you—into a folder, which of course is nonsensical.

NOTE   The Organize tool's most serious annoyance is that it always hides itself when you leave the current folder and there's no preference setting to make it stay visible, neither on an individual folder basis nor globally.

In the Using Colors tab you can color-code messages from specific recipients (again based on the currently selected message), or color-code messages of which you are the only recipient (see Figure 2-40). To drill down further on this feature called Automatic Formatting, select View → Current View → Customize Current View, then click on the Automatic Formatting button. You can add new conditions by clicking on the Add button and then the Condition button, which invokes the Filter dialog (more on this in Chapter 7). Once you've added the conditions, you can modify the font and color by clicking on the Font button (you can also set the format first, then create the conditions). Automatic formatting is available for any data type, not just mail messages.

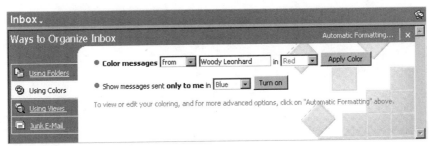

Figure 2-40: Color coding is very cool

We covered Junk E-Mail earlier in this chapter. With the Organize pane on, the other facilities in Outlook let you do unexciting things like create folders, assign items to categories, and change the displayed view—things usually done faster using other methods (which we'll cover in depth in Chapter 7).

We'd rather see Microsoft make existing interface features like the Rules Wizard more intuitive than to start spinning off new and esoteric interface options. Especially ones that are somewhat slow and convoluted to use.

Ready to Rock

If Outlook is purring like a kitten on your system and you've yet to see the first ripple on the Outlook pond, then you are totally blessed and should go directly to Chapter 4 and collect two hundred dollars...well, skip to Chapter 4 anyway. But keep a bookmark at the beginning of Chapter 3 and hope you never need it.

If, however, you've experienced some of Outlook's more vexing annoyances (like you can't get it to work), then roll up your sleeves, put on a pot of java (the kind you drink, not of the endless hype variety), and get ready to do battle with the beast you love to hate. Because when Outlook works, it is an outstanding piece of software, and Chapter 3 is dedicated to keeping Outlook working.

3

Outlook Repair Tactics

If you're one of the lucky few who works with Outlook day in and day out, never experiencing a GPF, mysteriously stuck message, corrupt profile, or other problem, lucky you. Let us make one thing perfectly clear: we're really annoyed with Outlook's unstable, obfuscatory, and unnecessary complexity in the realm of handling email. This is a natural for an "I'm mad as hell and I'm not gonna take it anymore" campaign. (On the other hand, we all depend on Outlook because when it's not making us crazy, it is an amazingly useful program.)

So, this chapter is devoted to tactics you'll need to solve Outlook problems—from the trivial to the catastrophic. We've organized Outlook problems into several different operational categories, and within each category we provide at least one (and occasionally more) Repair Checklist. Our favorite checklist employs what members of the military/industrial sector call the "scorched earth" policy: if all else fails, uninstall and reinstall (or delete and add back) the component in question, be it a profile, Outlook, or Office itself. But there's more to it than that, much more. In fact, we've put together the "Checklist of All Checklists" for this operation. It's complete and well-organized and when you're done, you'll never know you uninstalled Office. All your custom toolbars, keyboard shortcuts, options settings, the OSB, email and other information service settings, and so on—the whole Office enchilada—will be back the way they were. You won't find a list like this anywhere else, but it's worth its weight in gold. Guaranteed.

Meantime, here's a short wish list to Microsoft summarizing the most important changes that should be made to Outlook's email feature set.

1. A Problem Detection Wizard or Wizards—or a standalone tool like *Scanpst.exe*—to validate and repair Exchange profiles. Perhaps something similar to the Master Document Utility released by Microsoft to repair problems with Word 97 Master Documents.

2. Dramatically improved help file content in the area of problem-solving. Stop treating the Office Assistant as an excuse for getting lax about context-sensitive help.

3. Dramatically improved problem-related message box text with Help button links to the appropriate help topics.

Solving the Name and Address Storage Puzzle

Before we discuss how to solve problems that arise when sending email, receiving email, and using profiles, we need to talk about the different ways you can store names and addresses in Outlook. Outlook offers a confusing variety of places to store "name and address" information. Even the vocabulary can be confusing. The situation is worsened by the fact that the relevant settings are spread throughout Outlook in an inconsistent manner. Here is a list of terms along with their descriptions. Throughout the book, we supply the steps you need to create, add, modify, and delete these services and components, as well as discuss the pros and cons of using Contacts folders versus the Personal Address Book.

Contact Item

You can store name and address information about someone in a Contact Item. A Contact Item is stored in a Contacts folder, and the item is composed of fields like First Name, Last Name, Suffix, Title, and so on. In database terms, a Contact Item is a record in a database.

Contacts folder

You store Contact Items in a Contacts folder. The default Contacts folder name is, not surprisingly, "Contacts," but you can create new Contacts folders and give them unique names like "Personal Contacts" or "High School Alumni." Contacts folders are stored inside

---

Solving Outlook Problems Using Our Checklists

We suggest you read through these checklists as they appear in this chapter, even if you aren't currently experiencing any problems. We've sprinkled them liberally with suggestions and tips that may prove useful, even if you don't have an Outlook black cloud hanging over your head.

As you move through any of our checklists (for example, Checklist 3-1), we suggest you do so in order step-by-step, and each step's instructions assume this. For example, in Checklist 3-1, if you start at step 4 without having checked steps 1–3, then you might be wasting time, since an earlier step might actually be the solution to your problem.

Although our suggestion that you check prior steps may seem like stating the obvious, our goal in developing these checklists is to help you solve your problem as quickly and painlessly as possible. Many a time, under the pressure and strain of an Outlook mishap, we've forgotten to check an earlier step only to regret this terribly later. Save yourself this misfortune and follow through the checklists one step at a time.

These checklists apply primarily to those of you running Outlook on a single workstation, or a workstation on a peer-to-peer network. If you're using Exchange Server on a network, please consult your LAN Administrator first.

If you're running Outlook 98 in Corporate/Workgroup mode, then you are running in a state that very much resembles Outlook 97—that is, you can add, remove, and change services and data resources through profiles. In contrast, Outlook 98's Internet Only mode is account-centric, not profile-centric. In fact, as we pointed out in Chapter 2, *Vital Changes, Settings, and Customizations*, there is no such concept as a profile in Internet Only mode. In these checklists, we'll point out alternate tactics where appropriate if you're in Internet Only mode.

The best advice we can offer anyone having Outlook problems is simply this (apologies to Douglas Adams): "Don't panic."

---

a Personal Folders file, typically *C:\Outlook\mailbox.pst,** along with all your other Outlook data.

---

* Depending on your configuration prior to installing Outlook (97 or 98), this PST file could be in a variety of places, sometimes with a root filename of *outlook.pst* instead of *mailbox.pst*. Some other likely candidates are *C:\Windows\outlook.pst* and *C:\Windows\Application Data\Microsoft\Office\8.5\Outlook\outlook.pst* (if you have a user name when you log on, look in *C:\Windows\Profiles\<username>\Application Data\..*).

Outlook Address Book

A virtual collection of one or more Contacts folders. For example, you could have three separate groups of Contact Items—say, Personal Contacts, Business Contacts, and High School Alumni (where each of these is a Contacts folder)—all gathered under the umbrella of your Outlook Address Book.

Personal Address Book entry

You can store name and address information about someone in a Personal Address Book entry. A single entry is comprised of fields like First Name, Last Name, and so on. In database terms, a Personal Address Book entry is a record in a database.

Personal Address Book

Often referred to by the acronym "PAB," you store Personal Address Book entries in a Personal Address Book. The PAB is a vestige of Exchange, whereas the Outlook Address Book is unique to Outlook (and wasn't available with Exchange). A Personal Address Book is stored in a *.pab* file, typically *C:\Outlook\mailbox.pab*.

Next we answer some common questions:

Q: *Are a Personal Address Book and a Contacts folder the same thing?*

A: No, they are two entirely different objects for storing address information. The PAB was part of Exchange and is still supported by Outlook. Contacts folders are a new feature of Outlook. The differences? In a nutshell:

— A Contact Item has about four times as many fields as a PAB entry;

— A Contact Item can have custom user-defined fields (not possible with a PAB entry); and

— A single Contact Item supports three separate email addresses for one person. (This would require three separate PAB entries, one for each email address, thereby creating duplicate records for the same person.)

Q: *Can I migrate my Personal Address Book data into a Contacts folder?*

A: Yes, using the Import and Export Wizard. We describe this in detail in Chapter 6, *A Cookbook for Conversion.* (When you install Outlook 98 in Internet Only mode, it will automatically ask if you want to import your PAB entries to contacts.)

Q: *Do I lose anything when I migrate my PAB data into a Contacts folder?*

A: The PAB does have a built-in distribution list feature that Contacts folders don't have. However, a workaround for this is described in Chapter 7, *Beyond the Basics.*

Q: *How does Outlook know which email address to use when I type a person's name in a message's To field?*

A: That depends on settings you specify in the Address Book dialog (Tools → Address Book). We describe these settings later in this chapter. Rest assured that it is possible, once you know how, to have Outlook always look first in your Outlook Address Book instead of your PAB when checking email recipients.

Problems Sending Email

The scenario: you've composed a new message, asked Outlook to send it over the wire, and gotten a good handshake between your system and your email provider. But when the dust settles, the email's stubbornly sitting in your Outbox folder, not the Sent Items folder where it should be. Most annoying. The following extensive checklist takes you through the steps to correct this and numerous other email-related problems.

Email Repair Tactics

Checklist 3-1: Repair Tactics for Problems Sending Email

1. Make sure the message was not opened before it was sent.

   The line item representing a message waiting to be sent in the Outbox folder (typically showing the To, Subject, Sent, and Size fields) will be in italics. If you open a message before it gets sent, then close it without sending it (by clicking the Send button or File → Send), you'll notice the message's line item is in a normal—not italics—font.

   Solution: Open the message, click on the Send button, and fire up a new email session.

2. Make sure the current profile includes the appropriate email service (the official term is "transport service"*) for this type of message.

   Let's say you have an account with CompuServe, so you have a number of PAB and Contact entries that use the CompuServe email

---

* In Exchange- and Outlook-speak, a synonym for "transport service" is "transport provider."

type. If you create a message to a recipient with this email type but the current profile doesn't include the CompuServe Mail service, then it can't be sent using this profile. To check, open the message, right-click on the recipient's display name, and choose Properties. The Properties dialog reveals the email type; in the case of Figure 3-1, it's a CompuServe recipient and message.

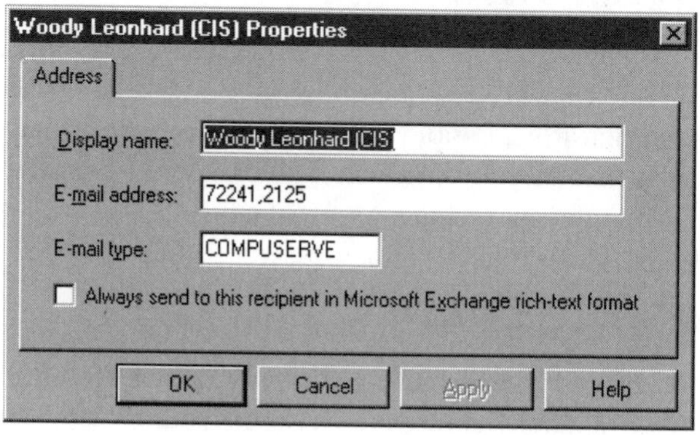

Figure 3-1: This recipient is a CompuServe subscriber

Solution: Add the CompuServe Mail service to the current profile or switch to a profile that includes the CompuServe Mail service. Adding a service to the current profile is simple. You can do so from within Outlook itself (select Tools → Services, click on Add, choose the desired service from the "Available information services" list, click on OK, close and restart Outlook to activate the change), or you can use Control Panel's Mail applet (close Outlook first, natch). What happens next depends on the particular service. For details and an example involving the Internet email transport service, see Checklist 3-3.

NOTE   Some services, like CompuServe Mail, install themselves, in which case you should refer to the manufacturer's installation instructions.

OUTLOOK 98 If you're running Outlook 98 in Internet Only mode, verify that you have the desired account set as the default (Tools → Accounts → Mail → Set as Default → Close).

3. Open the message, Check Names, then resend.

It appears to be impossible for an unrecognized name in any of the To, Cc, or Bcc fields to sneak past the Send click. In other words, you can't Send a message that contains a name that is not in one of your address books (Contacts folder, PAB, etc.) *or* is not in *address@domain.com* format. However, opening a message and doing a Check Names on a message that shouldn't—in theory— contain any invalid names has freed stuck messages for us on numerous occasions, so give it a whirl.

NOTE   Hopping on one leg while stripped down to your under-
                wear in full view of your work associates while chanting
                "annoyance be gone" over and over again has also been
                known to work. This invokes what Frederic Gordon so
                sagely refers to as the "voodoo effect" of PC problem solv-
                ing: try enough reasonably intelligent fixes, toss in a dash
                of unintuitive "what the heck" tweaking, and at some ran-
                dom and unexpected point the email-gods might smile on
                you and evaporate the problem. Sometimes shutting down
                the PC, getting a good night's sleep, and hoping the prob-
                lem will be gone when you boot up the computer the next
                morning can be a viable strategy.

Solution: Open the message, click on Check Names on the toolbar or in the Tools menu, then click on Send.

4. If just one message is stuck, re-create it and send it again.

    Occasionally, for no discernible reason, a message appears perfectly fine but still won't go. You've tried the previous tricks but to no avail. Before you try any of the more time-consuming solutions, just re-create the message from scratch.

    Solution: Open the message, select Edit → Select All, select Edit → Copy, close the message, create a new message to the same recip-ient(s), click on Send, then delete the original message.

5. Cold-boot your PC.

    This isn't a trick per se, but many folks flounder in the weeds tweaking their software settings when sometimes all it takes is a cold boot.

    Solution: Shut your PC down cold, including your modem (if external), then fire everything up after a minute or so.

6. If you repeatedly experience stuck email going to the same indi-vidual, check for duplicate address book entries.

If you begin to detect a pattern that outbound email to Mary Smith always gets stuck, you might have duplicate address entries for Mary Smith. For example, you might have one entry for her in your PAB that's routing email to her Internet address over MSN (email type MSNINET) and another entry for her in your Contacts folder that's routing email to her Internet account over the Internet (email type SMTP), both with the display name of "Mary Smith." Depending on the order Outlook uses to check names in your address lists (more on this in a moment), you might have a legal recipient but the underlying email type isn't supported by the current profile.

Solution: Connect to the appropriate service. As described earlier, you can add the desired service to the current profile or switch to a profile that includes that service. Also consider changing the display name for each of these duplicate entries in your PAB—say by appending a comment like "(MSN)" or "(CIS)" or "(Internet)" to the full name field so you won't be confused later about how the email is being routed (as discussed in Chapter 2). This isn't necessary in your Contacts folder since the three email fields automatically append "(E-mail)" or "(E-mail 2)" or "(E-mail 3)" to the addressee's display name.

Another trick is to replace the intended recipient's display name with his or her actual mailto address. In the case of Mary Smith, if you know you have an Internet email service in the current profile, just type in her Internet address (say, *marysmith@darnitall.com*) and see if the message is delivered.

Yet another trick in such a case is to delete and re-create the recipient's entry (or entries) in your address book(s).

7. Make sure your connectoid and modem are working properly.

Solution: Your connectoid might not be communicating properly (or at all) with your email provider, so fire it up and try to surf the Web. If your browser can surf the Web, then neither the connectoid nor your modem are the culprit. Otherwise, see Checklist 3-4.

8. Move the questionable transport service to the top of the delivery order.

Forcing the suspect service to be first in the delivery order is a common cure for a stuck message.

Solution: Select Tools → Services, click on the Delivery tab, use the up arrow button to move the service to the top of the "Recipient addresses are processed by these information services in the following order" list, then click on OK (see Figure 3-2).

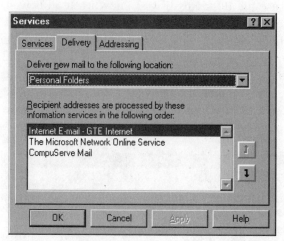

Figure 3-2: Who's on first in your Services dialog's Delivery tab?

OUTLOOK 98 If you're running Outlook 98 in Internet Only mode, the equivalent solution would be to reorder any installed directory services (Tools → Accounts → Directory Service → Set Order).

9. Try another dial-up access phone number.

   It might not be your system's fault! The problem might be on your email provider's end.

   Solution: Try using another—preferably local—dial-up access phone number (POP*) for your email provider. If the email remains stuck, this doesn't necessarily clear your email provider.

NOTE   If you suspect you're having dial-up networking or communications problems, see the *Microsoft Windows 95 Resource Kit* or search the MSKB on these topics.

10. In the case of Internet email, ping your email provider's SMTP server.

    Solution: To see if your email provider's SMTP server is available or busy, start an MS-DOS session while you're connected and type in `ping` followed by your email provider's SMTP server name, as shown in Figure 3-3; for example, `ping smtp.gte.net` works for GTE

---

* Point Of Presence—A term that indicates a city where the user can connect to a network (including the Internet), often with dial-up phone lines.

subscribers (you can use the IP address if you know it). If all is well, you'll see several lines of reply information showing the time it took a test packet to get there and back; otherwise you'll see an indication that the server has timed out. If the latter, you'll have to wait until the problem clears up on the provider's end unless you have an alternate provider. Meanwhile, ping another known server, like Microsoft's FTP server, *ftp://ftp.microsoft.com/.* If successful, then you know you're properly connected to the Internet.

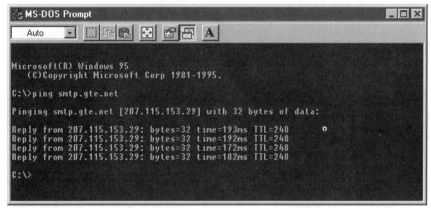

Figure 3-3: Running Ping in an MS-DOS window

11. Call your email provider's help desk.

NOTE   This step applies even if you're not having Internet email
                problems—for example, if you're sending email directly via
                CompuServe's front-end.

Even if Ping indicates that data is making the round-trip back to you, it's a minuscule tidbit of data—32 bytes. Call and ask a support engineer if the mail server is experiencing any difficulties. Sometimes you can get this information right off the provider's Web site as well. (We're describing a circumstance when the ISP connection is working but the mail server is down. One of the contenders for the All-Time Annoyance prize is being advised by a recording that you should get your questions answered online, while you're on hold for ISP technical support to discuss why you can't get connected.)

Some email providers (GTE, for example) have admitted their servers have problems with complex email packaging schemes used by "more modern"—that's a quote—front-ends like Outlook. Even a slight disruption of the mail server might be the cause of your stuck message. If you suspect the problem is on your provider's end, start a log of daily email behavior (there's no special feature in Outlook for this—you could keep a log on paper or store it electronically in Outlook, WordPad, or even Notepad).

12. Send the message using a different email type.

Although this isn't always feasible—particularly if you use only Internet email and have only one email provider—if you have a variety of email transport services installed (and have accounts with the related ISPs), try routing the message to the recipient using another email type.

Solution: For example, if Internet email to Mary Smith at *marysmith@darnitall.com* is stuck and you have the MSN service installed, create (or use an existing) address book entry for her using the "Internet over The Microsoft Network" type. If that message goes out, then the suspects are (a) the transport service (driver) that supports the original message's email type and (b) the email provider used to deliver that message type; the profile itself is not a likely suspect. Otherwise, if the message still cannot be sent, the profile might be the culprit.

13. Send the message using a different email program.

Use another email client. Windows 95 and Windows NT Workstation 4.x come with an Exchange email client, and Windows 98 will ship with Outlook Express (unless something really weird happens in the DOJ vs. Microsoft spat), so see if another client can send the stuck message. Since version 3.01, Microsoft Internet Explorer has come with a free Internet email program called Microsoft Internet Mail and News (IMN); beginning with IE 4.x, this program is referred to as Outlook Express. For information on where to get IMN and Outlook Express, see Chapter 2.

Solution: Shut down Outlook. If you're going to test with Exchange, find and run the file *Exchng32.exe* and use the same profile you've been using with Outlook. If the message gets sent, then you have a configuration problem limited to Outlook itself, not the transport service or the profile. If the message doesn't get sent, the profile is the prime suspect. Or copy the contents of the stuck message into a new message in Outlook Express or IMN and send it. If the Outlook Express or IMN message doesn't go out, the likely culprits are your connectoid, email provider, or dial-up adapter network protocols, roughly in that order.

14. Create a temporary new profile with just the information service in question.

    For example, if Internet email is giving you fits, first make note of your current profile's Internet email transport service settings and create a new profile using just that transport service.

    Solution: Select Tools → Services → click on the Services tab → click the Internet E-mail item → click on Properties; now note your settings for each dialog tab on paper or, even better, take screen shots (ALT+Print Scrn), copy 'em into a Word document, save and then print it. Create a new profile (for more information see Checklist 3-3) and add the Internet E-mail service. Copy the content of the stuck message, delete it, re-create it, then try sending it with this profile. If it goes out, then the original profile is suspect.

OUTLOOK 98   If you're running Outlook 98 in Internet Only mode, try removing all extant accounts (Tools → Accounts → Mail → Remove), then adding back only the account you use as your default.

---

15. Archive and clear out your email folders.

    This is one of those "why not give it a try" tricks that works sometimes. The key here is to weigh the cost in time to archive several folders—especially if you have hundreds or thousands of messages—and the hassle of not having them readily accessible for quick searching, versus the chance that this little exercise might jiggle things back into working order. Note that when we say "clear out your email folders," we mean delete *all* messages in *all* folders, including the Deleted Items folder.

NOTE   Remember that you can create a new PST especially for this archive, and then later, when you need to access the data, add it as a new service, import it, or open it directly (in Outlook 98, select File → Open → Personal Folders File (*.pst*); in Outlook 97, select File → Open Special Folder → Personal Folder).

---

16. Run the Inbox Repair Tool on your Personal Store file.

    Now is a good time to use the Inbox Repair Tool that we mentioned in Chapter 2.

Solution: Select Start → Programs → Accessories → System Tools → Inbox Repair Tool. Browse to your *mailbox.pst* file, then click on Start (see Figures 3-4 and 3-5).

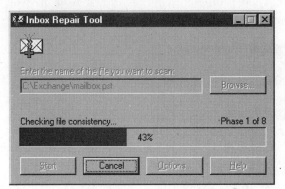

Figure 3-4: Inbox Repair Tool running through its paces

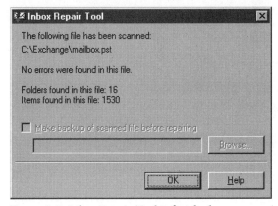

Figure 3-5: Inbox Repair Tool is finished

17. Compact your Personal Store file.

NOTE   The term "Personal Store file" is synonymous with "Personal Folders file." In the vocabulary of Exchange and Outlook, the Personal Folders service is a "message store" service. This is where messages (and, in the case of Outlook, other types of data as well) are stored.

Compacting your Personal Store file may shake some gremlins loose. It's best to do this right after running the Inbox Repair Tool.

Solution: In Outlook 98 Internet Only mode (this also works in Corporate/Workgroup mode, but not in Outlook 97), right-click on your Outlook Today – [Personal Folders] folder, choose Properties, click on the Advanced button, then click on Compact Now. In Outlook 98 Corporate/Workgroup mode or Outlook 97, select Tools → Services, click on Personal Folders, click on Properties, and click on Compact Now (see Figure 3-6). There's no status bar, so you'll have to wait patiently for the Compacting dialog to go away.

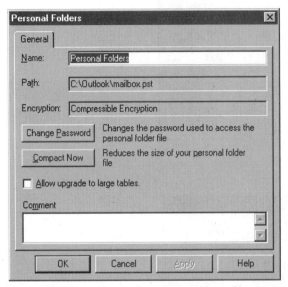

Figure 3-6: Compacting your personal store file

18. Uninstall any Outlook email add-ins.

    Outlook add-ins, whether from Microsoft or third-party vendors, have been known to cause email problems.

    Solution: You can try this one add-in at a time (if you have several installed) or uninstall 'em all at once—under the influence of the scorched earth policy. If this works, try adding them back one add-in at a time, testing outgoing email after each reinstall. When we say uninstall, we mean you should uncheck the add-in's checkbox in the Add-Ins dialog box, but don't click on the Remove button.

19. Create a new Personal Store file.

    The waters are getting deeper and more treacherous now, so steady as she goes. This step will help determine if your Personal Store file is corrupted, and may take up to an hour. You'll be setting aside your current Personal Folders file, creating a new one, and importing the contents of the original into the new one. For the details, see Checklist 3-2.

    Solution: First back up your working Personal Store file (see Checklist 3-2 for the detailed steps). Create a new Personal Store file and try sending a message *before* you import your old folders/data. Then import your data and try sending a message again. Be careful throughout this process not to accidentally delete your original Personal Store file.

20. Create a new profile along with a new Personal Store file and a new Personal Address Book (PAB).

    Gale-force winds are blowing, so batten down all the hatches and double-check your lifeline. This step requires some serious preparation and may take two hours to work through carefully. For the details, see Checklist 3-1.

21. Work through Checklist 3-4.

22. Install any Outlook patches or upgrades.

    Whether you're running Outlook 98 or 97, there may have been subsequent patches—this would not be a surprise, eh? If so, you should immediately download and install the latest one for your version of Outlook.

23. Uninstall and reinstall just Outlook.

    It may be that uninstalling and reinstalling only Outlook will resolve the problem. If not, proceed—with our sympathies—to the next step.

24. Uninstall and reinstall Office.

    <sigh> So it's come to this. We have stood at this crossroads (more than once for each of the co-authors), kicking the dirt, cursing the infernal and mightily annoying conglomeration of you-know-who's dysfunctional software—and that's putting a kind spin on things. But the buck has to stop somewhere, so let's nuke Office and see what we can rekindle from the smoldering ashes.

    Solution: See Checklist 3-5.

25. Upgrade Windows 95 or Windows 98 according to your system's current configuration.

    Microsoft's Web site provides an extensive list of Windows 95 upgrades. Check *http://www.microsoft.com/windows95/info/system-updates.htm* for links to Service Pack 1 and numerous upgrades that followed Service Pack 1, as shown in Figure 3-7. Similar upgrades will no doubt be available for Windows 98 as well.

NOTE   Until very recently, this page lacked date stamps. It's now fixed.

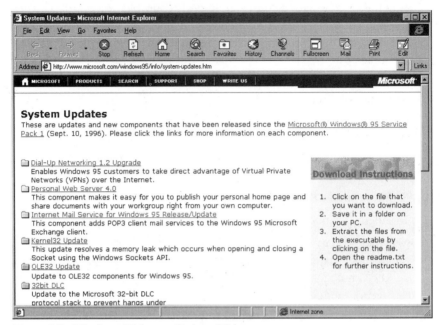

Figure 3-7: Windows 95 System Updates Web page

NOTE   Here's how to determine your operating system version: right-click on My Computer, then choose Properties, and you'll see a value of 4.00.950 for original Win95, 4.00.950a for Service Pack 1, 4.00.950 B for OEM Service Release 2 (OSR2), and so on.

                  If you decide to install one or more of the available upgrades, *we strongly suggest you document the details and date of each install* (an Outlook Note is a good place for this information) so you can review your system's configuration history should the need ever arise.

If you're already running Windows 95.0a, then your first upgrade when experiencing email or Internet connectivity problems should be the Kernel32 Update at *http://www.microsoft.com/windows95/info/ krnlupd.htm*. According to the documentation, "This update resolves a memory leak which occurs when opening and closing a Socket using the Windows Sockets [Winsock] API. Without this update, running a Windows Sockets application over a long period of time, especially one which opens and closes a large number of sockets, will result [in] a significant resource drain. This can cause the

Windows swap file to grow very large, overall deterioration of performance, and over time, possible system instability."

Needless to say, back everything up first.

If Your Email Woes Persist

You won't find the following discussion in any Microsoft documentation: if you still have an email problem after following all the steps in Checklist 3-1, then you've *really* got a problem. Maybe you're running an OEM version of Win95 that isn't happy about Exchange or Outlook. Contact your PC manufacturer's technical support staff and see what advice they have to offer. Perhaps—as thorough as we've tried to be with our checklists—we've omitted an issue that's the key to resolving your problem. So the next step is to query other experts on the problem: post messages on Microsoft's Outlook newsgroups, other relevant Internet newsgroups, and call Microsoft's technical support staff. When you emerge from the deluge of ideas and suggestions, a pattern may appear. Although completely unsolved problems are rare, they do occasionally occur. Remember Bill Machrone's series about a particular Micron that couldn't multitask more than two Windows 95 applications without crashing? As we recall, neither Micron nor Microsoft engineers were able to get that PC to function properly.

Problems with Personal Folders

The Personal Folders file (a.k.a. your Personal Store file or PST) maintains all your Outlook folders and your data, so don't go charging in willy-nilly. Instead, take some deep breaths, a walk around the block, do whatever it takes to work this through carefully. Even if you change your mind and decide to stick with your original Personal Folders file, you'll still lose any custom Outlook Bar settings (more on this shortly).

Checklist 3-2: Creating a New Personal Folders File

There is no way to dynamically remove your primary Personal Folders file from an Internet Only configuration of Outlook 98. In fact, it wouldn't make any sense to try this. (If you try, you'll be warned, "You cannot close the personal folders file that contains your calendar, contacts, and POP mailbox.") There are two solutions to a problematic PST under Internet Only mode; each is a variation on the same theme. (We describe these solutions at greater length below.) First (and less severe), you can close Outlook; temporarily move the PST where Outlook can't see it when it starts; use the Create/Open Personal Folders File dialog to create a new PST; then import your data from the suspect PST (we recommend import over copy since a copy involves physically exposing the profile of the suspect PST). Second (and more severe), you can uninstall Outlook; temporarily move the PST where setup won't see it; and reinstall Outlook 98 so it will create a new, clean Personal Folders file; then import as above. Try the less severe approach first; if it doesn't work, resort to the more severe technique.

With Corporate/Workgroup mode, since it supports multiple profiles, you can often avoid the harsh solution of an uninstall/reinstall and instead create a new profile from scratch, create a new PST, and then import as above. Alternately, as with Internet Only mode, you can close Outlook, temporarily move the PST where Outlook can't see it when it starts, use the Create/Open Personal Folders File dialog to create a new PST, then import as above.

With Outlook 97, we recommend you always create a new profile from scratch. In Outlook 97, we observed unpredictable results when using Create/Open Personal Folders to create a new PST.

Creating a New PST in Outlook 98 Internet Only Mode (a Less Severe Solution)

1. Back up your system.

2. Carefully make note of your current settings. Also, save any published forms to standalone Outlook Template (*.oft*) files.

3. Close Outlook.

4. Temporarily hide the PST so Outlook can't see it when it starts (either archive it with a utility like WinZip, or rename it).

5. Start Outlook. It automatically informs you "The file *filename.pst* could not be found." Click on OK.

6. Outlook then displays the Create/Open Personal Folders File dialog, so create a new PST by simply typing in the new name, then click on Open.

7. Outlook displays the message, "The location messages are delivered to has changed for this user profile. To complete this operation, you may need to copy the contents of the old Outlook folders to the new Outlook folders. For information about how to complete the change of your mail delivery location, see Microsoft Outlook help. Some of the shortcuts on the Outlook Bar may no longer work. Do you want Outlook to recreate your shortcuts? All shortcuts you have created will be removed." You can safely ignore the text in this message. In

Outlook 97, clicking on No here always caused problems, so out of habit you may wish to click on Yes in Outlook 98. (So far in our experience with Outlook 98, clicking on No has worked satisfactorily, but your mileage may vary.)

8. See if using this new (and empty) Personal Folders file solves your problem by sending a test message to a literal mailto recipient. If it does, import the contents of the original PST: first unarchive it, then select File → Import and Export; in Outlook 98 select "Import from another program or file" or in Outlook 97 select "Import from a personal folder file (*.pst*)" (see Figure 3-8). Click on Next. In Outlook 98 select "Personal Folder File (*.pst*)" and click on Next. In Outlook 98 or 97, you can select or type in the filename. Next set the Options to suit your needs ("Replace duplicates with items imported" is the default and really of no consequence here, since you're pouring data into an empty folder structure), then click on Next. In the next panel, accept these defaults: Personal Folders selected in the "Select the folder to import from" tree control, "Include subfolders" box checked, "Import items into the same folder in" selected with Personal Folders in the drop-down list, then click on Finish.* You'll see status bar indicators for each folder as it is imported, so sit back, relax, and enjoy the ride.

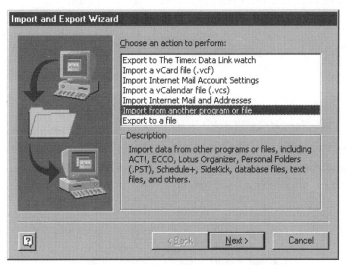

Figure 3-8: Outlook's Import and Export Wizard at work

---

* Depending on your system resources (primarily, how much RAM you have), you may experience severely low system resource levels—complete with message box warnings to that effect—while importing a large PST *en masse*. In such a case, we advise you to import one folder at a time.

9. Recreate your settings (see steps 15–22 in Checklist 3-3) and if needed, bring back your custom forms.

Creating a New PST in Outlook 98 Internet Only Mode (a Severe Solution)

1. Back up your system.

2. Carefully make note of your current settings. Also save any published forms to standalone Outlook Template (*.oft*) files.

3. Uninstall Outlook.

4. Temporarily hide the PST so Outlook setup can't see it.

5. Reinstall Outlook 98 so it will create a new, clean Personal Folders file.

6. See if using this new, empty PST solves your problem: send a test message to a literal mailto recipient.

7. Import your data from the suspect PST.

8. Re-create your settings (see steps 15–22 in Checklist 3-3) and if needed, bring back your custom forms.

Creating a New PST in Outlook 98 Corporate/ Workgroup Mode (a Less Severe Solution)

Follow the steps in the "Creating a New PST in Outlook 98 Internet Only Mode (a Less Severe Solution)" section.

Creating a New PST in Outlook 98 Corporate/ Workgroup Mode (a Severe Solution)

Since Corporate/Workgroup mode supports multiple profiles, you can often avoid the harsh solution of uninstalling/reinstalling Outlook and instead create a new profile from scratch, creating a new PST during that process.

To create a new profile from scratch, follow the steps in Checklist 3-3.

Creating a New PST in Outlook 97

With Outlook 97, we recommend you always create a new profile from scratch because we observed unpredictable results when using Create/ Open Personal Folders to create a new PST.

To create a new profile from scratch, follow the steps in Checklist 3-3.

Problems with Individual Information Services

If you suspect that a specific information service is the cause of an email problem, the simplest solution is to remove it and add it back. First, be sure you make note of the service's properties: go into Tools → Services, select the service in question, click on the Properties button, and work your way through all the settings on all the tabs of the resulting dialog box. Next, select the service and click on Remove. If you're feeling particularly superstitious, you could exit Outlook and then restart it before adding the service back. To add it back, select Tools → Services, then click on Add, select the service from the list, and click on OK.

OUTLOOK 98   In Outlook 98's Internet Only mode, you don't add services to a profile but instead add mail accounts or Internet directory (LDAP) servers to a single pseudo-profile that reaches out only over the Internet.

CompuServe Mail

You can get the CompuServe Mail service installation file directly from CompuServe. Access CompuServe using HyperTerminal or WinCIM (HyperTerminal is the Windows communications package, Start → Programs → Accessories → HyperTerminal; WinCIM is CompuServe's own proprietary communications package), type go csmail and download *CSMAIL.EXE* to an empty folder. It's a self-extracting file that creates all the setup files you need. Follow the *Readme.txt* file instructions to install the service. Figure 3-9 shows the Properties dialog for this service. The CompuServe Mail service—based on MAPI—will definitely bar the Internet Only version of Outlook 98 when upgrading from Outlook 97, and is probably not needed anymore anyway since CompuServe has adopted POP/SMTP.

Internet Email

If you have multiple Internet email providers, you'll need to add a transport service for each one. Figure 3-10 shows the Properties dialog for this service (in this case, GTE is the ISP). If you're running Outlook 8.02 SP-1 or earlier, you should also install the IMEP discussed in Chapter 2. Outlook 98 as well as Outlook 8.02 SR-1 Patch and SR-1 EU already include the IMEP upgrade's features.

Figure 3-9: Properties box for the CompuServe Mail service

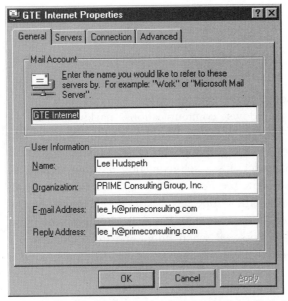

Figure 3-10: Properties box for the Internet E-mail service

OUTLOOK 98 In Outlook 98's Internet Only mode, you would add individual accounts via the Tools → Accounts interface.

Outlook Address Book

In the lexicon of Exchange and Outlook, an address book is a "directory service." For example, a Contacts folder is a directory service, ditto the PAB. If at some point you happen to remove all your Contacts folders from the Outlook Address Books list (in the Properties dialog shown in Figure 3-11), don't panic. The steps to recover are as follows:

OUTLOOK 98   In Outlook 98's Internet Only mode, the Outlook Address Book automatically includes your Contacts folders and its subfolders (if any). You don't have to manually do anything to set up this relationship.

---

1. Close Outlook.

2. Restart Outlook.

3. Go to the Contacts module, select File → Folder → Properties..., click the Outlook Address Book tab, make sure the "Show this folder as an e-mail Address Book" box is checked, then click on OK. (In Outlook 98's Internet Only mode, this box is checked but disabled.)

4. Select Tools → Services and verify the Outlook Address Book's properties. If necessary, repeat steps 1–3.

5. Now you need to tell Outlook to include your Contacts folder for use when selecting addressees, so select Tools → Address Book, select Tools → Options, and scroll down and select Contacts in the "Show this address list first" list. Now click on Add and select Contacts from the "Address lists" control; click on Add; and then click on Close; if you want Contacts at the top of the list and there are other items in the list here, click on the up button to move Contacts to the top of the "When sending mail, check names using these address lists in the following order" list; and then click on OK. At this point you should be in the Address Book dialog, so select Contacts in the "Show Names from the" list, then close the dialog. This convoluted, multiple dialog process is most annoying.

Personal Address Book

If you're going to rely solely on your Contacts folder for names and addresses, then you can remove the Personal Address Book (see Figure 3-12) from your profile. Since Outlook's address book (Contacts folder) doesn't support distribution lists and the PAB does, you may find it handy

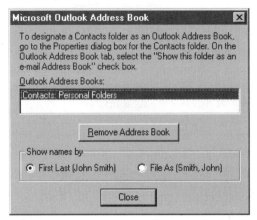

Figure 3-11: Properties box for the Outlook Address Book service

for that purpose alone. However, we describe a workaround to create a pseudo-distribution list for a Contacts folder in Chapter 7.

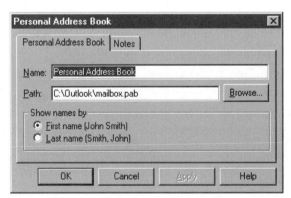

Figure 3-12: Properties box for the Personal Address Book service

---

OUTLOOK 98 There is no direct PAB support in Outlook 98's Internet Only mode. However, as mentioned previously, you can import PAB entries into your Contacts folder.

Personal Folders File

Figure 3-13 shows the Properties dialog for this message store service. As discussed earlier, the Personal Folders service is where messages (and, in the case of Outlook, other types of data as well) are stored, typically in the file *C:\Outlook\mailbox.pst*.

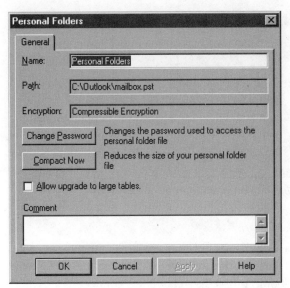

Figure 3-13: Properties box for the Personal Folders service

OUTLOOK 98 As mentioned earlier, in Outlook 98's Internet Only mode
you're stuck with a single pseudo-profile. To change PSTs
in Internet Only mode, see the sections "Creating a New
PST in Outlook 98 Internet Only Mode (a Less Severe Solution)" and "Creating a New PST in Outlook 98 Internet
Only Mode (a Severe Solution)," earlier in this chapter.

The Microsoft Network Online Service

Figure 3-14 shows the Properties dialog for this service. If you're having
problems with MSN, check the MSKB article *OL97: Using Microsoft
Outlook 97 with MSN version 2.0* (Q163162); it discusses causes and
workarounds for problems like Outlook hanging or GPFing when
opening, Fatal Exception errors during or after an MSN session, and mail
delivery not working. This article includes additional MSKB article references that you may find helpful. Unfortunately, as of the time of this
writing, the KnowledgeBase contains no articles about MSN version 2.5
(the MSN software that includes SMTP/POP support). If you have the pre-
MSN 2.5 service (which is strictly MAPI) installed in Outlook 97, this will
bar you from Outlook 98's Internet Only mode.

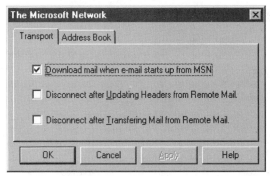

Figure 3-14: Properties box for the Microsoft Network Online service

Other Services

There are numerous other information services available, far too many for us to cover here. The Microsoft KnowledgeBase is the best place to consult when troubleshooting problems related to connecting to, and using Outlook with, a particular service. One good place to start:

http://premium.microsoft.com/support/kb/articles/q174/2/91.asp

Also, try searching on the name of your ISP.

Problems with Profiles

To determine if a problem is being caused by a profile, you're going to have to create a new one. An unenviable chore, but one we'll make as painless as possible with numerous tips and tricks in Checklist 3-3. It's easy to keep multiple profiles around and switch between them (as you learned in Chapter 2). However, it can be very time-consuming to switch between two profiles (say, from profile A—your original profile—that you suspect is corrupt, to a new from-scratch profile B) in order to migrate service settings from profile A to B. Instead, we suggest you make a complete record of all profile A's settings (as described in Checklist 3-1) and rebuild B to match A, one service at a time.

NOTE   You could create a profile with all your information ser-
               vices set up just the way you want them, and use this pro-
               file as a library from which you copy individual services
               (Tools → Services → Copy). The downside is that under
               some circumstances, a service in the library profile might
               become corrupted itself and thereby propagate the prob-
               lem when copied.

Checklist 3-3: Repair Tactics for Problems with a Profile (Creating a New Profile)

OUTLOOK 98 With Outlook 98's Internet Only mode, you're stuck with a single pseudo-profile. The equivalent in Internet Only mode to creating a new profile from scratch (as in Corporate/Workgroup mode) is to close Outlook, move your Personal Folders file where Outlook can't detect it, restart Outlook, and follow the prompts from there to create a new PST. See "Creating a New PST in Outlook 98 Internet Only Mode (a Less Severe Solution)" and "Creating a New PST in Outlook 98 Internet Only Mode (a Severe Solution)" earlier in this chapter for more information.

---

1. Carefully make note of the settings belonging to each service in your current profile, as described earlier. Also, save any published forms to standalone Outlook Template (*.oft*) files.

2. Close Outlook.

3. Open Control Panel and double-click on the Mail application.

4. In the default profile's Properties dialog box (see Figure 3-15), click on Show Profiles.

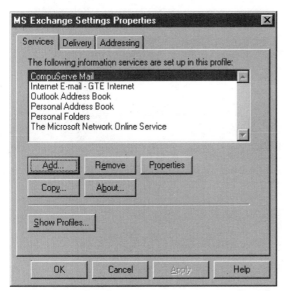

Figure 3-15: Start with the default profile's Properties dialog box

5. In the Mail dialog box, click on Add (see Figure 3-16). This starts the Inbox Setup Wizard.

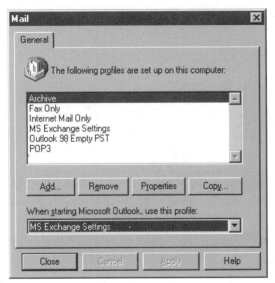

Figure 3-16: Add a profile from the Mail dialog box

6. Uncheck all the services but the one that should have delivered the stuck message. (Even though at this point in the problem-solving maze it appears that the service itself is okay, it's best to add and test services in the new profile one at a time.) For this case, we'll start with the Internet email service (see Figure 3-17). Then click on Next.

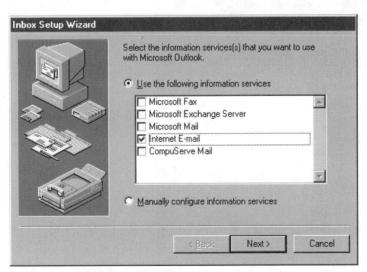

Figure 3-17: The first panel of the Inbox Setup Wizard

7. Enter a name for the profile—we used Do Not Panic—then click on Next (see Figure 3-18).

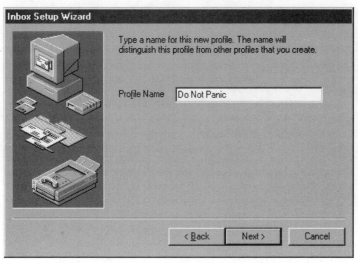

Figure 3-18: The new profile's name is, aptly, Do Not Panic

8. Click the Setup Mail Account button and fill out the subsequent fields as appropriate—the tab count will vary from service to service (see Figure 3-19). Back in the Wizard, click on Next.

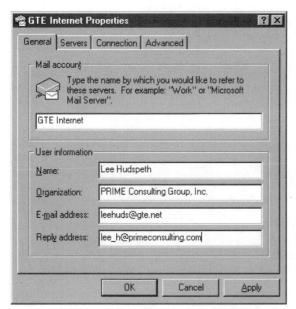

Figure 3-19: This dialog appears when configuring the Internet service in your new profile

9. Enter a completely new filename for a Personal Address Book (in this case we used *dnp_mailbox.pab*), then click on Next (see Figure 3-20).

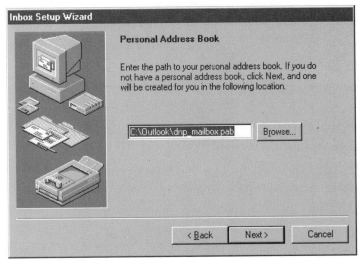

Figure 3-20: Type in a new PAB filename to have the Wizard create it for you from scratch

10. Enter a completely new filename for a Personal Folders file (in this case we used *dnp_mailbox.pst*), then click on Next (see Figure 3-21).

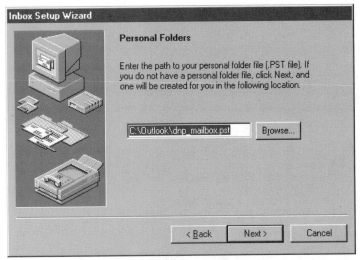

Figure 3-21: Type in a new Personal Folders filename to have the Wizard create it for you from scratch

11. In the next panel, choose whether or not to have Outlook (Exchange) run when you start Windows 95, then click on Next.

12. In the next panel (see Figure 3-22), click on Finish to complete the configuration process.

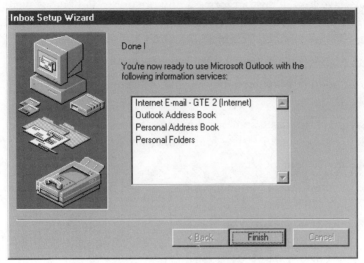

Figure 3-22: Finally, the end of the profile configuration trail

13. To have Outlook 98 use the new Do Not Panic profile, select the profile in the "When starting Microsoft Windows Messaging, use this profile" list. (In Outlook 97 the label reads "When starting Microsoft Windows Messaging, use this".) Click on Close. Alternately, from inside Outlook 98, select Tools → Options → Mail Services → select the "Always use this profile" button, and select the profile name from the drop-down list. (In Outlook 97: Tools → Options → General → select the "Always use this profile" button, and select the profile name.)

NOTE   When you're done, the new PAB file will be approximately
                32 KB and the new Personal Folders file will be around 48 KB.
                Because you're creating a new Personal Folders file, Out-
                look will automatically generate a default Outlook Bar.

---

14. Before importing any data from your original PAB and Personal Folders files, try to send a simple test message using a literal mailto. If the message is delivered, repeat the necessary steps to add the remaining services, then continue with the next step. If the message is stuck, then the trouble is probably the connectoid, your ISP, Outlook, or Office itself.

15. Some of your Tools → Options settings may have changed from your former profile. Work your way through each tab, updating the new profile.

16. You may have lost all custom forms if any of your form libraries were trashed. (If the old profile isn't recoverable or if you didn't back them up as standalone Outlook Template files, they're gone forever.)

17. Reset the AutoArchive settings for each folder in Personal Folders.

18. Reset your address book hierarchy (Tools → Address Book → Tools → Options...).

19. You may have to reset some add-in preferences. For example, in Outlook 97, the Chilton Preview font settings are disrupted.

20. Re-create any custom views.

21. Import data from your former profile's Personal Folders file and/or PAB.

22. You'll be using this profile for production work from now on and should consider deleting the original—and presumably corrupt— profile after, say, a week or so of reliable use.

Problems with Your Email Provider (ISP or Online Service)

Let's start by assuming there's a problem with your connectoid. (If you can surf the Web using your connectoid, then any email problems are not likely to be caused or abetted by the connectoid or your modem.) If you can't get connected to the Web, then try the following steps:

Checklist 3-4: Repair Tactics for Problems with a Connectoid

1. Verify the username and password settings that appear in the Connect To dialog box when you fire up the connectoid.

   Solution: Rekey your username and password, then click on Connect (see Figure 3-23). (Of course, the "GTE/" prefix shown in this figure is unique to GTE, so substitute the appropriate value for your ISP.)

NOTE   If you notice that suddenly the Connect To dialog's Password field is empty where before it wasn't (you had the "Save password" checkbox turned on), you may have a corrupt password file. This is a common symptom of a problem corrected by the Windows 95 Password List Update, available at *http://www.microsoft.com/windows95/info/passwd.htm*. Another common symptom is a GPF with the message "MPREXE caused an invalid page fault in module Kernel32.dll."

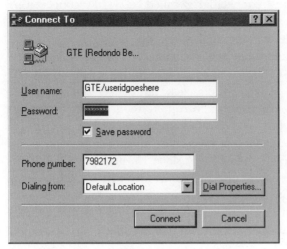

Figure 3-23: The Connect To dialog box

2. Verify the settings that appear in the Properties dialog box for the service you're having trouble with. (In Outlook 98 Corporate/Workgroup mode and in Outlook 97, select Tools → Services, select the service, and click on Properties. In Outlook 98 Internet Only mode, select Tools → Accounts, the same as previously.) For an image of the Internet email service's Properties dialog box (practically identical in Corporate/Workgroup mode and Internet Only modes), refer to Figure 3-10.

   Solution: Rekey critical values such as your account name and password, and verify the others. If you're using Internet email, carefully check both the SMTP and POP3 server addresses. If you're using DUN, make sure the correct DUN connection is selected in the Connection tab's "Use the following Dial-Up Networking connection" list. Click on OK when you're done.

3. Clear the NetBEUI and IPX/SPX Compatible network protocols for your connectoid.

   To access email and the Internet, the only network protocol your connectoid needs is TCP/IP, so clear all others.

   Solution: From the Properties dialog of the connectoid, click on Server Type, uncheck the NetBEUI and "IPX/SPX Compatible" checkboxes, then click on OK twice.

4. Make note of all your connectoid settings, delete the existing connectoid, and re-create it from scratch.

   This is another application of the scorched earth approach.

Solution: Say your local connectoid is called "GTE." Disconnect GTE if you're currently connected, double-click on My Computer, double-click on Dial-Up Networking, right-click on the GTE connectoid, choose Properties, and note the General tab settings (see Figure 3-24). Click on Server Type, note these settings, click on TCP/IP Settings, note these settings, then click on Cancel three times to dismiss all the dialogs. Remember to capture the Connect To dialog's username and password settings (they appear when you fire up the connectoid; see step 1). Actually, you must remember your password or have it written down somewhere, since it's masked. An Outlook Note is one possible repository, but remember that if Outlook goes down, you won't have access to the data, so to be on the safe side, keep this information in a plain text file. If you must go the Outlook Note route, be sure to copy/export the data routinely to a plain text file.

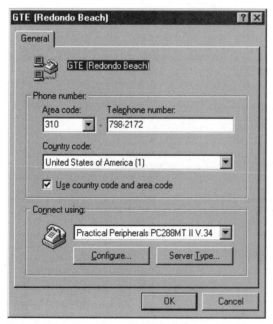

Figure 3-24: Properties dialog box for a GTE connectoid

NOTE   You can ALT+Print Scrn each dialog box's settings, paste the screen shot into a Word or WordPad document, and print or keep this file for safekeeping.

To delete the connectoid, right-click on it and choose Delete, then click on Yes to confirm.

To re-create this connectoid, select Connections → Make New Connection, which starts the Make New Connection wizard. Enter the previous connectoid's values and click on Next (do this for the two data-gathering panels), then click on Finish. When you next start this connectoid (in this example a connectoid to GTE), enter your user-name and password, click on the "Save password" checkbox (at your discretion), then click on Connect.

5. Install the Dial-Up Networking 1.2 Upgrade. While Microsoft originally billed this DUN upgrade as the "ISDN Accelerator Pack," it contains a number of general-purpose fixes, tweaks, and enhancements that we highly recommend you take advantage of, even if you aren't having any problems. You'll find it at:

http://backoffice.microsoft.com/downtrial/moreinfo/win95pptp.asp

or

http://www.microsoft.com/windows95/info/dialup.htm

The Ultimate Scorched Earth Solution

If *everything* you've tried has failed to resolve an Outlook behavioral problem (including reinstalling Outlook), uninstalling and reinstalling Office itself is an option. Admittedly, it's an unappetizing option, but there are cases where this is warranted. Routine GPF and other crashes or system hangs when running various Office applications—not just Outlook—warrant this flame-thrower approach. Or in the case of Microsoft's shipment of the first full maintenance release of Office 97 (the Enterprise Upgrade service release, or "SR-1 EU," as it's known in the trenches), Microsoft itself will advise you to uninstall and reinstall Office.

But what Microsoft doesn't mention are all the cherished settings you'll lose if you follow their upgrade steps literally. And that's a real shame. So we've put together Checklist 3-5 to rectify this. Be prepared to spend some quiet time getting ready for this process. It's a good idea to do this when there aren't any other demands on you, with at least 3–4 hours to spare in case something goes south. See Table 3-1 for a general overview and approximate times for each step. Of course, times will vary depending on your system and its configuration. And don't forget to dig up your Office CD beforehand.

NOTE   The times listed in Table 3-1 are based on a Pentium system replacing a 100% full installation of Office 97 Professional with a 100% full installation of Office 97 Professional SR-1 EU, followed by a separate on-top full installation of Outlook 98.*

Table 3-1: Office 97 uninstall/reinstall basic steps and completion times

Step	Time to complete
Backup	System dependent
Write down settings, etc.	30 minutes to one hour
Uninstall	10–20 minutes
Defrag	System dependent
Reinstall	20–30 minutes
Test and reconfigure all applications	Depends on how thorough you are, but it shouldn't take more than 45 minutes

Checklist 3-5: The Scorched Earth Solution—Uninstalling and Reinstalling Office 97

1. Do a complete system backup.

2. Note your add-in settings.

   We took a screen shot of each group of add-ins in each application's Tools → Add-Ins list (see Figure 3-25) and pasted those screen shots into a document for safe keeping. Among all the applications, only Access and Excel misbehaved. Access left the Print Relationships add-in installed but unloaded, so we had to manually reload it. Excel unloaded three add-ins that previously were loaded: Analysis ToolPak, Microsoft AccessLinks Add-in, and MS Query Add-in for Excel 5 Compatibility. Looks like Excel resets add-ins to some sort of factory default while the other Office applications don't. As for Access...go figure.

3. Note each application's Tools → Options settings for your default file location.

   The reinstall seems to properly preserve most Tools → Options settings; one notable and exasperating exception is your default file location. We set all our Office applications to use a default file

---

* A full install of all components of Office 97 Professional SR-1 EU sucks up 213 MB of disk real estate. Ouch.

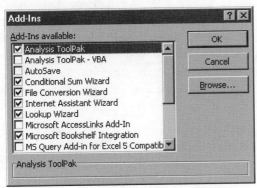

Figure 3-25: The first block of Excel's Add-Ins dialog's add-ins list (all items in the list are installed, only checked items are loaded)

location of *C:\Windows\Favorites** instead of the Office factory default of *C:\My Documents*. We were greatly disappointed to see this preference had been reset for all the applications during the reinstallation. The reinstall created *C:\Windows\Personal* and then changed every application's default file location to this folder on one test machine on which we had renamed the *My Documents* folder.

NOTE   Of all the Office applications, only the humble Binder preserves your custom default file folder setting when you reinstall (File → Binder Options).

---

4. Note several application's Tools → Options settings that don't get preserved.

   Excel is the worst offender in this department. It wants to reset all your Tools → Options settings to the factory defaults. Most annoyingly, Excel's MRU (most recently used) file list got whacked down to four from its previous setting of nine, and the current list was purged meaning you get an empty MRU list when you start Excel after the reinstall.

   Setting integrity varies from application to application, most likely depending on where each one stores its Tools → Options settings (you'd think they'd all work the same). Some of Access's settings get lost. Word's View settings survive, but if you have Outlook 97 spell checking your messages before they go out, it'll get reset and stop

---

* The setting *C:\Windows\Favorites* is simply our preference, you can of course use any default file location you like.

checking after the reinstall. In Outlook 97, we had Journal logging turned completely off, but after the reinstall all five applications (Access, Excel, Binder, PowerPoint, and Word) were checked in Outlook's "Also record files from" list. So you might want to make note of or print out screen shots of each panel in the Tools → Options dialog box for all your main applications (particularly those you've probably tweaked to work more like you want them to work).

Particularly annoying is Outlook 97's insistence on resetting your Address Book's "Show this address list first" preference from whatever it was before the uninstall—in our case, Contacts—to Personal Address Book. To fix this, select Tools → Address Book, then from the Address Book dialog select Tools → Options; now pick your preferred list from the "Show this address list first" control and click on OK.

NOTE   Outlook Bar customizations and Outlook folder view cus-
              tomizations are preserved when you reinstall.

---

5. Note OSB customizations.

   Annoyingly, your customizations of the Office OSB toolbar, among other settings, will be lost during this process. When the OSB starts after the reinstall, it will be in its factory default state (the Office OSB toolbar is showing). Although the folders "behind" any custom OSB toolbars survive (see *C:\Program Files\Microsoft Office\Office\Shortcut Bar*), the toolbars formerly associated with these folders are no longer in the Toolbars tab's "Show these Folders as Toolbars" list (see the Customize dialog box), and you'll have to re-create them.

   In addition, the default position is used, so if you moved your OSB from the left-docked position, you'll find that it's back over on the left side of your screen. AutoHide is also disabled by default, so if you use this feature, you'll have to reset it.

6. Note your Start → Programs settings.

   If you took our advice in *Office 97 Annoyances* and purged your Start menu of the multitudinous (and silly) additions Office makes to it, you'll have to purge them again. On the bright side, and not surprisingly, any of your customizations that involve added items are preserved (for example, consolidating all Office application shortcuts in a single Microsoft Office folder right below Programs itself).

You may also want to remove the Fast Find shortcut that gets added back to your Startup folder. Furthermore, you may want to get rid of the "Install Microsoft Internet Explorer" shortcut on the desktop and rerun the Change Inbox utility (its official moniker is Microsoft Outlook Inbox Icon).

7. Note Office Assistant settings.

The Office Assistant remembers its Gallery and Options settings (right-click on the Assistant and choose Options to access these settings). It will remember what avatar was selected and whether you had the "Make sounds" option checked or not. Annoyingly, the Assistant fires itself up the first time you start each of the reinstalled applications, even if you had it turned off previously. (Actually, the Assistant fires off to welcome you to Word and Excel but not Access or PowerPoint. Go figure.) You'll have to put up with it asking you if you need some help using the current application until you can click on the X in the Assistant's title bar, thereby putting him back to sleep.

8. Verify that you have a backup copy of *<username>8.xlb* (the storage location for changes to Excel command bars—toolbars, menu bars, and shortcut bars).

Any changes you make to Excel command bars are stored in *<username>8.xlb* (located in the folder where you installed Windows, typically *C:\Windows*). This includes command bars you add as well as changes to existing command bars. While the reinstall will not remove this file, Excel will act like it's never heard of it when you first start the upgraded version. You should be able to find your existing *<username>8.xlb* in the Windows folder (but make the backup copy just in case). To get Excel to recognize your custom command bars, just double-click on *<username>8.xlb* in the Windows folder (even if Excel is running) and everything should go back to normal.

9. Close all running applications.

This is, of course, a step you've probably learned to take after many uninstall runs with various applications. An alternate is to cold-boot, then after restarting, close any applications that are running by virtue of being in your StartUp folder. (Alternately, hold down the Ctrl key as Windows starts to bypass the Startup folder.)

10. Close the OSB if it's running (right-click on the OSB's control menu, then choose Exit).

11. In Control Panel, double-click on Add/Remove Programs.

12. If Microsoft Outlook 98 is listed, select it and click on Add/Remove, click on Remove Outlook 98, then click on Yes when prompted "This will uninstall all Microsoft Outlook 98 components. Do you want to continue?"

13. If Microsoft Outlook Internet Mail Enhancement Patch (IMEP) is listed, do this before proceeding: quit the Add/Remove Programs applet, remove the Internet Mail service from all your profiles (since they get trashed anyway and you have to put the information back in, this costs no extra time; just remember to jot down or record these settings), uninstall IMEP, then go back to Control Panel and double-click on Add/Remove Programs.

14. Select Microsoft Office 97 (Standard or Professional or whatever) Edition, then click on the Add/Remove button. You'll be asked to insert your original Office CD at this point so have it handy.

15. Click on the installer's Remove All button and when prompted "Are you sure you want to remove Microsoft Office 97?", click on Yes.

16. If Setup asks if you want to remove your Windows Messaging (meaning, Exchange) shared components while uninstalling Office 97, elect to keep all files by clicking on the Keep button.

17. When Setup is done, defragment your system (Start → Programs → Accessories → System Tools → Disk Defragmenter).

18. If you're feeling ultra conservative—as is usually best when it comes to matters like this—reboot before you install any piece of software.

19. Reinstall Office 97.

20. Reinstall Outlook 98 at this point if appropriate.

21. Test each application and reset preferences in accordance with details provided in the earlier steps in this checklist.

22. Repair the effects of any other anomalies generated by the reinstall (see the next section, "Office Reinstallation Anomalies").

Office Reinstallation Anomalies

Here are the other anomalies we experienced during repeated tests of the uninstall/reinstall cycle.

Exchange suddenly autostarts

Don't be surprised if you run into the unexpected. On one of our test machines after Setup's Restart Windows cycle was finished, the Exchange 5.0 client started of its own accord. This was odd because on the test PC neither Outlook nor Exchange were set to autostart. We rechecked the StartUp folder, *WIN.INI's* run= command, and the Registry, but couldn't detect the cause of the autostart.

Internet account data is missing

After Setup's Restart Windows cycle was finished, when we started either Exchange or Outlook 97 an Internet E-mail message box warned, "Your E-mail address cannot be found. Be sure your personal information provided on the General tab for Internet E-mail properties is correct." When we checked the properties for this transport service, all the fields on all the tabs were empty except the name of the Mail Account on the General tab. After filling them back in, the message box stopped appearing and Internet email worked as usual.

OUTLOOK 98 On the majority of our test PCs, this bug appears to be fixed in Outlook 98. However, on one PC, the bug persisted in Outlook 98.

Miscellaneous cleanup

If you don't like loose folders cluttering up your system, check to see if you have a *C:\~mssetup.t* folder that Office Setup sometimes annoyingly leaves behind.

On your desktop, you'll find the "Setup for Microsoft Internet Explorer 3.02" icon. If you're already running Microsoft Internet Explorer (MSIE) or if you prefer another browser for your Web surfing, you can delete this shortcut. Speaking of MSIE, if you already have MSIE installed and you re-install Office, you may find that the installation has reset your default home page to *www.microsoft.com/msoffice* (this happened consistently on one test PC, but never on another, all running the same version of MSIE...go figure).

If, like us, you keep Find Fast turned off, remember to turn it off yet again, because the reinstall adds it back to your StartUp folder and activates its indexing feature.

4

Enigmatic Journal

Outlook's Journal feature gets a lot of people scratching their heads, wondering what the heck it is, what they should do with it, and why they need it. Good questions all, and not answered anywhere in the help file that we can find. Sure, bits and pieces of the Journal facility are described, but nowhere is the whole *gestalt* of the Journal discussed. Talk about *annoying!* You'd think Microsoft's first foray into the PIM market would bend over backwards to get users familiar with its potentially most intrusive and least intuitive feature. No matter, we'll fill the void, and a great deal of what we discuss in this chapter on the Journal applies to Outlook's other facilities as well.

The Journal module in Outlook is indeed just that, a "journal." Of course if you're an accountant, a journal is a very different thing than if you're a journalist, but the underlying paradigm of recording data remains the same. This facility has often been described as a "diary," but diary, while close, isn't really accurate. Think of any date-based appointment book, planner, or time-tracker that you might keep open on your desk to jot things down in, and you're pretty much on target for what Outlook's journal facility is all about. You might record in it at what time and on what date you worked on a particular file for a particular client. Or on what day you called which contact, what you talked about, and for how long. Or maybe you'd record just when you sent an important email notice to someone. Not only does Outlook provide a place for you to record these things, it can do most of that recording *automatically*.

That's the good news. The annoying news is that Outlook's journal feature has more than its share of glitches and hiccups. It can, for example, cause your Personal Folders file to grow to gargantuan proportions, and while most features work, they may not work as you'd expect.

The trade-off is between what the Journal can do *for you* and what it does *to you* as it performs its job. We'll break it all down for you and try to provide workarounds for some of Outlook's more annoying habits in this chapter. Trust us, the results can definitely be worth the hassle.

Creating Journal Entries

Let's start at the granular level and try to put this entire facility into perspective. Outlook records *items* in its facilities. An item in Outlook is a collection of information about something. If you are of the database persuasion, you can think of an item as a record in the journal database (because this is exactly what it is). The "thing" you are recording information about consists of any valid "Entry type" that the Journal recognizes, and some associated information.

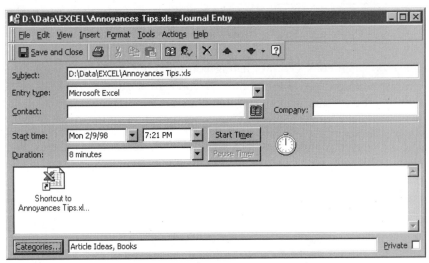

Figure 4-1: Outlook's journal entry form

In Figure 4-1, you see a fairly typical journal entry, in this case for an Excel file that was edited for a period of time (8 minutes) on a particular date (2/9/98). This entry consists of a subject (in this case the fully qualified path and filename of the Excel file), the entry type (Microsoft Excel), the start date and time, the duration, and the total amount of time the file was worked on. This entry was created automatically by Outlook's auto-journal feature, and a shortcut to the file was created so that, when viewing this journal entry, you can launch the actual file by double-clicking on the shortcut icon. Note that you can also add a name (or names) to the Contact field from any of your various address books. Clicking on the Address Book icon to the right of the Contact text box lets you browse your address book entries.

You'd think that if you picked a name from your Contact list, any company information for that person would automatically appear in the Company field. No such luck if you use the Address Book icon to select a name. You'll have to key in the company information yourself.

NOTE   As we'll discuss later in this chapter, you're better off skipping the Address Book icon altogether for names in Outlook's Contact list. Instead, use the Check Names feature to resolve the name. Type the name (or part of it) into the Contact field and press Ctrl+K. This solves a couple of problems when listing a contact from Outlook's Contact list, one of them being that if there is a company entry for that contact record, it does appear in the journal entry's Company field.

The Start Timer and Pause Timer buttons come in handy when you're timing a phone call or meeting. Click on the Start Timer button and the little stopwatch comes to life, letting you know the timer is running. The time is recorded in whole minutes (if you start the timer, pause it at 55 seconds, then restart it, you lose the 55 seconds as the counter restarts at zero, so don't plan on timing any horse races with this feature).

The Categories button pops up Outlook's Categories dialog box (see Figure 4-2), and you can use category keywords to group your entries (handy when you want to find everything you did last week for "Article Ideas" or "Books").

Last, way down in the right-hand corner you can check the Private box. Check this box if you're working in shared folders and you want the item to be hidden from anyone with access to the folder the item is stored in other than yourself.

Journal Entry Types

The Journal provides a log of events, and the kinds of events are defined by entry types. Some entries can be generated automatically by Outlook based on how it's configured, others can be generated when you create a new Journal item. It's always possible to create a journal entry after the fact—for example, for an Office document that was created before you decided to begin journaling it.

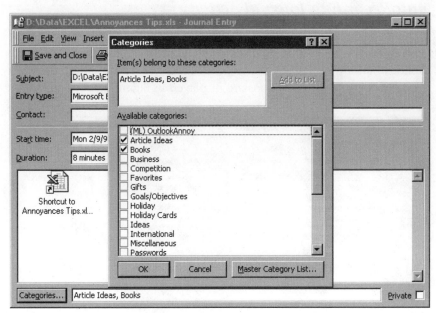

Figure 4-2: Adding Categories to a journal entry

Outlook supports 20 different journal entry types, as shown in Table 4-1.

Table 4-1: Outlook journal entry types

Outlook Journal Entry Types		
Conversation	Meeting request	Note
Document	Meeting response	Phone call
Email message	Microsoft Access	Remote session
Fax	Microsoft Excel	Task
Letter	Microsoft Office Binder	Task request
Meeting	Microsoft PowerPoint	Task response
Meeting cancellation	Microsoft Word	

Even though there are numerous entry types, the information for each item remains pretty much the same. The journal flags each entry with the date the item was created and the duration, if applicable. This lets Outlook show you journal entries in a timeline format, which we'll discuss later in this chapter. There are two ways to generate journal entries: manually, or you can let Outlook crank them out automatically.

AutoRecording Journal Activity

Outlook defaults to generating automatic journal entries right out of the box. In Outlook 98, click on Tools → Options, then click on the Journal Options button (in Outlook 97, click on Tools → Options, and then select the Journal tab). Journal options are displayed in Figure 4-3.

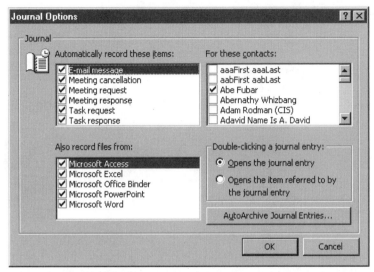

Figure 4-3: Journal facility command central

Email messages, meeting information, and tasks can all be automatically tracked, as well as any file activity from other installed Office applications. Needless to say, Outlook has the capability to generate an awful lot of journal activity if left to its own designs. After we go through the mechanics of what is happening, you might want to trim this automatic mania back a bit, as we mentioned in Chapter 2, *Vital Changes, Settings, and Customizations*.

Let's tackle the file-tracking features first.

Files: typed and cross-matched

Let's say you're in Word and you create a new document. Knowing a bit about document management, you take full advantage of Word's File → Properties dialog and record all sorts of pertinent information about this document, as shown in Figure 4-4.

Completing your work on the document in question, you close it. Now, assuming you have the settings in Outlook shown in Figure 4-3, you start Outlook or switch to it if it's already running. Click on the Journal icon in

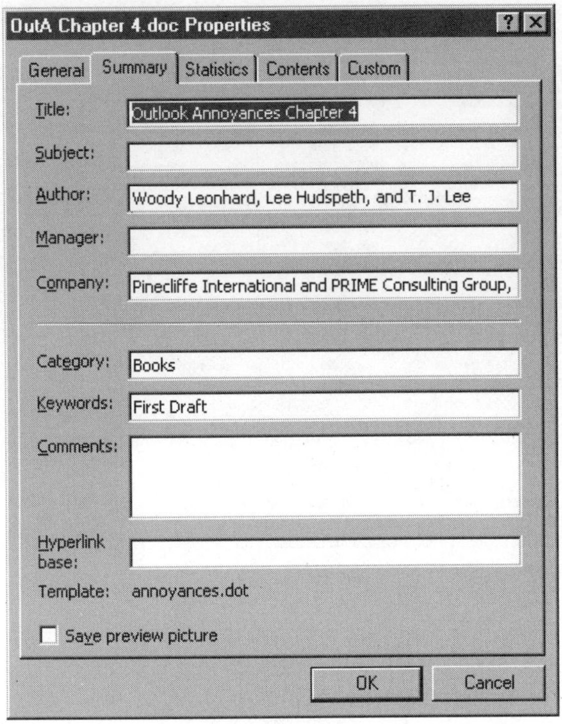

Figure 4-4: A Word document's File Properties dialog box

the Outlook Bar and there, big as life, is an entry chronicling your work with that document (see Figure 4-5).

Remember, the journal entries are listed by default with the most recent *start* time shown at the top of the list. This means a document you have had open all day may not be displayed at the top of the list. In Outlook 98 if you have Preview Pane on (or in Outlook 97 if you have the Chilton Preview add-in installed), you'll see the preview pane as well, which includes any text typed into the body field.

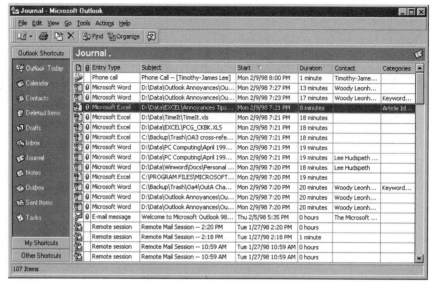

Figure 4-5: Journal facility displayed in Entry List view

NOTE   Journal entries for file activities are actually created in Outlook (or queued up for the next time Outlook starts if Outlook is not running) when the file is closed in the other
Office application. Note that each open/close activity for a
specific file is logged as an individual journal entry. If the
Journal facility is displayed in Outlook and you close a file
and then switch back to Outlook, the new journal entry
may not appear for a few seconds, up to a full minute. But
if you switch to another facility in Outlook (or if another facility is displayed when you switch to Outlook), the new
entry appears as soon as you display the Journal facility.

Opening this entry, you see the standard journal entry with a number of
fields already filled in, as shown in Figure 4-6. Note that the Author information from Word's Properties dialog is entered in the journal record's
Contact field. The Company information also maps across from Word's
dialog settings to the corresponding journal field, with some important
exceptions that are noted in Table 4-2.

But woe and annoyance when it comes to the Categories field. The Word
document's Properties dialog has a field named Category. You'd think
that anything you type into this field would appear in the Categories field
in the Outlook journal entry. Nope. The values in Word's Keywords field
wind up in the Journal's Categories field. Very confusing and annoying.
At least if you type a keyword on the Word side, and it *matches* an

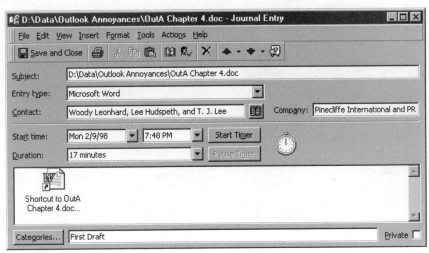

Figure 4-6: An automatically generated journal entry for a Word file

Outlook category, the keyword is treated as a legitimate category. But if you use a keyword in Word that is not in Outlook's Master Category List, the keyword still shows up in the journal entry's Categories field and is unique (available) *only* to journal entries for this specific file. No other journal entries will interpret this keyword as an Outlook category. Another way to look at this phenomenon is that you cannot add to Outlook's Master Categories List on the fly by typing keywords for Office documents that are being automatically tracked as journal entries.

If there is a single Author name, and it happens to exactly match the name of a Contact item in Outlook's Contact list, then the journal entry for this file is listed on the Journal tab in that person's Contact record. (If there are multiple authors listed in Word's Author name field, even if the names all match exactly with Contact items in Outlook, none of their Journal logs will reflect the document activity.) Create a file in Word for a client that is listed as a contact over in Outlook and change the Author name to the name of the client. That file is automatically associated with the client contact record, and you're able to look back over a timeline of all the files created for this client (see Figure 4-7).

Given this behavior it appears that Microsoft has made the assumption that you only want to associate files you create with...yourself. The Author field in the Word document's Properties dialog is not usually someone listed in your Contact List, but rather yourself, the actual author of the document. To further hamper your taking advantage of Author-to-Contact mapping, there is no way to browse Outlook's Contact or Category lists in Word when filling in a document's properties information—

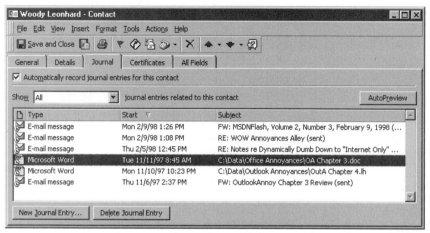

Figure 4-7: A Contact record's Journal tab—knows all, reveals all!

and it's confusing to list names other than the actual author in the Author field. Ditto for the Company field. So as a mechanism for associating files you are working on with client Contact records in Outlook, Microsoft definitely needs to rethink this integration.

It could simply be that this is a bug, not a feature (and one not corrected in Outlook 98). In one KnowledgeBase article, Microsoft states, "The 'Also record files from' portion of the Journal Options tab will automatically record activity in the programs listed, but does not associate this activity with a particular client." It's tempting to chalk up Word's behavior in this regard as a colossal glitch. Except that this is the same behavior you'll get with Excel, PowerPoint, and Access documents. Maybe it's a feature still in development. In summary, if you know which field in the Properties dialog box is stuffed into which field in Outlook journal entries, you can use this "feature" however you see fit (see Table 4-2).

Table 4-2: How Office document properties fields map to Outlook journal entries

Office Document Properties Field	Maps to Outlook 98 and 97 Journal
Title	No
Subject	No
Author	Contact (but only if Author field content includes one name and it matches exactly to a corresponding Contact)
Manager	No (if the document includes non-empty Manager text then this text is appended to the Author name and separated by a comma)

Table 4-2: How Office document properties fields map to Outlook journal entries (continued)

Office Document Properties Field	Maps to Outlook 98 and 97 Journal
Company	Company[1]
Category	No (see Keywords)
Keywords	Category (if a keyword matches an Outlook category, the keyword is treated as a legitimate category, but if a keyword is not in Outlook's Master Category List, it still shows up in the journal entry's Categories field but is available only to journal entries for this specific file)
Comments	No
Custom fields	No

[1] If there's no Author-to-Contact match, then the field text pours into the journal entry's field as is. If there is an Author-to-Contact match and the dialog's value is the same (or empty!), then the Journal shows the Contact's company. If the dialog's value is different, the journal entry takes on a paired value that looks like this: "*dialog_company_name, Contact_company*" where *dialog_company_name* is the value from the dialog and *Contact_company* is the value according to the Contact record. And if you subsequently change the value in the document, it replaces *dialog_company_name* only. A weird, head-shrinking annoyance indeed.

Last but certainly not least, a shortcut back to the actual file appears in the journal entry. Double-clicking on this shortcut opens the original file.

Through its Journal facility, Outlook promises to perform the role of a document management system (DMS) for the entire suite of Office applications. In reality, however, Outlook's Journal makes for a second-class document management system for several reasons:

- The inconsistent mapping of information between the source Office documents and their corresponding journal entries that we've discussed;

- The absence of a batch facility to create journal entries for all previously created documents*; and

- The absence of a full-text search engine that can find text inside the Office documents being "journaled" (not just comment text or other properties logged in a journal entry that points to a document). You might find the Journal useful for reviewing the timeline of the files you worked on during a particular period of time. However, if you simply need to find a file, the built-in search features—including full text searching—of the Office File Open dialog are vastly superior to Outlook's Journal.

---

* Robust document management systems typically come with a sophisticated built-in batch facility that allows you to finely tune which extant documents get added to the DMS database. In Outlook, you'd have to build this from scratch in VBScript, a non-trivial undertaking.

Tracking email, meeting, and task items

If you want the journal entries for email messages; meeting cancellations, requests, and responses; and task requests and responses automatically associated with those Contacts that the email, meeting, or task item relates to, you must check the checkbox next to that Contact's name in the Journal Options dialog. (You can't do this *en masse* by selecting multiple entries like a typical Windows dialog; you've got to painstakingly do it one by one.) Every name in your default Contacts list appears here. This is a colossal annoyance.

NOTE   When we say *all* Contact names appear in the Journal Op-
                tions dialog, we mean all the contact entries in the default
                Outlook Contact list. If you have created your own custom
                folders using the Contact data type, none of those entries
                appear in the Journal dialog.

By default these checkboxes are *not* checked. You can either check the boxes shown in the Journal Options dialog (in Outlook 97 the Options dialog's Journal tab) or you can check the "Automatically record journal entries for this contact" checkbox on the Journal tab of the individual's contact record. If you always want this box checked whenever you add a new Contact, you must create a custom Contact form and make it the default. This is not as hard as it sounds:

1. In Outlook, open the Contacts folder and create a new Contact (File → New → Contact). Don't enter any data for the new contact or the data will be bound to the form.

2. Pull down the Tools menu on the Contact form, select Forms, and choose Design This Form (in Outlook 97 it's Tools → Design Outlook Form).

3. Select the Journal tab and check the "Automatically record journal entries for this contact" checkbox.

4. Select the General tab (so this tab shows up as the default tab when you create new Contacts). From the form's Tools menu click on Forms, then choose Publish Form As (in Outlook 97, from the form's File menu click on Publish Form As). See Figure 4-8.

5. Give it a creative name like "MyContacts," make sure Look In (in Outlook 97, Publish In) is set to the Contacts folder, then click on Publish.

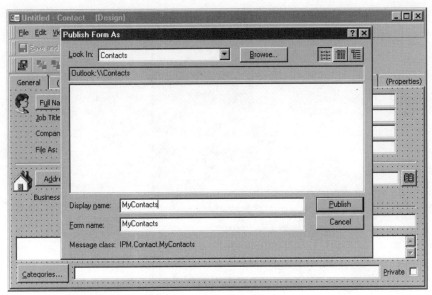

Figure 4-8: Publish your own custom Journal Entry form

6. In the Contact form, pull down the File menu and click on Close. Click on No when asked if you want to save changes.

7. In Outlook, if Folder List isn't already on, pull down the View menu and click on Folder List.

8. In the Folder List, right-click on Contacts and choose Properties from the pop-up menu (this works from the Outlook Bar also). In the "When posting to this folder, use" drop-down list, choose the MyContacts entry (see Figure 4-9).

9. Click on OK.

Now whenever you create a new contact, the checkbox for associating journal entries with the contact record will be checked by default. Seems like the long way around the barn, but it's the only way to accomplish this without resorting to code.

NOTE   Custom forms are a very powerful feature of Outlook. See Chapter 8, *Introduction to VBScript, the Outlook Object Model, and Custom Forms*, for more on creating, using, and managing custom forms.

Overall this is pretty handy if you need or want to automatically track these types of activities from the contact's perspective. You open a

Figure 4-9: Setting the default form for new contacts

contact record and the Journal tab lists all the activity—email, meetings, related tasks, documents, phone calls, and so on—for that person.

Manual Journal Entries

Auto recording is not the only way that journal entries can or should be created. You can manually create a journal entry several different ways. The most direct is to switch to the Journal facility and click on the New Journal button on Outlook's toolbar. Or you can create a new journal entry no matter which facility you are in by pressing Ctrl+Shift+J. In either case, Outlook opens a form like the one shown in Figure 4-10.

Notice that the default "Entry type" is Phone call. For us this is grand, as that's usually just what we want when we crank out a manual journal entry. If you want a different default, get used to being annoyed. Not even creating a custom form lets you change the default from Phone call to some other entry type.

You can enter the information for this item, start the timer if you want, associate this entry with a Contact, and type notes in the body.* And as we discussed earlier, you can also insert files or other Outlook items into the body.

---

* We use the term "body" to describe the large, scrollable area you type into that occupies the bottom half of most types of Outlook data items.

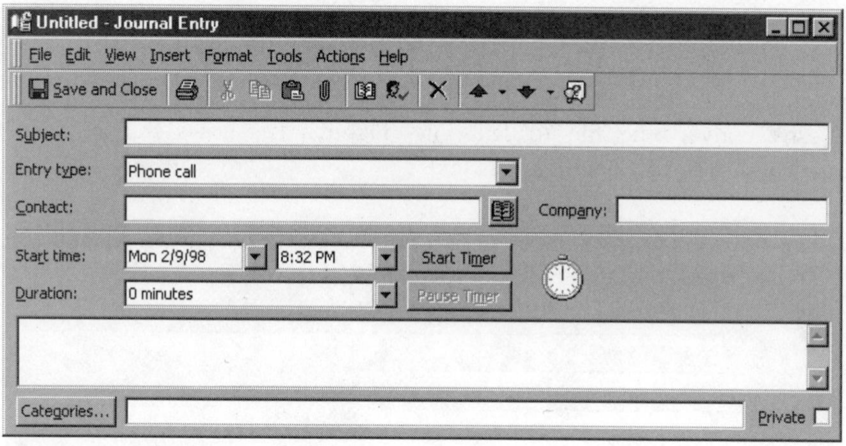

Figure 4-10: The default manual journal entry form

Inserting files in journal entries

Inserting a file, shortcut, object (object insertions aren't supported in Outlook 98's Plain Text mode for messages, which makes good sense), or the text content of a file is very straightforward. It doesn't matter which field your cursor is in within the journal entry (or any other Outlook form, like a Contact item for example)—the file is always inserted in the appropriate place. (However, the Object command is typically disabled unless the cursor is in the item's body field.) Pull down the Insert menu in a Journal form and click on File. The Insert File dialog pops up and you can browse for the file you want (see Figure 4-11).

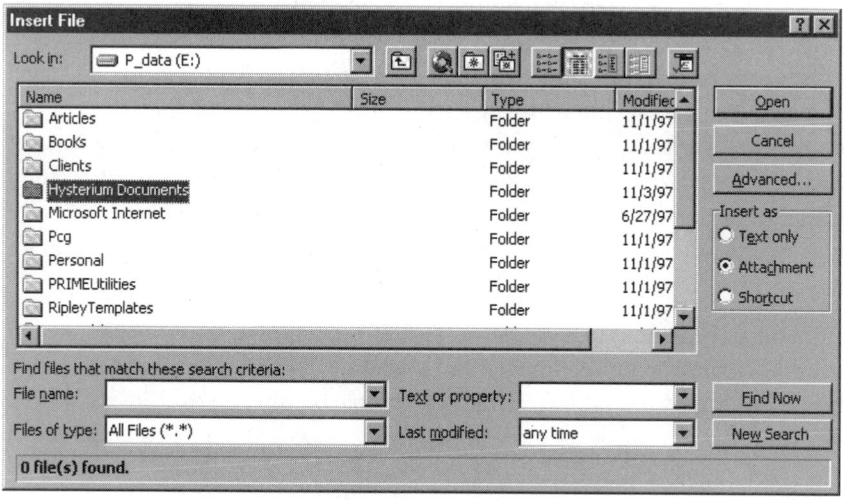

Figure 4-11: Inserting a file into a journal entry

Notice the "Insert as" options on the right side of the dialog box. You
have the choice of inserting the file as Text only, as an Attachment, or as
a Shortcut. If you choose "Text only" for a binary file (like a Word document, for example), you won't get the result you're looking for. Outlook
doesn't convert the file to text-only. Figure 4-12 shows the result of
inserting a Word 97 document as text.

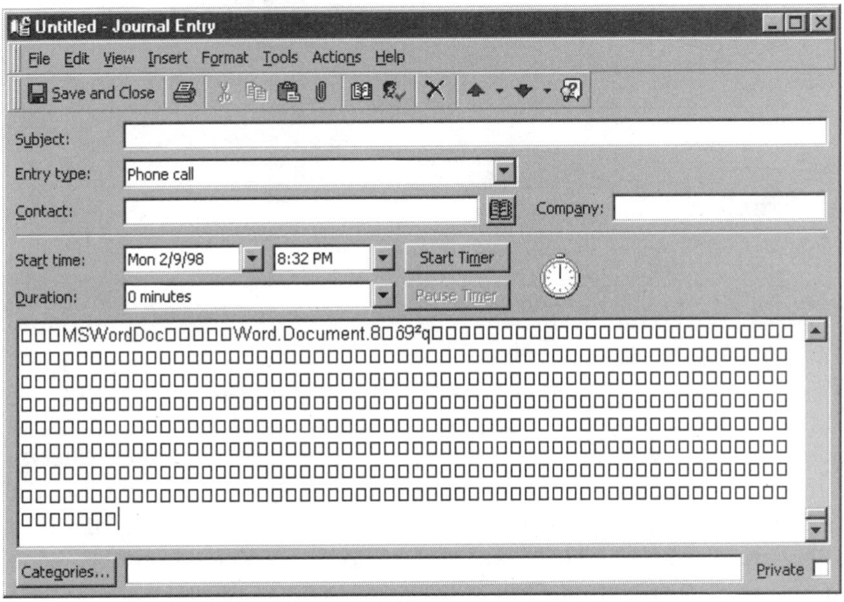

Figure 4-12: The Text only option works best with text files

If you choose to insert the file as an attachment, you actually embed a
copy of the file into the journal entry. Keep in mind that an embedded
object is not linked in any way to the original file. If you insert an Excel
spreadsheet as an attachment, then modify that file in Excel, the
embedded version in the journal entry won't reflect those changes. In
addition, since you are effectively making a copy of the file (and sticking
it inside the journal entry), you're using up hard disk real estate in addition to introducing a potential problem with multiple versions.

To avoid these problems, insert the file as a Shortcut. This creates a
shortcut that points to the location of the original file. Double-click on the
shortcut icon and the original file is opened. Note that if you delete or
move the target file later, the shortcut won't be able to find it, and you'll
get the error message shown in Figure 4-13 when you double-click on
the shortcut.

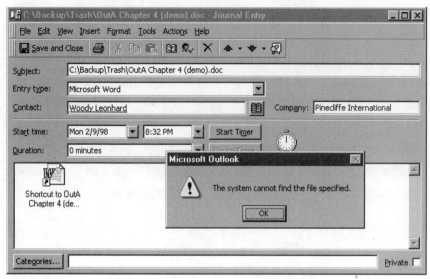

Figure 4-13: Those broken link blues!

Inserting Outlook items in journal entries

Just as files are inserted into the body of a journal entry, Outlook items like email messages, tasks, and calendar items can be inserted as well. In the journal entry, pull down the Insert menu and click on Item. You get a dialog box very similar to the Insert File dialog box, only this time you're browsing the folder structure within your Personal Folders file (see Figure 4-14).

Items for the selected folder appear in the list at the bottom of the dialog box; as with Insert File you have the choice of "Text only," Attachment, or Shortcut. These options work the same as when you insert a file. The good news is you don't have to worry about binary file formats if you choose the Text only option. Contact items, emails, and what-have-you come in as plain text very nicely. Figure 4-15 shows a Contact item that has been inserted as Text only in a Phone call journal entry.

Entries that are recorded automatically by Outlook's auto-journal feature default to inserting shortcuts for items and files. If there's a way to change this default we've not been able to find it.

Creating journal entries

A slick way to manually record a journal entry and get it associated properly with another item is to open the item, be it an email, appointment, contact, or whatever, and from the item's menu bar click on Tools → Record in Journal (or press Ctrl+J if you like keyboard shortcuts). This

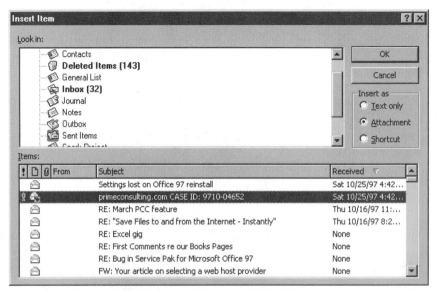

Figure 4-14: Inserting Outlook items in a journal entry

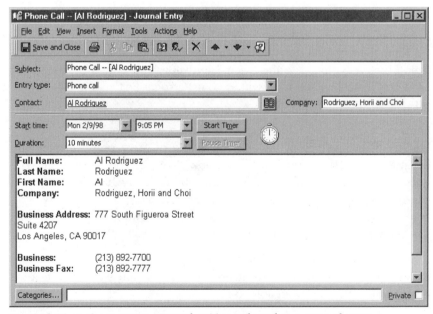

Figure 4-15: A Contact item inserted as Text only within a journal entry

fills out the appropriate information in the journal entry form and is the best method for creating journal entries for extant Outlook items. A slightly different way to do the same thing is to drag the item from the displayed list to the Journal icon in the Outlook bar. Both methods put a shortcut to the item being created in the body of the journal entry. Slick indeed.

OUTLOOK 98   The `Ctrl+J` technique works in both Outlook 98 and 97 but for some reason there's no menu bar interface for this operation in Outlook 98. You can customize your command bars in Outlook 98 to add back the Record in Journal command.

However, there are some serious gotchas with getting manually created journal entries associated with the proper Contact item. First, the `Ctrl+J` trick from within an email message only associates the created journal entry with a Contact item if the email's From field matches exactly with an email field in an existing Contact record. If it's not an exact match, but there is a Contact item for this person, you can try clicking in the Contact field in the journal entry and pressing `Ctrl+K` to do a Check Names and see if the proper association can be made.

Using the address book icon to associate a journal entry with a Contact item also has its problems. If Outlook is in Internet-only mode and you create a journal entry and use the address book icon (it's to the right of the Contact field) to pick a Contact, something unexpected happens. The journal entry won't appear in that Contact's Journal tab. The journal entry will exist, it just doesn't show up in that person's list of associated journal entries even though they are referenced in the Contact field of that journal entry.

Here's a specific example: create a manual journal entry, then click on the Address Book icon and search the list for the name you want. So far so good (see Figure 4-16). Now select a name from your Contacts address book, click on Add, then click on OK. Save and Close the journal entry. What could be easier? But if you're in Internet-only mode, when you open the Contact record and check the Journal tab, this journal entry is not listed. Talk about annoying! *It just doesn't work.*

Fortunately there is a way to sidestep this problem. Create your journal entry and click in the Contact field. *Do not click on the Address Book icon!* Instead, type in the name of the contact (or a partial name like "Bill") and press `Ctrl+K`. This triggers the Check Names feature we described earlier. If there are several entries in your Contact list that match what you've typed they'll be displayed in a list box and you can choose the one you want (see Figure 4-17).

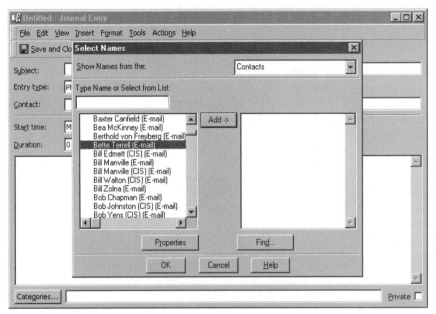

Figure 4-16: Using the Address Book button to pick Contact names for a journal entry

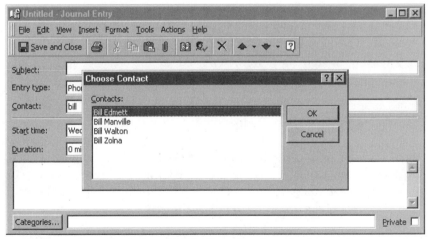

Figure 4-17: Using Check Names (Ctrl+K) to select from the Contact list

This method ensures that the journal entry ends up on the Contact's Journal tab as it's supposed to and has the added benefit of ensuring that any Company name in the contact record appears in the Company field in the journal entry.

Taming the Telephone

The Journal facility in Outlook is the only good repository for logging your phone calls. You can time calls, associate them with people in your Contact list, jot down information as you talk, and so forth. This is very handy for consulting your notes on just when you said what and to whom.

Unfortunately, Outlook only provides the bare minimum you need for phone call logging: a form to type your notes and time your calls with a contact. That's it. You can't mark a phone call journal entry as incoming or outgoing. You can't initiate a call, get a busy signal, and automatically generate a reminder to call back. Outlook won't let you sort phone call journal entries (or any other type of journal entries for that matter) by their Categories or Contact fields; instead you get the annoyingly terse message box "You cannot sort by this field" with no corresponding help topic or advice, just a stark OK button.* (The workaround is to select all desired records, then copy and paste into Access or Excel for sorting by these no-sort fields.)

Many other PIMs include a separate module called Phone Calls or Phone Log, the sole purpose of which is to log phone calls. Outlook's competitors recognize phone call management as a fundamental feature demanded by PIM users, so much so that they devote a unique data type to this function. Not so with Outlook. Instead, phone calls are set aside as a sub-type of the Journal (one sub-type among 20). Outlook has a long way to go to providing real utility to people who make their living on the telephone. In the ensuing sections we cover how to place a call using Outlook's telephony features as well as how Outlook fares (it falls way short) for time billing purposes.

Placing a call

As you saw in Chapter 2, you can set Outlook 97's dialing options via the Tools → Options → General → Dialing Options button. You can also get to the Dialing Options dialog by pulling down the Tools menu, choosing Dial, then clicking on New Call on the cascading menu (see Figure 4-18). In Outlook 98 it's a bit more awkward: although the keyboard shortcut Ctrl+Shift+D still displays the New Call dialog from any folder, the menu interface is only visible when the Contacts folder is active, in which case the steps are Actions → Call Contact → New Call. The solution to this

---

* You can sort on a field by simply clicking that field's column heading. Clicking a second time toggles the sort order.

annoyance is one we've been preaching for years: customize your tool-bars. Since Outlook 98 has grown up and now supports command bar customizations, you're all set. Add the New Call command to your menu bar or any toolbar of your choosing (you'll find several phone call commands in the Customize dialog box under the Actions category).

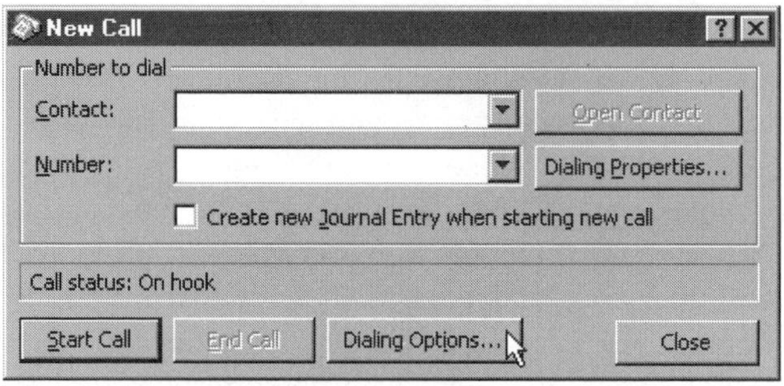

Figure 4-18: Outlook's New Call dialog

The Contact drop-down list holds the names that you have added to your speed dial list (we'll talk about the speed dialer shortly). Either pick a name from the drop-down list or type a name in the Contact field, then hit the Tab key to move the cursor to the Number field. Assuming the name is either a speed dial entry or is listed in your Contact list, the tele-phone numbers for that person appear in the Number field drop-down list.

Annoyingly enough, you must type in enough of the Contact name to allow Outlook to uniquely identify a single contact. You can't type in "bill" and run Check Names (Ctrl+K) as you did in the last section, where you were looking up a contact name to associate with a journal entry. Ctrl+K doesn't work in the New Call dialog. To retrieve "Bill Edmett" as we did in the last example, it would be necessary to type in "bill e" at a minimum to get a unique match on his contact record.

Then again, there's nothing that says a name *must* come from any address book. You can always just type in any name you want, then type in a phone number and click the Start Call button.

Outlook dials the number through your modem and presents you with the Call Status dialog box shown in Figure 4-19. The Call Status dialog lets you terminate the call via the Hang Up button, or use the Talk button to switch the call to the handset attached to your modem when you hear the party you're calling answer.

If you checked the "Create new Journal Entry when starting new call" checkbox of the New Call dialog (see Figure 4-18), a new Phone call type

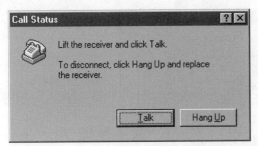

Figure 4-19: Using the modem and Outlook to place your calls

journal entry is automatically generated. The Subject is the name of the person entered in the New Call dialog box enclosed in square brackets, for example, Phone Call -- [Lee Hudspeth].

NOTE   You can activate the New Call dialog in Outlook 98 and 97 by right-clicking on any contact in a Contacts folder, then choosing Auto Dialer. This brings up the New Call dialog with that entry in place; all the contact's phone numbers are in the Number drop-down list.

Speed dialing

You can set up to a maximum of 20 speed dial entries. To create speed dial entries just fire up the Dialing Options dialog, as shown in Figure 4-20.

Enter the name and phone number for the entry and press the Add button. To automatically pull the name and phone number from the Contacts list, type in the name as it appears in Contacts (or enough of the name so it can be uniquely identified) and hit the Tab key or click in the Phone number field. All the numbers for that contact are listed in the drop-down list. Just pick the number you want and click on Add. Annoyingly, if the speed dial contact has multiple phone numbers, they're all listed without their associated field designation (like Business versus Pager), so you can't tell which number is which. Equally maddening is the fact that you can't sort the speed dial names; they're permanently stuck in the order in which you entered them (the only way to rearrange them is to delete and re-add entries).

In Outlook 98, you can only get to the speed dial interface from the Call Contact menu, and Call Contact is only visible on the Actions menu when a Contacts folder is active (see Figure 4-21). To see it in other contexts you'll have to add the Call Contact command to a command bar yourself.

Figure 4-20: Setting up speed dial entries

In Outlook 97, the speed dial entries appear as menu items on a cascading menu off the Tools menu. Click Tools → Dial → Speed Dial to display the speed dial menu (annoyingly, there's no keyboard shortcut for the Speed Dial dialog in either version of Outlook). Click on the name you want to call and Outlook pops up the New Calls dialog with the name and phone number filled in.

NOTE   That said, you can get to your speed dial data another way: Ctrl+Shift+D to fire up the New Call dialog, then click on the Contact control's drop-down arrow. This displays all your speed dial entry names; pick one and its associated number automatically pops into the Number field.

It's annoying that there is no way to have Outlook generate a speed dial-based journal entry *without* dialing the modem. If your system is not set up to shunt your modem to your handset it's a real headache to have to hit the Hang Up button before anyone at the other end of the call answers their phone and is greeted by the modem's squealing squelch.

Time is money

Despite the ability to record the elapsed time of a telephone call (or the duration of any of Outlook's items) there is no built-in methodology for

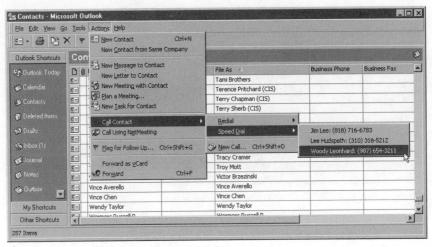

Figure 4-21: Working with the Speed Dial menu

grouping and summarizing time spent on calls, files, or anything else for billing purposes.

This is a major annoyance for anyone that bills for his or her time. He or she has to record everything in Outlook and then either reenter the information into some timekeeping application (cut and paste into Excel, for example) or export the Outlook data and effectively do the same thing to get it into some other application for summarizing.

Monitoring Activities over Time

In Outlook's Journal facility you can view the journal entries on a timeline. This type of view is unique to the Journal and is probably why the misnomer "diary" gets applied to this facility. It's better to think of the Journal as a large desk calendar where you jot down everything you do.

These timeline views are very interesting. Different types of activities recorded and spread across a horizontally scrolling timeline are available as built-in views. Different views for your journal entries are selected, logically enough, from the View menu. These built-in views let you group or categorize your information quickly (see Figure 4-22).

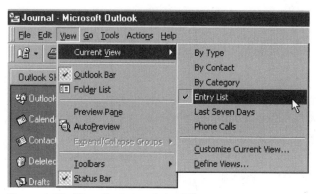

Figure 4-22: View the Journal six different ways

WARNING   If you create a manual journal entry in Outlook while the
current facility is the Journal, you can get bit by this bug: If
you are in By Type, By Contact, or By Category view, any
journal item you manually create will have a start time of
12:00 A.M. From any other view, the system clock time is
used. Sort of a temporal annoyance.

Figure 4-23 shows the Journal in By Type view. In this example you see
what journal entries have been recorded for email messages, phone calls,
and file activity across several different Office applications. To expand
any given type, just click on the plus icon to the left of the entry type
description. In Figure 4-24 you see the phone call journal entries spread
across a chunk of the timeline.

You can quickly see what calls were logged on which days. Each of the
journal types can be expanded and displayed across the timeline. The
timeline can be scrolled forward and backward. By Type, By Contact, and
By Category all function in roughly the same way. You can expand a
given Contact or Category and see all the transactions recorded for this
entry type spread across the timeline.

The Entry List view provides a row and column format for all journal
entries as they were entered (refer back to Figure 4-5), while the Last
Seven Days view reduces the same type of view to entries created within
the last seven days.

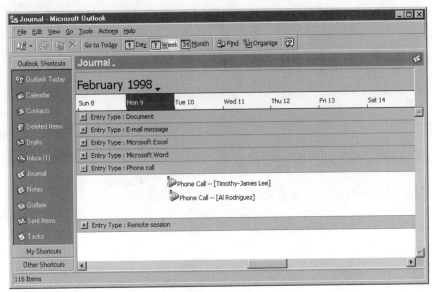

Figure 4-23: The Journal shown By Type

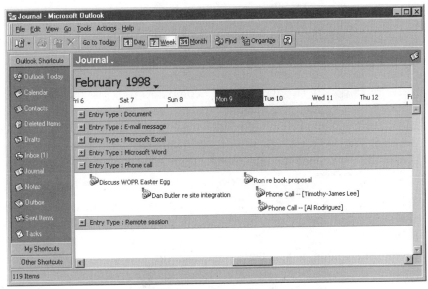

Figure 4-24: Viewing phone calls across the timeline

5

Outlook's Key Ingredients

In this chapter:
- *New Items, Less Annoyance*
- *Thick as a Post*
- *Calendar—or if This Is Tuesday It Must Be Outlook*
- *Making Contact*
- *The Task at Hand*
- *Make a Note of That*
- *Mastering Mail Messages*

Having dealt with the unique-to-Outlook Journal facility from soup to nuts in the preceding chapter, we'll now look at the remaining, more traditional facilities that make up Outlook.

The bread-and-butter attributes of any PIM are scheduling (meetings, events, and appointments), address book, to do list, and a place to record miscellaneous information that doesn't readily fit into any of the other facilities. Outlook provides these services within its respective Calendar, Contact, Task, and Notes facilities. And because email has become at least as important to the average computer user as the telephone, Outlook also acts as a full-featured email client that allows you to send and receive email. Combining email with a personal information manager provides you with a single piece of software that manages pretty much everything you need to effectively communicate with the rest of the world.

The first thing you need to do is get your data into Outlook. A super-annoyance is that once you begin using a particular manufacturer's brand of PIM software, they've effectively got you. "Get their data, and their hearts and minds will follow," because once you've stored all your precious data using their software, without their software it (and you) are up the old cybercreek without an oar. Fortunately, with Outlook, despite its sometimes annoying habits and quirks, you have a top-of-the-line PIM that will serve you well over the long haul.

We'll start with the basics of data entry in this chapter on a small scale, deal with creating and working with single items, and then move on to getting the most out of each facility with a minimum of annoyances. In the next chapter, we'll cover importing and converting data *en masse* from other programs.

New Items, Less Annoyance

Entering data into Outlook is as easy as filling out the onscreen forms that it presents for each of its facilities. Simple. You complete the form and create an *item*, such as a Contact, a Task, or an email message. Items can be created from the New option found on the File menu, as shown in Figure 5-1.

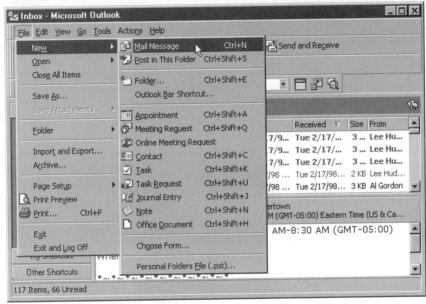

Figure 5-1: Creating a new item in Outlook

From the cascading menu, you can create any of the items that Outlook stores in its facilities, create a new folder in the Personal Folders file, choose a template or form (the template or form controlling what type of item you'll create), or create a new Office Document item, which encloses an Office document of the type you choose in the current Outlook item.

The order of the menu options (and the availability of some of the options themselves) depends on which facility is active at the time you access the menu. In computer palaver, we call this *context sensitivity*, and it's supposed to make your life easier by changing your available options depending on where you are in the program at the moment. If your Inbox is the selected facility, for example, the first option on the cascading menu is Mail Message, as shown in Figure 5-1. Note that next to the Mail Message option is the keyboard shortcut Ctrl+N. This shortcut pops open a new item for whatever the active facility is.

Ctrl+N works the same way as the first button found on the Outlook toolbar. This "New *item*" button also creates a new item when clicked, but what kind of item depends again on the active facility (also called folders, in Outlook lingo), as Figure 5-2 illustrates.

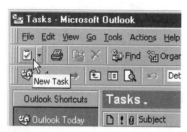

Figure 5-2: Create a new item from the toolbar

This takes context sensitivity to a wonderful or very annoying height, depending on how you work. People tend to keep one facility in Outlook active most of the time. Maybe you have your Inbox active all the time for email, maybe you keep your Calendar displayed at all times, or perhaps you always have the Task list available. You can get used to clicking on that first toolbar button or pressing Ctrl+N and getting a new item form for the facility you "live" in. But every time you switch to a different facility and press Ctrl+N, you'll get a form for the wrong type of item.

You could customize the toolbars in Outlook 98 (as discussed back in Chapter 2, *Vital Changes, Settings, and Customizations*) and add a button specifically for calling up the item you create most often. Heck, you could add a series of buttons, one button for each item you can create in Outlook. But not only would having specific email, appointment, contact, task, journal, and note buttons be cumbersome, you'd also have to modify the toolbar separately in each facility since the toolbars are also context-sensitive, and item buttons disappear as you change facilities. Still, if you only wanted one or two buttons for creating specific items from within any facility, you certainly could. An annoying but workable workaround.

There is a much easier and less painful way, however. We heartily recommend you memorize a few simple keyboard shortcuts that let you create any type of item no matter what the active facility is (see Table 5-1).

Table 5-1: Handy shortcuts for item creation

To Create This Item	Use This Shortcut
eMail Message	Ctrl+Shift+M
Contact	Ctrl+Shift+C
Appointment (or meeting or event)	Ctrl+Shift+A
Journal	Ctrl+Shift+J
Note	Ctrl+Shift+N
Task	Ctrl+Shift+K

Even if you're more a mouse person than a keyboard person, these shortcuts will make you more productive with Outlook in short order. It should be noted that these shortcuts call up a form for the *default* folder for each facility. If you have multiple Contact folders, for instance, Ctrl+Shift+C brings up the default form that belongs to the main Contacts folder.

Thick as a Post

The Post item is a handy feature that many Outlook users don't even know exists, which is why we bring it up. In Figure 5-1, there is an easily overlooked option labeled "Post in This Folder." A *post* is just like an email message, only you don't send it to anyone (see Figure 5-3). Rather you simply "post" it to a folder that others on your computer network have access to. Posting adds the message to the selected folder. The folder must have been created to contain Mail items; you cannot, for example, post to a folder created to hold Task items.

If you are using Outlook on a single machine and are dialing into an ISP for your email, then the ability to Post to email folders is of little practical use. However, if you're running Outlook with Microsoft Exchange as the back-end mail server on a network, you can set up *public* folders. Other users can post to and read from public folders, letting you readily disseminate information to and have ongoing conversations with a given group of people. The ability to create Posts in public folders lets you effectively have your own bulletin board, where you can post messages and other folks with access to the folder(s) can reply to your posts and make posts of their own.

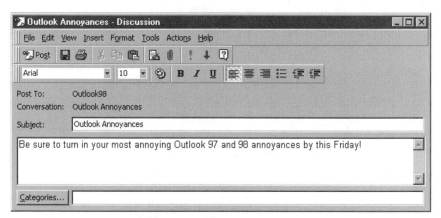

Figure 5-3: A Post is much like an email message

The shortcut for creating a Post, `Ctrl+Shift+S`, only works when the current facility/folder is an email type folder like the InBox, so we did not list it in Table 5-1.

Calendar—or if This Is Tuesday It Must Be Outlook

Calendar events in Outlook fall into three subcategories: Appointments, Meetings, and Events, each with its own shortcut key sequence. This apparent troika is a bit misleading since all three types of calendar entries start off with the same form, so you really only need to memorize the `Ctrl+Shift+A` keyboard shortcut to call up the Appointment form. Meetings and Events are easily created from this form.

An *appointment* is an activity you want to reserve some time for on a specific day at a specific time, and that you usually physically attend (although that is changing in this new cyberfrontier in which we live). When using the term in the context of Outlook, we like to think of an appointment as "a meeting without an electronic attendee list." For example, although a haircut appointment (you go to your barber's shop at a specific time) is semantically a meeting, it's not likely that you or your barber communicated this via an Outlook Meeting Request form, so to Outlook it's an *appointment*.

A *meeting* is the same as an appointment, only more people ("attendees" in Outlook parlance) are involved than just you, and the attendees are notified (or their names stored) electronically with Outlook. (You might be the meeting organizer, or just an attendee.) Continuing with the previous haircut example, a haircut activity would be an Outlook meeting if you and your barber did in fact communicate via an Outlook Meeting Request form. Another Outlook meeting example is your company's board of directors meeting, about which each director is notified by an Outlook Meeting Request form.

An *event* is an activity that occurs throughout a given day or days (and is usually an "all day" affair) and that happens whether or not you attend or are involved at all. For example, your spouse's birthday or a national holiday is an event.

NOTE   Use the same distinction between appointment and meeting if you are using Outlook to track resources in addition to, or instead of, human attendees. An example of a resource would be a conference room you have to reserve, or a VCR or monitor unit you have to check out from the company audio/video equipment lab.

Your Appointment Is Confirmed

An appointment is simple: "Teleconference with design team" entered for 9:15 A.M. on the 16th of the month qualifies as an appointment. Pressing Ctrl+Shift+A (refer to Table 5-1) pops up the Appointment form and you can easily enter the details of the appointment, as in Figure 5-4.

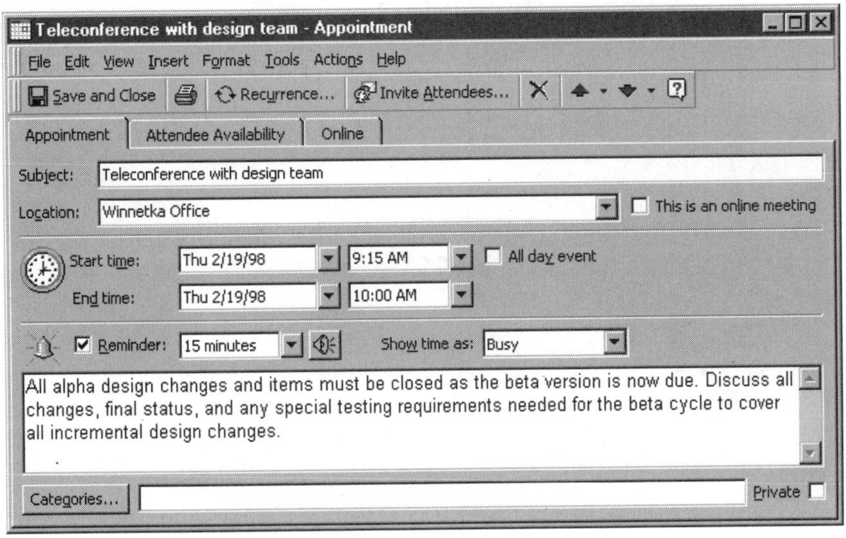

Figure 5-4: Creating an appointment

NOTE   Why, you may wonder, is a "Teleconference with design
                team" activity considered an appointment and not a meet-
                ing in our example? An Outlook meeting is an activity to
                which you actually invite people and track whether each
                of them will attend. An appointment is a meeting without
                an electronic attendee list. The "Teleconference with de-
                sign team" activity wasn't set up by you or anyone else
                through Outlook, but it's still an activity you need on your
                calendar, so it's an Outlook appointment. An appointment
                may be a meeting and a meeting an appointment...it's all
                in how you, or more exactly how Outlook, looks at it.

You can save yourself some steps if you highlight the block of time for
the displayed day in your calendar that you want for your appointment;
that time block automatically appears as the start and end times in your
appointment form. Appointment and meeting items default to creating a
reminder that pops up 15 minutes before the start time. You can change
this by picking a new time increment from the drop-down list or by
typing a time interval into the Reminder field yourself, or you can change
the default via Tools → Options → Preferences → Calendar Options,
where you can set a new default Reminder time span for appointments.
Changing the defaults to match what you normally want saves you from
constantly having to change settings when creating items. Changing the
reminder time whenever you create an appointment may not seem much
of an annoyance, but it adds up to lost productivity over time.

In addition to the subject line, there is a field for recording the location of
this appointment. Locations are remembered by Outlook, and previous
entries are available for quick selection by pulling down the drop-down
list (see Figure 5-5).

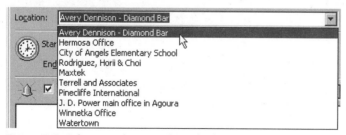

Figure 5-5: Selecting a location from the handy Location drop-down list

Outlook 98 tracks the last ten locations entered by you (up from seven in
Outlook 97). Once you have ten unique items, each new location
appears at the top of the list and the last line on the bottom is dropped.

These locations are stored in the Windows registry,[*] although unless you think in hexadecimal you won't be using a Registry editor like *Regedit.exe* to edit them. The strings are written to the registry as binary values. It would be nice if you could edit them as strings in the registry in those situations where you've entered a location with a typo and don't want to keep re-adding your most used locations just to push the misspelled one off the list.

NOTE   If you are registry savvy (kids, don't try this at home), you'll most likely find the name of the file containing location data in the registry at *HKEY_CURRENT_USER\Software\Microsoft\Windows Messaging Subsystem\Profiles\MS Exchange Settings\0a0d020000000000c000* with a value entry name of `101e0228`. The Registry key may be different on your system depending on how Office/Outlook was initially set up.

The Main Event

An event is simply an activity that lasts all day or extends over several days. This is handy for flagging a day as your spouse's birthday or as your anniversary. Vacations, seminars, occasions when you or someone you work with is out of the office—all these are good event candidates. An event shows up in the Day/Week/Month view of the Calendar at the top of the daily schedule (see Figure 5-6).

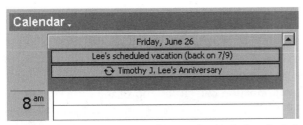

Figure 5-6: Events appear at the top of your daily schedule

To create an event, first create an appointment (`Ctrl+Shift+A`) as we did in Figure 5-4. Rather than providing the begin and end times, check the "All day event" checkbox, and like magic you have an Event. The

---

[*] For the straight scoop on the Windows registry, see *Inside the Windows 95 Registry*, by Ron Petrusha (O'Reilly & Associates), ISBN 1-56592-170-4. This book comes with a handy monitoring program that lets you monitor data as it is entered into the registry by your applications. Highly recommended.

Start time and End time fields disappear, the title bar changes the item's designation from Appointment to Event, and the "Show time as" entry changes from the default for Appointments (Busy) to the default for Events (Free).

It's as simple as that.

Take a Meeting

As we've mentioned, the only difference between an Appointment and a Meeting in Outlook is that you electronically invite other people to a meeting. Again, you start off with an appointment form (Ctrl+Shift+A). To make this into a meeting, you have several options, all of which *invite* people to attend the meeting via email.

You can invite others by clicking on the "Invite Attendees" button on the Appointment item's toolbar (see Figure 5-7). The Meeting Request option (found on the New cascading menu when the Calendar facility is active) is nothing more than an Appointment form with the "Invite Attendees" button already clicked for you.

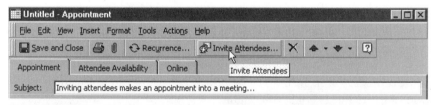

Figure 5-7: Invite Attendees to make your appointment into a meeting

Once you click on the "Invite Attendees" button, your appointment becomes a meeting, and the form takes on some of the aspects of an email message (see Figure 5-8). A Send button appears on the toolbar. A notice telling you the status of your invitation(s)—sent or not sent—appears in a dark gray "information bar" at the top of the form. A new To field appears that works the same as the To field of an email message form. You can type in a valid email address, type in a name and press Ctrl+K to Check Names, or you can click on the To button to call up the Select Attendees and Resources dialog (see Figure 5-9). Select the name(s) from your Contact list or PAB and add them as either Required or Optional attendees or as resources.

If the meeting time conflicts with any existing scheduled items, you are given a warning in the information bar. Outlook also warns you if your meetings/appointments are scheduled back to back (without any time between them), if you're creating an item with a start date that is earlier

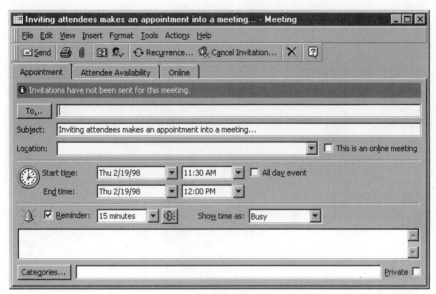

Figure 5-8: One click on Invite Attendees changes your Appointment form

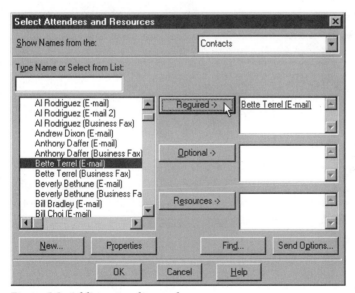

Figure 5-9: Adding attendees and resources

than the current day, if your invitations have not been sent yet, how many attendees have responded, and so on. Outlook is very good about providing you with helpful feedback.

Another way to make an appointment into a meeting is to click the Attendee Availability tab (called Meeting Planner in Outlook 97) that appears on an appointment form, as shown in Figure 5-10.

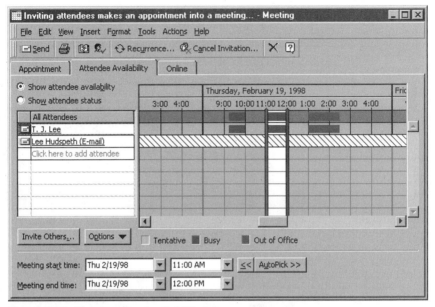

Figure 5-10: The Attendee Availability tab

The basic idea behind Outlook's handling of meetings is that every person is invited to a meeting via email, and that they'll respond to the request for meeting via email, indicating whether or not they can or will attend. In Figure 5-10, the first attendee, Lee Hudspeth, has a hashed bar across the timeline, indicating that his schedule is not available for reference. If everyone attending has made their schedules available via Exchange Server running on the network server, you can see not only your own conflicts, but also the available times of the invitees. The AutoPick feature lets Outlook calculate the time when all attendees are available at the same time.

You can type in your attendee list (using Ctrl+K to verify addresses) or you can use the Invite Others button, which calls up the Select Attendees and Resources dialog as you saw in Figure 5-9. Change the meeting time via the start and end time fields, or by dragging the start and end time bars on the timeline, if you need to adjust the time from this tab. Click on the Send button and meeting requests are generated as email and sent. For this example, we'll invite people using Outlook but who are not on our network, so our invitations will be emailed to the attendees over the Internet.

What happens when you want to add a meeting to your schedule and some of your proposed attendees are in your Contacts list and some are not? Say you don't want to send out email invitations to *any of them!* Or maybe you don't have email addresses for them. Or they already know they're coming and you just want to book the meeting in your calendar. Finally, what if, heaven forbid, they *don't use Outlook?* These questions point out the limitations of trying to use meetings in Outlook. If you're not going to go the whole nine yards through email, forget making it a meeting. Stick with an appointment and add a list of attendees in the note field.

NOTE   In Outlook 98, you can forward someone who's not using Outlook what's called a *vCalendar* item. Open the Calendar item and from the Actions menu choose "Forward as vCalendar." This creates an email message with a vCalendar (*.vcs*) file attached. If the recipient has a scheduling program that supports vCalendar, they can import this item into their calendar. If the recipient has Outlook they can open it and save the item directly into their Outlook Calendar.

If the recipient of a meeting request is running Outlook, the meeting is automatically added to their calendar as soon as the request hits their Outlook Inbox. If you open the email message in your Inbox, you won't get an email message form but a Calendar meeting form complete with Accept, Tentative, or Decline buttons included on the item's toolbar (see Figure 5-11).

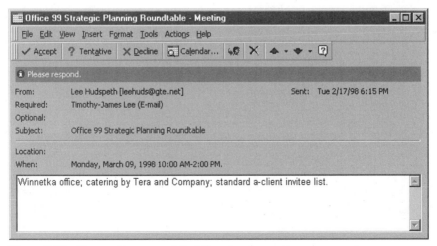

Figure 5-11: The meeting request that the attendee receives

If you looked in your Calendar and noticed a meeting item that you don't remember adding and open up the item, you see this same form marked with "Please respond" in the information bar.

Some users think this is handier than a pocket on a shirt. Others are none too happy to find stuff cluttering up their Calendar just because some email came in. When you respond (accept, tentatively accept, or decline) to the email message/meeting form, you'll be prompted to either edit, send now, or not send a response at all (see Figure 5-12).

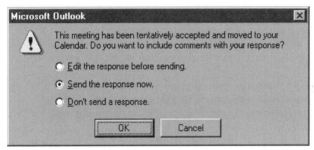

Figure 5-12: Responding to a meeting request message

Responding generates an email message back to the meeting's originator, telling that person that their request has been accepted, tentatively accepted, or declined, and updating the Attendee Availability tab in their meeting item. Declining removes the item from Outlook. When the origi-nator gets responses back, he or she can open the meeting item and click on the "Show attendee status" radio button as shown in Figure 5-13.

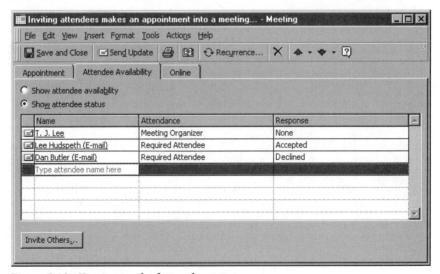

Figure 5-13: Keeping track of attendee status

The Response column shows the current status of each attendee's response to the meeting request. Any changes by the originator to the meeting's time or date, the addition or deletion of an attendee, or any material change with regard to the meeting is emailed to the attendee list with a click on the Send Update button.

Making Contact

If you're anything like us, then your contact list is one of your most important resources. In the next chapter, we'll show you how to import any existing address and phone information you have into Outlook *en masse*. Here, we'll cover the manual method of creating a Contact item. Pressing Ctrl+Shift+C pops up a pristine new Contact form, as Figure 5-14 shows.

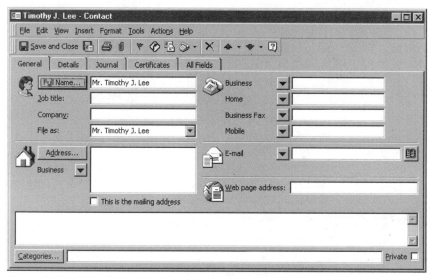

Figure 5-14: Outlook's Contact form

Naming Names

In the example shown in Figure 5-14, we've typed in a name using a title, first name, middle initial, and last name. Another of Outlook's really useful IntelliSense features is its ability to auto-parse a name into its various component pieces and stick those pieces into the appropriate field. Clicking on the "Full Name" button shows how Outlook has parsed our example name (see Figure 5-15).

The only annoying glitch we've run into is in dealing with suffixes. Type "Mr. Timothy J. Lee, CPA" and Outlook gets confused, thinking you are

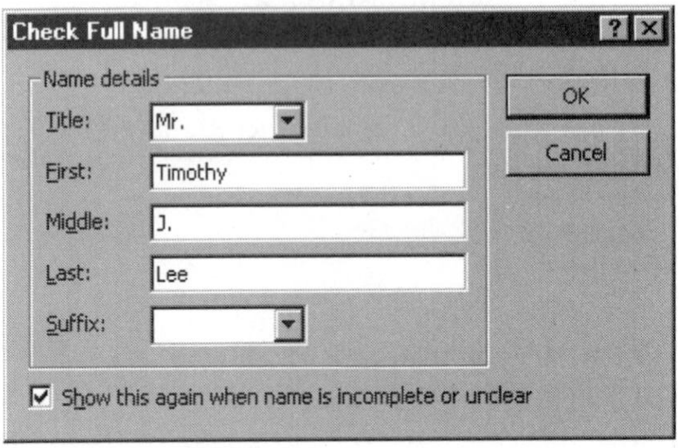

Figure 5-15: Outlook can automatically parse a name

using a *Lastname, Firstname* format. You get a first name of "CPA" and a last name of "Timothy J. Lee." But overall, it's still a nifty feature.

After you've entered a name, Outlook completes the "File as" field using data from the name entry as soon as you leave the name field. This controls how your contacts are sorted and presented in the Contact facility. The default is Last, First, Middle, but you can pull down the "File as" drop-down lists and choose from any of several formats, including (depending on the fields for which you've supplied contact information) Company or a combination of Company and Name. This is one of the flexible features found in Outlook that endear it to a lot of people (see Figure 5-16).

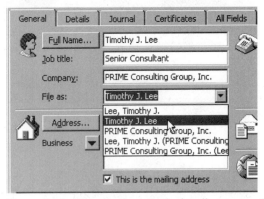

Figure 5-16: Choosing how Outlook will sort your Contacts

Let Me Address that Annoyance

Addresses are parsed as well. Just type in the street address with a hard return at the end of each line and Outlook will parse it into the appropriate fields. Type the following information into the address edit box:

2629 Manhattan Avenue
Suite 273
Hermosa Beach, CA 90254-2447

Outlook will parse it up. Click on the Address button and you'll see what we mean, as displayed in Figure 5-17.

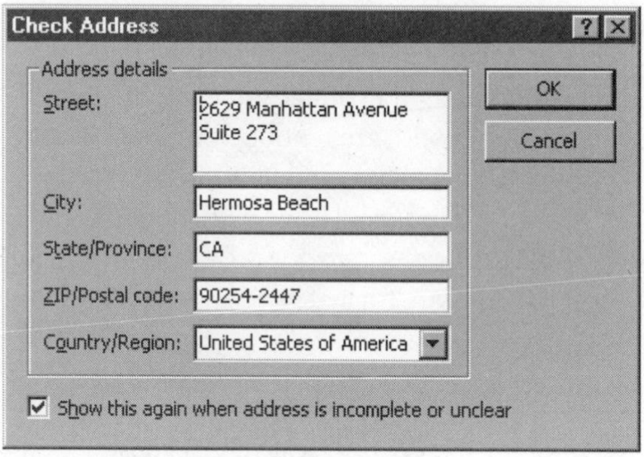

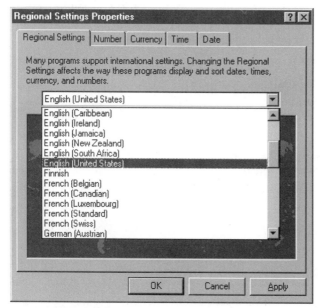

Figure 5-17: Auto-parsing addresses

If you don't enter a country in the Country field, Outlook fills in this field with the country from the Windows Regional Settings Properties dialog. To check this setting, start Control Panel and run the Regional Settings utility (see Figure 5-18).

Figure 5-18: Regional Settings influence Contact's Country field

The annoying aspect is that you typically don't want the country name to appear on domestic letters and envelopes. But that's exactly what happens when you do a mail merge to Word, as you'll see in Chapter 7, *Beyond the Basics*. If you create a Contact from scratch and want this field left blank, you'll have to clear it yourself.

Annoying Multiple Email Addresses

Email is rapidly replacing the telephone as the primary means of communication in the business world (you are nobody until you're *somebody@somewhere.com*). Outlook tracks three email addresses for individuals in your Contact list. You'd be surprised how many people have more than one email address. One for home, two for work (in case your ISP decides to shut down the email server for a few days—don't get us started!). You get the idea.

NOTE   We're assuming you're using the Contact facility in Outlook to maintain your email addresses, and that you have multiple email addresses for different contacts. The PAB requires you to create a new entry for each email address and as such doesn't suffer from this particular annoyance.

The trick is in figuring out which email address is which. When creating an email message based on names in your Contact list, you might type in the recipient's name and press Ctrl+K to verify the name. If this person has multiple email addresses, you could easily wind up with something like this (see Figure 5-19).

Now, which was the CompuServe address that Matt asked us to use when sending him a binary file? Tough to tell. You have the same problem if you click on the To button in the email message to call up the Select Names dialog—you'll find three entries labeled (E-mail), (E-mail 2), and (E-mail 3). What you have to do is select one of the addresses and click on the "Properties" button. On the email type tab you can see the actual email address (see Figure 5-20). From the Select Names dialog, you also click on the Properties button to sort out multiple email addresses.

If you're running Outlook 98 in Internet Only mode, *it's a whole other ballgame!* (We feel for any help desk people out there trying to support a mixed bag of users running both Corporate/Workgroup mode *and* Internet Only mode, we really do.) While the Contact record is the same in both modes, in Internet Only mode the first email address, "John Doe (E-mail)," is the *default* address. Create a new email message, type in

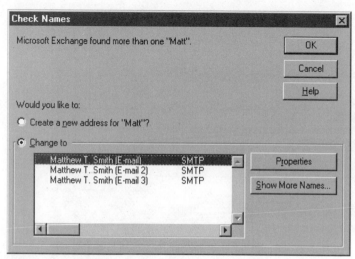

Figure 5-19: Hmmm, which is which?

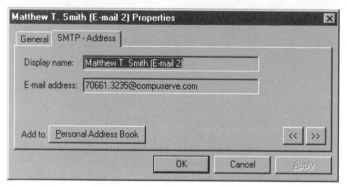

Figure 5-20: Finding the right email address

Matt, as in our previous example, and even if Matthew T. Smith's record has three email addresses, the first one is instantly dropped into your message when you hit Ctrl+K. Click on the To button to call up the Select Names dialog, and in Internet Only mode you see each Contact listed only once, even if they have multiple email addresses.

So what can you do in Internet Only mode to choose one of the other two possible email addresses that a given contact record could hold? If you right-click on the verified name (i.e., you type Matt and press Ctrl+K for Check Names and it appears in the message with the verification underline), you'll get a pop-up menu from which you can select one of the other two entries. If you click on the Properties option from this pop-up, you'll see how the Internet Only mode presents the Contact data.

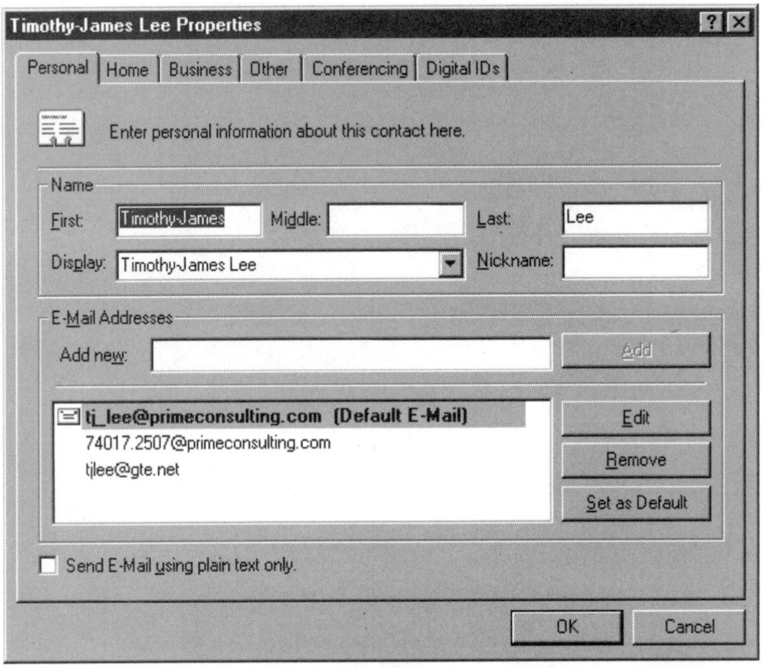

Figure 5-21: Properties—Internet Only style

NOTE　　　Contact records can easily be passed around between Outlook users. Select the Contact that you want to send to another Outlook user and choose "Forward as vCard" from
the Actions menu. This creates an email message with the
Contact record embedded in the message as a *.vcf* file. Just
send it to the Outlook user you want to have it, and he or
she can drag the embedded item to their Contact list. If
you send a vCard to a non-Outlook user, that user may still
be able to read the information. For example, Netscape
will add a vCard to its internal address book.

The Task at Hand

The Task facility is where you record and track your to-do list. Pick up a
quart of milk on the way home, write the great American novel, finish the
Snyder proposal—all these can be recorded and maintained as tasks in
Outlook. Lots of users fool around with the Task facility a bit, then go
back to putting yellow stickies around the edge of their monitors. But it
really is worth the trouble to get into the habit of using tasks, especially if
you assign tasks to others and have to keep track of what's been done

and what still needs doing. Enter a Task from scratch by pressing Ctrl+Shift+K (see Figure 5-22).

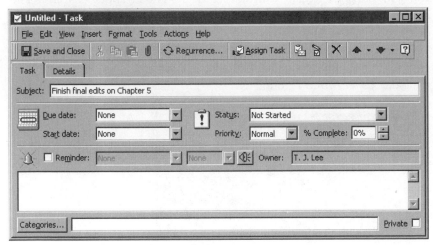

Figure 5-22: Creating a Task in Outlook

The Subject is the description of your task (some people call these to-do's, some tasks; we'll go with Microsoft's "task" nomenclature just to keep things consistent). You can set a due date (if it's a time-sensitive task) like "Buy anniversary gift BEFORE anniversary this year!" For a task that takes substantial time to complete, you can record the date you started the task in the Start field, and track the percent complete (especially handy if the task is assigned to you by someone else who is tracking your progress—more on this in a bit). There are several pre-set choices for the status of the task as well as the task's priority (see Figure 5-23).

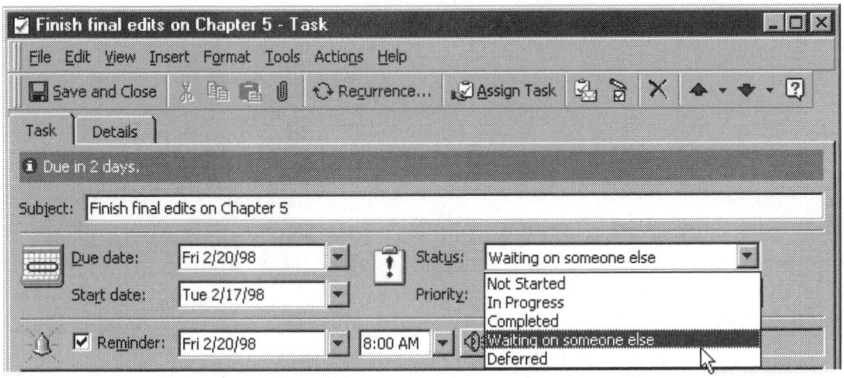

Figure 5-23: The Status drop-down list box

Notice that, like an email message, there is an information area to give you helpful notices related to your task. Check the "Reminder" checkbox and you can pick a date and time to be reminded about this task. The default for the alert, er, reminder, is the due date. If you don't enter a date, you get the current date and a time of 8:00 A.M. for the reminder. You can change the default time (8:00 A.M.) via Tools → Options → Preferences in the Tasks section. At the specified time Outlook pops up a reminder, as shown in Figure 5-24.

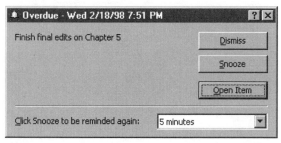

Figure 5-24: A reminder pop-up message for a task

When the reminder appears, it can be deleted by the Dismiss button, snoozed by clicking on Snooze (in Outlook 97 this button is labeled Postpone), or you can open the item itself (in this case the underlying task item) by clicking on the Open Item button. The drop-down list lets you specify how long to snooze or postpone the reminder before it pops up again. A huge annoyance is that you cannot postpone it for any interval other than those offered in the list. There's no workaround that we can find. This may not seem like a problem, but if you start tracking all your tasks, you'll soon run headlong into this limitation. Another annoyance is that the Dismiss button is selected by default when the reminder pops up. If you are typing away in another application when the reminder is fired off, you may very well dismiss it before you have a chance to see what it's about.

TaskPad

Recording your tasks in Outlook does you no good unless you can keep track of them. The TaskPad appears on the default view of your Calendar, showing you your current task list at a glance, as in Figure 5-25. The TaskPad is just the name of the task display area that appears on the Calendar default view. The TaskPad can be fine-tuned to display just the tasks you are interested in.

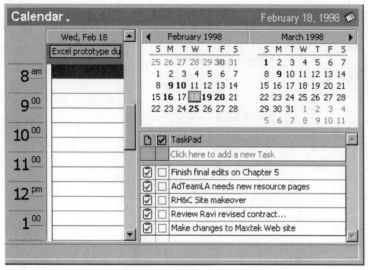

Figure 5-25: Outlook's default Calendar view displays the TaskPad in the lower right-hand corner

NOTE   How much of the TaskPad is displayed (or if it is displayed at all) is determined by how willing you are to give up precious screen real estate to its display. By placing your mouse pointer just below the calendar area (and above the TaskPad), you can resize the TaskPad window by clicking and dragging. Probably the biggest problem users have with the Task facility is the way tasks are dealt with for presentation in the TaskPad. Most of us assume that when you add a task, it'll appear as a task until it's marked as "done." Tasks without a due date do just that, but if you add a due date and that date passes, the task item is classified as "overdue" and the item just disappears unless you set the view to show you all overdue tasks. This is both annoying and confusing.

When in the Calendar view shown in Figure 5-25, right-click on an empty portion of the TaskPad and then click on the TaskPad View option to determine what task information is displayed (see Figure 5-26). The "All Tasks" option shows you just that—all the tasks you have in the task facility. Completed tasks have a checkmark in the Complete column and are shown "grayed out" and with a strikeout line through them (see Figure 5-27).

"Today's Tasks" shows you the tasks that have a due date of today or earlier and that have not been completed. If you complete a task, it

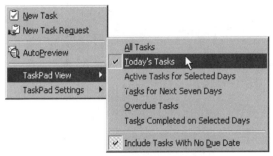

Figure 5-26: Tweaking the TaskPad settings

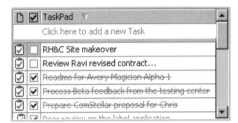

Figure 5-27: Completed Tasks shown in the TaskPad

remains on your TaskPad until the next day no matter what the due date or completed date within the task item itself is. This was very annoying until we figured it out. We expected a task to be gone from the list once it was completed, especially if, say, we completed it on Friday but did not update the record until Monday.

Assigning Tasks

Tasks can be assigned to others on your local network (assuming they are also using Outlook). We've had some success actually assigning tasks via email across the Internet. In fact, we had better luck with Outlook 98; with Outlook 97 we only had success when both people were using the same ISP. Go figure—universal email ain't a reality yet by a long shot. When using the Task facility in this way, you assign tasks to others and get back updates to track progress. This is one of the Task facility's most compelling features.

To assign a task once you've created it, if the task isn't open simply right-click on it and choose Assign Task; if it's open, then pull down the Actions menu and click on the Assign Task option. You can also click on the Assign Task button on the item's toolbar.

A task request is immediately generated. The item suddenly sprouts a To field, allowing you to email the task request to someone in one of your address books. This works exactly the same as addressing an email message (see Figure 5-28). In Outlook 97, everything in the item window is shoved downward when this happens, making the Categories field almost disappear. No vertical scrollbar appears, so you have to resize the window to see all of the controls again. This annoying bug is fixed in Outlook 98.

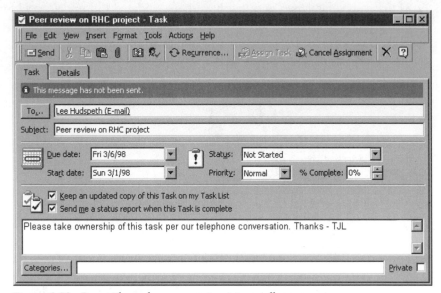

Figure 5-28: Dump the task on, er, assign it to a colleague

Note that there are now two new checkboxes in the item, one to allow you to keep a copy of the task on your task list (so you won't lose track of what you assigned) and one that, when checked, causes a status report to be sent to you automatically when this task is marked "complete."

When you assign a task, you are giving up ownership of that item (even if you retain a copy on your own Task list). If you have set a reminder, you'll see the message box shown in Figure 5-29 when you make the assignment. If you routinely assign tasks to others, this message box gets annoying really fast.

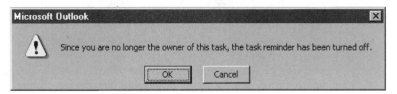

Figure 5-29: You don't get reminders on assigned tasks

The recipient can Accept or Decline the task in much the same way as the meeting request discussed earlier. Either way, you as the original owner are notified. If the assignee accepts the task, then he or she becomes the new owner. If declined, the originator remains the owner. While waiting for the potential assignee to respond, the task is "read-only."

Tasks that you've assigned and that have been updated (an update could also mean it was accepted or declined or that the assignee has made changes to it) or that are being assigned to you appear in the Task list and the TaskPad in bold, similar to the way unread email is displayed in your Inbox (see Figure 5-30).

Figure 5-30: Updated tasks show up in bold

In the icon column—get out your magnifying glass!—the task icon has a "hand" holding it on the left for tasks you've assigned, and on the right for tasks being assigned to you. In Figure 5-30, the "Acme Manufacturing" task is being assigned to us, while the "Peer review" task is one that we've assigned to someone else. Because the icons are small and difficult to read, we thought it would be handy to go this one better and create rules to show tasks assigned to us in one color and tasks we've assigned to others in another color. While we could create a rule for this in the Task facility, there's no way to make the color format show up in the TaskPad view. A major annoyance; maybe it'll be fixed in the next version of Outlook.

NOTE   If you want to set up this color-coding trick in the Task fa-
                cility, click View → Current View → Customize Current
                View → Automatic Formatting. Click on Add to add a new
                rule, and click on the Condition button to open the Filter
                dialog. In the Filter dialog, use the Advanced tab to define
                the criterion "Assigned" to equal "Assigned to me." Then
                set the font to be the color of your choice. Do the same
                thing for a second rule in which "Assigned" equals "As-
                signed by me."

Again, the ability to assign tasks and to monitor their status is an outstanding feature of Outlook. To recap: when someone assigns you a task, the item shows up in your Task list or TaskPad (and your email Inbox of course). When you open the item, you can either accept or decline the task. If you want to update the assignor of a particular task without modifying the task item itself, you can click on the "Send Status Report" button on the item's toolbar (or on the same command found on the Task menu). This generates an email message to the originator of the task with all the information from the task form in the body of the message.

Make a Note of That

The Note facility in Outlook is the catchall for bits and pieces of information that don't really fit into any of the other facilities. Notes are awesome as a simple free-form database of sorts. When you search the Notes facility (switch to Notes and click on the Find button), you are doing text searches on the contents of all notes in that folder. Once you've used this facility for a while, you'll wonder how you ever managed without it. To create a Note, press Ctrl+Shift+N (see Figure 5-31).

Figure 5-31: Creating a Note

Type up to 32K of text to complete your note. There are no fields, drop-downs, menu bars, or toolbars—nothing to deal with but just jotting down your note. The note is saved as you go, so you can leave a note open on screen and add to it as you think of things. Hit the X in the upper right corner to close it. Fast, simple, and efficient.

The few customizable features of Notes are controlled from the Tools → Options → Note Options (see Figure 5-32).

Outlook 98 Notes come in five colors: blue, green, pink, yellow, and white (up from four in Outlook 97 which lacked blue); and three default

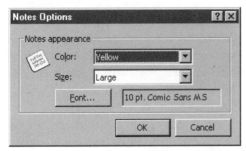

Figure 5-32: There are very few customizable defaults for Notes

sizes: small, medium, and large (see Figure 5-33). (Once created, you can
resize a note to any desired size like any Windows window; more on this
in a moment.) Use Tools → Options → Notes Options to set the defaults
you want to see when you hit Ctrl+Shift+N, including a default font. In
Outlook 97, you could also specify whether or not to display the note's
creation date and time. Set the color of an individual note if it's not open
by right-clicking on it and choosing Color, or if it's open, by clicking on
the note's upper left-hand corner to pull down the control menu, then
clicking on Color and choosing the shade you want from the cascading
menu.

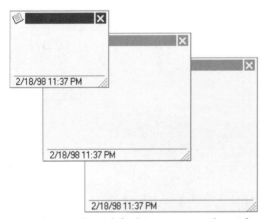

Figure 5-33: Three default note sizes to choose from

Despite the simplicity in design and lack of customizable features, Notes
are really very useful. There may only be three sizes of default note sizes,
but each note remembers its last window size (and you can resize them
by grabbing any side or corner and dragging); so if you resize a note, it'll
be that same size the next time you pop it open. The colors may be
limited, but each color is automatically categorized; that is, each color
becomes a category for grouping. So you can use green for notes relating

to specific projects and, say, yellow for general information (see Figure 5-34).

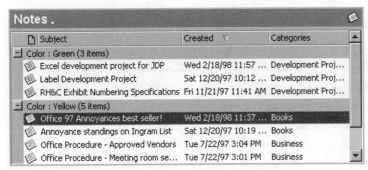

Figure 5-34: Notes automatically categorized by color

This is not to say that you can't also add other categories to each note. Just click on the control icon of the individual note and choose Categories from the menu.

NOTE   Here's a tip on creating Notes. The subject of a note is the first paragraph, or as much of it as can be displayed on screen. Instead of just typing away willy-nilly when you pop open a note window, take a second and type a short description of what this note is about, hit the period key, then a hard return. Then start the free-flow brain dump into the body of the note. This way you get a cogent description in the subject column of the Notes facility when you view your notes. Otherwise, it's tough to make heads or tails out of the stream of consciousness text that is liable to appear.

Mastering Mail Messages

It's only been with the explosion in connectivity caused by the Internet that email, once a separate category of software altogether, became an integrated component within personal information managers.

As an email client, Outlook is great. It's also very annoying. We talked about some firsthand experiences with Outlook's occasional recalcitrance in moving the mail in Chapter 1, *It's a Bit Like Whacking Your TV Set*, and then how to go about troubleshooting these foibles in Chapter 3, *Outlook Repair Tactics*. In this section we'll look at some of Outlook's email features that you may not be aware of and how to deal with their more annoying aspects.

Creating an email message is as simple as pressing Ctrl+Shift+M to pop up an email form (see Figure 5-35).

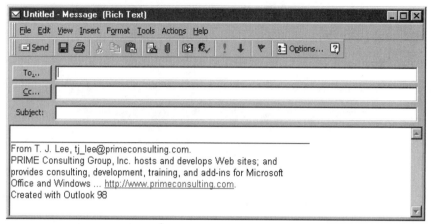

Figure 5-35: Outlook's email form

From and Bcc

By default you get the To, Cc, and Subject fields, along with the body area where you actually type in your message and add attachments. When you are in a new email message, you can pull down the View menu and click on the "From Field"* and "Bcc Field" options to add these address fields to the form. These fields are not displayed by default, but once you display them when creating a message, they stay visible in all subsequently created messages until you toggle them off by using the View menu.

The Bcc (blind carbon copy) field is something that many users overlook. Addressees and Cc recipients do not see the names of those who get a copy of the message via a Bcc; hence the term *blind.* If you get a blind carbon copy email, you see the original message, to whom it was sent, and who got a carbon copy; but no one knows that you, the Bcc recipient, got a copy of the message, nor can you see any other Bcc recipients.

The From field (in Outlook 97 and in Corporate/Workgroup mode in Outlook 98) is used when you send email *on behalf of another user.* According to the Help file, you have to have the proper "permissions" to send email on behalf of another person, but we've sent email out over the Internet using this feature in Outlook 98 without any special permissions using names in our Contacts list. In the example in Figure 5-36, T.J.

---

* The From field is not available in Internet Only mode in Outlook 98.

Lee was the actual sender of the message, and he entered Matthew T. Smith in the From field and sent the message to Lee Hudspeth. When the message hits Lee's Inbox, only "Matthew T. Smith" shows up in the From column, as shown in Figure 5-37.

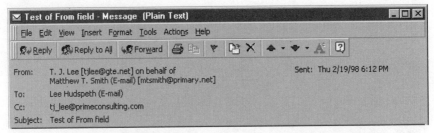

Figure 5-36: Email on behalf of...

Figure 5-37: Message from Matt, or is it?

This feature is about as scary as it sounds (and Outlook is not unique in this: many email clients offer this sort of alias feature). For example, Lee sees the message in his Inbox and thinks its something important from Matt, only to find out it's just a message that purports to be from Matt. *Assuming he looks at the From information in the message at all!* If he doesn't, he might think that the message really was from Matt. Oddly enough, the Outlook 98 Preview Pane does show the true originator of the message, in this case T.J. Lee, in the From address.

AutoSignatures

In Figure 5-35 you can see that a block of text appears in the message body. This is an example of Outlook's AutoSignature feature. An Auto-Signature can be inserted manually into any Outlook item except a Note, and it can be set to automatically appear in new email messages. Create your AutoSignature by clicking on Tools → Options → Mail Format → Signature Picker (we kid you not). The Signature Picker dialog box is shown in Figure 5-38.

Click on the New button, then on Next. Type in the signature text or closing you want added to the end of each new message. Formatting in the Edit Signature dialog is limited to basic font and paragraph formatting. Or you can create your signature in Word or WordPad and cut and paste

Figure 5-38: Create a single AutoSignature for use in Outlook

it into the Edit Signature dialog if you want something a bit fancier. The Advanced Edit button just fires up WordPad—with no instructions whatsoever telling you to create your signature and then copy it back to Outlook—sheesh! You can create multiple AutoSignatures in Outlook 98, but in Outlook 97 you can't create more than one AutoSignature.

Set the default AutoSignature for new messages in Tools → Options → Mail Format. If that's not the signature you want, you can insert a different one from the message's Insert menu.

Nicknames

There are several ways to address your messages. Typing a valid email address in the To field, like *matt@primeconsulting.com,* is one option. As long as it's a valid address for your connectivity setup (a local network, dial-up via the Internet, etc.), it'll work.

But it's easier if you maintain your email addresses in your Contact list or even the PAB (Personal Address Book, discussed back in Chapter 3). Then you can type in a portion of the recipient's name and let the Check Names feature fetch the proper email address. To use Check Names in Outlook 97 or Outlook 98 Corporate/Workgroup mode, first make sure that Outlook knows which address books you want checked. Pull down the Tools menu, click on Services, then click on the Addressing tab (see Figure 5-39). The list box at the bottom of the Services dialog shows which address lists are searched when you check names. Add any lists that you need to and set the order in which they're searched.

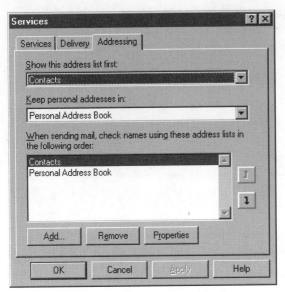

Figure 5-39: Address lists used by Check Names are set up in the Services dialog

Outlook 98 Internet Only mode works differently. Check Names works against the address book by default, but if you want other directory services included when checking names, click Tools → Accounts, select a directory service, click on Properties, and check the "Check names against this server when sending mail" checkbox. Once you've set up directory services to check for names, you can set the search order by clicking on Tools → Accounts → All → Set Order (see Figure 5-40).

An alternate (and usually faster) method is to type the addressee's name into the To field and click on the "Check Names" button on the message's toolbar or press Ctrl+K (a nifty shortcut that we strongly suggest you commit to muscle memory). If the name is in your address list and you've typed enough characters so that the search returns a unique name, the name appears with a solid underline indicating that it is an exact match to the address list entry. See the top entry in Figure 5-41.

If you type in a name that matches more than one entry in your address list, like "David," it'll be shown with a squiggly red underline to indicate several partial matches (the second entry in Figure 5-41). Right-click on the name at this point and a pop-up menu appears from which you can

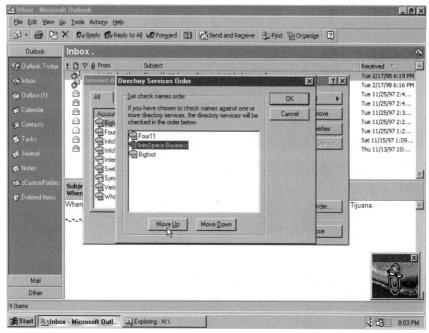

Figure 5-40: Setting the search order in Outlook 98 Internet Only mode

select the name you want to use. In Figure 5-42, for example, "David" was typed into the To field, but the Contact list has three different names that include the string "David."

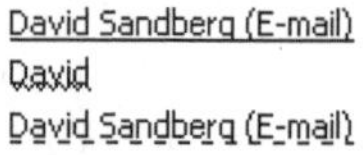

David Sandberg (E-mail)
David
David Sandberg (E-mail)

Figure 5-41: Straight, squiggly, and dashed underlines all tell a story

---

NOTE   You have to turn name checking on. In Outlook 97 click
            on Tools → Options → Send and check the "Automatic
            name checking" box. In Outlook 98 it's Tools → Options →
            Preferences → E-mail Options → Advanced Email Options,
            and check the appropriate checkbox (whew!).

Let's say you click on David Sandberg, as shown in Figure 5-42. That name then appears in the To field with the solid underline. No problems and far from annoying—this actually seems pretty handy. But beware, once you select a name in this manner, that particular name (in this case David Sandberg) is always matched when you type just "David" in the To

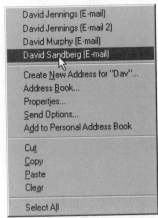

David Jennings (E-mail)
David Jennings (E-mail 2)
David Murphy (E-mail)
David Sandberg (E-mail)

Create New Address for "Dav"...
Address Book...
Properties...
Send Options...
Add to Personal Address Book

Cut
Copy
Paste
Clear

Select All

Figure 5-42: Choosing one "David" among many

field. "David" becomes the nickname for the "David Sandberg" entry. Create a subsequent email message, type "David", and as soon as you leave the To field, "David Sandberg (Email)" replaces the partial entry and is given a green dashed underline. (See the bottom entry in Figure 5-41.) If you want to use one of the other Davids in your address book, you'll have to right-click on the dashed underline entry and select another name from the pop-up menu. When you do, this new name is what you get from then on when you use that nickname.

WARNING   The "nickname" feature we're describing here is not to be confused with a Contact record's Nickname field. They have nothing in common.

Getting rid of a nickname once it gets created is a bit trickier than just changing it to a different record. You can create a new profile which gets you a new nickname file, but that seems like overkill. If you look in your *C:\Windows\Application Data\Microsoft\Office\8.5\Outlook* folder, you should find a file with your current Outlook profile name as the filename and *.NICK* as the extension (for example, *MS Exchange Settings.NICK*). This file holds the nickname information for that profile. Rename this file (while Outlook is not running), and Outlook will create a new nickname file the first time you use or set the nickname (even if you do so unwittingly).

To avoid nickname issues altogether, *don't* right-click on the squiggly red underlined name to resolve the address. Run Check Names (Ctrl+K) before you leave the To field, and if there are multiple entries for that name (as in our example with a plethora of Davids), pick the one you want from the Check Names dialog and go on about your business.

Outgoing Message Flags

Outlook provides the ability to "flag" messages, which adds some informational text and possibly a date and time to the message to hopefully get the recipient's attention and let them know something about the message. A flag shows up in the information area of the outgoing message form just below the Message and Options tabs on the message itself, as shown in Figure 5-43.

Figure 5-43: A flag appears as additional information on the message

Set a message flag by clicking on the "Flag for Follow Up" button on the message's toolbar. The Flag for Follow Up dialog (see Figure 5-44) lets you pick from a pre-defined number of flag-text choices. You'll find all the usual suspects, such as Call, Forward, Follow up, Reply, For Your Information, and others. The Reminder drop-down list lets you choose a date from a calendar. If you assign a date, it starts off with a default time of 5:00 P.M., but you can edit the time to any time of day you want.

Figure 5-44: Outlook's Flag Message dialog

What's nifty is that you can type whatever you want as a flag message in the Flag field, as we did in Figure 5-43. What's annoying is that you can't permanently add your own custom flag messages to the drop-down list; they are not saved to the list, and you have to type custom flag text each time from scratch.

Truly outstanding is that in Outlook 98, setting a reminder on an outgoing message triggers an alert on the recipient's system that's displayed when the designated time is reached (assuming the recipient is also running Outlook 98).

Incoming flagged email messages show a red flag icon in the Inbox's Flag Status column. You as the recipient can also set flags on messages in your Inbox, and this is a handy way to organize your Inbox. But too many flags detract from their usefulness as a way to, well, *flag* messages so they stand out. We'd like to see a different color flag icon if the sender had flagged the message; this would complement the red flag you get if you (the recipient) flag a message.

We'll discuss flags and the new reminder feature in Outlook 98 at length in Chapter 7.

Messaging Options

Last but not least when creating email are the Options that Outlook allows you to set for each outgoing message. Click on the Options button on the message toolbar (in Outlook 97 click on the Options tab in the message form). The Message Options dialog box appears, as shown in Figure 5-45.

Sensitivity is a setting of which not many Outlook users are aware. The settings range from Normal to Personal, Private, and Confidential. The "sensitivity" of the message shows up in the message information area as "Please treat this as Confidential" or "Please treat this as Private" when the user opens it.

NOTE   The Private sensitivity setting is the most interesting setting. Besides the "Please treat this as Private" admonition, the message itself cannot be edited by the recipient. With any other setting, you can edit the message all you want (just open it and click on Edit → Edit Message) and save it, but with the Private setting the message is permanently read-only.

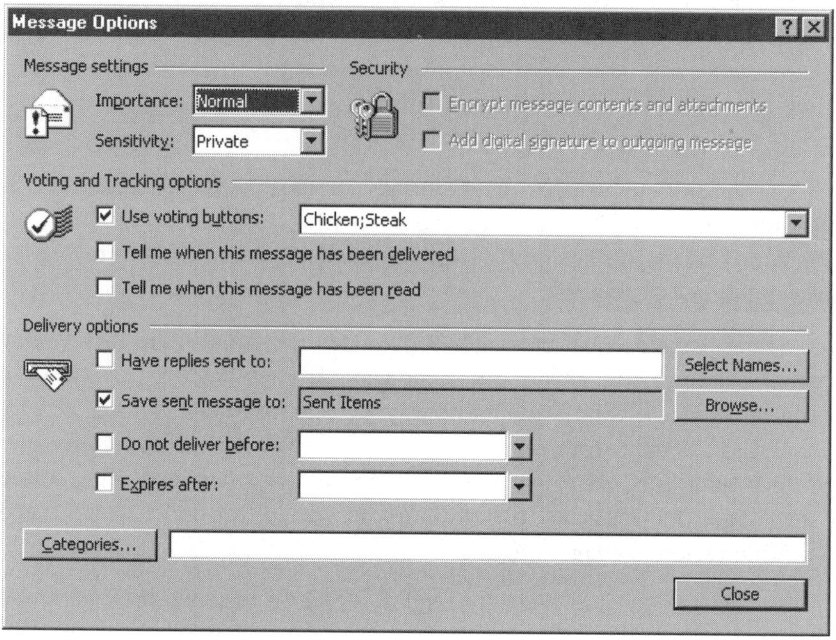

Figure 5-45: Setting message Options

Voting is another easily overlooked feature (sorry, voting isn't supported in Outlook 98's Internet Only mode). Voting buttons are very cool. You can select Accept;Reject, Yes;No, and Yes;No;Maybe from the drop-down list. The recipient of the message gets an actual set of buttons just below the message toolbar (see Figure 5-46).

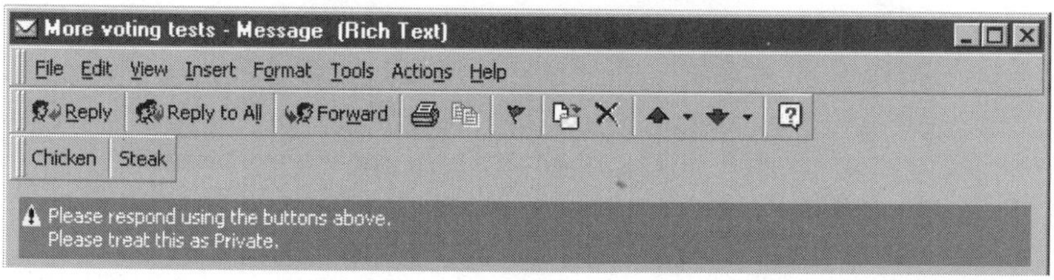

Figure 5-46: Voting buttons let you quickly poll people via email

As you can see, Outlook is not limited to the three stock button choices. Modify the text in the "Use voting buttons" drop-down separating each button name with a semi-colon; for example, add the entry "Chicken;Steak" when you need to get a consensus on an entrée for the company picnic. As the people you poll vote, you'll get back messages telling you which button they clicked on (see Figure 5-47).

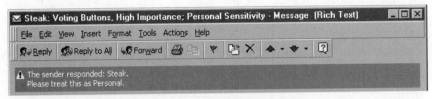

Figure 5-47: A response from someone you asked to vote

The original message, which is in your Sent Items folder (unless you utilized the "Save sent message to" option to store your voting message somewhere else), keeps track of the votes as they come in (see Figure 5-48). Once responses start coming in, the original message sprouts a Tracking tab and each person included in the original voting message is listed along with the status of their responses.

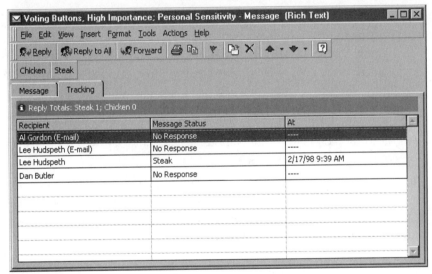

Figure 5-48: Keeping a tally on the voting

Feature Unavailable?

A major annoyance in Outlook 98 has to do with what feature is available in which mode—Corporate/Workgroup versus Internet Only. Outlook 98 in Corporate/Workgroup mode does things that the Internet Mode does not do or does differently.

To complicate things further, you can use Outlook 98 in Corporate/Workgroup mode (or Outlook 97) with Exchange Server on the back end of your network to manage your email traffic, or not use Exchange Server and instead dial into an ISP for email service. Some of Outlook's features require Exchange Server (ES) in order to work and some don't. The problem is that you don't know if a feature needs ES or not. The options are available in Outlook Corporate/Workgroup's interface, but your first clue that something won't work is when it fails. Thankfully, Outlook 98 Internet Only mode knows that ES is not an option and omits those features from its interface.

Message Recall is one example. Send a message, then open the message from your Sent Items folder and from the Actions menu you can elect to recall it. If the recipient has not opened the message, you can snatch it out of their Inbox, but *only* if ES is on the back end to do the house-keeping. If there's no ES, then you just get back a Message Recall Failure notice telling you your message could not be recalled. You might just think you did not recall it fast enough, but the reality is that without ES there is no recall feature. Potentially very annoying.

According to Microsoft's documentation, there are a number of features that require ES. But our empirical tests show that some of them do and some don't. Voting buttons, for example. Microsoft says ES is required to use voting, but we've tracked votes going through an ISP (Outlook 98 Corporate/Workgroup mode on each end, of course). Message flags work without ES even between Outlook 98 users running Internet Only mode. Delivery notices don't work without ES, but Read receipts work just dandy. So the key is to try the various features and see which ones work for you given your particular setup.

Being productive is often just a matter of knowing what features are available, and as you've seen in this chapter, Outlook is loaded with hidden, obscure jewels well worth discovering and using. Another of Outlook's more endearing and productivity-enhancing features is its own integration between facilities. Mutate an Appointment into a Task, zap a piece of email into a Contact—it's a snap to turn an item from one facility into an item in another facility. We'll cover Outlook's ability to transfer information between facilities as well as to convert extant data and bring it into Outlook in Chapter 6, *A Cookbook for Conversion*. Then in Chapter 7 we'll show you the tips and tricks you'll need to know to be productive with Outlook and to help keep your annoyance level under control.

6

A Cookbook for Conversion

Your personal information can take many forms. Names, addresses, and phone numbers for friends, prospective clients, prospective spouses, surf report services, vendors, suppliers, and so on. Meetings, to-do lists, random notes, and email threads. The flotsam and jetsam of your busy life, all stuffed into a single bucket, Outlook.

You need to know how to expediently and accurately get data into Outlook from outside sources, and that's this chapter's first priority. You also will benefit from Outlook's own "inside Outlook" data conversion capabilities; for example, you can drag-and-drop an email message onto the Tasks folder to create an instant follow-up mechanism for that message's subject. Last, but certainly not least, you must adhere to some sort of backup/archival strategy for your priceless personal information (if not, shame on you); we'll show you the best backup and archival tips, tricks, and annoyances to avoid.

Importing Data from Outside Repositories

Since Outlook came out in its first release as part of Office 97, you're definitely going to have to import your data from another source, or—shudder—do the unthinkable and type it all in again. In this section we'll cover the data sources for which Outlook supplies converters, data sources for which there are third-party import add-ins, and the issues to watch for when matching fields and content.

183

First let's address what you should do before importing a single byte of data. Checklist 6-1 shows the basic steps.

Checklist 6-1: Preparing for an Import

1. Clean up your source data using its current host program. This includes:

   a. Eliminating duplicate records.

   b. Archiving or deleting any records that are outdated or of no current use to you. This reduces the amount of data being imported and then inspected after the import.

   c. If you use keywords or other descriptive terms to categorize your data, making a full sweep through all records to verify you have consistently used the same terms. Updating as needed; for example, fixing any misspellings or keywords applied to the wrong records.

   d. Now's the perfect time for bringing your data up-to-date. For example, say your contacts repository isn't integrated with your email program; in particular, you've been keeping all the information about your contacts in ECCO except for a hand-written list of birthdays for key clients and vendors. Whatever the case or whatever type of "set aside" data you have in your desk drawer, take a few minutes now to roll this information into your main data repository.

2. If your host application supports field names (for example, Excel's database feature), you'll want to include them. The benefit is a much smoother mapping of your source data fields to Outlook 97's field structure (more on this in the "Performing an import" section later in this chapter).

3. Outlook 98's initial release does not support mapping, the ability to say "this field in my source file maps to this field in Outlook," as Outlook 97 does. Therefore, in Outlook 97, you'll use the Import and Export Wizard's Map Custom Fields dialog; in Outlook 98, you have to rename the fields in your source file to match the field names in Outlook 98 *exactly*. This is a colossal annoyance, and we can only hope Microsoft corrects this in a maintenance release soon.

4. If your data includes phone numbers, take the related steps detailed in the section "Performing an import."

5. Make a backup copy—compressed, if you like—of your source data and store it somewhere safe and clearly marked. (This may be one file or several; don't forget any index files.) Also, put your host

program's master diskettes or CD somewhere safe, again, clearly marked. This way, if you have a problem with the imported data that you don't discover until some time *after* the import, you can access the original data and take corrective measures.

6. As a further precaution, we recommend you have your host program export all your data to the highest-level, most persistent, ubiquitous format that it supports. This might be Excel workbook (*.XLS*) or dBase file (*.DBF*) format, or a less robust format like comma-separated value (*.CSV*). The point is that now you'll have a snapshot of your data in its original format (possibly a proprietary format, as in the case of, say, the defunct but ever-popular PackRat) *as well as* in a different (possibly more portable) format.

7. Before starting the actual import, back up the destination *.pst* file.

8. Make sure the destination disk drive has enough free disk space on it. In fact, make sure it has more than twice the disk space you estimate you'll need. (There's nothing worse than running out of disk space and hanging your system halfway through a 100 MB import.)

9. Defragment the destination disk drive.

At this point you've done all you can to prepare your source data and your system for the import process.

Native Import Support

Outlook ships from the factory with the ability to import the types of data listed in Table 6-1 using the Import and Export Wizard. Outlook 98 includes over a dozen built-in converters that were not available in Outlook 97.

NOTE   If you did a Typical Installation during Office setup, or otherwise elected not to install all Outlook 97 converters, you may need to rerun setup to install the appropriate converter. Start Office 97 setup, click the Add/Remove button, click Microsoft Outlook, click Change Options, select the desired converter(s), and continue with the setup as usual.

Table 6-1: Import formats supported by Outlook 98 and 97

Import Data Format	Outlook 98	Outlook 97
ACT! 2.0	Yes	Yes (ValuPack)
ACT! 3.0	Yes	No
Comma Separated Values (DOS and Windows)	Yes	Yes
dBase	Yes	Yes
ECCO 2.0	Yes	No
ECCO 3.0, 3.01, and 3.02	Yes	Yes (ValuPack)
ECCO 4.0	Yes	No
Eudora Light and Pro (mail and address book)	Yes	No
Internet mail account settings[1]	Yes	No
Lotus Organizer (1.0, 1.1, and 2.1)	Yes	Yes
Lotus Organizer 97	Yes	No
Microsoft Access	Yes	Yes
Microsoft Excel	Yes	Yes
Microsoft FoxPro	Yes	Yes
Microsoft Internet Mail and News (mail and address book)	Yes	No
Microsoft Mail File (*.mmf*)	Yes	Yes
Netscape Mail (mail and address book)	Yes	No
Netscape Messenger (mail and address book)	Yes	No
Outlook Express (mail and address book and rules)	Yes	No
Personal Address Book	Yes	Yes
Personal Folder File (*.pst*)	Yes	Yes
Schedule Plus Interchange (*.sc2*)	Yes	No
Schedule+ (1.0 and 7.0)	Yes	Yes
Sidekick 1.0/95	Yes	Yes (ValuPack)
Sidekick for Windows 2.0	Yes	No
Tab Separated Values (DOS and Windows)	Yes	Yes
vCalendar file (*.vcs*)	Yes	No
vCard file (*.vcf*)	Yes	No

[1] The email and server name, and so on for Eudora Pro and Light, Netscape Mail and Messenger, MS IMN, and Outlook Express.

In a subsequent section, "Conversion du Jour: PAB to Contacts," you'll see a detailed example of how to use the Import and Export Wizard to convert data from a PAB.

Other Sources for Converters

Quite a number of additional direct PIM-to-Outlook 97 converters are available for free on Microsoft's Web site and on the Office 97 CD. Other converters are scattered across cyberspace as detailed in this section, so check the following online sources:

- *www.microsoft.com/OfficeFreeStuff/Outlook/*—free stuff (or from Outlook just click on Help → Microsoft on the Web → Free Stuff).

- *www.microsoft.com/Outlook/documents/thirdparty_addons.htm* — Microsoft's own listing of third-party add-ins.

- *www.slipstick.com/exchange/add-ins-outlook.htm* — the Slipstick Exchange center includes a great listing of Outlook and Exchange add-ins (including converters).

- Your favorite search engine, which you can use to search the Web for Outlook add-ins that might not be listed in the above sources.

ACT!, ECCO, SideKick, and other goodies for Outlook 97 in the ValuPack

You'll find six additional Outlook 97 converters in the Office 97 CD's ValuPack folder: ACT! 2.0; ECCO 3.0, 3.01, and 3.02; SideKick 1.0/95; Outlook Journal folder; Outlook Notes folder; and Outlook Inbox folder. Follow these steps to install the converters:

1. Close Outlook 97 if it's running, and close Word if you use WordMail.

2. In Explorer, double-click on the *Valupk8.hlp* file in the CD's Valu-Pack folder.

3. Click on the link button to view the "Microsoft Outlook import and export converters" topic.

4. At the bottom of the topic, click on the button corresponding to the operating system you use; this installs the converters. When the installation is finished, you'll see the message, "Optional Import/Export translators have been successfully installed," so click on OK.

5. The new converters will now be available in Outlook 97's Import and Export Wizard. Once installed, there is no provision to remove them that we're aware of.

NOTE Outlook 97 includes a two-way converter for the moribund Lotus Organizer (import-only in Outlook 98), but import-only for the vigorous SideKick, ECCO, and ACT!.

CompuServe address book

CS2Exchange is a shareware utility that converts a variety of CompuServe software formats, as well as the CompuServe Address Book directory service, into your PAB. You'll find this utility at *www.slipstick.com/files/ cs2ex20.exe*.

Windows address book

To import data from your IMN Windows Address Book (WAB) using Outlook 97, check out the freeware utility WabOut at *www.empire.net/ ~level/WabOut.html*.

OUTLOOK 98 The ability to import data from the IMN Windows Address Book (WAB) is built right into Outlook 98.

Business cards

CardScan from Corex is a business card scanning and import utility compatible with a variety of PIMs, including Outlook. Check it out at *www.corex.com*. For your electronic business card needs, be sure to peruse the Outlook vCards Copier (for Outlook 97) at *www.microsoft.com/ OfficeFreeStuff/outlook/default.htm*.

OUTLOOK 98 Once again, Outlook 98 ships with a native vCard converter.

Other

For any other data sources not listed in this section, be sure to check the Microsoft KnowledgeBase. For example, although there's no direct converter for the old Windows Cardfile format, there are several workarounds as explained in the article *OL97: Converting Windows Card- file Files to Outlook* (Q164994). Or, you can use the *Transfile.exe* utility— available at *ftp://ftp.slipstick.com/pub/slipstick/cardxlt2.zip*—to convert Cardfile records to tab-delimited format, then let the Import/Export Wizard take it from there.

Keep in mind that if you have a data source for which there currently is no direct converter, you can try using the source's own export capabilities to export the data to the highest-level format common to the source application and to Outlook.

Conversion du Jour: PAB to Contacts

If you've been using Windows 95 and Outlook's predecessor, Exchange, you probably already have all your names and addresses tucked in your PAB. For reasons we'll be discussing shortly, you should consider getting your PAB data into Outlook. Here's how.

NOTE   If you're running Outlook 98 Internet Only mode, as we discussed in Chapter 2, *Vital Changes, Settings, and Customizations*, the installer will detect a prior PAB and ask if you want to convert its entries to Contacts. If you've already converted that PAB, then you won't need to manually perform the steps in this section, but you will still benefit from reading along to gain insight into the general procedure for converting data into Outlook.

If a PAB has been added as a service to your current profile (in Outlook 97 or 98 in Corporate/Workgroup mode), then the referenced *.pab* file is automatically used as the import source when you tell Outlook to import a Personal Address Book. To see if this is the case, check your profile using what you learned in Chapter 2 to see which *.pab* file the profile refers to (assuming you have more than one *.pab* file on your system; note that a profile can't have more than one Personal Address Book service installed at a time). If this is the PAB you want to import, you are now ready to proceed. If it is not the PAB you want to import, you'll have to remove the PAB service from your profile so that the Wizard will prompt you to explicitly select a source *.pab* file.

Outlook has a default Contacts folder for storing your contacts, but you can create multiple Contacts folders. This is useful if you want to separate your business contacts from your personal contacts, for example. Or you might create a Contacts list for a special project and isolate the people on that list from all other contacts. Alternately, you might need a temporary folder to store incoming contact data before you move it to another folder.

Creating a new Contacts folder—or any folder for that matter—should work the same way in both Outlook 98 and 97, but it doesn't. First, keep in mind that the parent folder's descriptions are different: in Outlook 98, it's "Outlook Today – [Personal Folders]" in the Folder List and "Outlook Today" in the Outlook Bar; in Outlook 97 it's "Personal Folders." In Outlook 98, with the focus on Outlook Today in either the Outlook Bar or the Folder List, when you select File → New there's no Folder command as there is in Outlook 97. So in Outlook 98 you must either go into the Folder List and *right-click* Outlook Today – [Personal Folders] and choose New Folder (this doesn't work from the Outlook Bar in either version) or select a facility other than Outlook Today and click on File → New → Folder. This displays the Create New Folder dialog box (see Figure 6-1). In the folder tree, be sure you select the folder under which you want to create your subfolder. Otherwise, Outlook will offer a default that's based on the folder that was active when you clicked on the File menu. Unless you want the subfolder to be a subfolder of a subfolder, you want to start with Outlook Today – [Personal Folders] in Outlook 98 and Personal Folders in Outlook 97.

Type in a Name for your folder and be sure to tell Outlook what type of data this folder will contain. Under the label "Folder contains" is a drop-down list of the types of data your Outlook folders can contain. You must select Contact Items or you will not be able to import PAB data to it. Click on OK to return to Outlook.

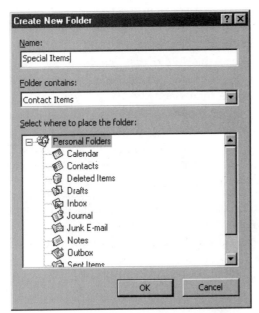

Figure 6-1: Creating a new folder in Outlook

NOTE   Remember that the folders you create within Outlook are
              not the same as those you create on your hard disk to hold
              your data. Just think of all your Outlook folders as being
              tucked inside your Personal Store file (*.pst*).

Next, pull down the File menu and click on the Import and Export option. This starts the Import and Export Wizard (see Figure 6-2). Preposterous as it may seem, there is no specific choice for importing a personal address book. How obvious is it that when you want to import a PAB, you should choose the "Import from another program or file" item (in Outlook 97 the description is "Import from Schedule+ or another program or file")? This category turns out to be the catchall for most of the formats from which you would likely import data. Anyway, that's the option you want. Click on Next to proceed.

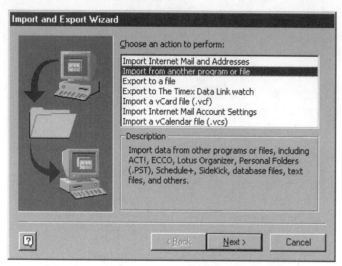

Figure 6-2: The PAB qualifies as "another program or file"

This next list is much less cryptic (see Figure 6-3). Scroll down the list and you'll find an option for Personal Address Book. Select this option and click on the Next button.

If you are importing a PAB that is installed as a service in your current profile, you'll next be prompted to select the destination folder (the *.pab* file referenced in the service's Properties dialog is the file that will be imported). Otherwise you'll see the Import a File panel, in which case you should type in (or browse to) the filename of the PAB you want to import, then click on Next.

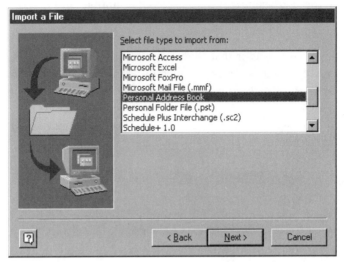

Figure 6-3: Selecting the type of data to import

WARNING   Before you click on the Finish button to start the import process, verify the source file and the destination folder. Both will be listed in the "The following actions will be performed" list (see Figure 6-4). You can change the destination by clicking on the Change Destination button. We don't recommend importing into your primary Contacts folder, regardless of the data source, since it's virtually impossible to unwind this once you've done it. Also, it's so much easier to verify that the import went properly and to do any last-minute data cleansing from inside a temporary folder. Later, when you're ready, you can move the data from the temporary folder to your Contacts folder, then delete the temporary folder (more on this shortly).

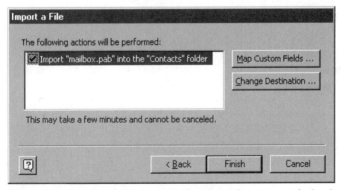

Figure 6-4: Ready to import a PAB, but don't forget to verify the destination first!

Once you click on Finish, you'll see the Import and Export Progress status box that lets you monitor the progress as the PAB is imported to Outlook. When the import process is complete, the status box disappears, and you can unveil people as Contacts who were formerly PAB records. You can't filter the PAB during the import, so it's an all-or-nothing proposition, but once you have the data translated into Contact items, you can search the list and prune records as needed.

If you followed our recommendation and imported into a separate, custom Contacts folder, now's the time to go ahead and verify that all the records were imported, prune any duplicates, and tidy up as appropriate. Next, to move all these records *en masse* to your default Contacts folder, you can use drag-and-drop or menus. To drag-and-drop: click on the temporary folder, select Edit → Select All (Ctrl+A), then right-drag the selected items onto your main Contacts folder and choose Move.* With menus: click on the temporary folder, then select any item displayed in this folder (this puts the focus on the item list instead of on the parent folder icon, giving you the desired options when you select the Edit menu), Edit → Select All, select Edit → Move to Folder, select your main Contacts folder, then click on OK. During this move operation if there were any item matches with your temporary folder, Outlook conservatively—and thankfully—preserves the original items and adds the new ones, so you may need to resolve these duplicates.

NOTE   You may want to verify that you moved stuff to the correct
              folder before you do anything else, so you can use the Edit
              → Undo command if you messed up. It's fairly easy to drag
              to the wrong folder in the Folder List.

Contacts provide more flexibility in Outlook than trying to work with the PAB, for two reasons. First, a Contact item comes with between 104 to 111 built-in fields (depending on which dialog box you base the count on—see Table 6-2 for a complete listing of Contact item fields in all their manifestations), whereas a PAB entry supports a paltry 28 fields. Second, you can create custom fields for Contact folders but not so for the PAB. However, don't discard the Personal Address Book from your profile just yet. Outlook 98 Corporate/Workgroup and Outlook 97 have no built-in provision for email distribution lists and the workaround available is far from perfect (we provide it in Chapter 7, *Beyond the Basics*), so you might want to keep that PAB if you're using those versions.

---

* The true paranoid *copies* the imported data, then archives the import target folder before getting rid of it.

A Walk Through the Data Mapping Minefield

Let's work our way through the process of importing a small sample database with six records from an Excel workbook list into Outlook's Contacts folder. Along the way, we'll examine data mapping options and how to deal with duplicate records. The overall scenario is that you've got about 3,000 records in a defunct PIM for which there's no built-in or third-party converter to Outlook format. You've already created about 300 critical records in your Contacts folder for use primarily with email correspondence; most, but not all of these records are duplicates of records in the defunct PIM, and many are more current for certain field values.

NOTE   We use Excel in this scenario because many of you are licensees of Office 97 Standard which includes Excel but not Access, which comes with the Professional version of Office. For those of you who do have Access, and even those who don't, keep in mind that Access is an excellent tool for organizing, massaging, and pruning source data of any type.

A list of contact item fields

While contemplating the list (shown in Table 6-2) of all the Contact item fields that Outlook makes available to you through its own user interface, consider the headaches imposed by this hornet's nest of fields.[*]

- The fundamental problems with this morass of fields and dialogs are: (1) the names aren't consistent and (2) a common set of fields is not available consistently from one dialog/view to the next. While it's true that certain fields must be excluded from a particular view or context (for example, the new Categories... "button" field that pops up the Categories dialog box shouldn't be available from the Show Fields dialog), the vast majority should be equally accessible.

- There is no comprehensive help content describing these fields, their meanings, and data types. You often have to reverse-engineer from the VBScript help file property descriptions or resort to the help topic "Standard fields in a contact." This topic is a meager start, but it is missing many fields and doesn't address the abundant inconsistencies.

---

[*] Back when Outlook 98 was but a twinkle in a Microsoft developer's eye, Helen Feddema first pointed out this discontinuity between Outlook's various "user interface" lists of Contact item fields and the object model for a ContactItem object. We all owe her a rousing cheer for persevering in her pioneering search for the correct matches between the user interface lists and the object model.

- The minimal help that is available in Outlook 98 should be available for the selected field from the context of whatever dialog in which you're seeing the field name. This has long been possible in Word when constructing fields.

- Besides all the fields Outlook lets you "see" listed through its interface, there are 41 additional Contact item fields in the Outlook object model that you simply can't access from any of the field or control property dialogs. Some of these don't need to be accessible outside of code because it wouldn't make sense or serve any useful purpose (for example, the Application property). But the majority of these additional fields should be accessible via the standard user interface, and not just through code.

Table 6-2: Outlook's myriad and divergent lists of Contact item fields

Show Fields Dialog	Field Chooser Dialog	Control Properties Dialog	Map Custom Fields Dialog[1]	Object Model
				Actions
				Application
				Class (new in Outlook 98)
				Companies
				CompanyAnd-FullName
				CompanyLastFirst-NoSpace (new in Outlook 98)
				CompanyLast-FirstSpaceOnly (new in Outlook 98)
				Conversation-Index (was not applicable to ContactItem object in Outlook 97, but is in Outlook 98)
				Conversation-Topic (was not applicable to ContactItem object in Outlook 97, but is in Outlook 98)
				Email1Address-Type

Table 6-2: Outlook's myriad and divergent lists of Contact item fields (continued)

Show Fields Dialog	Field Chooser Dialog	Control Properties Dialog	Map Custom Fields Dialog[1]	Object Model
				Email1EntryID
				Email2Address-Type
				Email2EntryID
				Email3Address-Type
				Email3EntryID
				EntryID
				FormDescription
				FullNameAndCompany
				GetInspector
				Importance
				LastFirstAndSuffix (new in Outlook 98)
				LastFirstNoSpace (new in Outlook 98)
				LastFirstNoSpaceCompany (new in Outlook 98)
				LastFirstSpaceOnly (new in Outlook 98)
				LastFirstSpaceOnlyCompany (new in Outlook 98)
				LastNameAndFirstName
				MailingAddressCity
				MailingAddressCountry
				MailingAddressPostalCode
				MailingAddressPostOfficeBox
				MailingAddressState
				MailingAddressStreet

Table 6-2: Outlook's myriad and divergent lists of Contact item fields (continued)

Show Fields Dialog	Field Chooser Dialog	Control Properties Dialog	Map Custom Fields Dialog[1]	Object Model
				NetMeetingAlias (new in Outlook 98)
				NoAging
				Parent
				Saved
				SelectedMailing-Address
				Session (only in Outlook 98)
				UnRead
				UserCertificate
				UserProperties
Account	Account	Account	Account	Account
Address Selected (new in Outlook 98)	Address Selected (new in Outlook 98)	Address Selected (new in Outlook 98)		
Address Selector (new in Outlook 98)	Address Selector (new in Outlook 98)	Address Selector (new in Outlook 98)		
Anniversary	Anniversary	Anniversary	Anniversary	Anniversary
Assistant's Name	Assistant's Name	Assistant's Name	Assistant's Name	AssistantName
Assistant's Phone	Assistant's Phone	Assistant's Phone	Assistant's Phone	AssistantTele-phoneNumber
Attachment	Attachment (this field eerily pops in and out of the list on different PCs while in normal Outlook mode, but always appears in the list when in Form Design View; go figure)	Attachment		Attachments

Table 6-2: Outlook's myriad and divergent lists of Contact item fields (continued)

Show Fields Dialog	Field Chooser Dialog	Control Properties Dialog	Map Custom Fields Dialog[1]	Object Model
Billing Information	Billing Information	Billing Information	Billing Information	BillingInformation
Birthday	Birthday	Birthday	Birthday	Birthday
Business Address	Business Address	Business Address	Business Address	BusinessAddress
Business Address City	Business Address City	Business Address City	Business City	BusinessAddress-City
Business Address Country	Business Address Country	Business Address Country	Business Country	BusinessAddress-Country
Business Address PO Box	Business Address PO Box	Business Address PO Box		BusinessAddress-PostOfficeBox
Business Address Postal Code	Business Address Postal Code	Business Address Postal Code	Business Postal Code	BusinessAddress-PostalCode
Business Address State	Business Address State	Business Address State	Business State	BusinessAddress-State
Business Address Street	Business Address Street	Business Address Street	Business Street; Business Street 2; Business Street 3	BusinessAddress-Street
Business Fax	Business Fax (appears only in Form Design View)	Business Fax	Business Fax	BusinessFax-Number
Business Home Page	Business Home Page	Business Home Page		BusinessHome-Page
Business Phone	Business Phone (appears only in Form Design View)	Business Phone	Business Phone	BusinessTele-phoneNumber
Business Phone 2	Business Phone 2	Business Phone 2	Business Phone 2	Business2-TelephoneNumber
Callback	Callback	Callback	Callback	CallbackTelephone Number

Table 6-2: Outlook's myriad and divergent lists of Contact item fields (continued)

Show Fields Dialog	Field Chooser Dialog	Control Properties Dialog	Map Custom Fields Dialog[1]	Object Model
Car Phone	Car Phone	Car Phone	Car Phone	CarTelephone-Number
Categories	Categories (appears only in Form Design View)	Categories	Categories	Categories
	Categories... (new in Outlook 98)	Catego-ries... (new in Outlook 98)		
	Check Address... (new in Outlook 98)	Check Address... (new in Outlook 98)		
	Check Name... (new in Outlook 98)	Check Name... (new in Outlook 98)		
Children	Children	Children	Children	Children
City	City	City		
Company	Company (appears only in Form Design View)	Company	Company	CompanyName
Company Main Phone	Company Main Phone	Company Main Phone	Company Main Phone	CompanyMain-TelephoneNumber
		Company Yomi		YomiCom-panyName
Computer Network Name	Computer Network Name	Computer Network Name		ComputerNet-workName
Country	Country	Country		
Created	Created	Created		CreationTime
Customer ID	Customer ID	Customer ID		CustomerID
Department	Department	Department	Department	Department
		Directory Server (new in Outlook 98)		NetMeetingServer (new in Outlook 98)

Table 6-2: Outlook's myriad and divergent lists of Contact item fields (continued)

Show Fields Dialog	Field Chooser Dialog	Control Properties Dialog	Map Custom Fields Dialog[1]	Object Model
E-mail	E-mail	E-mail	E-mail; E-mail Address; E-mail Display Name	Email1Address; Email1Display-Name
E-mail 2	E-mail 2	E-mail 2	E-mail 2; E-mail 2 Address; E-mail 2 Display Name	Email2Address; Email2Display-Name
E-mail 3	E-mail 3	E-mail 3	E-mail 3; E-mail 3 Address; E-mail 3 Display Name	Email3Address; Email3Display-Name
E-mail Selected (new in Outlook 98)	E-mail Selected (new in Outlook 98)	E-mail Selected (new in Outlook 98)		
E-mail Selector (new in Outlook 98)	E-mail Selector (new in Outlook 98)	E-mail Selector (new in Outlook 98)		
File As	File As (appears only in Form Design View)	File As		FileAs
First Name	First Name	First Name	First Name	FirstName
Flag Status (new in Outlook 98)	Flag Status (new in Outlook 98, appears only in Form Design View)	Flag Status (new in Outlook 98)		
Follow Up Flag (new in Outlook 98)	Follow Up Flag (new in Outlook 98)	Follow Up Flag (new in Outlook 98)		
FTP Site	FTP Site	FTP Site		FTPSite
Full Name	Full Name (appears only in Form Design View)	Full Name	Name	FullName

Table 6-2: Outlook's myriad and divergent lists of Contact item fields (continued)

Show Fields Dialog	Field Chooser Dialog	Control Properties Dialog	Map Custom Fields Dialog[1]	Object Model
Gender	Gender	Gender	Gender	Gender
	Given Yomi			YomiFirstName
Government ID Number	Government ID Number	Government ID Number	Government ID Number	GovernmentID-Number
Hobbies	Hobbies	Hobbies	Hobby	Hobby
Home Address	Home Address	Home Address	Home Address	HomeAddress
Home Address City	Home Address City	Home Address City	Home City	HomeAddressCity
Home Address Country	Home Address Country	Home Address Country	Home Country	HomeAddress-Country
Home Address PO Box	Home Address PO Box	Home Address PO Box		HomeAddressPost-OfficeBox
Home Address Postal Code	Home Address Postal Code	Home Address Postal Code	Home Postal Code	HomeAddress-PostalCode
Home Address State	Home Address State	Home Address State	Home State	HomeAddressState
Home Address Street	Home Address Street	Home Address Street	Home Street; Home Street 2; Home Street 3	HomeAddress-Street
Home Fax	Home Fax	Home Fax	Home Fax	HomeFaxNumber
Home Phone	Home Phone (appears only in Form Design View)	Home Phone	Home Phone	HomeTelephone-Number
Home Phone 2	Home Phone 2	Home Phone 2	Home Phone 2	Home2Telephone Number
Icon	Icon (appears only in Form Design View)	Icon		Icon
In Folder	In Folder	In Folder		Parent.Name
Initials	Initials	Initials	Initials	Initials

Table 6-2: Outlook's myriad and divergent lists of Contact item fields (continued)

Show Fields Dialog	Field Chooser Dialog	Control Properties Dialog	Map Custom Fields Dialog[1]	Object Model
Internet Free/Busy Address (new in Outlook 98)	Internet Free/ Busy Address (new in Outlook 98)	Internet Free/Busy Address (new in Outlook 98)	Internet Free Busy Address (new in Outlook 98)	InternetFreeBusy-Address (new in Outlook 98)
ISDN	ISDN	ISDN	ISDN	ISDNNumber
Job Title	Job Title	Job Title	Job Title	JobTitle
Journal	Journal (appears only in Form Design View)	Journal		Journal
			Keywords	
Language	Language	Language	Language	Language
Last Name	Last Name	Last Name	Last Name	LastName
Location	Location	Location	Location	
Mailing Address	Mailing Address	Mailing Address		MailingAddress
Mailing Address Indicator (new in Outlook 98)	Mailing Address Indicator (new in Outlook 98)	Mailing Address Indicator (new in Outlook 98)		
Manager's Name	Manager's Name	Manager's Name	Manager's Name (only in Outlook 98)	ManagerName
Message Class	Message Class	Message Class		MessageClass
Middle Name	Middle Name	Middle Name	Middle Name	MiddleName
Mileage	Mileage	Mileage	Mileage	Mileage
Mobile Phone	Mobile Phone (appears only in Form Design View)	Mobile Phone	Mobile Phone	MobileTelephone-Number
Modified	Modified	Modified		LastModification-Time
Nickname	Nickname	Nickname		Nickname

Table 6-2: Outlook's myriad and divergent lists of Contact item fields (continued)

Show Fields Dialog	Field Chooser Dialog	Control Properties Dialog	Map Custom Fields Dialog[1]	Object Model
Notes	Notes		Notes	Body
Office Location	Office Location	Office Location	Office Location	OfficeLocation
Organizational ID Number	Organizational ID Number	Organizational ID Number	Organizational ID Number	OrganizationalID-Number
Other Address	Other Address	Other Address	Other Address	OtherAddress
Other Address City	Other Address City	Other Address City	Other City	OtherAddressCity
Other Address Country	Other Address Country	Other Address Country	Other Country	OtherAddress-Country
Other Address PO Box	Other Address PO Box	Other Address PO Box		OtherAddressPost-OfficeBox
Other Address Postal Code	Other Address Postal Code	Other Address Postal Code	Other Postal Code	OtherAddress-PostalCode
Other Address State	Other Address State	Other Address State	Other State	OtherAddressState
Other Address Street	Other Address Street	Other Address Street	Other Street; Other Street 2; Other Street 3	OtherAddressStreet
Other Fax	Other Fax	Other Fax	Other Fax	OtherFaxNumber
Other Phone	Other Phone	Other Phone	Other Phone	OtherTelephone-Number
Outlook Internal Version	Outlook Internal Version	Outlook Internal Version		OutlookInternal-Version
Outlook Version	Outlook Version	Outlook Version		OutlookVersion
Pager	Pager	Pager	Pager	PagerNumber
Personal Home Page	Personal Home Page	Personal Home Page		PersonalHome-Page

Table 6-2: Outlook's myriad and divergent lists of Contact item fields (continued)

Show Fields Dialog	Field Chooser Dialog	Control Properties Dialog	Map Custom Fields Dialog[1]	Object Model
Phone 1,2,3,4,5,6,7, 8 Selected (new in Outlook 98)[2]	Phone 1,2,3,4,5,6,7,8 Selected (new in Outlook 98)[2]	Phone 1,2,3,4,5,6,7, 8 Selected (new in Outlook 98)[2]		
Phone 1,2,3,4,5,6,7, 8 Selector (new in Outlook 98)	Phone 1,2,3,4,5,6,7,8 Selector (new in Outlook 98)	Phone 1,2,3,4,5,6,7, 8 Selector (new in Outlook 98)		
PO Box	PO Box	PO Box	PO Box	
			Priority (new in Outlook 98)	
Primary Phone	Primary Phone	Primary Phone	Primary Phone	PrimaryTelephone-Number
Private (only in Outlook 98)	Private (only in Outlook 98)	Private (only in Outlook 98)	Private	
Profession	Profession	Profession	Profession	Profession
Radio Phone	Radio Phone	Radio Phone	Radio Phone	RadioTelephone-Number
Read	Read	Read		
Referred By	Referred By	Referred By	Referred By	ReferredBy
Reminder (new in Outlook 98)	Reminder (new in Outlook 98)	Reminder (new in Outlook 98)		
Reminder Time (new in Outlook 98)	Reminder Time (new in Outlook 98)	Reminder Time (new in Outlook 98)		
Reminder Topic (new in Outlook 98)	Reminder Topic (new in Outlook 98)	Reminder Topic (new in Outlook 98)		
Send Plain Text Only (new in Outlook 98)	Send Plain Text Only (new in Outlook 98)	Send Plain Text Only (new in Outlook 98)		
Sensitivity	Sensitivity	Sensitivity	Sensitivity (only in Outlook 98)	Sensitivity

Table 6-2: Outlook's myriad and divergent lists of Contact item fields (continued)

Show Fields Dialog	Field Chooser Dialog	Control Properties Dialog	Map Custom Fields Dialog[1]	Object Model
Size	Size	Size		Size
Spouse	Spouse	Spouse	Spouse	Spouse
State	State	State		
Street Address	Street Address	Street Address		
Subject	Subject	Subject		Subject
Suffix	Suffix	Suffix	Suffix	Suffix
		Surname Yomi		YomiLastName
Telex	Telex	Telex	Telex	TelexNumber
Title	Title	Title	Title	Title
TTY/TDD Phone	TTY/TDD Phone	TTY/TDD Phone	TTY/TDD Phone	TTYTDDTele-phoneNumber
User Field 1	User Field 1	User Field 1	User 1	User1
User Field 2	User Field 2	User Field 2	User 2	User2
User Field 3	User Field 3	User Field 3	User 3	User3
User Field 4	User Field 4	User Field 4	User 4	User4
Web Page	Web Page	Web Page	Web Page	WebPage
ZIP/Postal Code	ZIP/Postal Code	ZIP/Postal Code		

[1] The Map Custom Fields dialog's fields are not in this order, in fact they're in no logical order whatsoever, as far as we can determine. If you are importing to Outlook 98, you have to use these exact names for the field names in your source file, since Outlook 98 does not support field mapping.

[2] To simplify the table, we list the eight separate fields Phone 1 Selected through Phone 8 Selected together in a single row, and do the same for Phone 1 Selector through Phone 8 Selector.

There are three ways to see these dialog field listings:

1. The Show Fields dialog (see Figure 6-5). In Outlook 98, select View → Current View → Customize Current View → Fields (or add the Show Fields command, found in the View category, to a toolbar). In Outlook 97, from any folder, select View → Show Fields. In the "Select available fields from" list choose "All Contact fields."

WARNING   The Show Fields dialog contains two list boxes: "Available fields" on the left and "Show these fields in this order" on the right. When you first display the dialog, the "Show these fields in this order" list is populated with the fields used in the current view. When you change to "All Contact fields" as described in the previous step, the "Available fields" list shows all Contact fields *that are not already in the view*. So the dialog now reveals Contact fields in two separate lists: Contact fields that are not already in the view are on the left, and Contact fields that are already in the view are on the right. If you want to see a *single* list of all Contact fields, the trick is to select all the items in the "Show these fields in this order" list, then click on the Remove button. (An annoyance common to both Outlook versions: when you click on the Remove button the "Select available fields from" control snaps back to its default value "Frequently-used fields" so you must manually set it back to "All Contact fields.") Now the "Available fields" list displays all Contact fields. Be sure to click on Cancel when done or you may unintentionally change the current view's settings.

The net effect is that if you don't remember that the complete Contact field list is initially spread across two list boxes, you might wrongly assume the list on the left is incomplete.

---

2. The Field Chooser dialog (see Figures 6-6 and 6-7). In Outlook 98, this command is not provided on any built-in toolbars or the menu bar unless you have a form open in Design View, so you'll have to add the Field Chooser command to a toolbar yourself (it's listed as a command in the View category) to use it outside that context. In Outlook 98, click on the Field Chooser button you've just added to a toolbar and then choose "All Contact fields." In Outlook 97 this dialog isn't available from every folder, or from every view: select your Contacts folder, activate the Phone List view, select View → Field Chooser, and then choose "All Contact fields."

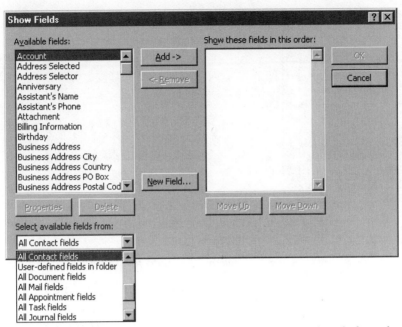

Figure 6-5: The Show Fields dialog with "All Contact fields" selected, shown here after performing the important Remove process

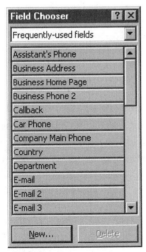

Figure 6-6: The Field Chooser dialog in its default state

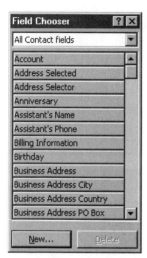

Figure 6-7: The Field Chooser dialog with "All Contact fields" selected

---

NOTE   You can also activate Field Chooser in Design view (more
                on this in Chapter 8, *Introduction to VBScript, the Outlook
                Object Model, and Custom Forms,* but here are the quick
                steps). Create a new scratch record (say, a Contact). In Out-
                look 98 select Tools → Forms → Design This Form; Field
                Chooser should appear automatically (if not, select Form →
                Field Chooser or click on the Field Chooser button on the
                Form Design toolbar). In Outlook 97 select Tools → Design
                Outlook Form, click on the (P.2) tab, click on the Field
                Chooser button (or Form → Field Chooser).

---

3. Control Properties dialog (see Figure 6-8). From the Design view, add
   a TextBox control to the form. To do this in Outlook 98 and 97, the
   steps are identical: click on the Control Toolbox button (or select
   Form → Control Toolbox), click on the TextBox control, then draw
   the control anywhere on the form. Now right-click it, choose Properties, click on the Value tab, and click on the Choose Field button.

As you can see by examining Table 6-2, Outlook's own user interface
isn't consistent about which Contact fields are exposed in which dialog.
Since these lists are built-in, there's nothing we can do about this annoyance except be aware of it and hope for a consistent reworking in a
future version of Outlook.

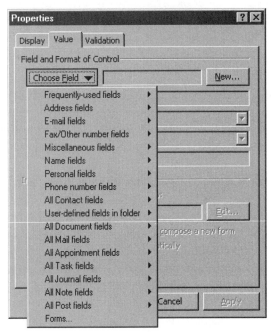

Figure 6-8: The Control Properties dialog's Choose Field list

Performing an import

Follow the steps in Checklist 6-2 to perform an import. We use the test Excel database and a destination of a new Contacts folder.

Checklist 6-2: Performing an Import

1. If you want to do any preprocessing on the source data, do so now. Refer to Checklist 6-2. (The model Excel database named *Import to Outlook.xls* is available at *ftp://ftp.ora.com/published/oreilly/windows/outlook.annoy.*)

   a. We strongly suggest you include field names in your source data-base. If you don't, you won't be able to make sense out of your source data structure when you get to the Wizard's Map Custom Fields panel. Remember, in Outlook 98 you don't have data mapping capability at all, and you *must* include field names and they have to match *exactly* the field names in Outlook. Other-wise, no data will be imported.

   b. If you're importing phone numbers, here are some tips. If the phone number data is stored in a numeric type field in the source application, the imported value may have ".000" appended to it and the root number itself may be completely

different. This is because Outlook expects to receive the phone number data as text (a series of characters like "(310) 555-1212") not numeric data (the number 3105551212). Look carefully at phone number data in your source application, and if necessary, convert it (if only temporarily) to raw text.

In Excel, if you select a cell containing the number 3105551212 and then format it as a phone number (Format → Cells → Number → Special → Phone Number), the result in Outlook will be wrong. This is to be expected, since in Excel, formatting as a numeric value only changes a cell's appearance, not its underlying value. The trick is to completely transform the data to text using a formula like this: =TEXT(A1,"(###) ###-####"). Once transformed, you can then copy and paste the formula-based cells back on top of the neighboring source cells using Paste Special Values. The same logic applies to Access. If your Access phone number field is numeric, even if you format it as a phone number using an input mask (say, !\(999") "000\-0000), when you import the data into Outlook it will be garbage. So in Access you would also need to transform the numeric phone number data into text.

c. Although we discussed this earlier in Checklist 6-1, it's vitally important. This is the time and place to clear out any unwanted duplicate records. Duplicate records are a hassle to contend with, so the fewer the better, unless of course you have them by choice (for example, if you correspond with two John Smiths). If you eliminate unwanted duplicate records in your source and then import the data into a temporary Contacts folder, you won't have any unwanted duplicates in this folder either. As you'll see shortly, the next and final step is to move these imported records into your main Contacts folder. This is the point where you would contend with any resulting new duplicates.

2. Select the entire data range in Excel and give it a unique range name (one that's different from any column header label); otherwise, you'll get the annoying message shown in Figure 6-9, and the workaround would only be discovered if you searched the Microsoft Knowledge-Base to locate article Q161556. (This information should be in Outlook's help file and also referenced by a Help button on this very message box.) Specifically, select the source data range, then choose Insert → Name → Define, type in a unique range name like Export-Data, and click on OK. Now close *Import to Outlook.xls*. If your source is not Excel, you can skip this step.

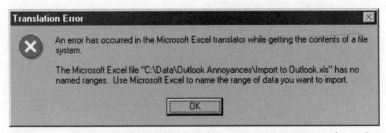

Figure 6-9: This annoying and unhelpful error message occurs if you don't name the range of your Excel source data

3. Create a new, temporary Contacts folder for the imported data. In this example, name it `Imported from Excel`.

NOTE   Remember, never import directly into your main Contacts folder. Instead, you should always create a new Contacts folder and import into it. That way, if something goes wrong with the import, it doesn't mess up the existing contacts list. Once the new imports are sorted out, putting them into the main contacts folder is a simple drag-and-drop (or Edit → Move to Folder) procedure.

---

4. To gain some experience with duplicate records, let's force one to exist in the Imported from Excel folder before the import. Add a new Contact item with the name Dr. William Santana, a company of Redondo Beach Medical Center, and, to uniquely identify this contact, set the Manager's Name field to "I was here first." Now Save and Close this Contact item.

NOTE   This step is provided to give you some practical experience with duplicate records. If you're importing into an empty folder, naturally this step is moot.

---

5. Start the Wizard by selecting File → Import and Export, choose the "Import from another program or file" item from the "Choose an action to perform" list (in Outlook 97 the description is "Import from Schedule+ or another program or file"), then click on Next.

6. Choose the appropriate file type (in this example, Microsoft Excel) from the "Select file type to import from" list, then click on Next.

7. Locate and select the source file (in this example, *Import to Outlook.xls*), select the "Allow duplicates to be created" option

(which causes a new, second record to be created), then click on Next.

If you were to choose "Replace duplicates with items imported," the original record for Dr. William Santana would be replaced by the imported record.

If you were to choose "Do not import duplicate items," nothing would happen; that is, the original Dr. William Santana record would be left alone and a duplicate record would not be created.

8. In the folder tree control labeled "Select destination folder," select the destination folder (in this example, *Imported from Excel*), then click on Next.

9. In Outlook 97, click on the Map Custom Fields button, which displays the Wizard's Map Custom Fields panel (see Figure 6-10). This dialog allows you to drag-and-drop field names from the From frame on the left (the source data map; here it's Excel) onto the To frame on the right (the destination data map, which is an Outlook Contact Items folder). Thankfully, both the From and To field lists have horizontal and vertical scroll bars, and all the column widths are adjustable. The From list allows you to see the value behind each field, and you can even browse through the data source one record at a time using the Previous and Next buttons. Excellent!

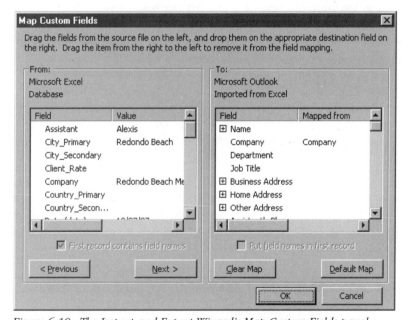

Figure 6-10: The Import and Export Wizard's Map Custom Fields panel

The Wizard attempts to match up source and destination fields with identical field names, so if this is an option for the data source you're working with—it is an option with Excel—you may prefer to change source field names *before the import* to match Outlook's field names; this minimizes the amount of manual drag-and-drop mapping you have to do.

NOTE   The Wizard matches field names on an exact basis. This means that an incoming field name of "BillingInformation" or "Billing_Information" will not be automatically matched to Outlook's "Billing Information" field. Only an incoming field name of exactly "Billing Information" gets auto-matched.

By the way, Outlook builds its Full Name field based on the fields Title, First Name, Middle Name, Last Name, and so on. When you're mapping imported data, map to these lower-level fields, not to Full Name.

The Clear Map button, not surprisingly, clears any destination (Outlook) data mapping that was done automatically by the Wizard or that you did by hand. There's no "undo undo"; once cleared, it's gone. You can remove a mapped field by dragging it from the To column to any part of the From list box. This feels a bit weird at first, since elsewhere in Outlook you remove fields—say, from a View—by dragging them anywhere out of their starting zone, but in this case you actually have to drag the mapped field back to the From list box; otherwise, you'll just see the no-drop mouse pointer. If you drop an unmapped field right on top of a source field, the source field gets highlighted—again, the design of this operation strikes us as rather bizarre—but rest assured there's no effect on the source data map.

The Default Map button clears any manual mapping you've done and resets the mapped fields to their "automatic" state.

10. In Outlook 97, you can map the incoming Excel database fields shown in Table 6-3 to their Outlook equivalents. Click on OK when you're ready to start the import.

In Outlook 98, you have to edit the Excel column titles to match the Outlook equivalents precisely, again using the fields shown in Table 6-3. Microsoft has a KnowledgeBase article that explains why the mapping feature is not in the released version of Outlook. Check out Article ID Q182728 for all the annoying details.

NOTE   If you have created any custom fields in the folder that are
              receiving the imported data, they won't be listed in the Wiz-
              ard's Map Custom Fields dialog box. This oversight should
              definitely be corrected in the next version of the Wizard.
              There are two workarounds: (1) import data into any of
              the four built-in Contact fields (User Field 1, User Field 2,
              User Field 3, and User Field 4), then manually or program-
              matically redistribute it to custom fields; or (2) import the
              data programmatically into Contact custom fields.

              The same problem exists when exporting: you can't use
              the Wizard to export data from custom fields. Instead, you
              either have to: (1) define a Table type view, copy the data
              in that view and paste it into the destination application
              (for example, Excel); or (2) export the data programmati-
              cally.

Table 6-3: Excel to Outlook—sample conversion field equivalents

Map Custom Fields Dialog Fields	Import Fields (from Excel)
Assistant's Name	Assistant
Business Address City	City_Primary
Business Address Country	Country_Primary
Business Address Postal Code	Zip_Primary
Business Address State	State_Primary
Business Phone	Phone_Number_1
Business Phone 2	Phone_Number_2
Business Street	Street1_Primary
Business Street 2	Street2_Primary
Company	Company
Department	Dept_Primary
E-mail	Email_Name
E-mail 2	Email_Destination
First Name	First_Name
Full Name	Don't map intentionally (let component fields "build" this value)
Home Address City	City_Secondary
Home Address Country	Country_Secondary
Home Address Postal Code	Zip_Secondary
Home Address State	State_Secondary
Home Phone	Phone_Number_3
Home Phone 2	Phone_Number_4
Home Street	Street1_Secondary

Table 6-3: Excel to Outlook—sample conversion field equivalents (continued)

Map Custom Fields Dialog Fields	Import Fields (from Excel)
Home Street 2	Street2_Secondary
Job Title	Position
Last Name	Last_Name
Organizational ID Number	Nickname
Title	Title
User Field 1	UserKey1
User Field 2	UserKey2
User Field 3	UserKey3
User Field 4	UserKey4

Now let's examine the resulting Contacts folder data (see Figure 6-11) for any import anomalies.

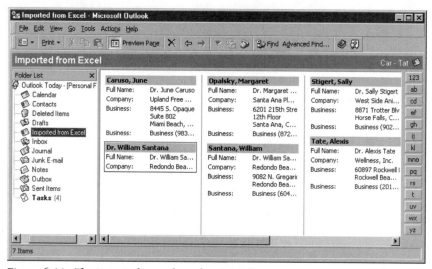

Figure 6-11: The imported records as they initially appear in the Imported from Excel folder, including the previously mentioned Dr. Santana record

You can set the standard Contact form to reveal all Contact fields. To do this, open the Contact item, click on the All Fields tab, and select "All Contact fields" in the "Select from" list box. (The field name list in the All Fields tab's "All Contact fields" is the same as the Control Properties dialog column, as seen in Table 6-2.) Figure 6-12 displays Dr. June Caruso's record in this format. You can scroll up and down this list, verifying that the import was successful.

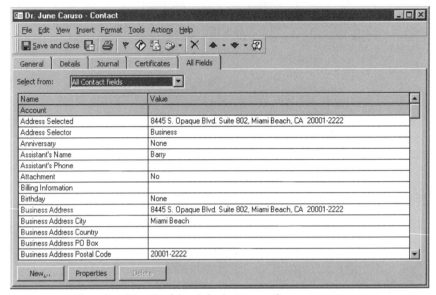

Figure 6-12: The All Fields tab of the default Contact form

NOTE   Should you need to return to the source file and re-import
              the data, Outlook 97's Map Custom Fields conveniently re-
              members the field mapping for the source file *until you
              point to a different file of the same data type.* You can also
              use this behavior to import a new set of data with the
              same field structure, without having to repeat the drag-and-
              drop operations. Just eliminate all but the first row (the col-
              umn headers) of the original source workbook and replace
              the data with new data, then repeat the import. Of course,
              if all your import file field labels match Outlook's field
              names, this is moot.

The import itself is now finished, but you still need to clean up any imper-
fect field mappings. We cover that in the next two sections.

Cleanup

It's very unlikely that you'll have a perfect one-to-one field correspondence between your source application and Outlook. Although the way
you go about the cleanup is a subjective decision, you'll quickly learn
that the fastest solution when dealing with more than a few dozen
records is writing some VBScript code to perform the cleanup operation
for you. In this example, there are several things we need to clean up.
Keep in mind that this six-record database is only the tip of a much larger

iceberg, in our case, a 3,000-record database. We're just using the six records as a test so we'll be prepared for problems and can handle them when the entire database is imported. The problems that our attempt to import the Excel data revealed include:

1. The source application has two address field groups—Primary and Secondary—with no way to differentiate between home versus business address fields, so you're going to have to write some heuristics in VBScript. For example, if the contact's company name is empty, move the business address values to home address fields, unless the home address fields aren't all empty, in which case do nothing (or write this exception to a log file for later handling).

2. The source supported a set of default phone number labels and allowed us to customize these labels and to then store numbers in any order. We arbitrarily mapped the source's first two phone numbers to Outlook's Business Phone and Business Phone 2 fields, then the source's next two phone numbers to Outlook's Home Phone and Home Phone 2 fields. Now you need some VBScript code to read each of these four phone number fields, determine the label, and use the label to decide where to put the phone number itself—minus the label. For example, "Business" should map to the Business Phone field and "Pager" should map to the Pager field. And this all has to happen in memory without disrupting the contents of the extant Outlook fields that our post-processing code hasn't yet filtered.

3. The source's email fields aren't being used to store email information at all (we mapped them anyway, but they're all empty). Once the 3,000 records are in a temporary Contacts folder, you have to meld email data that—in this fictional scenario—you already have in a production Contacts folder for some 300 contacts. You would write some VBScript code to find any duplicate records in the production Contacts folder, grab the E-mail field contents, and put that content in the matching temporary folder's record. Later you'll move all records from the temporary folder to the production folder, *replacing* duplicates in the production folder.

4. For some reason, the Map Custom Fields dialog in Outlook 97 doesn't include Outlook's own Nickname field for Contact items. This is odd because it's available in the object model as one of the ContactItem object's properties. It also appears in the other field dialogs (see Table 6-2): the Show Fields, Field Chooser, and Control Properties (Choose Field) dialogs. Go figure. The consequence here is that you have to map (or rename the field in Excel, if you are using Outlook 98) the incoming nickname data to a different field in Outlook (we

chose Organizational ID Number, since in this scenario there's no pre-existing ID data), then move it to Nickname, an awkward and annoying inconvenience.

5. Our source used the UserKey1–UserKey4 fields in the same way that Outlook uses Categories, but with delimited keyword lists. The VBScript challenge here is to take comma and semi-colon delimited keyname lists from the imported fields (a string like "TUG COMP; PRIME PRESS"), parse them into individual new Categories, add those Categories if they don't already exist, then set all those Categories for the current record.

The final step

Once you've cleaned up the contacts in your temporary Contacts folder, it's time to move them over to your main Contacts folder. Follow the steps provided in the earlier section, "Conversion du Jour: PAB to Contacts."

Other Conversion Considerations

So far in this chapter we've focused on how to get data into Outlook from an outside repository, but there's another important area to consider: shuffling data around *inside* Outlook. Microsoft bills this as one of Outlook's many IntelliSense features; it's called AutoCreate. Here's a quick example: you compose an email to your Mom with a subject of "When I Was a Little Tyke" asking her for a list of your childhood illnesses and inoculations. You send it, and while it's sitting in your Outbox, you Ctrl+drag the message onto the Tasks icon in the Outlook Bar or the Folder List. Poof! Instant Task, complete with a Subject that's the same as the message's and the body of the message itself (with a brief header comprised of From, Sent, To, and Subject fields), including any formatting. Assign a due date, set a reminder, and forget about it, letting Outlook fret over this new to-do item. (Yes, there are other ways to flag an email message for follow-up action, but this is the one we prefer so that all pending tasks are reflected in one place, our Tasks folder.) We don't have to print out paper copies of messages that are awaiting a reply or worry about tracking them at all. Instead, Outlook does it for us, and the cool part is how easy it is to AutoCreate an email message into a task.

Here's another example. If you're like us, you scribble lots of little notes on pieces of paper and Post-it Notes that end up scattered all over the place. We've forced ourselves to dispense with paper lists, instead relying entirely on Outlook to help us manage these little idea/to-do snippets. Outlook's rich viewing, grouping, and sorting features make it a far superior technology for managing these types of information tidbits than pencil and paper. (We cover viewing, grouping, and sorting in Chapter 7.)

Specifically, we suggest you create a Note item whenever you have an information tidbit that has no particular deadline. Perhaps a list of books you'd like to read, fantasy home improvement projects, that sort of thing. You can always drag-and-drop a Note (say, one of the book titles) to a Task, in which case the Note's Subject (the first paragraph of the Note) becomes the Task's Subject; the Task's content includes the modification date/time of the Note plus its content. Now you can set a due date and reminder by which to tackle this Note.

Of course, you can directly create a Task instead of a Note when you're creating a time-based to-do (or even a no-deadline to-do) from scratch. But if you already have content on hand, it's handy to AutoCreate new Tasks using the technique described above.

Transmogrify with AutoCreate

Let's take a look at all the possible combinations of AutoCreate data items. In Table 6-4, we show what happens for each such AutoCreate transformation using the traditional left mouse button drag-and-drop technique.

NOTE We use the term *body* to describe the large scrollable note-taking area found in every Outlook data type—except for a Note item, where we call it *content* due to the Note's physical appearance (the Subject field melds into the content, even though in the object model they are two distinct properties).

Table 6-4: Results of all possible AutoCreate combinations

Source Item Type	Destination Item Type	AutoCreate Results
Inbox or any email folder	Calendar	The message's subject and content becomes the Appointment's subject and body. The Appointment's start/end dates are set to today and the start time to the next half-hour increment, with a duration of 30 minutes.
Inbox	Contacts	The message sender's display name becomes Full Name; email address becomes Email (display name is correctly preserved; email address itself is the sender's From address *not* his Reply-To address; and email type will always be SMTP); and content becomes the Contact's body.
Inbox	Tasks	The message's subject and content become the Task's subject and body respectively.
Inbox	Journal	Creates a Journal Entry using the message's subject for Subject, puts the sender's display name in the Contact field (will display name underlined to indicate a matching Contact if one already exists), plus a shortcut to the message object in the body (attachments are preserved within the message object itself).
Inbox	Notes	The message's subject does *not* become the Note's subject, so you have a subject-less Note that looks weird in any view. Message's content (including standard From, Sent, To, Subject, and the actual message material) becomes the Note's content. Since a Note's content is text-only, no binary attachments are preserved.
Calendar[1]	Inbox	The activity's subject becomes the message's subject. The activity's organizer and attendees are *not* placed in the message's To field even if they're in the Contacts folder. The activity's key field values (like Subject, Location, Start/End, Recurrence, etc.) become the message's body.

Table 6-4: Results of all possible AutoCreate combinations (continued)

Source Item Type	Destination Item Type	AutoCreate Results
Calendar	Contacts	The activity's organizer becomes the Contact's name, and key field values become the Contact's body.
Calendar	Tasks	The activity's subject becomes the Task's subject, date becomes the due date, key field values become the Task's body. *The reminder is set for 8:00 A.M. on the due date no matter what the activity's start time is.*[2]
Calendar	Journal	The activity's subject becomes the Journal's subject and its start date/time and duration map accordingly. The organizer is reflected in the Journal's Contact field *only if the organizer is not you.* Meeting attendees are added to the Contact field. We think this is a good thing.
Calendar	Notes	The activity's subject does *not* become the Note's subject, so you have a subject-less Note. (Workaround: the first bit of copy in the note will be white space and a dashed line followed by "Subject:" so erase all that and "subject" becomes the subject.) The activity's key field values become the Note's content.
Contacts	Inbox	The message that's created is smart enough to know it belongs in the Outbox no matter which email folder you drop the Contact on. The Contact is used in the To field; if multiple Contacts are dropped onto an email folder, they are all listed in the To field (letting you create a distribution list of sorts, as covered in Chapter 7). If the contact has multiple email addresses, all are placed in the To field.[3]
Contacts	Calendar	The Contact is placed in the Meeting Request form's attendee list. Ditto for multiple Contacts (one Meeting, multiple attendees). See the "Take a Meeting" section in Chapter 5, *Outlook's Key Ingredients*, for a discussion of the Meeting Request Form.

Table 6-4: Results of all possible AutoCreate combinations (continued)

Source Item Type	Destination Item Type	AutoCreate Results
Contacts	Tasks	The Contact is placed in the Task Request form's recipient list. Ditto for multiple Contacts (one Task, multiple recipients).
Contacts	Journal	The Contact's full name becomes the Journal Entry's subject (and the Journal Entry is a Phone call type). A pointer to the person appears in the Journal Entry's Contact field in the form of the person's full name, underlined. A shortcut to the person's Contact record appears in the entry's body. If more than one Contact is selected, only one Journal Entry is created; the Subject and Contact fields are blank, and shortcuts to each Contact appear in the body.
Contacts	Notes	The Contact's name does *not* become the Note's subject, so you have a subject-less Note. The Contact's Full Name and E-mail field values become the Note's content. Ditto for multiple Contacts (one Note, multiple Contacts listed in the Note's content). As before, the Note starts with a blank space, a dashed line, then "Full Name:" and then the name. Erase everything up to and including "Full Name:" and it then becomes the Note's subject.
Tasks	Inbox	The Task's subject becomes the message's subject. The Task's key field values (like Subject, Due Date, Status, etc.) become the Task's body.
Tasks	Calendar	The Task's subject becomes the Appointment's subject. The Task's due date is ignored—whether it's recurring or not—and the Appointment's start and end date/times are all set to the next quarter-hour increment from now. The Task's key field values become the Appointment's body.

Table 6-4: Results of all possible AutoCreate combinations (continued)

Source Item Type	Destination Item Type	AutoCreate Results
Tasks	Contacts	The Task's owner becomes the Contact's name and key field values become the Contact's body. Maybe this makes sense in a corporate environment, but on a single-user system, why would anyone want a function that adds oneself as the contact?
Tasks	Journal	The Task's subject becomes the Journal Entry's subject for a Task entry type, and a pointer to the Task is in the body. The Task's original due date becomes the Journal Entry's start date/time. In Outlook 98, if it's an unstarted Task, the Task's original *due date* becomes the Journal Entry's start date, and the time is set to exactly 12:00 A.M. If it's an in-progress Task, the Task's original *start date* becomes the Journal Entry's start date, and the time is set to exactly 12:00 A.M.
Tasks	Notes	The Task's subject does *not* become the Note's subject, so you have a subject-less Note. Use the workaround described previously to fix this. The Task's key field values become the Note's content.
Journal	Inbox	The Journal Entry's subject becomes the message's subject, and its key field values (Subject, Entry Type, etc.) become the message's body.
Journal	Calendar	The Journal Entry's subject becomes the Appointment's subject, and its key field values become the Appointment's body. The Appointment acquires a start/end date of today, a start time beginning at the nearest half hour, and a 30-minute duration.
Journal	Contacts	The Journal Entry's key field values become the Contact's body. No other field mapping occurs, regardless of the Journal Entry's type.

Table 6-4: Results of all possible AutoCreate combinations (continued)

Source Item Type	Destination Item Type	AutoCreate Results
Journal	Tasks	The Journal Entry's key field values become the Task's body. The Journal Entry's subject becomes the Task's subject but no other field mapping occurs, regardless of the Journal Entry's type. The Task has no due date.
Journal	Notes	The Journal Entry's subject does *not* become the Note's subject, so you have a subject-less Note. Use the workaround described previously to fix this. The Journal Entry's key field values become the Note's content.
Notes	Inbox	The Note's subject becomes the message's subject, and its key field values (like Modified and Categories), along with the content, become the message's body.
Notes	Calendar	The Note's subject becomes the Appointment's subject, and its key field values along with content become the Appointment's body. The Appointment's start/end dates are set to today, the start time to the next half-hour increment, with a duration of 30 minutes.
Notes	Contacts	The Note's key field values along with the content becomes the Contact's body. No other field mapping occurs.
Notes	Tasks	The Note's subject becomes the Task's subject, and its key field values along with the content becomes the Task's body. The Task has no due date.
Notes	Journal	The Note's subject becomes the Journal Entry's subject for a Note entry type, and a shortcut to the Note is in the body. The Journal Entry's start date/time is set to today at the current time.

1 If the Calendar item (meeting, appointment, or event) is recurring, the AutoCreated item points to the original date/time of the source event, not the next recurring date/time.

2 In all relevant Outlook modules, the reminder always defaults to the start of your defined "Calendar working hours Start time" in Tools → Options → Calendar.

3 In Outlook 97, when you have a contact stored in a customized Contact form, this doesn't work; the contact information appears in the body of an unaddressed message. This is fixed in Outlook 98.

For the most part, these AutoCreation transformations are sensible and actually quite elegant. Here's a list of annoyances and characteristics we'd like to see improved or added:

- When a Calendar activity is AutoCreated from a message, it would be useful if you could choose whether the spawned email address should be the From or Reply-To address (ditto for the email fields when AutoCreating a contact from a message). In this day and age of volatile ISP service, it's very common for people to use one email address (the Reply-To) as a switching station for two or more ISPs, each with its own address (the From address for a given message). In an effort to reduce spam traffic, some ISPs disallow masking the From address by setting it to your preferred Reply-To address. So if you had this choice during AutoCreation, you'd grab the sender's preferred (Reply-To) email address.

- When a Note item is AutoCreated, it never takes on the source's subject, so it ends up with a blank subject. This is annoying because *all* data items in Outlook's object model have a Subject property. You can see a Note item's subject in several of the Notes folder's default views. You can see a Note item's subject via VBScript and VBA code, and you can see a Note item's subject when you AutoCreate it into another data type (say, Note-to-message). As explained in the table, the most likely information that you would want to use as a subject appears as the first "real" text in the note; if Microsoft simply did away with that wasted blank space and dashed line, this feature would work properly.

- When a message is AutoCreated from a Calendar activity, the activity's organizer (and attendees, if any) don't land in the To field, even if these contacts are in the main Contacts folder. Seems to us that these folks should appear in the To field by default. Although it's arguable that at least half the time the organizer is you, why would you want a message addressed to yourself? Microsoft should make AutoCreate smart enough to omit you from the To list when you're the organizer.

- When a Task is AutoCreated from a Calendar activity, it's annoying that the Task's reminder is set for 8:00 A.M. on the due date no matter what the activity's start time is.

- When a Calendar activity (Appointment) is created from a Task, the Task's due date is ignored and the Appointment's start and end date/ times are all set to the next quarter-hour increment from now. We're ambivalent about this particular outcome; some of you might find this sensible, and some of you might balk. What would be really helpful is for AutoCreate to allow you to choose—in the appropriate AutoCreate combinations involving a time-stamped source item—whether to have the new item's due date become (a) today; (b) the original date of the non-recurring source item; (c) the date of the non-recurring source item's reminder; or (d) the date of the recurring source item's next recurrence, and then provide these options for the time component of the date/time stamp.

NOTE   As is often the case when doing a drag-and-drop operation (like dropping an Inbox item on the Task facility), you have more control if you use the right mouse button during the drag-and-drop. The right mouse button, when released, causes a pop-up menu to appear (shown in Figure 6-13) from which you can choose between copying or moving (when you choose Move…, the original item is copied into a new target item and the original item is then deleted, i.e., sent to the Deleted Items folder). You can also control whether to put a shortcut back to the original item in the new item's body or a copy of the original item embedded in the body as an attachment.

Interestingly, Outlook is programmed to presuppose that when you drag an item—using the standard left-drag technique—between modules of the same type, you intend to move it rather than clone a new one, so the item will disappear from its original module. Ctrl+left-drag guarantees that the original item is copied, not moved.

Archive and Backup

We've repeatedly stressed throughout this book—and will continue to do so—how important your personal information is. Of course, none of us typically appreciates just how important it is until we lose it, or lose access to it. Let's face it—stuff happens. The disaster could be as subtle as a corrupted Personal Store file or—as was the case for one of us while writing this book—as dire as a disk crash rendering a 2 GB drive into a useless heap of unaligned metal oxide particles. So, you've got four choices for backing up the *PI* of your *PIM*, and they're not all mutually exclusive:

- Do a traditional backup of your entire system, whether full or incremental, at your discretion. We do strongly suggest, though, that you maintain a daily incremental backup of *mailbox.pst* (and *mailbox.pab*, if you use a PAB). Do backups routinely even if you export, archive, or AutoArchive.

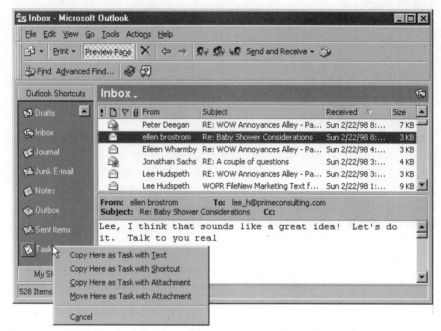

Figure 6-13: Using the right mouse button to expand your drag-and-drop options

- Do a manual export (File → Import and Export).
- Do a manual archive (File → Archive).
- Use Outlook's handy AutoArchive feature.

We're going to assume you have an automated, routine, robust daily backup strategy in place, so the rest of this section will concentrate on exporting, archiving, and AutoArchive.

Export

The most important difference between export and archive is that an export operation *copies* a folder's data to another repository and leaves the original data in its folder, whereas an archive operation *moves* a folder's data to another Personal Store file, meaning that the data is moved and is no longer in its original folder. The second most important difference is that an export operation supports many different types of destination file formats (as we discussed at the beginning of this chapter), whereas an archive operation only supports a Personal Store file type.

There's a special consideration for source data items that include binary attachments or objects; these objects won't survive the export process, but are preserved with an archive.

Archive

Besides backing up, archiving your Outlook data is essential to keeping *.pst* file sizes from getting out of control. To perform an archive, select File → Archive, which displays the Archive dialog box (see Figure 6-14). In this example, only the Sent Items folder is being archived; we're ignoring any AutoArchive settings; we're archiving all items older than October 1, 1997; we're selecting the "Include items with 'Do not AutoArchive' checked" box in order to force a complete archive; and we're using the default archive Personal Store file, *C:\Exchange\archive.pst*.

OUTLOOK 98 The new folder size utility in Outlook 98 is quite helpful. Right-click your Outlook Today folder → Properties → Folder Size to see statistics on all your folders. Contrary to our initial hypothesis that a lot of space is consumed by high-maintenance features like the Journal, most of a *.pst* file is typically eaten up by old messages. (Your mileage may vary, natch.) This utility is very useful in that respect. By simply creating one or more archive *.pst* files for old messages, you'll see useful performance gains. Archiving messages is a Very Big Deal in optimizing Outlook performance.

In this particular test, messages with Sent values of 9/30/97 were not archived, although common sense would interpret the dialog box's label of "Archive items older than" to indicate that they should have been archived. So it's a good idea to always verify that what you wanted to be archived actually was archived, including quickly checking the cutoff date.

NOTE If you want to know what date Outlook uses when performing an archive operation, ask the Office Assistant for the "date used to archive items" and select the topic of the same name. The date used varies depending on the type of data item being archived.

You can always get archived data back in one of two ways. First, you can simply add *archive.pst* as a new Personal Store information service: File → Open → Personal Folders File (**.pst*). To quickly see the new Personal

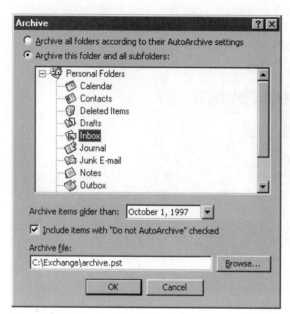

Figure 6-14: The Archive dialog box

Folders hierarchy represented by *archive.pst*, turn on Folder List if it isn't already on (click on the Folder List button), and then you'll see the new Personal Folders node at the bottom of the folders list. This technique has the benefit of keeping your current data segregated from the archived data. The second technique is to import one or more folders from *archive.pst*. Keep in mind that this will commingle your archived and current data in your current folder hierarchy, so you might want to create a temporary holding folder if you opt for this approach.

AutoArchive

We suggest you first set each individual folder's AutoArchive options, then activate the overall feature itself. Let's say you want your Sent Items folder to be AutoArchived. Right-click on the Sent Items folder, click on the AutoArchive tab as shown in Figure 6-15, accept the default values "Clean out items older than 2 months" and "Move old items to C:\Exchange\archive.pst," then click on OK. (If you have never examined your other folders' AutoArchive settings and want to follow along literally with this exercise, cycle through all remaining folders and turn AutoArchive off for each one.)

There's no way to set defaults for any of this other than Outlook's presets. It would be good to set your own generic specifications for AutoArchive. In one test, we moved *archive.pst* from the C: to the D:

drive (we recommend that if you have more than one hard drive, you put the archive or backup on a different one from the main Personal Store file), and there was no way to set this new location without changing it for each AutoArchived folder. Blecch.

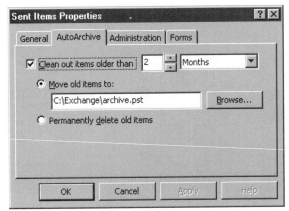

Figure 6-15: The Folder Properties dialog's AutoArchive tab

To turn AutoArchive on in Outlook 98, select Tools → Options → Other → AutoArchive (in Outlook 97 select Tools → Options → AutoArchive); the AutoArchive dialog box is shown in Figure 6-16. Now configure the settings as follows. Checking the "AutoArchive every 14 days" box causes AutoArchive to look at each folder's AutoArchive settings every time it starts up, but only to perform an archive once every 14 days. When checked, the "Prompt before AutoArchive" option (which we suggest you leave on at all times) prompts you first, as shown in Figure 6-16. The "Delete expired items when AutoArchiving (e-mail folders only)" box gives you the option to actually *delete* expired email items instead of archiving them, so turn this on at your own risk (we leave it off); this feature applies only to email folders. Lastly, set the "Default archive file" to the same *archive.pst* file referenced in your individual folders' AutoArchive settings.

Here are the factory default AutoArchive settings for each Outlook folder:

- Calendar—on (six months)

- Contacts—off (can be manually archived, but cannot be Auto-Archived)

- Deleted Items—on (two months)

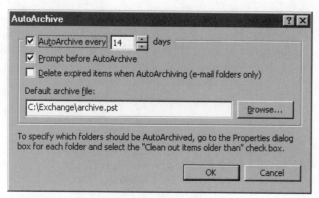

Figure 6-16: The AutoArchive dialog

NOTE   The Deleted Items folder's default AutoArchive settings are
            for a two-month cleanup and to *permanently delete old
            items* (this is the only folder that has "Permanently delete
            old items" set from the factory). If you prefer archival to de-
            letion for the Deleted Items folder, be sure to change this
            setting.

- Inbox—off

- Journal—on (six months)

- Notes—off

- Sent Items—on (two months)

- Tasks—on (six months)

Set each of your folders' AutoArchive options in accordance with your
own preferences and remember, please be sure to do a routine daily
backup that includes your *mailbox.pst* and *archive.pst* files (and
mailbox.pab, if you use a PAB).

NOTE   How do you set the "Do Not AutoArchive" property for an
            individual item? It's buried in a very obscure place: open
            the item and choose File → Properties, then check the "Do
            not AutoArchive this item" box.

7

Beyond the Basics

Getting information into Outlook consists primarily of filling out forms for the various items, as discussed in Chapter 5, *Outlook's Key Ingredients*, or of bringing the data into Outlook *in bulk* via the import and conversion processes, covered in Chapter 6, *A Cookbook for Conversion*. In this chapter, we focus on how you *use* Outlook—on the tips and tricks to make it do useful things, both when it's behaving nicely and when you bump into some of the stranger annoyances that lurk under the surface.

Finding, Viewing, and Filtering

Once you have all your information in Outlook, life's a breeze, right? Not quite. You still have to be able to *find* the one piece of information you need that's floating somewhere in the data-sea, and if your workday is anything like ours, you probably need to find it in a big hurry. Outlook is pretty handy at letting you slice and dice your data without folding, spindling, or mutilating it.

New and Simplified Find

Outlook 98 introduces a simplified Find feature with a decidedly Web-like interface. To perform a simple search on the current facility, click on the Find button on the toolbar (or Tools → Find from the menus) and the Find pane appears at the top of the facility's display data (see Figure 7-1).

By default the checkbox "Search all text in the contact" is checked (where "contact" will change depending on what facility you're in at the time), and whatever you type in the "Look for" text box for your *search*

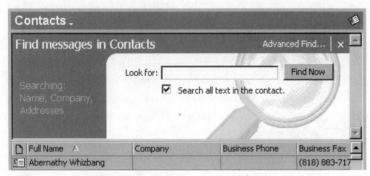

Figure 7-1: Outlook 98's kinder, gentler Find feature

criteria will be matched against text appearing anywhere in each record in the selected facility/folder. Uncheck the "Search all..." checkbox and only the fields shown at the left of the Find pane (Name, Company, and Addresses in the case of a Contacts folder) are searched.

WARNING   Be aware that assigned Categories are not treated like plain text within a field. For example, if an item is assigned to the Business category, you can search for "business," but the item won't be found. However, it will be found if the word "business" appears in, say, the Note field.

Type in the text to search for and click on the Find Now button. Simple. The Find pane changes when a search is completed, telling you that it's Done! and offering you two additional choices, "Go to Advanced Find..." and "Clear Search," as shown in Figure 7-2.

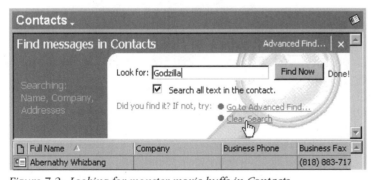

Figure 7-2: Looking for monster movie buffs in Contacts

Notice that both of these new options appear *grayed out*. According to Windows graphical user interface (GUI) standards, a selectable option that has turned gray means it is currently unavailable. But Microsoft is promoting a Web browser type of user interface here, and the underlining indicates a selectable option. Who knows why Microsoft elected to make the color a light gray, but it's very confusing and a tad annoying.

Put your mouse pointer over the text (or the Find Now button, for that matter) and instead of a northwest-pointing arrow mouse pointer you get the hypertext-pointing index finger pointer common to help files, Web browsers, and Office hyperlinks.

The Find pane is not sticky, so once you invoke it, it's only displayed while you are working in that particular facility. If you switch to another facility and then switch back, the Find pane is closed and you have to click on the Find button again to redisplay it. Likewise, it is not displayed across sessions; close Outlook with the Find pane displayed, and when you restart Outlook, the pane is gone. We'd like to see this fixed, along with providing user preference settings to govern whether the Find pane should (or should not) be persistent across facilities and Outlook sessions.

NOTE   Find doesn't report the number of matched items, but Advanced Find does. Also, Find doesn't remember your previous search phrases, but Advanced Find does, even across Outlook sessions.

Advanced Find

Searching is something you'll be doing a lot of; it's inherent in the very nature of databases. The Find pane in Outlook 98 may be more than adequate for your search needs, but if you need a bit more flexibility in your searching, especially the ability to search several facilities at once, then you need to utilize the Advanced Find feature. You can pop up the Advanced Find dialog from the Tools menu by pressing `Ctrl+Shift+F`, or by selecting Find from the Tools menu (Tools → Find Items in Outlook 97). You can also click on the Advanced Find button on your Outlook-Annoy Standard toolbar (see Figure 7-3).

NOTE   Outlook 97 did not have the Find feature at all. What was called Outlook 97's Find feature became Outlook 98's Advanced Find feature, so everything in this section applies to both Outlook 97 and 98.

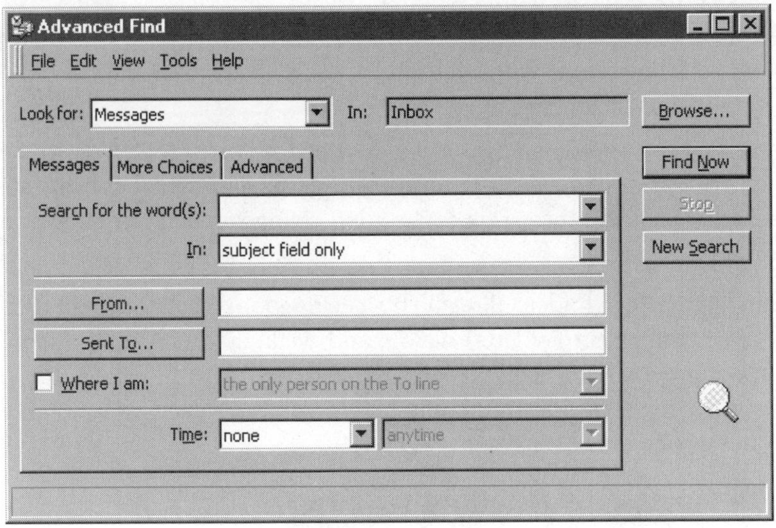

Figure 7-3: Searching for Messages

The Advanced Find dialog (the Find dialog in Outlook 97) is context-sensitive, and the choices in the "Look for" drop-down list and on the three option tabs depend on which facility is active when the dialog is opened. In Figure 7-3, the Inbox is the active facility. In Figure 7-4, the Calendar is the active facility.

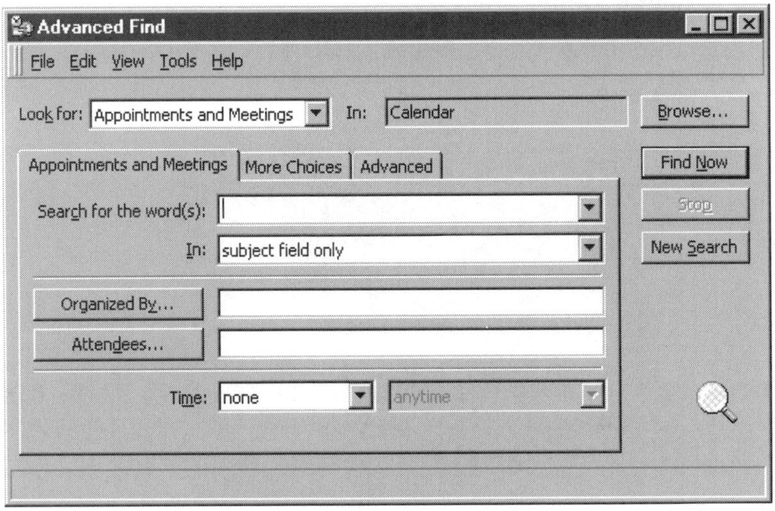

Figure 7-4: Searching for Appointments and Meetings

Most often, your basic search criteria consist of some text that you remember was somewhere in the message or the appointment description. You use the specialized controls like Organized By or Sent To in order to narrow a given search.

The "Look for" drop-down list lets you choose what folder is to be searched so you don't have to be in the correct facility when you initiate your search. Changing the "Look for" setting changes the folder shown in the "In" field.

You can also select folders directly by clicking on the Browse button, which opens the Select Folder(s) dialog, and walking your Personal Store file's folder tree. The Select Folder(s) dialog lets you choose multiple folders (including subfolders), thereby letting you search across a number of facilities at one time (see Figure 7-5).

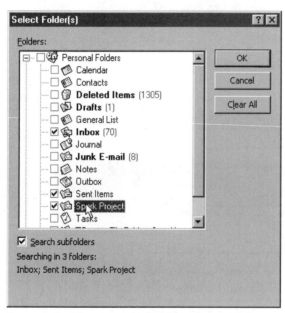

Figure 7-5: Selecting multiple folders for a search

On the Advanced tab, you can set criteria for any field found in any type of item, and you can set a criterion for more than one field (see Figure 7-6).

Once your search criteria have been entered, you click on the Find Now button to start the search. The search results appear in a scrollable window at the bottom of the Advanced Find dialog. You can open a record from the Advanced Find dialog simply by double-clicking on it (see Figure 7-7). This is different from using the Find pane in Outlook 98,

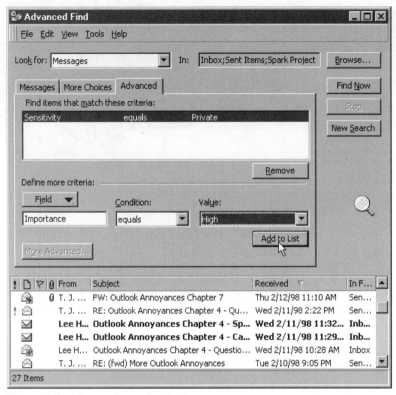

Figure 7-6: Advanced search criteria

where the search results are displayed right in the facility data area in Outlook.

The tools and techniques you use when searching for Outlook items are the same ones you'll use when filtering information to create custom views of your data, as you'll see in the following section.

How to Use and Customize Views

A view is simply a customizable collection of fields (and their formatting) for the current facility/folder. Changing a view has no effect on the underlying data, only on how it's displayed. Outlook provides a number of "pre-set" views for each facility, and you can easily create your own custom views. In Figure 7-8 for example, you see the Contact List displayed in the "Detailed Address Cards" view.

You can change views via a drop-down list that appears on the Outlook 98 Advanced toolbar (select View → Toolbars → Advanced to display it).

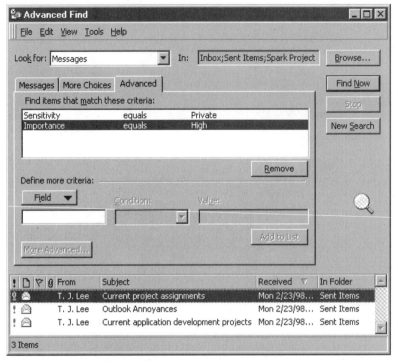

Figure 7-7: Search results displayed in the Advanced Find dialog

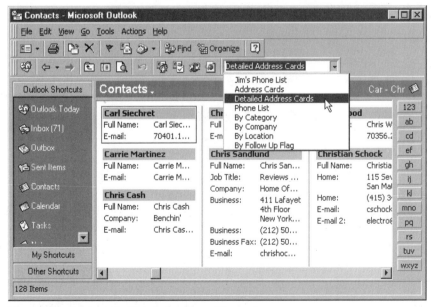

Figure 7-8: Contacts in Detailed Address Cards view

Or you can use View → Current View to display a cascading menu of view choices.

Phone List tip

If you use your Contact List as we do to quickly look up phone numbers or address information, you'll find the Phone List to be the most productive view. Switch to the Contacts facility, then pull down the View menu, click Current View, and then choose Phone List from the cascading menu. The Phone List view is shown in Figure 7-9.

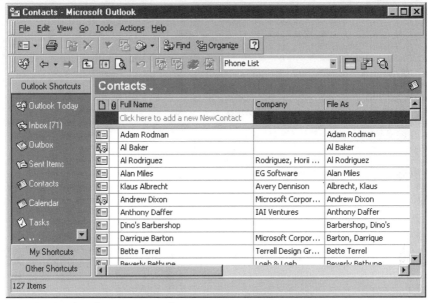

Figure 7-9: The Phone List view for Contacts

No, wait, come back! It really is useful; you just have to make it less annoying with a few customizations of this basic view. First, go to the View menu and click on Current View → Customize Current View → View Summary → Other Settings. (In Outlook 97, View → Format View.) The Other Settings dialog box appears, as shown in Figure 7-10.

First you need to decide how you want to deal with columns displayed in the Phone List view. You have two options. If you uncheck the "Automatic column sizing" parameter (it's labeled "Allow column sizing" in Outlook 97, but has the same effect), a horizontal scroll bar appears at the bottom of the Phone List display. This lets you set the width of each column and then scroll left and right if all the columns won't fit within

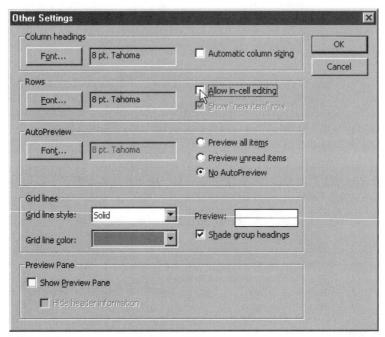

Figure 7-10: Formatting the Phone List view

the display. If you check the "Automatic column sizing" box, all the columns in the view are squished together in order to make them all fit into the display space.

Back in Figure 7-8 you saw the Detailed Address Cards view, which includes buttons along the right side of the window that let you drill down to a given part of the alphabet when looking up names. Unfortunately in the Phone List view, you get no such navigational aid. If you're like us, you'd like to be able to type a letter on the keyboard and have the displayed list jump directly to that letter.

NOTE   If you follow our tip and set up your Phone List to let you
            type a letter to jump the list to that part of the alphabet,
            you should be aware that what Outlook looks for in an al-
            phabetical search is the first character in the File As field.
            This trick works for any table view of information as long
            as in-cell editing is turned off for that view, as described in
            the next paragraph.

By default, if you type a letter key when in this view, Outlook assumes you want to create a new contact record and lets you type in the Full

Name field in the entry record shown as the first line of the Phone List view. To force Outlook to search alphabetically when you type a letter, you need to uncheck the "Allow in-cell editing" checkbox in the Other Settings dialog box (it's the Format Table View dialog in Outlook 97). Then if you type a letter, you'll get the first contact that begins with that letter (as defined in the "File As" field). Type another letter *very quickly* and you get the first contact that starts with both letters. If there are no contacts that have both letters, the second letter is treated as a new search and you get the first record that begins with that letter. You'll value this very fast and easy (to say nothing of intuitive) way to search your Contacts list.

Next, select View → Current View → Customize Current View → Fields (in Outlook 97, select View → Show Fields). From the Show Fields dialog, you can add and remove fields so your Phone List displays only the information of interest to you (see Figure 7-11).

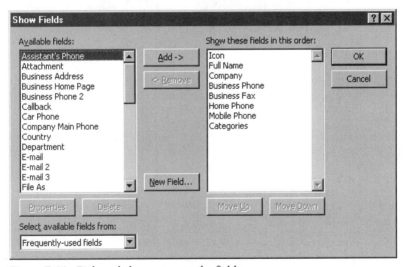

Figure 7-11: Pick and choose among the fields

In Outlook 97 if the view is customized in this manner be aware that changes made on the fly are temporary. When you next change views, you'll see the warning dialog shown in Figure 7-12. You can simply discard the changes (the default setting), update the current view with your changes (the third choice, and one we don't recommend), or you can create a custom view (the second choice).

This changed radically in Outlook 98. Now any changes you make to a view are *automatically* treated as if you had checked the "Discard the current view settings" option. You don't get the dialog box asking what

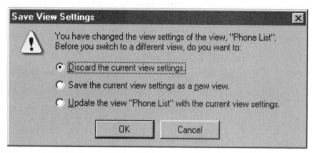

Figure 7-12: Three choices for temporary view changes in Outlook 97

you want to do, it just happens. This means it's easy to permanently change your views. The way to deal with this is to create custom views, which give you the flexibility to keep the preset views intact and let you experiment on potentially more effective ways of presenting your data.

NOTE   In Chapter 2, *Vital Changes, Settings, and Customizations,*
                we discussed Outlook's start-up switches. The /clean-
                views switch can reset all your default views back to their
                factory settings, which is handy if you wind up with chang-
                es to your views that you don't want. It also wipes out any
                custom views, so be careful with it. As mentioned in the
                previous paragraph, we recommend you keep the default
                settings in their original state and create custom views to
                present your data just the way you like it.

Custom views

Each facility has a number of built-in views you can choose from (View → Current View), and we strongly suggest you experiment with each one to see if Outlook already has a ready-made view that suits your needs. But if there is no built-in view that brings you nirvana, you can and should create your own.

Let's say none of the provided calendar views tickle your fancy and you just want a view that lists all appointments chronologically in a table (list) format. No problem. Here's how to do it:

1. Switch to the Calendar facility.

2. Pull down the View menu and choose Current View → Define Views (in Outlook 97, View → Define Views), then click on the New button in the Define Views for Calendar dialog box (see Figure 7-13).

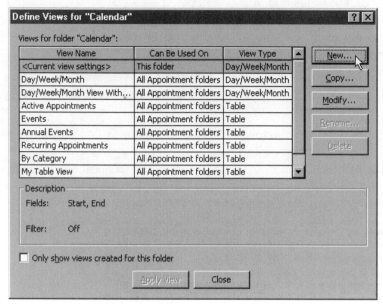

Figure 7-13: Creating a custom view

3. Select Table as the type of view, type in a name for your custom view (in our example, "My Table View"), and because you want this view available in any folder that houses appointment information, check the "All Appointment folders" option button. Next click on OK in the Create a New View dialog box.

4. The View Summary dialog appears (see Figure 7-14).

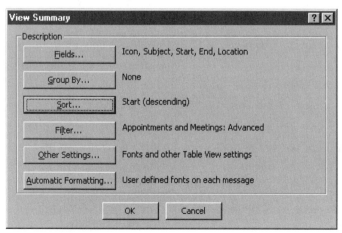

Figure 7-14: Setting up View parameters

5. Click on the Fields button and select the Fields you want displayed in your custom view. Click on OK when you've got the fields you want displayed in the order in which you want them. (We'll cover Outlook's Group By feature in just a bit.)

6. Click on the Sort button and determine how you want the records sorted when first displayed. In our example, we opted for sorting by the Start field in descending order.

7. Click on the Filters button. You'll notice that filtering a custom view utilizes the same dialog box and controls that you saw earlier when doing Advanced Find, and they work in an identical manner (see Figure 7-15). In our example we used the Advanced tab to display any items whose Start field met the built-in "anytime" condition.

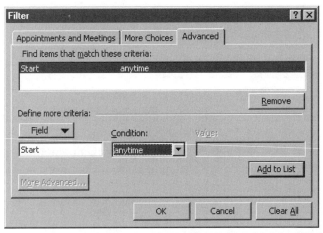

Figure 7-15: Filtering is identical to the Advanced Find controls

8. Click Other Settings to format your table (similar to the Other Settings dialog you saw in Figure 7-10). To close the View Summary dialog, click on OK.

9. You're now back in the original "Define Views for Calendar" dialog box. Click on Close.

Now whenever you're in the Calendar facility, you can display your custom view (View → Custom View → My Table View). Our example, "My Table View," is shown in Figure 7-16.

Finally, the Start and End columns are not optimal for what we want—they're too wide. Format the individual columns in a view by right-clicking on the column heading and choosing Format Columns from the pop-up menu. (In Outlook 97 click on View → Format Columns.) We set

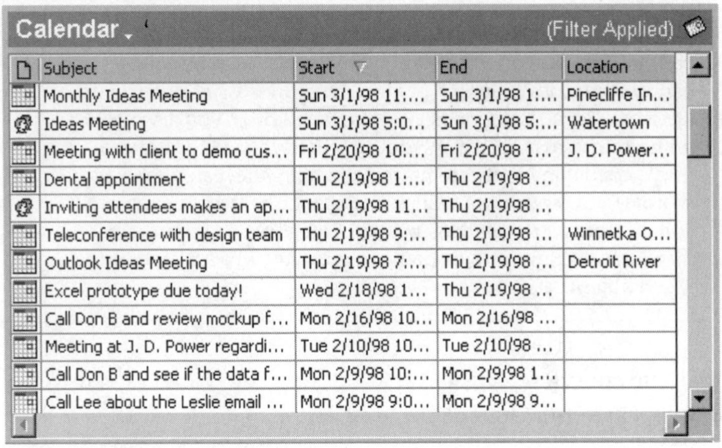

Calendar (Filter Applied)

	Subject	Start	End	Location
	Monthly Ideas Meeting	Sun 3/1/98 11:...	Sun 3/1/98 1:...	Pinecliffe In...
	Ideas Meeting	Sun 3/1/98 5:0...	Sun 3/1/98 5:...	Watertown
	Meeting with client to demo cus...	Fri 2/20/98 10:...	Fri 2/20/98 1...	J. D. Power...
	Dental appointment	Thu 2/19/98 1:...	Thu 2/19/98 ...	
	Inviting attendees makes an ap...	Thu 2/19/98 11...	Thu 2/19/98 ...	
	Teleconference with design team	Thu 2/19/98 9:...	Thu 2/19/98 ...	Winnetka O...
	Outlook Ideas Meeting	Thu 2/19/98 7:...	Thu 2/19/98 ...	Detroit River
	Excel prototype due today!	Wed 2/18/98 1...	Thu 2/19/98 ...	
	Call Don B and review mockup f...	Mon 2/16/98 10...	Mon 2/16/98 ...	
	Meeting at J. D. Power regardi...	Tue 2/10/98 10...	Tue 2/10/98 ...	
	Call Don B and see if the data f...	Mon 2/9/98 10:...	Mon 2/9/98 1...	
	Call Lee about the Leslie email ...	Mon 2/9/98 9:0...	Mon 2/9/98 9...	

Figure 7-16: My Table View

the Start column to show the day, date, and time, but the End column to only show the time (see Figure 7-17).

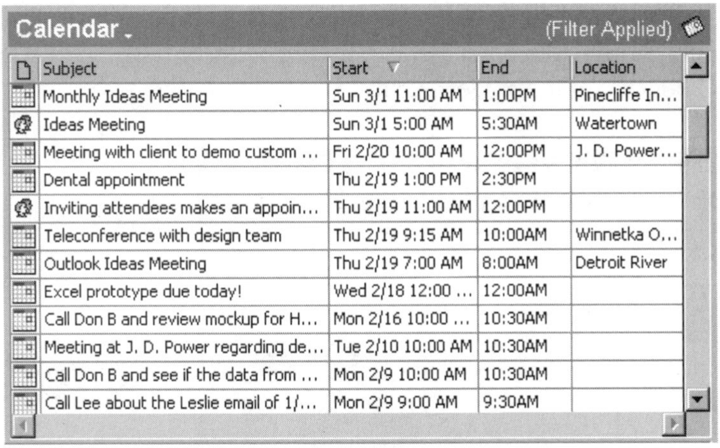

Calendar (Filter Applied)

	Subject	Start	End	Location
	Monthly Ideas Meeting	Sun 3/1 11:00 AM	1:00PM	Pinecliffe In...
	Ideas Meeting	Sun 3/1 5:00 AM	5:30AM	Watertown
	Meeting with client to demo custom ...	Fri 2/20 10:00 AM	12:00PM	J. D. Power...
	Dental appointment	Thu 2/19 1:00 PM	2:30PM	
	Inviting attendees makes an appoin...	Thu 2/19 11:00 AM	12:00PM	
	Teleconference with design team	Thu 2/19 9:15 AM	10:00AM	Winnetka O...
	Outlook Ideas Meeting	Thu 2/19 7:00 AM	8:00AM	Detroit River
	Excel prototype due today!	Wed 2/18 12:00 ...	12:00AM	
	Call Don B and review mockup for H...	Mon 2/16 10:00 ...	10:30AM	
	Meeting at J. D. Power regarding de...	Tue 2/10 10:00 AM	10:30AM	
	Call Don B and see if the data from ...	Mon 2/9 10:00 AM	10:30AM	
	Call Lee about the Leslie email of 1/...	Mon 2/9 9:00 AM	9:30AM	

Figure 7-17: Each column can be individually formatted

Filtering Views by Categories

We started this chapter talking about how to search for information in Outlook. Filtering is just an extension of the searching concept. You filter a view so that it only shows you items that match your search criteria, your *filter*. We've found that the filtering we do most often involves filtering by Categories.

NOTE   As we discussed back in Chapter 4, *Enigmatic Journal,* you
                can assign categories to items you create in Outlook. You
                can use any of Outlook's built-in categories or you can cre-
                ate your own. Categories are like keywords you associate
                with your items. This way you can filter your views by cate-
                gory, displaying only items that contain the category key-
                word(s) you specify. A minor annoyance is that you cannot
                sort a table view of data by the Categories column, since
                there may be more than one category keyword assigned to
                a given item.

To filter the current view, click View → Current View → Customize
Current View → Filter (in Outlook 97, just View → Filter) and you'll see
the Filter dialog box. If you want to change the filter of a custom view,
click View → Current View → Define View, select your extant custom
view, and click on Modify, then Filter (see Figure 7-18). This three-tab
dialog contains the same search controls you saw earlier when doing
Advanced Find searches in Outlook 98. The first tab has search criteria
controls unique to the facility you are filtering. The More Choices tab
allows you to choose which categories an item must be associated with
in order to be included in the view results.

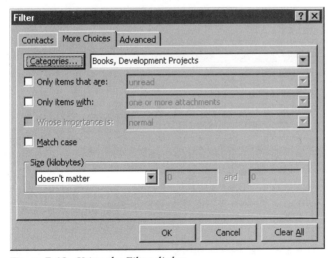

Figure 7-18: Using the Filter dialog

The More Choices tab's Categories drop-down list keeps track of the last
five category settings you've used, assuming you might want to reuse the
same criteria. Click on the Categories button to select from any categories

to filter the view (see Figure 7-19). Note that if you include multiple categories, Outlook connects them with a logical OR for the search, so that an item with any category specified is returned.

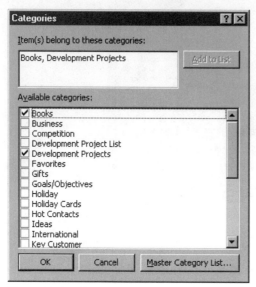

Figure 7-19: Choosing categories to filter the view

The third tab in Figure 7-18 is the Advanced tab. Here you can specify filter criteria based on the fields found in the type of item stored in the facility in which you are working. You pick the field by clicking on the Field button, then choosing the condition from the drop-down list. Finally, you specify a value for the test and then add the criterion to the list. You can specify multiple criteria, but Outlook applies the logical OR to them all (see Figure 7-20).

Once you have specified all the criteria for filtering your data, click on OK. If you want to rapidly unwind the filter, return to the Filter dialog and click on the Clear All button, then click on OK. To create a filter that you can use whenever you want, use a custom view and add your filtering criteria by clicking on the Filter button shown in Figure 7-14.

The "Group By" Feature

Every Outlook item is made up of a number of fields (Full Name, Job Title, Categories, etc.). You can *group* items displayed in a table view by the type of information contained in a field. For example, in your Contact List, each record is a person, and we usually think of contacts in terms of a collection of individual names. But if you group your Contact List by

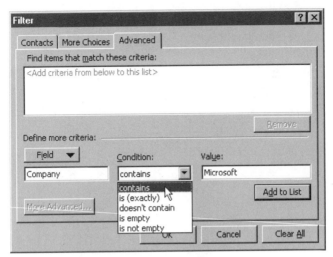

Figure 7-20: Advanced filter criteria

the Company field, you now have a collection of companies: all contact items are now segregated into groups by company name, with a general catchall of "none" for those entries that have no entry in the Company field.

You can further refine this feature by grouping items first by Company and then by Department. You get a table view showing all the companies in an expandable outline form. Expand a given company and you see the various Departments, with all the individual contacts for that company grouped by department (see Figure 7-21).

When you group information, the records are shown in an outline view with all the headings expanded to show you the detail for all records. To give you a better idea of how grouping can be used, we've "rolled-up" the outline shown in Figure 7-21 and have only expanded the record for PRIME Consulting Group, Inc., letting you see the three department groups that are one level below the Company field. Each department can then be expanded to show all the individual contacts for that department.

If you've worked with outlines in Excel, then this will look very familiar to you. To group information, you first select the facility you want to work with—remember that it has to be displayed in a table or timeline type view—then select View → Current View → Customize Current View → Group By, which displays the Group By dialog box. As shown in Figure 7-22, you can group records up to four levels. (Don't forget that changes to a view are saved automatically in Outlook 98, so always create a custom view if you don't want changes to the default view saved.)

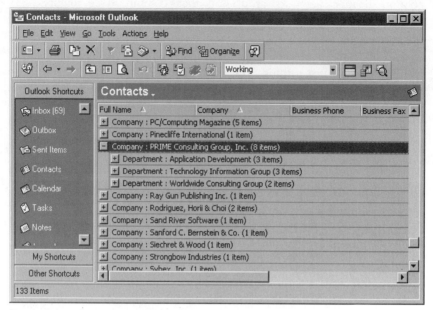

Figure 7-21: Contacts grouped by Company, then by Department

Figure 7-22: Setting up groups and subgroups

Outlook 97 sports a very cool drag-and-drop interface, allowing you to bypass the Group By dialog. In Outlook 97, pull down the View menu and click on the Group By Box option. This causes a space to appear above the field names in your view, along with the instruction "Drag a column header here to group by that column" (see Figure 7-23). Grouping is as simple as clicking on a column heading and dragging it up into the Group By Box. As in the Group By dialog box, you can only have four levels to a group. Be careful though. If you start dragging a heading without first turning on the Group By Box (or if you fail to drop the column heading within the Group By Box), that column is removed from the view. This is the equivalent of selecting View → Show Fields and removing a field from the show list in Outlook 97. When Microsoft opted to simplify Outlook's interface for the 98 version, this drag-and-drop grouping feature bit the cyberdust.

Figure 7-23: Outlook 97's Grouping by drag-and-drop

If you group data using the Group By dialog box (in either Outlook 98 or 97), the "Show field in view" checkbox is checked by default (meaning this field will still appear as a column in the view). Annoyingly, if you drag-and-drop, this setting is not checked, so if you want this field to quickly re-appear in the table view, select View → Group By, then check the "Show field in view" checkbox and click on OK. However, this puts the field at the far right of the display, not back to its original position in the field order, so you may have to readjust the column order.

Also, it's not as easy as you might think to unwind a grouping. If you call up the Group By dialog box and click on the Clear All button followed by the OK button, the group is removed. But any grouped fields that do not have the "Show field in view" button checked are removed from the view, and you'll have to add them back manually. Very annoying. In Outlook 97, you can ungroup via drag-and-drop by simply dragging any field from the Group By Box back to its proper position in the view.

User Interface Tips

Let's start off with some simple things that you need to know when working day in and day out with Outlook that are somewhat less than obvious.

A Date by Any Other Name

One of the highly touted IntelliSense™* features found in Office is Outlook's automatic date-recognition feature. While many of Microsoft's massively over-hyped IntelliSense features are really "IntelliNonSense," its implementation in Outlook is impressive. Automatic date recognition is a big winner.

Anywhere you might want to enter a date when creating (or modifying) an Outlook item, you can type in a plain language equivalent line such as "a week from Tuesday," and Outlook will calculate the exact date for you. A few examples of the text typed into the Start day field found in an Appointment or Task item and what Outlook returns are shown in Table 7-1. All examples assume the current date is July 1, 1998.

Table 7-1: Outlook's automatic date-recognition feature

Type This in a Date Field	Outlook Calculates This Date
Ten days from today	7/11/98
12 days from yesterday	7/12/98
in two weeks	7/15/98
three days	7/04/98
tenth of next month	8/10/98

What's more, say you've set a Start date for 7/29/98. Select that date and type "five days" into the date field and the date changes to 8/3/98. Impressive indeed.

Folder Hierarchy View

Outlook is chock full of new and completely non-standard user interface features. Take the Outlook Bar. Please. Actually, the Outlook Bar is sort of a throwback to pre-tabbed dialog box days (circa Word 2) when Microsoft tinkered around with displaying a number of icons on the left side of a dialog box that determined what options were displayed on the right side. Ah, but we digress.

The Outlook Bar...some love it, and some find it annoying. If you're in this latter group, you'll be glad to know that you can do something about

---

* Here's a little known fact. Microsoft claims a trademark on IntelliSense, and uses it rather liberally (even indiscriminately) for any MS product feature the marketing folks think is cool enough to sell more software. Whirlpool also claims a trademark for the term Intellisense™. In Whirlpool's case, the word refers to their washing machines' ability to determine how much water is in the tub. There's a metaphysical hyperlink lurking in there somewhere.

it. Like replace the Outlook Bar altogether with a folder hierarchy view, which is very similar to how Exchange—Outlook's predecessor—looks.

On the View menu in Outlook, click on the Folder List option and uncheck the Outlook Bar setting. This presents your Outlook folders in a tree view (see Figure 7-24). If you have screen real estate to burn, you can display both the Outlook Bar and the Folder List at the same time.

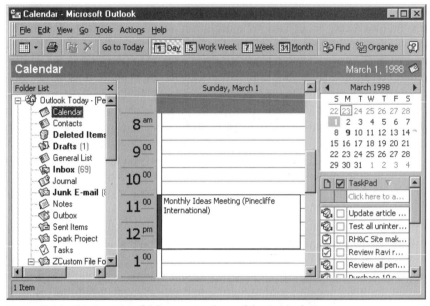

Figure 7-24: Display your folder tree in place of the Outlook Bar

Right-Mouse-Clicks Galore

There are several interesting things you can do with the right mouse button in Outlook. If you don't want to change the currently displayed facility, right-click the facility you want in the Outlook bar and choose "Open in New Window." Figure 7-25, for example, shows a Notes window opened in this manner while the Calendar facility is open in the main Outlook window.

You can open several facilities inside different windows in this manner. If you leave them open and you exit by using File → Exit and Log Off, they'll be restored automatically when next you start Outlook.

In Calendar, you can right-click on the daily times column, the TaskPad bar, on an item in the list of tasks, or on the gray bar that shows today's date. Each of these pops up a separate menu making a number of settings and actions that are only two mouse clicks away. This applies to

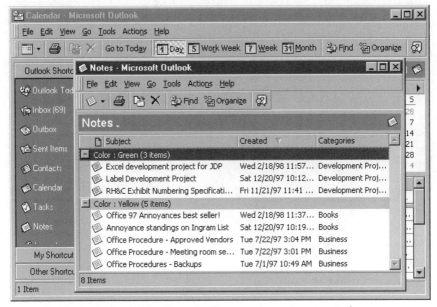

Figure 7-25: Outlook with the Notes facility open in a separate window

most of the facilities in Outlook; when in doubt, just right-click on something to see if there's an underlying shortcut menu lurking about.

Enable Horizontal Scroll Bars

Do you get annoyed when columns in your table views get squished more and more as you display more columns? Us too. The bad news is that automatic column sizing is turned on for that facility. The good news is that you can easily enable a horizontal scroll bar, so if you want more fields displayed than comfortably fit onscreen, they won't get squished so small as to make readability a joke.

Select any table view for a facility. For example, switch Contacts to Phone List view (View → Current View → Phone List). Then on the View menu, select Current View → Customize Current View → Other Settings and uncheck the "Automatic column sizing" checkbox.

Categories

Outlook lets you assign items to various categories, which is quite useful, especially when you want to search for different types of data in Outlook that are somehow related. You may be working on a big project that involves a number of contacts, meetings, appointments, tasks, and notes. If you want to gather a list of all these items for review, use categories.

Think of categories as keywords. You stick a keyword in a field and later you can search and filter based on that keyword. Keywords in Outlook are called categories. It's as simple as that.

Assigning Categories

Outlook starts you off with a number of built-in categories. Select any item in an Outlook facility and from the Edit menu, click on Categories (see Figure 7-26).

Figure 7-26: Outlook's Categories dialog box

If the selected item has been assigned to a category, that category is checked in the available categories list and it appears in the "Item(s) belong to these categories" text box. You check the box next to any of the categories to which you want to assign the current item.

You can create your own custom categories in one of two ways. First, you can open the Categories dialog box and just type the category name into the "Item(s) belong to these categories" text box, then click on the Add to List button. According to the sparse documentation, this should only add the new category to the active facility, but we've found that it adds the category to the Master Category List as well. You can add multiple categories by separating the entries with a comma. Second, you can open the Master Category List dialog box, which is discussed in the next section.

The Master Category List

If you click on the Master Category List button in the Categories dialog box, the Master Category List dialog box is displayed (see Figure 7-27).

Figure 7-27: Working with the Master Category List

In the Master Category List dialog box, you can *both* add and delete categories, as well as reset the list. Be very careful with the Reset button, however. It offers to return Outlook's factory category settings, and wipes out any and all custom categories you've created. You do get a chance to reconsider, since it displays the warning message shown in Figure 7-28.

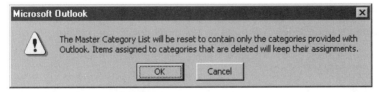

Figure 7-28: Resetting the Master Category List

WARNING   The OK button is the default selection in this warning dialog. A slip of the finger can be disastrous unless you do in fact want to remove all your custom categories.

Searching for Items by Category

Once categories are assigned, you can filter your views by category (as discussed earlier in this chapter) and search for items across facilities by category. Let's say you want to find all items assigned to the "Books" category:

1. From the Tools menu select the Advanced Find option (Tools → Find in Outlook 97).

2. In the "Look for" drop-down list, select "Any type of Outlook item."

3. Click on the More Choices tab. Click on the Categories button and choose the category (or categories) you want to search for from the Categories dialog box. Click on OK.

4. Click on the Find Now button.

All Outlook facilities are searched and the results returned in the Advanced Find dialog box. This list of items can be treated like any other view in Outlook. You can sort the results by left-clicking on a column heading, or right-clicking on a heading and grouping, customizing, or formatting the view by making the appropriate selection from the pop-up menu (see Figure 7-29).

Reminders

In Outlook 97, *reminders* (pop-up alerts that are triggered at a pre-set time) can only be set for calendar items such as Appointments, Meetings, and Events, and for task items. Outlook 98 also has follow-up alerts for Contact items (and email messages, both inbound and outbound). Reminders are set for some time interval preceding the scheduled time of the appointment (see Figure 7-30).

Reminder Sounds

The interval you set determines how far in advance of the scheduled time the reminder will pop up. You can select from the drop-down list or type some interval of your own. The small speaker icon to the right of the drop-down lets you set the *.WAV* sound file to be played when that particular reminder is triggered (see Figure 7-31).

To change the reminder sound globally in Outlook 98, click on Tools → Options → Other → Advanced Options → Reminder Options, and change the default sound file setting. (In Outlook 97 click Tools → Options → Reminders.)

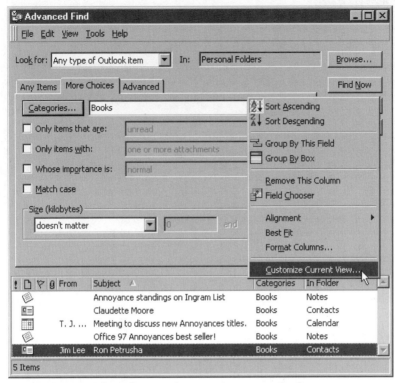

Figure 7-29: Searching for items by Categories across facilities

Figure 7-30: Setting a reminder for an appointment item

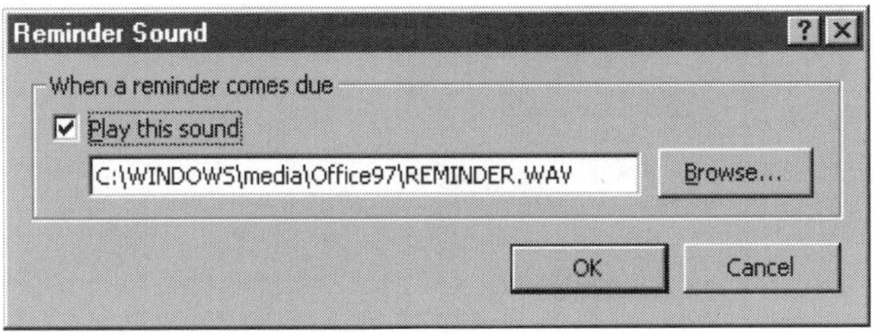

Figure 7-31: Choosing a reminder sound file

Task Reminders

Reminders for Task items work a little differently. A task reminder can be set for any date and time independently of the task due date or start date (as long as it is sometime in the future). To accomplish this, click on a date on the calendar that appears when you click the reminder pull-down (or you can type in a date or plain language equivalent). The pull-down calendar is shown in Figure 7-32.

Figure 7-32: Setting a task reminder

Intractable Postponements

When a reminder is triggered, you can dismiss it, open the underlying item, or postpone it. Despite the flexibility with dates and times in other aspects of Outlook, you cannot postpone a reminder for any length of time that is not provided on the drop-down list. This limitation is most annoying (see Figure 7-33).

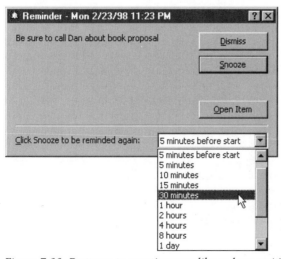

Figure 7-33: Postpone to any time you like as long as it's on the drop-down list

Set a Recurring Activity

Some of your calendar activities occur with regularity. The daily mid-morning staff meeting. The weekly sales team get-together on Fridays for breakfast. Perhaps a monthly meeting in which your department is completely reorganized (this occurs more frequently than you might realize, especially if you work at Microsoft). Entering all these recurring items manually would be time consuming and tedious. Fear not, Outlook provides for recurring items.

Create your calendar item, pull down the Action menu, and click on the Recurrence option (or click on the Recurrence button on the toolbar). This displays the Appointment Recurrence dialog box, shown in Figure 7-34.

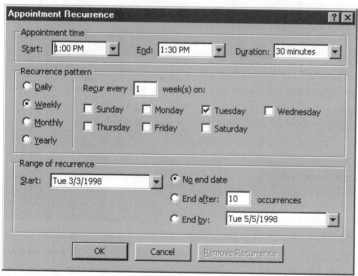

Figure 7-34: Setting a recurring appointment

Enter the recurrence pattern by checking the appropriate option buttons, checkboxes, and the range of times over which you want the item to recur. Tasks can also be set up as recurring items. In a task item, pull down the Action menu and click on the Recurrence option (or click on the Recurrence button on the toolbar). The Task Recurrence dialog box is almost identical to the one for appointments (see Figure 7-35).

Editing a recurring item adds a new wrinkle. Outlook considers a recurring *task* item as one seed item with numerous clone tasks extending off into the future; however, *the clone tasks are not individually editable.* Outlook considers a recurring *calendar* (appointment, meeting, or event)

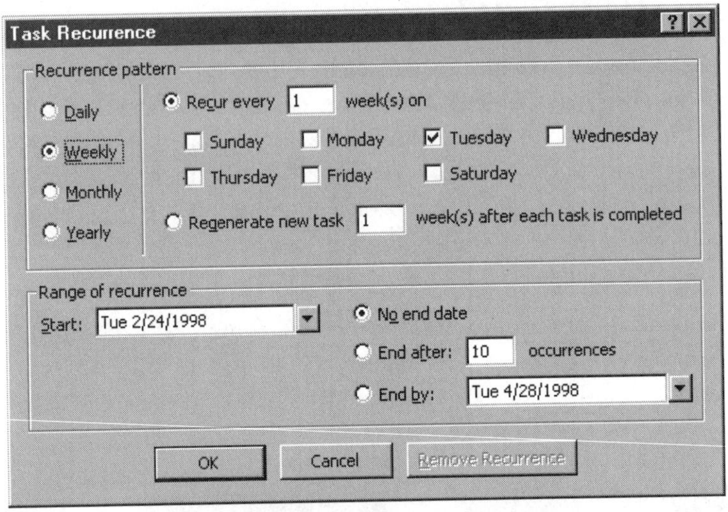

Figure 7-35: Setting a recurring task item

item as a series of individual—and independently editable—items. Quick proof: create a recurring task, open it, and Outlook opens it normally. Now create a recurring appointment, open it (today's instance of the appointment or any future instance thereof), and you have two choices: open the single occurrence (the one item you have selected) or the entire *series*. If you opt for the single occurrence and make a change, the change will only be reflected in that one item. If you open the series, it looks like you're only editing the one item, but any changes are reflected *in all items* for that recurring series.

To delete an entire series of recurring items at one time, open the item (in the case of a task, open the seed task; in the case of a calendar item, open either the single instance or the series), then click on the Recurrence button and then on the Remove Recurrence button. This deletes all the recurring items *except* the one instance of the item you have open. The fastest way to delete all items in a recurring series—including the one at hand—is to select it and choose Edit → Delete. Outlook will display a dialog box and allow you to delete all, delete this one, or cancel.

Recurring Reminders

Reminders are an attribute of an item (like a task, contact, or event), so there is no reminder item *per se.* You can display items that have reminders, but what if you want a reminder without an actual appointment on your calendar to which to attach the reminder? You create reminders for which the associated item is *not* displayed.

For example, you want to be reminded every day at 10:00 A.M., 2:00 P.M., and 4:00 P.M. to imbibe your favorite soft drink, but you don't want to see daily appointments for this Epicurean excess cluttering up your calendar. Here's what you do:

1. Create a custom category by selecting an item and clicking on Categories on the Edit menu. Name it `Reminders`.

2. Create a recurring appointment item for the appropriate time and be sure to assign it to the Reminders category you created in step 1.

3. In your Calendar facility, pull down the View menu and select Current View → Customize Current View, and then click on the Filter option. (In Outlook 97, View → Filter.) In the Filter dialog, click on the Advanced tab.

TIP   You can avoid the menu shuffle of getting to the View Summary dialog to customize a view if you can right-click on an unused portion of the currently displayed facility (this works for any facility, by the way, although in some views you might have to look hard for open space to right-click on). For example, in the Calendar view, right-click on a portion of the daily appointment area that does not have an appointment on it. From the resulting pop-up menu, you can select the Customize Current View option. This works both in Outlook 98 and Outlook 97, although the latter's pop-up commands are worded a bit differently.

---

4. Define a criteria to hide any items where Categories doesn't contain the value "Reminders," as shown in Figure 7-36. Click on Add to List, then click on OK.

5. In Outlook 98 the filter kicks in immediately. In Outlook 97 you have to refresh your calendar view (View → Current View → Day/Week/ Month) and when prompted, check the 'Update the view "Day/Week/ Month" with the current settings' option button and click on OK.

The recurring times won't be displayed on your calendar, but the reminders will fire off as scheduled. Bottoms up.

Get Email Smart

Email is probably the most important and most annoying aspect of computer life today, no matter what software you're using. Here are some tips on getting along with Outlook on a day-to-day messaging basis.

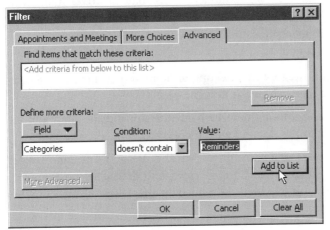

Figure 7-36: Filter out any calendar items in the Reminders category

Message Headers

The term "message header" has a couple of different meanings in Outlook. First, there is the Message Header option found on the View menu of each email item (in Outlook 97, click the Message Header button on the open message's toolbar). This controls how much of the received email message header is displayed when that item is opened. Normally, you see the From, To, Cc, and Subject lines, which eat up an annoying amount of screen space. (In Outlook 97, you see Message and Options tabs, too.) Most of the time, you only need to see whom the message was from and what it says; just toggle the Message Header off from the View menu and you see only the From line (in Outlook 97, click on the Message Header button), as shown in Figure 7-37.

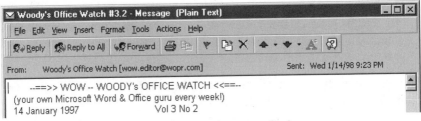

Figure 7-37: Use Message Header to control message display

In outgoing messages, you can reduce the header to just the To line; even the Subject field disappears. This may be too much screen economy, though—we always recommend you put a subject in your messages.

The other header we refer to in Outlook is on the Options panel of received messages. Open a message and from the View menu select Options. (In Outlook 97, click on the Options tab—turn your Message Header back on if you don't see your Options tab—and at the bottom of the message you'll see a scrollable window labeled "Internet headers.") This shows you the actual message header that is part of the email data stream. It's full of all kinds of arcane stuff, but if you puzzle through it, you can see every transaction for a message as it traversed across the great Internet void (see Figure 7-38).

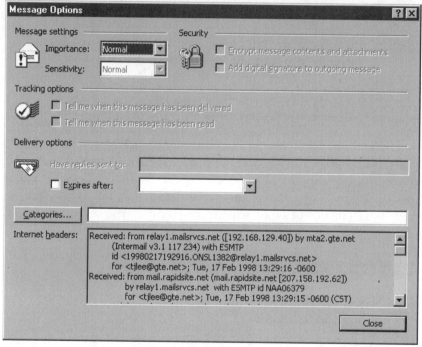

Figure 7-38: Puzzle out the many and varied stops on the road to your Inbox

Flags and Reminders on Incoming Messages

If you're like a lot of Outlook users, you probably let incoming messages stack up in your Inbox until you can deal with them. Email drives us on a day-to-day basis. Messages come in every day asking you to do this or that, or you get a reminder about something that's overdue, or maybe someone sends you a URL that "you've just got to see," and so on. Most of us run triage on our Inbox several times a day, dealing with the most immediate issues of the moment, deleting whatever we can, and letting everything else pile up to the cyberrafters. How can you manage this constant influx of messages? Flags can help, as can transmuting emails into tasks (as discussed in Chapter 6's "Transmogrify with AutoCreate" section).

Incoming flags

In Chapter 5 we discussed how you set flags for outgoing messages. The flag feature can also help you manage your incoming messages. There are two ways to set a flag on a message. First, you can right-click on a message line in the Inbox (or in any email type folder) and choose Flag for Follow Up from the pop-up menu to display the Flag for Follow Up dialog box.

NOTE   In Outlook 97, right-clicking and choosing Flag Message
            from the pop-up menu sets the flag. You actually have to
            open the message and click on the Flag button on the tool-
            bar in order to choose from the other types of flags avail-
            able or to create your own custom flags. You cannot set
            reminders for flags in Outlook 97.

You can also set a flag by opening a message and clicking on the Flag icon on the message's toolbar to display the Flag for Follow Up dialog box (see Figure 7-39). "Follow up" is the default flag, but as you can see, there are a number of other settings, or you can type in your own flag message.

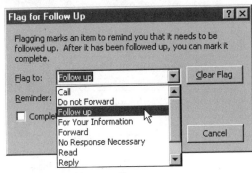

Figure 7-39: Setting a flag type

A flagged message shows up in the Inbox with a red flag in the flag column (see Figure 7-40). The message can be marked as completed by calling up the Flag for Follow Up dialog and checking the Completed checkbox. This changes the flag icon to a clear flag (it almost appears grayed out). Lastly, you can clear the message flag entirely—again via the Flag for Follow Up dialog—by clicking on the Clear Flag button. When you clear the flag, there is no icon displayed at all (as though the message had never been flagged). A message with no set flag is considered by Outlook to have a "Normal" flag. More on this in a moment.

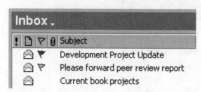

Figure 7-40: The first message's status is Flagged, the second Completed, and the third is Normal

What makes all this flagging worthwhile, you ask? If you're struggling to keep all the messages flooding into your Inbox organized, it's very worthwhile. As you read each message in your Inbox, you assign it a flag. Use the flag text Outlook provides or create custom flags like "PANIC TIME! Do this now!" or "Read later." The flag text shows up in the message information area (see Figure 7-41).

Figure 7-41: Flag text appears in the information area

While you can type custom flag text, it is not added to the drop-down list or remembered. And you can't change the default flag text—the flag selected when you open the Flag for Follow Up dialog for an unflagged message—it's always "Follow up." It's most annoying that Outlook does not support a way to add items to the drop-down list and to reset the default choice.

Flags can let you add text to the information area of a message, as you've seen. You can also filter your displayed list of email messages by their flag settings. Click View → Current View → By Follow Up Flag (By Message Flag in Outlook 97). This sorts the messages into three main categories, or what Outlook calls Flag Status. A message has a flag status of "Flagged," "Completed," or "Normal" (in Outlook 97 this last category is called "(none)"). Expand the Flagged category and then sort the list by the Follow Up Flag column, as we have done in Figure 7-42. This sorts the messages alphabetically according to the text of the flag message.

! ▯ ◌ Follow Up Flag ▵	Due By	From	Subject

Pending Emails .

▣ Flag Status : Flagged (4 items)

	Follow up	None	Klaus Al...	International Installation
	Must discuss with Lee ASAP	None	Lori Ash	RE: Microsoft Office & Visual ...
	PANIC TIME! Do this now!	None	Bill Brad...	Cantina Frame Scripts
	PANIC! Act on this now!	None	Vincent...	GetAddress()

▣ Flag Status : Completed (4 items)

	Follow up	None	Steve....	PCG Feedback
	Follow up	None	Vincent...	RE: Ideas Meeting
	Follow up	None	mcc@w...	RE: WOW Annoyances Alley
	PANIC TIME! Do this now!	None	Vincent...	Current book projects

▣ Flag Status : (none) (2 items)

		None	Lee Hu...	Annoyances FAQ on our site...
		None	Katie G...	O'Reilly Transitions

Figure 7-42: Messages viewed by Message Flag and sorted by flag message text

---

NOTE   Creating custom email type folders into which you can sort
              and hold different types of incoming messages would let
              you further organize email messages.

Reminder flags

Outlook 98 has a very cool new feature that allows you not only to flag a
message, but to set a reminder for it also. This effectively gives the
message a due date. Outstanding! In the Flag for Follow Up dialog box,
click on the Reminder drop-down list and select a date from the
displayed calendar (see Figure 7-43).

Figure 7-43: Setting a Reminder for a flagged message

By default, the time is set for 5:00 P.M. for the selected date. You can, however, edit this and change it to any time of day you desire. When the reminder is triggered, you get a traditional Reminder dialog with the message's subject displayed (see Figure 7-44).

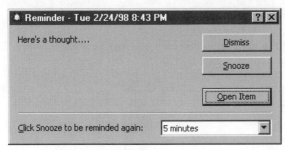

Figure 7-44: An email reminder

Once the reminder is past, the email message is considered "overdue" and becomes subject to the overdue email rule which by default colors the message line in the Inbox to red. To change this rule (or any of the other formatting rules that impact the current view), click on View → Current View → Customize Current View → Automatic Formatting. Select the "Overdue e-mail" rule and you can change the formatting applied to a message that becomes overdue (see Figure 7-45).

Figure 7-45: Setting formatting for the Overdue e-mail rule

Clearing the flag resets the message formatting back to a non-overdue state. With flags to keep you organized and reminders to keep you from procrastinating on answering that important email from your boss, you may for once get the upper hand on your Inbox.

NOTE   The reminder flag feature in Outlook 98 works as advertised, although the overdue rule does not always kick in instantly once the reminder is triggered. The view has to be refreshed by switching to another facility and then back again, or by closing and then restarting Outlook.

Distribution Lists

One of the main reasons that so many Outlook 97 and Outlook 98 users (in Corporate/Workgroup mode) maintain their contacts in the Contacts list *and* in the Personal Address Book is because the PAB lets you easily create an email distribution list. In Outlook, you can have distribution lists too (of a sort), but you have to jump through some hoops along the way.

OUTLOOK 98   Outlook 98 Internet Only mode provides for painless email distribution lists. Click on Tools → Address Book → New Group. Give your group a name and click on Select Members to add entries from your Contacts list to the group.

To create a Contacts-based distribution list in Outlook 98 Corporate/Workgroup and Outlook 97, here's what you need to do. Open each contact item that you want in a given distribution list and assign that person to a unique category. It's best to use a custom category, since you don't want to unintentionally send the wrong message to someone. A unique category like "Xmas mailing list" probably won't be used by accident for the wrong contact name. Then display your Contact list by category (View → Current View → By Category). Click-and-drag the desired category title to the Outbox icon in the Outlook Bar or the Folder List (see Figure 7-46).

This creates a new email message addressed to everyone in that category. If you don't want each person in the list to be able to see all the other names, cut and paste the addresses from the To field to the Bcc (blind carbon copy) field.

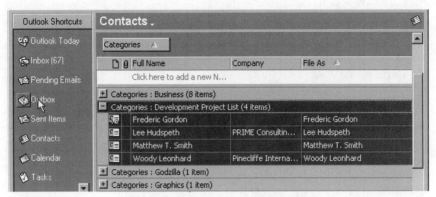

Figure 7-46: An email distribution list for contacts via category assignments

Integration with Word

We worry about Microsoft sometimes, we really do. Not only have they saddled their customers with a bewildering array of address books, but *no single address book lets you easily drop a name and address into a Word document.* Now maybe email will one day make actual letters obsolete, but by golly, we create documents in Word and would like to be able to get names and addresses from Outlook or the PAB into Word without jumping through flaming hoops.

The good news is that we'll show you not only how to get a name and address into Word, but how to do a mail merge with Outlook or PAB contact data. The bad news is that there are still plenty of hoops to traverse, flames and all.

Getting Names and Addresses into Word

Since many Outlook users keep their contact data in the PAB, we'll take a look at pulling data into Word from both the Contacts and PAB address lists. Let's take a look at a letter to a single person from inside Outlook first.

Contacts to Word—take a letter

In Outlook, select one of your Contacts. Then pull down the Actions menu (Contacts in Outlook 97) and click on New Letter to Contact. Word starts. If Word is already running, it is ignored, and a new instance of Word is started. Jeez, we just started and already we're annoyed.

Next, the Letter Wizard in Word kicks in. This Wizard is a bit unique in that each of the four tabs shown in the Letter Wizard dialog in Figure

7-47 corresponds to the steps in the Wizard. The Letter Format tab is Step
1, the Recipient Info tab is Step 2, the Other Elements tab is Step 3, and
the Sender Info tab is Step 4. This Wizard helps you create a letter in
Word and pops in the Contact's name and address into what it decides is
the appropriate spot. From the "Choose a page design" list, you can pick
from several letter templates that ship with Word. You can click on the
Next button or you can click on the individual tabs at the top of the
dialog box to work your way through the Wizard. In Step 2, Recipient
Info, you'll see the Contact information that will be plunked down in
your Word letter (see Figure 7-48).

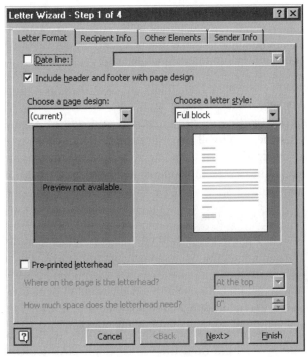

Figure 7-47: The Word Letter Wizard

If this isn't the name and address you want, you can click on the "Click
here to use Address Book" icon and search your address books for a
different name. You'll notice that the Address Book icon has a drop-
down arrow next to it. It saves the last 16 names you accessed in a drop-
down list under the assumption that you'll use one of these names again
soon.

Overall, this method is pretty brain-dead. First, there's the multiple
instances of Word problem (if Word is already running when you start a
new letter from within Outlook). Next, apparently, it's impossible to tell

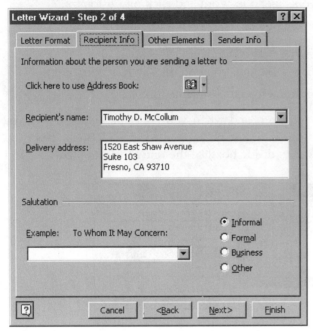

Figure 7-48: Your Contact item information

the Wizard exactly where you want the name and address dropped into the document (if it's not impossible, how to do it has completely eluded us). Instead, the Wizard is intent on putting the name and address on the first line in the document. Third, to get the address, you're required to use the Wizard. For a full discussion of Word's Letter Wizard, and particularly its deficiencies, see "Dealing with the Letter Wizard" in *Word 97 Annoyances*, by Woody Leonhard, Lee Hudspeth, and T.J. Lee, published by O'Reilly & Associates (ISBN 1-56592-308-1).

Word to Contacts—give me an address

If you ask the Office Assistant in Word to find a topic like "Getting an address from Outlook," the closest topic you'll receive is "Insert an address from my personal address book." And if you follow the instructions there, you'll go to the Tools menu, then click on Envelopes and Labels. This lets you find the Insert Address icon in Word, but the best you'll do with it is create a label or an envelope with a Contact address in it.

Not so good for the letter you want to create. To get the Insert Address icon out where you can actually use it to get a name and address into a document is annoyingly cumbersome:

1. Pull down the Tools menu in Word and click on Customize.

2. In the Customize dialog box, click on the Commands tab.

3. In the Categories list, select Insert.

4. Scroll the Commands list until you find the Address Book entry.

5. Drag the Address Book icon to a suitable toolbar.

Now you can create a letter, and when you have the cursor where you want the name and address, just click on the Address Book icon. This displays the Select Names dialog box like the one shown in Figure 7-49.

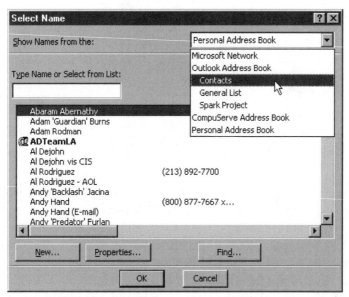

Figure 7-49: Selecting names from various names lists in Outlook

Notice that the various and sundry address lists that Windows/Office supports are selectable in the "Show Names from the" drop-down list. You can select a contact from Outlook, the Personal Address Book, or other lists, depending on which online service you may be using and whether you're in Outlook 98's Corporate/Workgroup or Internet Only mode. Pick a name from your Contacts list, and that name and address is inserted into the document like this:

```
Timothy D. McCollum
1520 East Shaw Avenue
Suite 103
Fresno, CA 93710
United States of America
```

Actually, you may get more *and* less than you want. In this example, we inserted a name from the Outlook Address Book's Contacts list, and while the Company name was omitted, we got the text "United States of America" appended to the end of the address. When you add a contact to Outlook, it likes to fill in the Country field for you. PAB entries that are imported into the Contact list only get a Country field value if the PAB record had one. The only way we've found to turn this off is the hard way: open the Contact item in Outlook, click on the General tab for the displayed contact, click on the Address button, then delete the entry in the Country field and do a Save and Close.

If you want it, you'll have to add the Company information manually by typing it yourself into Word. Incredibly annoying. But given that the Insert Address button in Word allows you to control which address book to query and how contact information is placed within the Word document, this is the recommended way to bring in names and addresses for single documents, lame though it is.

At *support.microsoft.com/support/kb/articles/Q134/9/01.asp* is a Microsoft KnowledgeBase article that has a semi-workaround for this problem. The address layout in Word is determined by an AutoText entry named "AddressLayout." You can create your own AutoText entry by the same name and add the company name field like this:

```
<PR_GIVEN_NAME> <PR_SURNAME>
<PR_TITLE>
<PR_COMPANY_NAME>
<PR_STREET_ADDRESS>
<PR_LOCALITY>, <PR_STATE_OR_PROVINCE> <PR_POSTAL_CODE>
```

Read the KnowledgeBase article for details on using this workaround.

Mail Merge in Word

Doing any kind of mass mailing requires using the Mail Merge feature built into Word (yes, even in this electronic age, many of us still need to send form letters, invitations, notices, and the like, from time to time). You can use your Personal Address Book or your Contacts list as a data source for a Word mail merge.

When Microsoft designed the Exchange PAB and later the Outlook Contacts list, they adopted a, er, uh, *unique* method for handling mail merges. The way merges work can cause you some major annoyances, so we'll discuss each step in depth.

Let's see what happens using the PAB as your data source. To do a mail merge to generate labels in Word linked directly to your PAB:

1. Create a new Word document.

2. Select Tools, Mail Merge, click on the Create button, choose Mailing Labels (we'll use Mailing Labels for all the examples in this section, but this technique works equally well for any other type of mail merge), click on the Active Window button, click on the Get Data button, choose Use Address Book, select Personal Address Book in the Use Address Book dialog (see Figure 7-50), and click on OK.

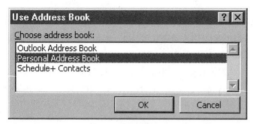

Figure 7-50: Word's Use Address Book dialog appears when mail merging with Outlook

3. Click the Set Up Main Document button, make your choices in the Label Options dialog (we selected Avery standard 5162), and click on OK.

4. In the Create Labels dialog, click the Insert Merge Field button and select the desired fields (one at a time) from the cascading menu. Click on OK when done. See Figure 7-51 for the list of fields we chose.

Figure 7-51: Word shows you a sample label in "merge field" format in its Create Labels dialog

5. To merge without any filtering (querying), click on the Merge button, accept the Merge dialog's defaults (Merge to – New document, Records to be merged – All, Don't print blank lines...) and click on Merge. Word reports the record numbers on its status bar as it merges them. The time it takes for the merge depends, of course, on the number of records in your PAB.

6. You can save, print, or discard the mail merge output document at your discretion (see Figure 7-52). Currently it has a name like Labels1.

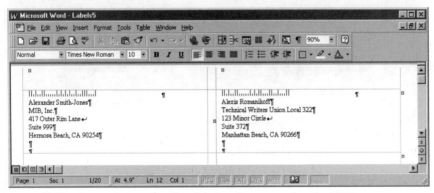

Figure 7-52: Output from a mailing label mail merge using the PAB

7. Save your mail merge main document now with the filename *PAB mail merge (postal info).doc*.

So far so good, right? Wrong. Something's about to hit the fan. Go ahead and close *PAB mail merge (postal info).doc*. Word (sometimes) prompts you, "PAB mail merge (postal info).doc is a mail merge main document that is attached to a data source Personal Address Book that has not been saved. Do you want to save Personal Address Book?" Maddeningly, there's no Help button on this red herring message box.

NOTE   In addition to the headaches of just getting your data into Word, Outlook has another annoying gotcha you need to watch out for.* If you're merging from the Contact list and you have a company name that starts with "The," as in "The Big Bag Corporation," Outlook helpfully changes that to "Big Bag Corporation, The" in the File As field so it will alphabetize nicely in the Contact list. That's all well and good, but you wind up with it showing up this way in a Word mail merge as well. Ouch!

---

* Hats off to Helen Feddema, Outlook maven and Access guru, for pointing out this annoying anomaly to us here at Annoyances Central.

If you choose Yes, you'll next see a message box, "This document will be saved in Word format. Do you want to continue?" Click on Yes. The next message box has to be seen to be believed; it's shown in Figure 7-53 (note that the message box text is oddly truncated at the end). The first time we saw this message was on a PC with 230 MB free on a 1.2 GB drive and plenty of free system resources. Subsequent tests on this and other PCs yielded the same result, so this is not a case of a machine-specific glitch. Something's terribly wrong here.

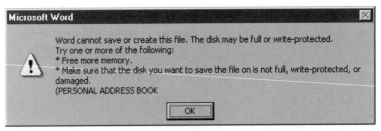

Figure 7-53: Clear evidence that Word has lost its way (and mind) while tidying up after a simple mail merge with a Personal Address Book

Word wants to create a background copy of the PAB, but mismanages the process horribly.

Without making any changes to your PAB, immediately open *PAB mail merge (postal info).doc*, then select Tools → Mail Merge (this invokes the Mail Merge Helper dialog), click on the Data source section's Edit button, and notice the bizarre data filename: *C:\~~\~~~_virtual_file_~~~.pab** (see Figure 7-54).

As bizarre as this is, you can still perform a successful merge using this main document. *However, if you subsequently edit your PAB in Outlook, this main document will never see any changes to existing records or any new records.*

Proof: close the main document, add a new record to your PAB—we used a name of aaaFirst aaaLast with bogus information in the appropriate data fields for easy identification—and run a new merge. *The new record is not in the new merge.* Update a record that was present in the previous merge and run a new merge. *Changes to the record are not reflected in the new merge.*

---

* You can actually view this file in Word like this: click the Mail Merge Helper button, click on the Data source section's Edit button, choose the bizarre item entitled Data: C:\~~..., and click on View Source in the Data Form dialog.

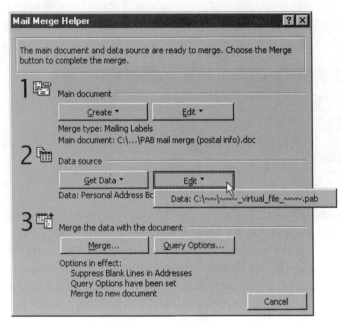

Figure 7-54: The Mail Merge Helper dialog reveals the existence of the "~~~_virtual_ file_~~~.pab" virtual file

It gets even worse. Close Outlook and Word. Restart Outlook and then Word. Open *PAB mail merge (postal info).doc,* and you'll see the weird message in Figure 7-55. Click on Yes to make a copy, and you'll see the dismaying message in Figure 7-56.

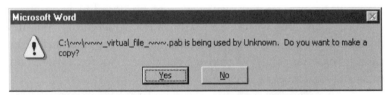

Figure 7-55: Word descends deeper into PAB mail merge hell

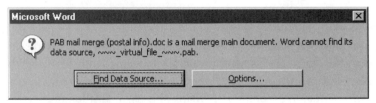

Figure 7-56: Word descends even deeper into PAB mail merge hell

Click on Options (don't bother with the Find Data Source button—you'll never locate the non-existent file), and then writhe in the agony of

Microsoft's obfuscatory hell with the message in Figure 7-57. Note the annoying truncated text (it looks like the developers didn't plan for long filenames in the message prompt).

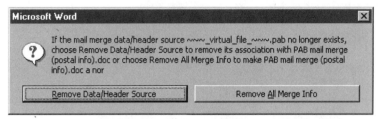

Figure 7-57: Nowhere left to go in the PAB mail merge inferno's inner circle

Microsoft suggests this workaround: click Remove Data/Header Source, select Tools, choose Mail Merge, click Get Data, choose Use Address Book, select Personal Address Book, and click on OK; all in order to create a new virtual file based on the current PAB. We've found this technique doesn't work reliably. In some tests, this caused the Merge button to be disabled in the Mail Merge Helper dialog. Ouch, there's a belly-up main document. In others, the technique worked. Go figure.

Could it possibly get any worse, you ask? Oh yes. Say you've just given up in disgust on this particular fubar* main document. With the same session of Word still running (the one in which Word's been misbehaving like a wolverine on amphetamines), add a new record to your PAB. Back in Word, create a new main document and work your way through all the normal merge steps. You'd think you'd be establishing a nice, clean link to your PAB—albeit a link that's going to be hosed as soon as you close the document, but we digress. Wrong. Do a merge and this new main document fails to see the new record. You have to exit and restart Word, and invoke the clumsy "Remove Data/Header Source" workaround to re-establish (sometimes) a direct PAB link.

Here's what the Microsoft KnowledgeBase has to say about this, "This behavior is by design to prevent you from accidentally overwriting the original Outlook 97 (Schedule+) contact list with a format not recognized by Outlook 97 (Schedule+). Since this file [~~~_virtual_file_~~~.pab, .olk, or .scd] is a temporary file, it is deleted when you exit Word." By design? Well, what this really means is that Microsoft decided not to make the link simple, elegant, dynamic, and one-way (for safety's sake) and instead kludged this virtual file solution. Perhaps this is a MAPI limitation, or perhaps there's a more deeply rooted problem here. It's an inexcusable annoyance nonetheless.

---

* Fouled up beyond all repair.

Mail merge and the Contacts list

Mechanically, using a Contacts list as your data source for a mail merge works the same way as using the PAB. However, there's good news and bad news.

First, the bad news. All of the infuriating problems with a PAB-direct mail merge that we described in the previous section apply to a Contacts-direct mail merge. (The terms "Contacts list," "Contacts module," and "Outlook Address Book" are all synonymous.) After you set up your Contacts-direct main document, run a mail merge, close Word, open Word, and open up the Contacts-direct main document. Here comes that series of message boxes you love to hate (see Figure 7-58), only this time the virtual file has an extension of *.olk*.

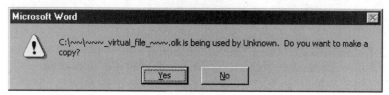

Figure 7-58: Déjà vu—a Contacts-direct mail merge has all the problems of a PAB-direct mail merge

Setting up a Contacts-direct link from your main document involves the same steps you used for a PAB-direct link. The only difference is that when you select Outlook Address Book in the Use Address Book dialog box (see Figure 7-50), you then have an additional dialog box to contend with, as shown in Figure 7-59.

Figure 7-59: Word's Mail Merge from Contacts Folder dialog shows a list of all the available Outlook Address Book folders

In the Mail Merge from Contacts Folder dialog box, you can choose any Contacts folders that are set up in Outlook to display as resources in the Outlook Address Book. The default Contacts folder—named, not surprisingly, Contacts—is already set to appear in your Outlook Address Book.

To prove this, right-click on the Contacts icon in the Outlook Bar, choose Properties, click on the Outlook Address Book tab, and you should see that the "Show this folder as an e-mail Address Book" box is checked (and the name is "Contacts"), as shown in Figure 7-60.

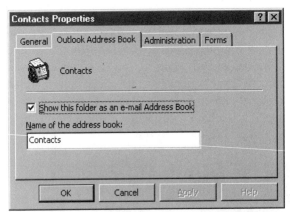

Figure 7-60: Look at the default Contacts folder's properties, then its Outlook Address Book tab settings, to verify that it will appear as an Address Book

This checkbox and name designation can be applied to any folder containing Contact items. This brings us to the (sort of) good news: with a Contacts-based mail merge, you don't have to use filtering on the Word side to narrow down the desired records. Instead, you can create a new temporary Contacts folder—say, Contacts Mail Merge—to store records for your mail merge, copy records from Contacts to it, and then use it in the mail merge. Here are the steps:

1. To create a new folder, select File → New → Folder, enter **Contacts Mail Merge** in the Name field, select Contact Items in the "Folder contains" drop-down control, select Contacts in "Select where to place the folder," and click on OK.

2. Verify that the Contacts Mail Merge folder's properties designate it as "Show this folder as an e-mail Address Book" on the Outlook Address Book tab.

3. Add a shortcut to the Outlook Bar when prompted. Copy the Contact items you want to merge to this folder.

4. When you set up a mail merge, point to this folder instead of Contacts.

While this approach is still fraught with all the virtual file problems we discussed earlier, it introduces the new problem of duplicate records existing in multiple Contact item folders. A kludge is still a kludge, but it's a tad easier than dealing directly with the PAB.

Mail merge—conclusions and workarounds

We'd like to think that Microsoft has a crack team of programmers working on the fundamental issue of effortlessly shuffling and inserting names and addresses between Outlook and *any* other Office application. We'd like to think so, but it's hard to get worked up to that level of optimism.

First, we recommend you move all your names and addresses from your PAB to an Outlook Contacts list. Not that this solves the mail merge problems we've discussed, but it's one step towards consolidation of the diverse address books that Windows and Office has foisted on you.

Then you need to decide if working with the *virtual file* methodology is going to drive you nuts or not. If you can live with having to remove the Data/Header source every time you want to remerge a mail merge main document, then you're all set.

Well, almost all set. Outlook has another annoying flaw: you can't merge all of the Contact item fields. Of the 100+ Contact item fields, you can only merge 40 of them (the ones that appear in Word on the Insert Merge Field menu). How big an annoyance this is depends on what information you need to merge.

There is one other workaround to avoid the use of the virtual file method and the limits on which Contact item fields you can merge.[*] You can export the Contacts list to another application—like Excel or Access—and merge from there.

Exporting a Contacts list is very easy:

1. In Outlook, select the Import and Export option from the File menu. This starts the Import and Export Wizard. Select the "Export to a file" option and click on the Next button.

WARNING   In Outlook 97 the order of steps in the Import and Export Wizard are different. In this example, steps 2 and 3 should be reversed. You select the folder you want *before* you choose the file type.

---

2. You have a fairly complete choice of file types to which you can export your Contacts list. Pick the file type you are most comfortable doing mail merges with and click on the Next button.

---

[*] Or most of the limits. Under no circumstances can you merge custom user-defined fields.

3. In the next panel, select the Contacts folder you want to export.

4. Type a path and filename for the file that will receive the data. You can use the Browse button to choose a folder on your hard disk if you wish. Click on the Next button to proceed.

5. The last panel, which is shown in Figure 7-61, reveals what actions will be performed and admonishes you that this may take a while (depending on the number of contacts you have) and that you can't cancel the process once it starts. Click on Finish and you're done.

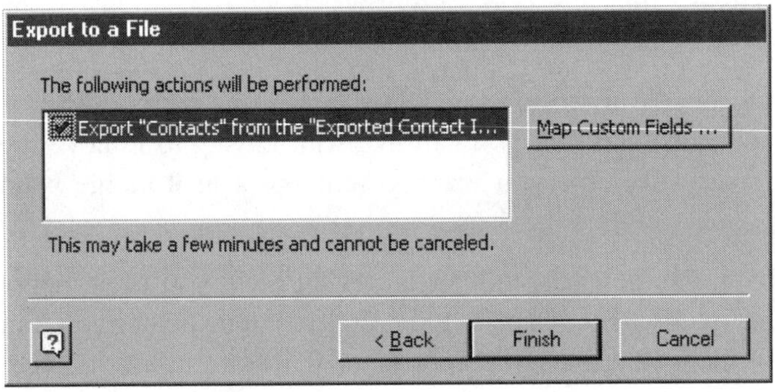

Figure 7-61: Ready to rock and roll, er, export!

Is this the panacea for all your mail merge headaches? No, you will still have the annoying problems of subsequent updates to your Contacts list in Outlook, and the usual problems with line breaks included in text fields, but on the upside, you have a great deal of control over your data once you get it in an exported format.

8

Introduction to VBScript, the Outlook Object Model, and Custom Forms

The macro language that lives inside Access, Excel, PowerPoint, and Word is called Visual Basic for Applications (VBA). Outlook, on the other hand, supports VBScript, a subset of the Visual Basic language.

Shocked? Confused? Dismayed?

You should be. Oh, Microsoft has put some marvelous spin doctoring on this shortcoming, but before we cover what's missing in Outlook/ VBScript and what you can do to be productive anyway, first we'll provide a quick VBA history lesson. Then we'll describe how Office programming with VBA works, and how it contrasts with Outlook/ VBScript. Once you're fully informed about the differences, we'll explain common uses for Outlook/VBScript, and then delve into the mechanics (which comprises the bulk of this chapter). When you're done, you'll have learned the basics of Outlook programming using either VBScript or VBA and the Outlook object model, the fundamental concepts of Office programming from VBA's point of view, plus plenty of sample code to illustrate the points.

Outlook and VBScript versus Office and VBA

NOTE	Since this is a fairly long chapter with plenty of technical material, we provide signposts like this one at the beginning of most sections. They are intended to help you keep a perspective on where you've been so far and where the next section is going.

VBScript is a subset of Visual Basic, originally available starting with Microsoft Internet Explorer 3.0. It is intended to be an Internet programming tool compatible with the widely popular and diverse range of Microsoft products. You could say that VBScript is Microsoft's answer to JavaScript. Anyway, by definition and design VBScript is limited because it needs to function safely across the World Wide Web as part of an HTML page. To meet this safety standard, it can't interact with files on the host PC, can't interact directly with the host's operating system, and it supports no user interface other than simple message boxes. If you're accustomed to Office/VBA, these limitations will frustrate you, and you'll long for the day—as we do—when Outlook will include VBA as its development platform. If you're not familiar with Office/VBA, then you'll be able to more easily cope with this shotgun wedding of Outlook and VBScript.

VBA was first introduced in Excel version 5.0 (Office 4.x), at which time Excel earned the distinction of being Microsoft's first Office application to use VBA.* In this and other books in the *Annoyances* series, when referring to the specific dialect of VBA that comes inside an Office application, we'll refer to "VBA/Excel," "VBA/PowerPoint," or "VBA/Word." Microsoft insists that the VBA inside Excel is the same VBA that's inside Word and PowerPoint and Project, and to a point that's true. Still, a program written in VBA/Excel usually won't run, unchanged, in its sibling applications, so we'll continue to draw the distinction. By "program" here we mean a macro or procedure that calls upon application-specific components or behaviors. It's true that a general-purpose VBA procedure—say, one that replaces a marker in a string variable with some text—could be written in Excel/VBA and also be used unmodified in all the other Office applications that host VBA.

---

* Both Excel 5 and Project 4 simultaneously released VBA to the world, but since Project has never been part of the official Office family, we give the vote of pioneering distinction to Excel.

A string-swapping VBA function would probably *not* run unmodified in VBScript, since a good VBA program uses rigorous data typing, but VBScript only supports one generic variable type—Variant. So at the very least you'd have to strip any Dim statements of their As type clause, and rework your code to allow for the numerous language constructs not supported in VBScript (more on this shortly).

What's the neatest part about VBScript in Outlook—setting its shortcomings aside for a moment—and VBA in the other Office applications? You don't have to buy anything. It's sitting right there inside its host Office application, waiting for you to bring it to life. All it takes is a little learning and a little gumption, and we'll give you a good dose of both in this chapter.

Once you're underway, the major conceptual hump for VBScript and VBA involves understanding the behavior and features of the host Office application and its object model. VBScript poses its own special problems in having to downshift your thinking to its minimalist development environment and capabilities. Not to worry. We'll take you by the hand and show you the way.

NOTE   If you're new to programming altogether, and Outlook/ VBScript is going to be your first foray into programming, read this note carefully. You might be tempted to conclude—based on what we've said thus far, and what we're going to say in the following sections—that Outlook/VB-Script's minimalism will benefit you. Not so. Although there is more to learn when using VBA and its integrated development environment, just a few minutes of immersion in that environment will convince you that, in the case of Outlook, less is definitely not more.

Why Use Outlook/VBScript?

There are three compelling reasons to learn Outlook/VBScript:

1. You need to be able to programmatically manipulate data from inside Outlook. For a sample program that illustrates accessing Outlook data, see the section, "Outlook Controlling Outlook."

2. You need to access or manipulate Outlook data from another application, like Access, Excel, or Word (among others). This chapter includes a sample program that does just that; see the section, "Print-FolderList: Use Excel to Interact with and Control Outlook."

3. You're developing enterprise solutions involving custom folders and forms.*

In other words, VBScript is decidedly *not* a tool for fixing Outlook's annoyances. This is in contrast to VBA, which *does* provide this benefit for Excel, Word, and the other VBA-enabled Office applications, as explained in our other Annoyances books.

Why can't Outlook/VBScript fulfill this annoyance-busting role in Outlook? The tools simply aren't there. (Bear with the terminology, all these concepts are explained more fully later in the chapter.) Outlook forms aren't fully customizable dialogs; they're based on built-in forms hard-wired for specific types of data, so you can't mimic or embellish Outlook's dialogs with your own. For example, Ctrl+Shift+J produces a new Journal form that defaults to a "Phone call" entry type. This is similar to the "float over text" gaffe in Word that we describe in *Word 97 Annoyances*, but there's no way to use Outlook's programming language or environment to fix this. As another example, Outlook uses a hard-wired list of reminder time intervals that we'd like to change by adding options for 3, 5, 6, and 7 hours, values that are currently missing. Since Outlook/VBScript has no access to this dialog, no programmatic workaround is available.

Outlook/VBScript provides no connection between its user interface and your programs, so you can't attach macros to Outlook's user interface components. Outlook/VBScript doesn't support calls to the Windows API, so you have no direct access to advanced capabilities provided by the API. Outlook has no Application-level events, so you can't customize its behavior as you can VBA-enabled applications.

That said, Outlook's incredibly rich object model *does* give you easy access to data from inside Outlook using VBScript and from outside Outlook using VB/VBA and OLE Automation. Also, it's handy that you can easily display Outlook's built-in forms—like Contact, Appointment, or Journal—programmatically, complete with all the attendant data without spending any time tediously building fields and data bindings for them. So don't be put off by the design differences between Outlook/VBScript and Office/VBA, just be aware of them and then get to work designing programs that make sense for your needs.

---

* Enterprise development is beyond the scope of this book. We recommend *Building Applications with Microsoft Outlook 97* (Microsoft Press) and Sue Mosher's *The Microsoft Exchange User's Handbook* (Duke Communications).

NOTE   VBScript is also used by the Windows Scripting Host
        (WSH) component of Windows 98, a quantum leap over
        the MS-DOS batch command language. WSH enables
        scripts to be run on the Windows desktop, and those
        scripts don't have to be embedded inside an HTML docu-
        ment. So by learning VBScript you'll be ready to use this
        new functionality to control your Windows environment.

The Concepts Behind Office Programming

NOTE   "Office programming" is a term that includes development
        using VBA in Access, Excel, PowerPoint, and Word;
        VBScript in Outlook; as well as the use of OLE Automation
        to control these applications from within each other, Visual
        Basic, and even non-Microsoft products. If you're reading
        this chapter, you're probably running Office Standard or
        Professional and therefore have easy access to Outlook's
        sibling applications. You'll probably use one of those sib-
        ling applications to extract data from or add data to Out-
        look, so you need an overview of VBA development.

Practically anything you can do in a host Office application, you can do
with a VBA program, including controlling Outlook from another Office
application.* Many things that you *can't* do in the host Office application
you *can* do with a VBA program. Indeed, anything you can accomplish
with a program in Windows itself can be done in a VBA program. The
full range of Windows programming—from simple offerings for the
Windows gods, to complex delving into Windows' innards using the
Windows API (WinAPI)—is at your beck and call from a VBA program.
Mind boggling. As shown in Example 8-1, with a single call to the
WinAPI function *GetDriveType*, you can find out if a particular drive is
removable, fixed, remote (network), CD-ROM, and so on. (You can put
this code into any VBA or VB project and run it.)

VBScript doesn't support use of the Windows API, and this constrains
what you can accomplish with this language.

---

* You can call 'em "macros" if you like, but they're really full-fledged programs. We'll use the
terms "macro" and "program" interchangeably throughout the book. Technically, in VBA a
"macro" is a subroutine with no parameters. In practice, self-impressed bit twiddlers use "macro" as a term of derision, e.g., "Oh, it's just a *macro!* I thought you had a program going." Those
of us who have been working with macros for many years know better: "Oh, it's just a *program?*
I thought you guys knew how to write real *macros.*"

Example 8-1: The WinAPI Function GetDriveType Handily Returns a Drive's Type

```
Declare Function GetDriveType Lib "kernel32" Alias "GetDriveTypeA"
  _
    (ByVal nDrive As String) As Long

Sub Demo_GetDriveType
    ' NOTE: the trailing backslash is CRITICAL!
    ' 0 is DRIVE_TYPE_UNDTERMINED (drive type cannot be determined)
    ' 1 is DRIVE_ROOT_NOT_EXIST (root directory doesn't exist)
    ' 2 is DRIVE_REMOVABLE
    ' 3 is DRIVE_FIXED
    ' 4 is DRIVE_REMOTE
    ' 5 is DRIVE_CDROM
    ' 6 is DRIVE_RAMDISK
    Dim lngRC as Long
    lngRC = GetDriveType("C:\")
    MsgBox "GetDriveType returned " & lngRC
End Sub
```

Once you learn VBA, the skills and tips (and bugs and workarounds) you learn in VBA/Excel, for example, transfer over, nearly intact, to Visual Basic, VBA/Word, VBA/PowerPoint, VBA/Visio, and many others. All this knowledge won't transfer over to using VBScript with Outlook, but much of it will, and vice versa if you start with VBScript and move on to VBA. With either macro language, you still have to learn the application—in Outlook you're manipulating folders and items, in Excel it's cells and ranges, in Word it's paragraphs and sentences, in Visio it's shapes and connectors—but the structure that holds all the macros together stays the same. That's leverage on a grand scale.

Paradise Lost

NOTE   In this section we take a look at the Office/VBA features that are not included in Outlook/VBScript to help those of you who write—or will be writing—code in both environments. This will save you significant time, particularly by pointing out things natural to VBA that won't fly in VBScript.

Outlook's programming gestalt falls short of the standard of excellence defined by Office 97. In this section, we'll work you through the differences between the two environments, which we'll refer to as "Outlook/VBScript" and "Office/VBA." At the end of this section, we quote Microsoft's official position supporting their conscious decision to use VBScript, not VBA, in Outlook, and provide our own counter-argument.

Then you be the judge. You can vote, if so inclined, at Microsoft's own Web site (we'll explain how).

Let's work our way through the contents of Table 8-1, which compares VBScript with the features available in VBA. First, macro recording. For any application supporting a programming language, a macro recording feature is a must-have. Outlook/VBScript doesn't provide macro recording; Office/VBA does.

A programming language can be a syntactic marvel and possess a rich set of data types, constructs, and built-in functions, but without a development environment—a home in which you the programmer breathe, eat, and sleep—to match these linguistic features, the language and its user suffers. Office/VBA is blessed with all these features. In fact, it's the wonderful balance between the VBA language itself, the development environment, and the various Office object models that makes developing Office applications—simple or complex—such a joy. Outlook/VBScript doesn't include Office/VBA's integrated development environment; instead, what you get with Outlook/VBScript is called the Script Editor, effectively Notepad with a Run command. As you can see in Table 8-1, here's what you're missing in this arena:

Table 8-1: Feature comparison between Outlook/VBScript and Office/VBA

Feature	Outlook/VBScript	Office/VBA
Record macros	No	Yes
Integrated Development Environment	No	Yes
IDE Project Explorer	No	Yes
IDE Property Window	Yes (two separate Properties dialogs)	Yes
IDE Code Window with IntelliSense	No	Yes
IDE Object Browser	No	Yes
IDE Debugging Tools	Yes in Outlook 98 (included with IE4); No in Outlook 97 (you must download a free debugger)	Yes
UserForms (Microsoft Forms 2.0)	No (Outlook uses only portions of the Microsoft Forms 2.0 object library; Outlook forms are not UserForms)	Yes

Table 8-1: Feature comparison between Outlook/VBScript and Office/VBA (continued)

Feature	Outlook/VBScript	Office/VBA
Separate repository for code and forms	No	Yes
Import/Export forms to/ from other VBA applications and Visual Basic 5	No	Yes
Events	Yes (none for the Application object, far fewer than Office/VBA for controls, 11 for Outlook items)	Yes
Connect custom command bar controls to macros	No	Yes
Import/Export VBA code modules	No	Yes
Your source modules can be compiled into Office add-ins	No	Yes
Syntax and language features	VBScript is a subset of VBA	VBA in Office includes the full syntax and features of VBA
Named arguments	No	Yes
Class modules	No	Yes
Programming help files are an Office setup option	Yes in Outlook 98; No in Outlook 97	Yes

- Since an Outlook form supports only one script, there's no Project Explorer.

- In Outlook, the window that equates to the Visual Basic Editor's Properties window is called Advanced Properties in the Script Editor's interface, even though its title bar reads "Properties." Outlook's Properties dialog (selected from the interface by clicking on the Properties command) also has a title bar that reads "Properties." To further confound things, you have to manually re-invoke the Script Editor's Properties dialog for each control, whereas the Advanced Properties window—like its Office/VBA cousin—remains visible as you select different controls.

- The Properties window does not display a subset of the properties shown in the Advanced Properties window, as you might think. Some crucial properties (such as the field to which a control is bound) can only be set in the Properties window.

- Instead of a Code Window with IntelliSense features galore, you write code in a Notepad-like application called Script Editor, which is shown in Figure 8-1. Compare this with VBA's integrated development environment, which is shown in Figure 8-2.

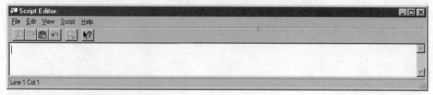

Figure 8-1: Outlook's Script Editor

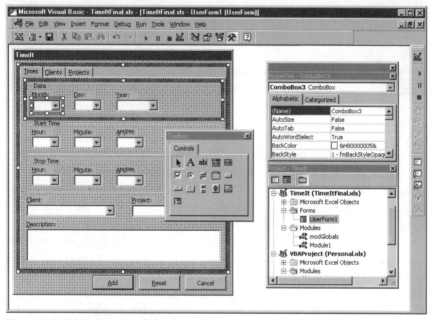

Figure 8-2: VBA's integrated development environment

- Outlook/VBScript doesn't include a tool like Office/VBA's Object Browser for navigating through Outlook's object model. Outlook 98 includes a rudimentary object browser that looks only at Outlook's own type library. We show you how to mitigate this in the upcoming section, "The Object Browser."

- In Outlook 97, no debugging tools ship with Outlook/VBScript; instead you have to download one (free) from Microsoft's Web site. We show you how to get and use the debugger in the section "The Microsoft Script Debugger." Outlook 98, by virtue of its mandatory coupling with Microsoft Internet Explorer 4, includes a script debugger.

In Outlook, a form (see Figure 8-3) is the repository for your source code, whereas in Office/VBA, code and forms are stored in separate repositories.

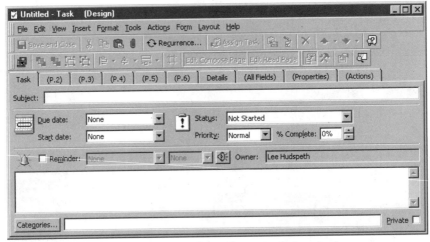

Figure 8-3: An Outlook built-in Task form (shown in design view)

An Outlook form and a VBA form (officially called a UserForm) are both customizable spaces on which you place controls. But unlike a dialog box type form (a UserForm), an Outlook form cannot be constrained to a fixed size; this means the user can resize it at will. Outlook uses a forms technology that's an eclectic blend of some parts of UserForms—like the Control Toolbox, the Controls collection, the Page object—and some parts proprietary to Exchange/Outlook. Unlike UserForms, they can't be exported to (or imported from) another Office application or Visual Basic since Outlook forms are proprietary. An Outlook form's controls support only one event (Click), and only the command button control can actually use the Click event. By contrast a UserForm's controls support 18 events, from Click to Zoom. In the section "Editing Forms with the Script Editor," we show you how to create and save a custom Outlook form.

Outlook 97 lacks customizable command bars,* so you can't create custom command bar controls (like a button on a toolbar, for example), much less connect them so they call your macros, as you can in Office/ VBA. Although Outlook 98 includes support for customizable command bars, you still can't connect them to your macros.

---

* Beginning with Office 97, Microsoft coined the term "command bar" as a fancy way of generally describing toolbars, menu bars, and shortcut menus.

Outlook/VBScript provides no built-in way to import or export code. To export, you must manually copy code into a text file and then manually save it; you'd reverse the process for an import. On the other hand, Office/VBA has a nice user interface built into the IDE for importing and exporting VBA code modules.

Outlook add-ins can only be developed in C/C++, whereas Office add-ins can be developed in VBA or C/C++.

VBScript is a subset of VBA. The list of Visual Basic features not present in Outlook/VBScript is extensive. Earlier, we explained the logic for this— primarily to operate safely when running scripts in a client/server environment like the Internet. Figure 8-4 shows a part of the *VBScript Language Reference's* list of VBA features not in VBScript.

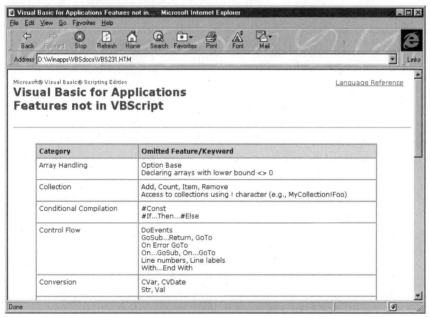

Figure 8-4: The VBScript Language Reference's report on VBA features not in VBScript

---

NOTE   As we take you on a tour of the differences between VBScript and VBA, keep this in mind. We aren't objecting to the specifications or design of VBScript itself, but to Microsoft's decision to couple Outlook with VBScript instead of VBA.

One of the many nice features of the VBA language is its support for named arguments. Simply put, this means you can refer to a function or method's arguments by name and put them in any order instead of having to present them without names in a predetermined, positional order (called "positional arguments"). VBScript lacks named arguments, making the code harder to read, harder to debug, and complicating your efforts to port VBA code to VBScript. You decide which of the following statements is easier to read:

```
' this is Office/VBA using named arguments
rc = MsgBox(Title:="Test", Buttons:=3, Prompt:="Are you there?")

' this is Outlook/VBScript using positional arguments
rc = MsgBox("Are you there?", 3, "Test")
```

A class module is a special type of module that allows you to define a custom object. Procedures you write in a class module become the methods and properties of that object. Classes have the benefit of being reusable in other projects, and you can create multiple instances of a class at run-time. Office/VBA supports class modules, but Outlook/VBScript does not.

In Outlook 97, help files for Outlook/VBScript can't be installed as an Office setup option; instead, you have to manually install them (and in one case, the file isn't shipped with Outlook 97 at all, but must be downloaded). We explain how to do all this in the section "Getting VBScript, Forms, and Object Model Help in Outlook."

In the KnowledgeBase article *OL97: General Information About Using VBScript with Outlook* (Q167138), Microsoft explains its choice to implement VBScript instead of VBA in Outlook as follows:

> Outlook's implementation of VBScript is by design and there are no current plans to implement Visual Basic for Applications within Outlook. VBScript is Microsoft's programming environment for all 'enterprise' (or 'distributed') solutions, mainly for two reasons: [1] Because VBScript code is interpreted and not compiled, Outlook items are relatively small (in terms of bytes). This means they consume less corporate and Internet server resources and also result in faster performance. [2] VBScript is designed to be a secure programming environment. It lacks various commands that can be potentially damaging if used in a malicious manner. This added security is critical in enterprise solutions.

In this quotation, Microsoft has missed the point about the real benefits of Office/VBA versus Outlook/VBScript. Office programming with VBA is about mastering VBA, both the language and its powerful, intelligent, integrated development environment, and having to do this only once with instant recognition and comfort whether programming in Excel, Power-Point, or Word (and, partly, Access).

As for security, well, the WordBasic language in Word 6 was the genesis of macro viruses—the most prolific breed of computer viruses yet produced by our civilization.* Did Microsoft gut the WordBasic language to provide "a secure programming environment?" No. Macro viruses now exist using VBA in Office 97. Did Microsoft lobotomize the VBA language to render Office "a secure programming environment?" No, and they have no plans to do so. That would be tossing the baby out with the bath water. Microsoft knows that Office/VBA is integral to enterprise solutions around the world. Certainly they aren't complacent about macro viruses. They themselves are working feverishly to solve—or at least contain—the macro virus problem, as is an entire sub-industry (the macro virus divisions of all the major anti-virus manufacturers). For these reasons we completely reject Microsoft's circular logic that the "added security [of VBScript] is critical in enterprise solutions."

It's odd that Microsoft would take this position, since its white papers about VBA and Office development repeatedly praise VBA's learn-it-once gestalt and its code reusability, *particularly across the enterprise.* You don't get these features with Outlook/VBScript. But they say that's on purpose. To make the code consume "relatively" (their term) fewer corporate resources and run "relatively" (again, their term) faster. Relative to what metric, performance standard, or comparison norm? This is an unreasonable trade-off, and we prefer the ease of use, intelligence, reusability, and portability that comes with VBA over the potentially marginally faster, marginally safer VBScript.

It's just speculation, mind you, but perhaps there were some technical hurdles in implementing full VBA in Outlook 97. In other words, Microsoft couldn't delay Office 97 any longer for lack of VBA in Outlook, so they bolted VBScript onto the side and shipped the thing. This is further suggested by the fact that the Outlook volume of the five-volume *Microsoft Office VBA Language Reference* documents Outlook using VBA examples; it looks like Outlook was intended to support VBA when that manual went to press. So we're taking bets that by the next major release of Office, Outlook will incorporate a full VBA implementation. Granted, it might not be an easy undertaking. The biggest hurdle is an architecture that accounts for the huge volume of email messages that flows every day, 365 days a year, and provides a safe mechanism for coupling/decou-

---

* The first macro virus, now known as WM/Concept.A, was discovered in July or August 1995. It was written with (and infected) Word 6.

·pling code from these emails (or their parent form receptors). On the other hand, Office documents are created and passed around in large daily doses as well, they are readily susceptible to being macro virus carriers, and the marketplace has shown that it's willing to take that risk. By this standard, it makes no sense to draw a line in the sand with email and say Outlook can't have full VBA.

Microsoft needs to know how you feel about this. If you feel as strongly as we do that Outlook should include VBA, you can provide Microsoft direct feedback. To make your voice heard, fire up your Web browser and from Microsoft's home page at *www.microsoft.com*, click on the Write Us button, then choose the "Send a product suggestion to Microsoft Wish" option (see Figure 8-5) and fill out the form.

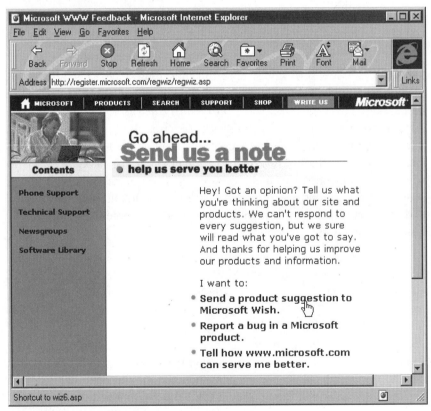

Figure 8-5: Microsoft's feedback page on the Web

Recording Macros...Not!

Pick up any book on Office applications or Office itself, whether written by us or our esteemed colleagues, and one of the first and most important things you'll read in the chapter introducing the application's programming language—including VBA and even the venerable Word-Basic and XLM macro languages of bygone Office versions—is how to record a macro. Macro recording is common to most heavy non-Microsoft applications as well. Trying to use an application that supports a programming language but lacks a macro recorder is like learning to drive a car without any rear view or side view mirrors: you can't see where you've been! Newcomers to Office/VBA benefit tremendously from being able to record some actions, study the resulting code, and learn something new about the application's object model. Recording an action as a macro is also a quick way to generate code for a repetitive process, although you may want to optimize that code later, since a recorded macro's code may be relatively inefficient.

The bad news is that Outlook does not support macro recording. Period. This is one of those annoyances for which there is no workaround.

The Script Editor

NOTE This section covers how to edit a form using the Script Editor and how to get help (it's not as easy as you'd think). Next, we move on to how to use the Outlook Form Designer's Properties and Advanced Properties dialogs to inspect and change form settings. Then we provide a step-by-step example of running sample VBScript code. We'll end with some debugging hints.

Editing Forms with the Script Editor

NOTE   A form is the basic unit of customization in Outlook. Data,
             fields, controls, actions, events, and your code are all at-
             tached to a particular form. Developing Outlook forms is
             unique in that you can't create a new form from scratch; in-
             stead, you must start with a built-in existing form. If you're
             using Outlook in a standalone setting, you would most like-
             ly create a custom form as a vehicle for storing code—and
             perhaps some controls—to manipulate your data inside
             Outlook or to communicate that data with another applica-
             tion like Access or Word. If you're using Outlook with Ex-
             change Server, you'd probably create a custom form as
             part of an enterprise solution. For example, take a look at
             the sample forms supplied on the Office CD (this section
             explains how to install these forms).

One consequence of the Outlook/VBScript mind-set that a new form
must be based on an existing form is that you can't start the Script Editor
directly. You must access it from inside the form you are trying to create/
customize. For example, here's how to edit a new message form* based
on the built-in message form in Outlook 98:

1. Choose Tools → Forms → Design a Form → select Message from the
   Standard Forms Library → Open. (Tools → Forms produces a fly-out
   menu with the following choices: Choose Form, Design This Form,
   Design a Form, Publish Form, Publish Form As, and Script Debugger,
   the latter of which is disabled at this point. We'll cover these shortly.)
   This opens a Message form in design view.

2. Choose Form → View Code, or click on the View Code button to
   open the Script Editor (see Figure 8-1).

In Outlook 97, the user interface for editing forms is not as friendly or
straightforward. Here are the steps to edit a new message form in
Outlook 97:

1. Compose a new mail message item (Ctrl+Shift+M).

2. Choose Tools → Design Outlook Form. Annoyingly, there's no corresponding toolbar button, and the button that looks like the Access
   form/design view toggle button does something quite different
   (Publish Form As).

---

* You can edit any form type with the Script Editor; we've simply chosen the Message form
for use in these examples.

3. Choose Form → View Code, or click on the View Code button to open the Script Editor.

Types of Outlook forms

There are four categories of Outlook forms:

- A Message form, which is perhaps the most common Outlook form. To see what one looks like, simply click on File → New → Mail Message (see Figure 8-6).

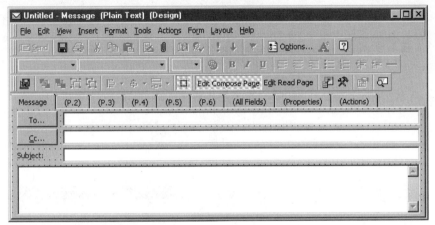

Figure 8-6: A Message form (shown in design view)

- A Post form, which allows you to post, read, and respond to items in a folder. The most common use of a Post form is for threaded folder-based conversations (discussions). When you look at a standard Post form, its title bar reads "Untitled - Discussion" as shown in Figure 8-7. To create one, select any email folder, then select File → New → Post in This Folder (Ctrl+Shift+S).

- An Office Document form, which includes either an Excel, Power-Point, or Word document embedded inside an Outlook form. To create one, select File → New → Office Document, then choose from the templates available in the New Office Document dialog (see Figure 8-8), and click on OK. Respond to the resulting message box to either Post the document in this folder or Send the document to someone, then click on OK. Figure 8-9 shows an Office Document form based on a Word document, and Figure 8-10 shows an Office Document form based on an Excel worksheet. The most common use for such a form is to post the wrapped Office document to a public folder or email it to a colleague. Since an Office Document form is an Office document wrapped inside an Outlook form, it has full

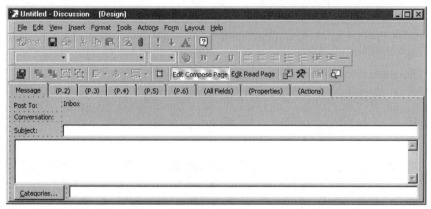

Figure 8-7: A Post form (shown in design view)

access to VBA. This is the key that separates this technology from simply enclosing the document as an attachment. If you're curious about this marginally useful technology, see the Microsoft KnowledgeBase article *OL97: Programmatically Accessing Office Form Documents* (Q168021).

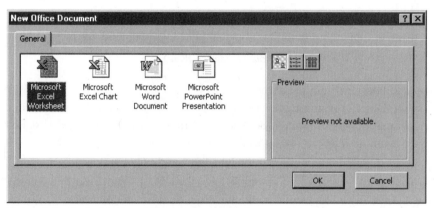

Figure 8-8: Outlook's New Office Document dialog, used to create Office Document forms

- A built-in module form (a Calendar, Contact, and Task), which allows you to use the specific capabilities of each module. To see what one looks like, click on File → New and choose the appropriate module. (Figure 8-11, for example, shows a Contact form in design view.)

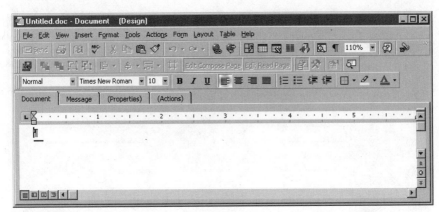

Figure 8-9: An Office Document form based on a Word document (shown in design view)

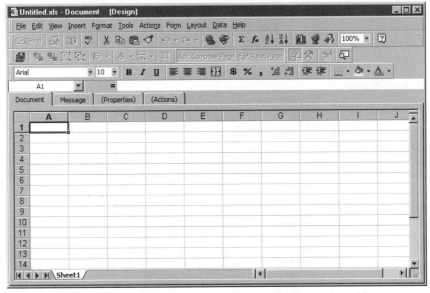

Figure 8-10: An Office Document form based on an Excel worksheet (shown in design view)

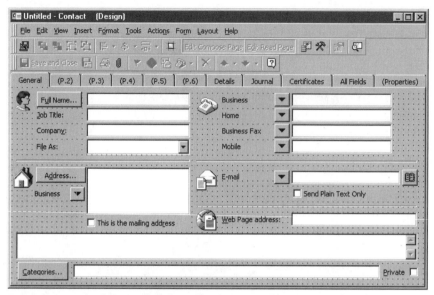

Figure 8-11: A built-in module form (here it's a Contact form shown in design view)

NOTE   If you ever modify a built-in module form (say, your Con-
            tact form) that's been used to create extant items, then you
            need a way to update all those items that are bound to that
            form—via their message class—to use the new form. This
            can only be done programmatically, and that code has al-
            ready been written for you. Go to the USEast Outlook De-
            velopers Site at *www.outlook.useast.com/outlook/*, click on
            the "Update message class of a Form" link, and take it from
            there. Many thanks to Helen Feddema and David Good-
            hand for authoring this helpful Reset Message Class utility.

            By the way, this is a rare example in which Outlook/VB-
            Script solves one of Outlook's user interface shortcomings.
            Since there's no way to change the message class of sever-
            al contact records at once, you have no recourse but to re-
            sort to code. Thanks again, Helen and David.

Sample forms

Microsoft has developed sample forms for such purposes as training and
sales. To see a list of these sample forms, check the help topic "Sample
forms supplied in Outlook." Note that none of these forms (except While
You Were Out) are installed when you install Outlook; you'll find them
on your Office CD. Go to *Valupack\Template\Outlook*, right-click, and
open the file *Outlfrms.exe*, then follow the instructions. The file *Forms.pst*

is placed on your local hard disk, typically in *C:\Program Files\Microsoft Office\Office*. In Outlook, select File → Open Special Folder → Personal Folder, then browse to *Forms.pst* and click on OK (see Figure 8-12).

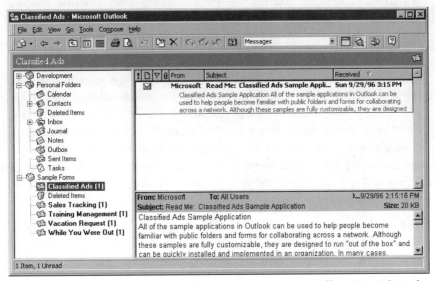

Figure 8-12: The sample Outlook 97 forms available in your Office CD's ValuPack folder

Additional sample forms are available on the *Microsoft Office 97 Resource Kit** CD-ROM. They are: Corporate Calendar, Employee Handbook, Office Expense Report, Help Desk, Job Candidates, Job Postings, Knowledge-base, Project Management, Office Supplies/Equipment Requisition, and Sales Tracking.

More on form commands and the Script Editor

In Outlook 98, when you start from a *new item's* Tools → Forms command, you get these choices:

- Choose Form: displays the Choose Form dialog

- Design This Form: puts the form into design view, ready for editing

- Design a Form: displays the Design Form dialog

- Publish Form: displays the Publish Form As dialog (similar to the familiar File Save As dialog)

- Publish Form As: displays the Publish Form As dialog

- Script Debugger: only enabled for a previously published item/form that is currently running

---

* Published by Microsoft Press, ISBN 1-57231-329-3.

If the item is based on a previously published form, these commands respond accordingly. For example, choosing Publish Form for a previously published form would publish (save) it back on top of itself; for an unpublished form, if you choose Publish Form, then Outlook needs to know where to publish it, so it displays the Publish Form As dialog.

Now back to the Script Editor. As you can see from Figure 8-1, the Script Editor is a desolate place. In Outlook 98, you get five menus: File, Edit, View, Script, and Help. (In Outlook 97, you get four menus: File, Edit, Script, and Help.) The File menu has one command—Close. The Outlook 97 version's Edit menu contains Undo (one level only); the traditional Cut, Copy, and Paste commands, plus a Go To (to advance directly to a particular line of code) and a Select All. The Outlook 98 version adds the much-needed Find, Find Next, and Replace commands. The Outlook 98 version's View menu has two commands that toggle the Status Bar and Tool Bar on and off.

The Outlook 98 version's Script menu has Event Handler and Object Browser commands. (This is a minimalist object browser that, unlike its Office/VBA and Visual Basic browser cousins, can't examine the object models of other applications, only its own.) Unlike Outlook 97, you can't run or stop a script from the Outlook 98 Script Editor, only from the form's user interface. In Outlook 97, the Script menu supports Event, Run, and Stop. The Help menu has one command—Microsoft Outlook Object Library Help. All these features are self-explanatory, although we'll cover the Insert Event Handler dialog box (triggered by Script → Event Handler) later in the chapter. Remember that the Microsoft Outlook Object Library Help (title bar reads "Microsoft Outlook Visual Basic") provides help on the Outlook object model, not VBScript. To get help on forms in Outlook 98, you have to switch to the form's user interface or Outlook's user interface and choose Help → Microsoft Outlook Forms Help. In Outlook 97, you must have first installed the Microsoft Outlook Forms help add-in, as described earlier. Unfortunately, there are no workarounds for the Script Editor's annoyances.

With the Script Editor, you get no environmental preferences, no real user interface to speak of, no docking windows, and no IntelliSense code-writing or help features. Add to this list of missing features in Outlook 97: no search and replace, no toolbars, no debugger, and no Object Browser.

NOTE   You can also open forms in Outlook 98 via Tools → Forms
→ Choose Form. (It's Compose → Choose Form in Outlook
97, where "Compose" is the menu to the right of "Tools"
and its name changes with the folder context, i.e., "Calendar" for a Calendar folder, "Contacts" for a Contacts folder,
"Compose" for any messages folder, and so on; this menu
is consistently named "Actions" in Outlook 98 regardless of
the folder context.) You can also use File → New →
Choose Form (see Figure 8-13). In Outlook 97, you should
get in the habit of holding down the Shift key while opening any form to edit it; this prevents any VBScript event
handler code from running when you open the form.

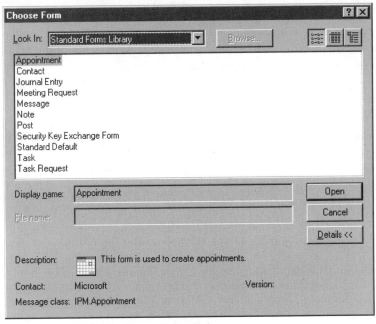

Figure 8-13: Outlook's Choose Form dialog

Getting VBScript, Forms, and Object Model Help in Outlook

NOTE	Now that you know the mechanics of editing a form with the Script Editor, let's explore where and how to get help on VBScript, forms, and Outlook's object model before going any further. Outlook 98 is dramatically improved in this arena; in fact, the only missing component in Outlook 98 is the VBScript language reference (see below for how to get it free on the Web).

For help on VBScript in Outlook 97, since Microsoft didn't include VBScript documentation, you'll have to look elsewhere:

1. *Do this if you're running Outlook 97...*Start by installing the complete version of the Microsoft Outlook Visual Basic help file (that's the description appearing in its title bar, but annoyingly it's called something different in the Script Editor, namely Microsoft Outlook Object Library Help). This help file, *Vbaoutl.hlp*, really documents the Outlook object model, *not* VBScript, and all its code examples are VBA, not VBScript. To install it, go to Outlook and ask the Office Assistant to "get help for visual basic," then select the "Get Help for Visual Basic in Microsoft Outlook" topic. Click on the button at the end of the first paragraph "To do this procedure ... click" and follow the instructions.* Once installed, choose Help → Microsoft Outlook Object Library Help from the Script Editor.

OUTLOOK 98	In Outlook 98, this help file is installed automatically during setup, and it includes both VBScript and VBA code examples. To access it, from the Script Editor choose Help → Microsoft Outlook Object Library Help.

2. *Do this if you're running Outlook 97...*Microsoft Outlook Forms Help—an indispensable Outlook add-in—is available from a variety of sources. Browse to *support.microsoft.com/support/kb/articles/Q161/0/82.asp* and download *Olfrmhlp.exe* (376 KB), which extracts to *Formshlp.exe* and *Readme.txt*. See the latter for installation instructions. This add-in provides much-needed information on Outlook's form design interface and Outlook/VBScript. It integrates into Outlook's help menu: select Help → Microsoft Outlook Forms Help.

---

* Credit to Helen Feddema for initially pointing out these help file discrepancies.

OUTLOOK 98 In Outlook 98, this help file is installed automatically during setup. To access it, select Help → Microsoft Outlook Forms Help from Outlook's user interface or an open form's user interface.

---

3. *Do this in both Outlook 98 and Outlook 97...*Download the *VBScript Language Reference* from *www.microsoft.com/vbscript*. Look for the 32-bit VBScript documentation download for Windows 95 and NT (*VBSDoc.exe*, 247 KB). After running *VBSDoc.exe*, you'll have two new options on your Start → Programs → VBScript Documentation flyout menu: VBScript Language Reference and VBScript Tutorial. Keep in mind, however, that this reference is geared to the IE developer, not the Outlook developer.

4. For help on controls, use Microsoft Outlook Forms Help: from Outlook select Help → Microsoft Outlook Forms Help, go to the Contents tab, double-click on the Outlook Forms Help book, double-click on Control Reference, and finally double-click on Objects. If you haven't installed Microsoft Outlook Forms Help, you'll have to turn to another Office application, like Excel, and use its Office Assistant or the Object Browser. The library you're interested in is called Microsoft Forms 2.0 Object Library in the References dialog (and is referenced by default in VBA projects), and MSForms in the Object Browser's Project/Library box.

Basic Functions

NOTE Let's see how VBScript actually works in Outlook by typing in a program and running it.

In Outlook/VBScript, unlike Office/VBA, you can't type in a subroutine and run or test it directly. Instead, the subroutine must be inside, or called by, a procedure that's connected to a control or other Outlook event. The easiest way to accommodate this is to write a subroutine, then add a bogus command button, CommandButton1, to the form and use the CommandButton1_Click event to call your subroutine. Here's an example:

1. Compose a new mail message item.

2. Choose Tools → Forms → Design This Form (in Outlook 97, choose Tools → Design Outlook Form).

3. Choose Form → View Code.

4. In the Script Editor, type in the code shown in Example 8-2. (We'll explain the purpose of the Option Explicit statement shortly, in the section "Creating a New Program." However, even though we list the Option Explicit statement here, we won't list it in subsequent short examples in order to conserve space.)

Example 8-2: A Simple One-line Outlook/VBScript Subroutine

```
Option Explicit

Sub HelloWorld
    MsgBox "Hello world"
End Sub
```

5. Back in the form, if the Control Toolbox isn't visible, choose Form → Control Toolbox.

6. Click on the form page tab labeled "(P.2)." Locate the command button control in the Toolbox. It's the last control on the second row and has a tooltip of "CommandButton." Click on it once. Now click on the custom form and click-and-drag to paint a command button on it. By default it will have the name and caption CommandButton1 (see Figure 8-14).

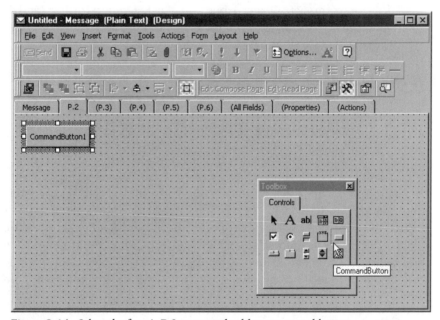

Figure 8-14: Select the form's P.2 page and add a command button

7. Choose Form → View Code and type the code shown in Example 8-3. If you were in Office/VBA, you would be able to right-click on the command button control and choose View Code, which automatically creates a new event procedure named CommandButton1_Click, complete with beginning Sub and ending End Sub statements.

Example 8-3: Using the CommandButton1_Click Trick to Call a Subroutine for Testing Purposes

```
Sub CommandButton1_Click
    HelloWorld
End Sub
```

8. Back in the form, choose Form → Run This Form (in Outlook 97, choose Tools → Design Outlook Form) to switch to run mode. The form in run mode looks like Figure 8-15.

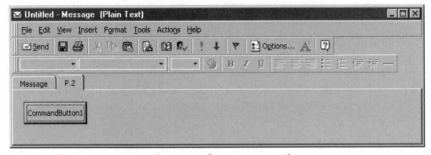

Figure 8-15: Your customized message form in run mode

9. Click on CommandButton1 and you should see a message box like the one shown in Figure 8-16. If you have the Script Editor visible alongside the form, notice that the Script Editor in Outlook 97 is grayed out while in run mode, whereas in Outlook 98 the Script Editor just idles.

Figure 8-16: Your first Outlook/VBScript message box

10. To stop the running script, choose File → Close from the running form's menu (in Outlook 97 it's Tools → Design Outlook Form); this switches to design mode. You'll be using the Script Editor and this form again, so leave them open.

NOTE   VBScript is not case sensitive. Although you can enter
                VBScript code in all lower case or mixed case or whatever
                case and have it run normally, it's a good idea to get in the
                habit of using different cases for the language's keywords
                as you find them in the help file and for variable/constant
                names in accordance with a well-established naming con-
                vention (for one such system, see the Microsoft Knowledge-
                Base   article   *Microsoft   Consulting   Services   Naming
                Conventions for VB* (Q110264)). This way, your code will
                be more consistent and readable for you and your associ-
                ates.

The Microsoft Script Debugger

In Outlook 98, the Script Debugger comes with your installation as part
of the marriage between Outlook and Internet Explorer 4. It's available
from a form's Tools → Forms fly-out menu, but only while the form is
running, and only for forms that have code attached. At the time of this
writing, it works less effectively with Outlook than with Internet Explorer,
but your mileage may vary. As with earlier versions, the latest Script
Debugger's window is still read-only, so you can't edit code during execution as you can in VB and VBA.

You can download the latest version of the Microsoft Script Debugger
from *www.microsoft.com/scripting/debugger/*. From that page, select the
"Microsoft Script Debugger 1.0" link and follow the instructions. What
you get when you install the debugger will depend on when you download it. Some months back, the file *Scrdebug.exe* would be installed on
your system, typically in *C:\Program Files\Internet Explorer.* With
Outlook 98, the filename appears to be *Msscrdbg.exe* in *C:\Program
Files\Microsoft Office.* Currently, the posted debugger is only compatible
with IE4. Microsoft has apparently stopped supporting pre-IE4 versions of
the debugger. There are copies of some of the different, earlier versions
of the debugger at *ftp://ftp.useast.com/Microsoft/VBScript/*.

A discussion of the debugger's capabilities are beyond the scope of this
book, but it does come with online help and there are some FAQs on
Microsoft's site (see the aforementioned URL).

One final caveat. If you're running Outlook 97 and Internet Explorer 3.02
and manage to get your hands on a pre-IE4 script debugger, the
Microsoft KnowledgeBase article *Internet Explorer 3.02 Problems After
Installing Script Debugger* (Q166399) warns, "After you install Microsoft
Script Debugger for Internet Explorer on a computer on which Internet

Explorer 3.02 is installed, the new security features included with Internet Explorer 3.02 may not function properly." The article goes on to suggest a workaround of removing the debugger and reinstalling IE 3.02. Of course, this won't do you any good if you want to use the debugger and upgrade to IE 4. How annoying.

Writing Outlook/VBScript Programs

NOTE　　　You've covered a big chunk of conceptual material so far in this chapter. Now it's time to take VBScript for another spin around the block and do some more hands-on coding. After that, we'll proceed to a discussion of concepts that sound ominous at first glance, but are really quite simple. They are in fact the tools of your trade when developing in either Outlook/VBScript or Office/VBA: objects, properties, methods, and events.

Before we dive into the big, bad world of events and object models, let's take a few minutes to write and run a couple of simple VBScript programs. These will give you a fighting chance of easing into the Outlook/VBScript way of thinking.

Creating a New Program

Let's keep working with the form we created in the previous section and add another subroutine. This one is called *LoopPractice* and it iterates a variable through a series of values from 1 to 10 while displaying the value in a message box each time it loops. Type in the code shown in Example 8-4 in the Script Editor.

Example 8-4: The LoopPractice Subroutine

```
Option Explicit

Dim i

Sub HelloWorld
    MsgBox "Hello world"
End Sub

Sub CommandButton1_Click
    HelloWorld
End Sub

Sub LoopPractice
    For i = 1 to 10
```

Example 8-4: The LoopPractice Subroutine (continued)

```
        MsgBox i
    Next i
End Sub
```

NOTE   This example includes the `Option Explicit` statement at
                  the beginning of the script, as should all your scripts. Even
                  though VBScript doesn't support strong typing,* if you ex-
                  plicitly declare all variables, it will be easier to spot one of
                  the most common bugs in programming: a misspelled vari-
                  able or constant name. The variable *i* has been declared at
                  the top of the script with the `Dim i` statement.

Change *HelloWorld* to *LoopPractice* in the CommandButton1_Click procedure, then run it. (If you prefer, Example 8-5 shows how you can
"remark out" one statement without having to delete it: the single apos-
trophe at the beginning of the HelloWorld statement is a remark character
and causes the interpreter to skip the statement altogether.)

Example 8-5: Tell the CommandButton1_Click Procedure to Call a Different
Subroutine

```
Sub CommandButton1_Click
    'HelloWorld
     LoopPractice
End Sub
```

NOTE   From this point on, when we say "run it," we mean this:
                  switch the form to run mode and click on the button or
                  control that's calling the test procedure.

Hey, what's this? Your first Outlook/VBScript error message (see Figure
8-17). And it's an annoying one. Welcome to the arcane and misleading
world of Outlook/VBScript debugging. First of all, you won't find help on
errors in any of Outlook's scattered help files. You are truly on your own
here.

First go to the alleged offending line number—click on OK to clear the
message box, and ordinarily the cursor will be in that line; if not, select
Edit → Go To and enter the line number. In this particular case, it turns

---

* Strong typing refers to the enforced use of specific variable types when declaring a variable,
like Byte, Boolean, Integer, Long, Currency, String, Object, and so on. VBScript doesn't use
strong typing.

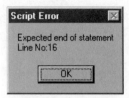

Figure 8-17: Your first Outlook/VBScript error message

out it's a goofy VBA versus VBScript syntax difference that's causing you grief. In Visual Basic and Visual Basic for Applications, the Next clause of a For...Next loop can include the counter or not; it's optional. In VBScript, it *cannot* be included, or you get the error we're dissecting. This syntax idiosyncrasy may confuse unwary Outlook/VBScript newcomers, and also frustrate anyone attempting to port code from VB or VBA to Outlook/VBScript.

To squelch the error, delete i from the Next i statement. (Specifically, to implement the corrected macro: close the running form, go back to the form's design view, fix the offending statement, then run this form again.)

This is a fully functional VBScript program. Translated into English, it goes something like this:

1. This is a subroutine called *LoopPractice*.

2. Do the following two steps, with *i* first set to 1, then to 2, then to 3, and so forth, and finally with *i* set to 10.

3. Put a message box up on the screen that contains the current value of *i*.

4. Repeat with the next value of *i*.

5. This is the end of the subroutine called *LoopPractice*.

If we were writing this procedure in Office/VBA, we would follow good programming practice and explicitly dimension *i* as an integer variable, like this:

```
Dim i As Integer
```

But Outlook/VBScript only supports one variable type—Variant—and it applies by default, so we used the simpler form of Dim i. As we mentioned earlier, it's beneficial to use the Option Explicit and Dim statements to declare all your variables, despite Outlook's lack of strong variable typing.

Embellishment

The best way to learn about Outlook/VBScript is to play with it a bit. Try these variations.

The `For` statement can do lots of things. Replace `For i = 1 to 10` with:

```
For i = 5 to 10
For i = 1 to 10 Step 2
For i = 5 to 1 Step -1
```

The *MsgBox* function has three commonly used parameters:

```
Msgbox(Prompt, Buttons, Title)
```

The first parameter (*Prompt*) is just the message that appears in the box. The second parameter (*Buttons*) specifies the buttons (OK, Cancel, etc.) and the icons (none, exclamation mark, question mark, etc.) that appear in the box. The third parameter (*Title*) appears as the box's window title. Try these in place of `MsgBox i`, and in each case see if you can guess what will happen before you run the program:

```
MsgBox i*10
MsgBox i, vbOKOnly
MsgBox i, vbYesNoCancel
MsgBox "The value of i is: " & i, vbExclamation, "My Loop Practice
Routine"
```

A message box produced by the last *MsgBox* statement is shown in Figure 8-18.

Figure 8-18: An embellished VBScript message box

`vbOKOnly`, `vbYesNoCancel`, and `vbExclamation` are examples of Visual Basic constants (available to VBScript effective with language engine version 2.0 and higher). They're numbers predefined by Visual Basic and given relatively easy to remember names. For example, `vbYesNoCancel` is pre-assigned the value 3. You could try to remember that the number 3 will produce Yes, No, and Cancel buttons on a Visual Basic message box. But you'll undoubtedly find it much easier to remember the constant `vbYesNoCancel`. Since these general-purpose constants are the same across all Visual Basic programs and the Office applications that support VBA (including Outlook/VBScript), your learning curve is lessened dramatically.

Saving and Updating Forms

If you want to save the form you're working on in one of your forms
libraries so you can use it later, here are the steps.

NOTE   Even after you've saved the form in a forms library, there's
an additional prompt asking if you want to save the form.
This creates a copy of the form in an active folder (for example, stores a message form in your Drafts folder). So unless you want to do this, it's safe to select No.

1. In Outlook 98, select Tools → Forms → Publish Form As (in Outlook
   97, select File → Publish Form As) and enter a form name, as shown
   in Figure 8-19. (For our purposes, use the name Outlook
   Annoyances.)

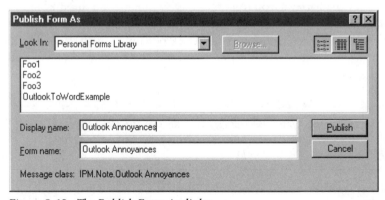

Figure 8-19: The Publish Form As dialog

2. Outlook sets the message class automatically, based on the class of
   the source form plus the form name as a suffix. See Table 8-3 for
   more information about standard message classes.

3. To work with a form privately before publishing it to others via email
   or a network, store it in your Personal Forms library.

Outlook includes a dialog box from which you can manage your custom forms. In Outlook 98 Corporate/Workgroup mode, select Tools → Options → Other, click on the Advanced Options button, click on the Custom Forms button, and click on the Manage Forms button, which displays the Forms Manager dialog. From here you can copy, update, delete, and examine properties of your custom forms. Annoyingly, Outlook 98's Internet Only mode omits this dialog from its user interface, meaning that the feature is simply not accessible. In Outlook 97, select Tools → Options → Manage Forms and click on the Manage Forms button.

For backup or distribution purposes, you can save your custom forms as standalone files in a format Outlook calls Office Template (*.oft). From a form's design view, select File → Save As, then save the form with a name of your choosing to the desired folder. To open an existing Office Template, choose Tools → Forms → Design a Form, select "Templates in File System" in the Look In control, and select the desired file followed by Open.

Important Outlook Constants

The next two tables provide you with important programmatic values for Outlook item types and Outlook folder types. Table 8-2 displays folder types, values, and their Outlook constant names. Annoyingly, Outlook/VBScript doesn't support these Outlook constants (with an "ol" prefix); these are only available if you're controlling Outlook from another application (like Word or Excel) via OLE Automation. Outlook does support Visual Basic constants (with a "vb" prefix) beginning with VBScript 2. Table 8-3 displays item types, values, Outlook constant names, and message classes.

NOTE   Beginning with VBScript 2, you can use the Const statement to add these Outlook constants to each script and overcome this limitation.

Table 8-2: Programmatic values for Outlook folder objects

Folder Type	Value	Constant
Calendar	9	olFolderCalendar
Contacts	10	olFolderContacts
Deleted Items	3	olFolderDeletedItems

Table 8-2: Programmatic values for Outlook folder objects (continued)

Folder Type	Value	Constant
Journal	11	olFolderJournal
Mail (Inbox)	6	olFolderInbox
Mail (Outbox)	4	olFolderOutbox
Mail (Sent Items)	5	olFolderSentMail
Notes	12	olFolderNotes
Tasks	13	olFolderTasks

Table 8-3: Programmatic values for Outlook item objects

Item Type	Value	Constant	Message Class
Appointment	1	olAppointmentItem	IPM.Appointment
Contact	2	olContactItem	IPM.Contact
Journal	4	olJournalItem	IPM.Activity
Mail message	0	olMailItem	IPM.Note
Note	5	olNoteItem	IPM.StickyNote
Post	6	olPostItem	IPM.Post
Task	3	olTaskItem	IPM.Task

WARNING   The message classes for mail messages and notes are deceptively similar. A mail message's message class is IPM.Note and a note's message class is IPM.StickyNote.

VBScript's Role in Designing Custom Forms

NOTE   In the next several sections, we take a quick look at the other parts of Outlook/VBScript—valuable parts that you may want to exploit in your programs somewhere down the line. As before, we won't even try for completeness (which would take another book's worth of pages). Instead our goal is to give you an idea of the major chunks of the language that are available, and how they all fit together.

So far we've covered the "Basic" part of VBScript. But the programming language itself is only part of the story, and only one of the tools at your disposal to customize Outlook to work for you and, if you develop custom Outlook applications for others, your users.

The "visual" part of Outlook/VBScript consists of a drag-and-drop construction kit of controls on forms, plus hooks to associate controls* on the forms—command buttons, text boxes, checkboxes, spin buttons, ActiveX controls, and more—with your program code.

Four kinds of hooks between the "visual" and the "Basic Script"—the forms and program code—come into play:

1. Your program can set many of the controls' characteristics. For example, you can write a program that changes the name that appears on a command button, or one that changes the color of the entire form. These characteristics are called control *properties.*

2. Your program can retrieve controls' characteristics (i.e., control properties). For example, if you have checkboxes on the form, your program can look to see if a particular box has been checked.

3. You can set up certain programs to be run when specific things happen to the form. For example, you can tell VBScript "run the program called Foobar whenever the user clicks on this button."† The things that can happen are called *events.* We call the programs that handle control events *event handlers.*

4. Finally, you can make your program "trigger" or "fire" events. For example, you can write a program to tell VBScript to behave precisely the same way it would've behaved if the user had clicked the OK button. Think of this as an invisible hand that you can manipulate from inside your programs. Sure, the user can click an OK button. But your program can "click" the OK button just as well.

Let's take a look at custom forms, how they're constructed, and what options are available to you. Then we'll tie together the "visual" and the "Basic" with a demonstration of control event handlers.

---

* As far as we're concerned in this discussion of Outlook/VBScript, "controls" are simply the things that sit on a form. In the larger Windows world, controls can sit on forms, dialogs, Excel sheets, Word documents, Web pages, and many other places. You can create your own controls with Visual Basic 5.0, Control Creation Edition.

† Remember that in Outlook/VBScript the Click event is only available to CommandButton controls, whereas in VBA the Click event applies to *any* form control.

NOTE   The terms "event" and "event handler" need a context in order to be correctly understood. In the context of custom forms (dialog boxes in Office/VBA), these terms refer to *control* events. In the context of an application's event model (referred to in some Microsoft documentation as the "code behind documents" feature), these terms refer to application and/or object events that you can control with code—for example, events occurring at the application (Excel and Word), document (Word), sheet (Excel), and Workbook (Excel) level. PowerPoint doesn't support application events, not even the old Auto macros (except for a loaded add-in, which runs an Auto_Open macro when loaded and when PowerPoint starts, and which runs an Auto_Close macro when the add-in is unloaded or PowerPoint closes). Outlook doesn't support any application events. In the context of Outlook, an event could refer either to the one supported control event (Click) or an item event (see Table 8-4).

The Properties and Advanced Properties Dialogs

NOTE   These two dialogs are your tools for examining and changing properties of the fields and controls on a form.

The Properties and Advanced Properties dialogs* reveal all the possible properties—their names and settings—for a property sheet or a particular control on the form designer's grid, and allow you to change those settings. (We discuss properties, objects, methods, events, and their relationship to Outlook and your code in upcoming sections.)

As shown in Figures 8-20 through 8-22, the Properties dialog has three tabs: Display, Value, and Validation. These self-explanatory tabs control these aspects of the control. (These figures were produced like this: on (P.2) of a standard Message form, drag Subject from the Field Chooser dialog and drop it onto the grid, then right-click on the text box control and choose Properties or Advanced Properties.)

---

* These dialogs appear when you select Form → Properties, or Form → Advanced Properties, respectively, from the design mode form's menu, or when you right-click on a particular object and select either the Properties or the Advanced Properties option.

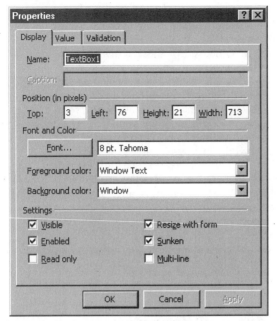

Figure 8-20: Display tab of the Outlook Form Designer's Properties dialog for a text box control

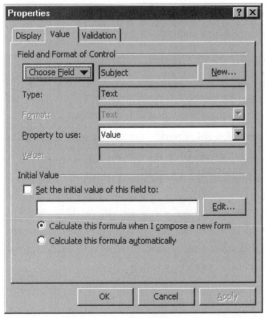

Figure 8-21: Value tab of the Outlook Form Designer's Properties dialog for a text box control

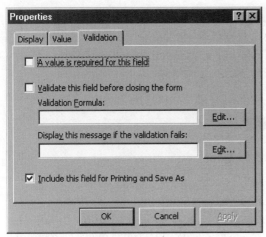

Figure 8-22: Validation tab of the Outlook Form Designer's Properties dialog for a text box control

The Advanced Properties dialog—which confusingly has a window title of "Properties" just like the regular Properties dialog—controls additional properties and their settings, as shown in Figure 8-23.

NOTE   If you want both of these dialogs open at once, you have to open Advanced Properties first, then Properties. Some important properties in the Properties window are not on the Advanced Properties window, so you can't do everything from the more convenient modeless Advanced Properties window (the most important is the bound field).

More on the Outlook Form Designer

NOTE   Let's experiment some more with the Outlook Form Designer's ability to place controls on a custom page.

In Outlook you design custom forms, not custom dialog boxes. Although in general the term "form" has come to be synonymous with "dialog box," an Outlook form is only vaguely related to a dialog box. For a bit of Office perspective, the UserForms forms engine is shared by Excel, PowerPoint, and Word. Access uses its own proprietary forms engine, and Outlook uses yet another proprietary forms engine.

Figure 8-23: The Outlook Form Designer's Advanced Properties dialog for a text box control

To see what's going on, let's construct a new, simple custom form. If you're not in the Script Editor already, create a new message form, switch to design view, click on the (P.2) tab, and choose Form → View Code. Now choose Form → Control Toolbox.

For this simple exercise we're going to place a single command button control on the form. To do so, follow the steps we used earlier in the chapter. Only this time we want the command button to say something slightly more interesting than "CommandButton1." The text that appears on a command button face is simply the Caption property of the command button. Right-click on the command button, choose Advanced Properties (if not already checked), double-click on the Caption field, change it from CommandButton1 to "Push Me!", then click on Apply. The result is shown in Figure 8-24.

Congratulations. That's all it takes to build a custom form in Outlook/ VBScript. In fact, you've now done it twice! Granted, it doesn't do much just yet, but adding intelligence to a form remains the provenance of event handlers. To see what this form can do, run it. Your custom form will spring to life, as shown in Figure 8-25. Note how you can push the command button, but it doesn't do much, aside from looking marvelous. When you're bored (should take about two seconds), return to design mode.

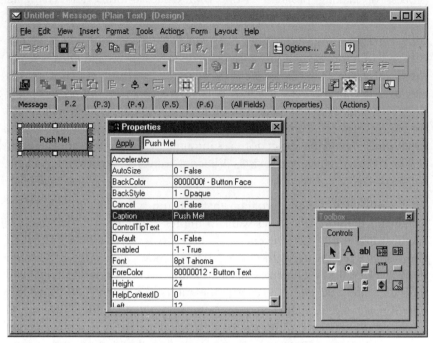

Figure 8-24: Changing the Caption property of CommandButton1

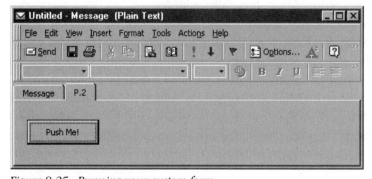

Figure 8-25: Running your custom form

Control Events and Control Event Handlers

NOTE   Now that you've learned how to add controls to a custom
               form, it's easy to link a control's behavior to your code.

Let's write an event handler that will accomplish something when you
push the form's command button. We think you'll be intrigued with the

process of making programs work with Outlook forms, and changing those forms from inside a program.

We're going to write a program that runs whenever the user clicks this command button. To put this another way, the program should run when CommandButton1's Click event occurs (fires). The way VBScript associates events with their event handlers is simplicity itself, and relies on the names of the event handler subroutines. For example, our command button is named CommandButton1. When CommandButton1's Click event fires, VBScript looks for a subroutine called CommandButton1_Click. If that subroutine exists, VBScript runs it; otherwise, nothing happens. Easy.

So if we want to write a program that will run when the user clicks on CommandButton1—or, if you want to impress your boss, "a handler for CommandButton1's Click event"—we need to write a subroutine called CommandButton1_Click. In Office/VBA, whenever you want to write an event handler for any control's most common event, you just double-click on the control and Office/VBA gets the subroutine going for you. In this case if you were to double-click on CommandButton1, Office/VBA would automatically move you into the code window and start a subroutine for you called CommandButton1_Click, including the starting and ending statements (Sub and End Sub). In Outlook/VBScript, you'll have to switch to the Script Editor manually and type in *all* the statements. (Double-clicking on an Outlook form control does nothing, and right-clicking it pops up a shortcut menu, but without a View Code option, whereas Office/VBA includes a View Code option in its menu.)

Type in the VBScript program shown in Example 8-6.

Example 8-6: CommandButton1's Click Event Handler in Outlook/VBScript

```
Option Explicit

Sub CommandButton1_Click()
    Dim objControl
    Dim objPage
    Set objPage = Item.GetInspector.ModifiedFormPages("P.2")
    Set objControl = objPage.CommandButton1
    If objControl.Caption = "Push Me!" Then
        objControl.Caption = "Push Me AGAIN!"
    Else
        objControl.Caption = "Push Me!"
    End If
End Sub
```

The program works by looking at the text on the face of the command button and changing it according to what it sees there. Or, in VBScript-speak, it examines and sets the Caption property of the CommandButton1 control object. But what's all this gibberish about Set, and why does the code refer to some abstract thing called *objControl* instead of CommandButton1? The answer lies deep in the heart of Outlook/VBScript's approach to building forms. And it's acutely annoying.

In Outlook/VBScript, when you refer to a form in code, you must do so through the object model hierarchy. Look at the first of the two Set statements. First, you have to point to the Item object (that's the item you create when you compose a new item or choose a form). Then you must use the GetInspector property to return an Inspector object, which is simply the current item's form. Next, by using the ModifiedFormPages property, you get back the Pages collection object that contains all the pages for this form. You point to the current page by name (here it's "P.2"), and now you have created a bona fide object expression in VBScript that, on the right side of the assignment statement, points to the current page. Set it to a variable (here we call it *objPage*), and you're ready to drill down to the controls on that page.

Look at the second Set statement. The variable *objPage* now points to the P.2 page, and all that's left to do is somehow point to one of the controls on that page. Do it by control name. Set a variable called *objControl* to point to *objPage*'s CommandButton1 control. The remainder of the subroutine refers to this *objControl* variable.

If you're accustomed to Office/VBA, the code would look like Example 8-7. In Office/VBA, when writing code for a specific UserForm's control event handlers, the development environment knows you're referring to the local form, thereby saving you the referencing overhead.

Example 8-7: CommandButton1's Click Event Handler in Office/VBA

```
Sub CommandButton1_Click()
    If CommandButton1.Caption = "Push Me!" Then
        CommandButton1.Caption = "Push Me AGAIN!"
    Else
        CommandButton1.Caption = "Push Me!"
    End If
End Sub
```

Now, back to Outlook....Once you're done typing in the code shown in Example 8-6, run the form. Click on the command button a few times to make sure all is well (see Figure 8-26). Then choose Tools → Design Outlook Form. The form stops; and you'll return to design mode.

The enormous number of events available for Office/VBA UserForms gives you unprecedented leeway in making custom dialog boxes work the way you want them to work. Not so in Outlook, with its severely

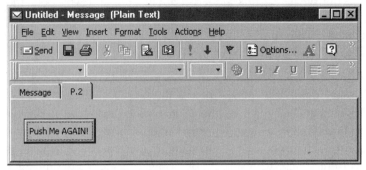

Figure 8-26: The CommandButton1_Click() event handler in action

limited forms event model, as shown in Table 8-4. With no application events, a constrained and proprietary form design environment, and VBScript as a subset of Visual Basic, many developers interested in manipulating data stored in Outlook have turned to OLE Automation. With OLE Automation, you can use all the power and intelligence of Visual Basic or Office/VBA to have, say, Excel simply "call" Outlook invisibly in the background and return data, unfettered by Outlook's limited form and user interface capabilities. We cover this OLE Automation approach later in the chapter.

On the other hand, Outlook does provide eleven distinct events that apply to items (see Figure 8-27); these events are included at the end of Table 8-4.

Table 8-4: Comparison of the Outlook/VBScript and Office/VBA event models

	Forms		Controls	
Event Name	Outlook/ VBScript	Office/VBA	Outlook/ VBScript	Office/VBA
Activate	No (closest Outlook equivalent is Open)	Yes	—	—
AddControl	No	Yes	—	—
Before-DragOver	No	Yes	No	Yes
Before-DropOr-Paste	No	Yes	No	Yes
Click	No	Yes	Yes (only the Command-Button control)	Yes

Table 8-4: Comparison of the Outlook/VBScript and Office/VBA event models (continued)

Event Name	Forms		Controls	
	Outlook/ VBScript	Office/VBA	Outlook/ VBScript	Office/VBA
DblClick	No	Yes	No	Yes
Deactivate	No	Yes	—	—
Enter	—	—	No	Yes
Error	No	Yes	No	Yes
Exit	—	—	No	Yes
Initialize	No (closest Outlook equivalent is Open)	Yes	—	—
KeyDown	No	Yes	No	Yes
KeyPress	No	Yes	No	Yes
KeyUp	No	Yes	No	Yes
Layout	No	Yes	—	—
Mouse-Down	No	Yes	No	Yes
Mouse-Move	No	Yes	No	Yes
MouseUp	No	Yes	No	Yes
Query-Close	No	Yes	—	—
Remove-Control	No	Yes	—	—
Resize	No	Yes	—	—
Scroll	No	Yes	—	—
Terminate	No (closest Outlook equivalent is Close)	Yes	—	—
Zoom	No	Yes	—	—
Close	Item event	No (closest Office equivalent is Terminate)	—	—
CustomAction	Item event	No	—	—

Table 8-4: Comparison of the Outlook/VBScript and Office/VBA event models (continued)

Event Name	Forms		Controls	
	Outlook/ VBScript	Office/VBA	Outlook/ VBScript	Office/VBA
Custom- Property- Change	Item event	No (closest Office equiva- lent is a control's Change event)	—	Yes (via a control's Change event)
Forward	Item event	—	—	—
Open	Item event	No (closest Office equiva- lents are Acti- vate, Initialize)	—	—
Property- Change	Item event	No (closest Office equiva- lent is a control's Change event)	—	Yes (via a control's Change event)
Read	Item event	—	—	—
Reply	Item event	—	—	—
ReplyAll	Item event	—	—	—
Send	Item event	—	—	—
Write	Item event	—	—	—

Outlook Events

NOTE Here's an example of how to create code for a specific item event, in this case the **Item_Open** event.

As shown at the end of Table 8-4, Outlook has eleven item events that fire as these events occur. Here's an example of writing an event handler for a form's Open event:

Figure 8-27: Microsoft Outlook Forms Help table of contents with the Events book open

1. In the Script Editor, select Script → Event Handler (Script → Event in Outlook 97), choose Open, then click on Add. This creates the new procedure shown in Example 8-8 for you.

Example 8-8: An Item's Event Handler Procedure (Item_Open) Looks Like This When You First Create It

```
Function Item_Open()

End Function
```

2. Type the code shown in Example 8-9. This code causes the P.2 page to always be selected when opening the form (instead of Message), then runs the CommandButton1_Click procedure that switches the command button's label between "Push Me!" and "Push Me AGAIN!"

Example 8-9: A Modified Item_Open Event Handler

```
Function Item_Open()
    ' select the P.2 page
    GetInspector.SetCurrentFormPage("P.2")
    ' invoke the label-switching code you wrote earlier (call
    '    the CommandButton1's Click event handler)
    CommandButton1_Click
End Function
```

3. Republish the form, close it, and then reopen it (Tools → Forms → Choose Form, or in Outlook 97 it's File → New → Choose Form). The Item_Open event procedure will be invoked automatically when the form loads, the P.2 page will be on top (instead of the Message page), and the command button's caption will change from the value it had when the form was last published.

Outlook Controlling Outlook

Back in Chapter 6, *A Cookbook for Conversion*, we set up a scenario in which you imported a sample Excel database into a temporary Contacts folder named *Imported from Excel*. Since the source application has two address field groups—Primary and Secondary—with no way to differentiate between home and business address fields, we need some code to help us. The rule we need to code is: if the contact's company name is empty, move the business address values to the home address fields, unless the home address fields already contain information (i.e., aren't all empty), in which case do nothing.

Here are the steps to create and test this program.

1. Create a new Contact form and add one command button with a caption "Outlook to Outlook (Example)".

2. Add the code shown in Example 8-10.

*Example 8-10: An Outlook/VBScript Program Using Rules to Move
Data Between Business and Home Address Fields (Based on the Chapter 6
Import Example)*

```
Option Explicit

'   ------------------------------------------------------------------
' Purpose:   Run rules described in Chapter 8 to swap address data
'            between home and company fields (see text for details).
'
' Inputs:    None
'
' Updated:   03/05/98 (PCG) - written for Outlook Annoyances
'   ------------------------------------------------------------------
Sub CommandButton1_Click
    ' ----- Declarations/initializations
    Dim objItem
    Dim objItems
    Dim objNameSpace
    Dim objNewContactFolder
    Dim objPersonalFolders

    ' ----- Main body
    ' get the NameSpace object
```

*Example 8-10: An Outlook/VBScript Program Using Rules to Move
Data Between Business and Home Address Fields (Based on the Chapter 6
Import Example) (continued)*

```
Set objNameSpace = Application.GetNameSpace("MAPI")
' get the root PST
Set objPersonalFolders = _
    objNameSpace.Folders("Personal Folders")
' get the temporary Contacts folder one level below the root
Set objNewContactFolder = _
    objPersonalFolders.Folders("Imported from Excel")
' get the collection of all items in "Imported from Excel"
' folder
Set objItems = objNewContactFolder.Items
' walk through all the items
For Each objItem In objItems
    If Len(objItem.CompanyName) = 0 Then
        ' there's no company name for this contact,
        '    so it's not a business contact
        If fblnNoHomeAddress(objItem) Then
            ' if all Home address fields are empty,
            '    move all Business address values to
            '    corresponding Home address fields
            objItem.HomeAddressStreet = _
                objItem.BusinessAddressStreet
            objItem.HomeAddressCity = _
                objItem.BusinessAddressCity
            objItem.HomeAddressState = _
                objItem.BusinessAddressState
            objItem.HomeAddressPostalCode = _
                objItem.BusinessAddressPostalCode
            ' empty all Business address fields
            objItem.BusinessAddressStreet = ""
            objItem.BusinessAddressCity = ""
            objItem.BusinessAddressState = ""
            objItem.BusinessAddressPostalCode = ""
            ' save the changes to this record
            objItem.Save
        Else
            ' not all Home address fields are empty,
            '    so don't overwrite Home with Business addresses
        End If
    Else
        ' there is a company name for this contact,
        '    so it's a business contact, therefore do nothing
    End If
Next
End Sub
```

Example 8-10: An Outlook/VBScript Program Using Rules to Move
Data Between Business and Home Address Fields (Based on the Chapter 6
Import Example) (continued)

```
' ----------------------------------------------------------------
' Purpose:  Returns True if all Home address fields are empty, else
'           returns False.
'
' Inputs:   objContactRecord - the Contact record of interest
'
' Returns:  Boolean sub-type
'
' Updated:  03/05/98 (PCG) - written for Outlook Annoyances
' ----------------------------------------------------------------
Function fblnNoHomeAddress(objContactRecord)
    If Len(objContactRecord.HomeAddress) = 0 Then
        fblnNoHomeAddress = True
    Else
        fblnNoHomeAddress = False
    End If
End Function


' ----------------------------------------------------------------
' Purpose:  Set P.2 active.
'
' Inputs:   None
'
' Returns:  n/a
'
' Updated:  03/05/98 (PCG) - written for Outlook Annoyances
' ----------------------------------------------------------------
Function Item_Open()
    ' select the P.2 page
    GetInspector.SetCurrentFormPage("P.2")
End Function
```

3. Publish this form with the name `OutlookToOutlook`.

4. Make sure your Imported from Excel folder is as you left it when you completed Chapter 6.

5. Add a new test Contact to the Imported from Excel folder: Mary Smith, no company name, no other values, but completely fill out all Business address fields (Street, City, State/Province, ZIP/Postal Code) with any test values you like.

6. Run this form and click on its command button. When done, the business address values for *only* the Mary Smith record will have been moved to her corresponding Home address fields. No other records' addresses will have been changed, since in this scenario they are all business contacts (i.e., have non-empty company names).

Controlling Office Applications Using Object Models

So much for the introduction to Outlook/VBScript, its programming environment, and the way VBScript influences—and is influenced by—custom forms. If you're a newcomer to programming, what you learn about VBScript will be immediately useful in Visual Basic or any of the Office applications that host VBA, because VBScript is a dialect of Visual Basic. If you're already familiar with VB or VBA, then—as we've pointed out in the past few sections—you'll be a leg up on Outlook/VBScript.

Now let's examine the ways in which Outlook/VBScript can control Outlook.

A Grammatical Take on Objects, Properties, and Methods

NOTE   It all boils down to nouns (objects), adjectives (properties), and verbs (methods).

Buzzwords, buzzwords.

Wherever you look in Outlook/VBScript and Office/VBA, you'll find references to objects, properties, and methods. They constitute the ruling triumvirate of the VBA/VBScript party. You'll see the terms mentioned so often that you might be tempted to believe they represent some sort of cosmic truth. That they're a literary shorthand for The Fundamental Concept Behind VBA/VBScript, Life, the Universe, and Everything. That somehow understanding the difference between an object, property, and method will bestow instant transcendental illumination on your road to VBA/VBScript enlightenment.

Ha.

Chances are good that you're reasonably well versed in the tenets of grammar. If so, here's what you need to know: an object is a noun; a property is an adjective; and a method is a verb. That's it. Well, one small embellishment: a collection is simply an object that contains—you guessed it—a collection of related objects. The position of any object in a collection can change and is therefore unpredictable. Think "nouns rolling about freely inside a box."

Fortunately, object modeling hasn't yet descended to the level of adverbial clauses and the subjunctive case. But those days are coming.*

Objects are things. In Outlook, that includes the active window, the MAPI message store, folders, items, custom forms, controls on forms, and so on. The most fundamental object in Outlook is the item, of which there are seven distinct types, as shown earlier in Table 8-3. In Excel, one of the most fundamental objects is the range—a conglomeration of cells that could be a single cell, an entire column or row, a selection of cells that includes one or more contiguous blocks of cells, or a 3-D range. In Word, objects includes documents, paragraphs, words, bookmarks, footnotes, built-in dialog boxes, and much more. One of the most fundamental objects in Word is also the range—a block of text with a beginning point and an ending point, that includes everything in between the two. In PowerPoint, you'll work mostly with the presentation object (analogous to a Word document or Excel workbook), which in turn contains slide objects.

The following shared Office components have object models, too: Office Assistant, Office Binder, Office CommandBars, Office FileSearch, Data Access for ODBCDirect Workspaces, Data Access for Microsoft Jet Workspaces, Microsoft Forms, Microsoft Map 97, and the Visual Basic Editor. In Office/VBA, you can view these object libraries with the Object Browser (in Outlook/VBScript—which has no object browsing capability—you'll need to fire up another Office application, say, Excel): simply go into any VBA code module and select Tools → References, then check the appropriate library in the list and click on OK (some are already included in

---

* A quick question to you object modelers out there—and we know you're reading this. What do you call a property of a property? (Grammatically, that's an adverb.) How long before you draw a distinction between methods that operate directly on associated objects, changing the object itself, and methods that merely change the contents or appearance of an object? (Akin to the distinction between transitive and intransitive verbs.) Better brush up on your Latin, folks.

another object library). Now you can browse through that component's object library. Try it with Microsoft Map 97 (called "MSMap" in the Object Browser). MSMap's first-level objects are Templates (map templates), Features (features in the specified map), Datasets (a range of cells used to create a map), Themes (themes that are displayed in the specified map), and PinMaps (pin maps that you can plot on the specified map).

Programs are considered to be objects, as are custom dialog boxes and controls on them (true for forms and controls in Outlook/VBScript). Whenever you're tempted to point at something on the screen and call it a "thing," chances are very good it's an object.

Properties refer to the characteristics of objects. You've already worked with the Caption property of the command button control object. It probably won't surprise you to learn that Name is a property of the MAPIFolder object (a fancy way of saying an Outlook folder object), or that Subject is a property of a MailItem object as well as many other types of Outlook items.

Methods do things to objects. For example, the Add method applied to Outlook's Folders object (a collection object, actually) adds (creates) a new folder. The Delete method applied to a NoteItem object deletes the specified note. In Word, the expression Application.GoBack would apply the GoBack method to the Application object and move the insertion point back through its last three locations (the same as pressing Shift+F5), one for each execution of the Application.GoBack statement.

In modern parlance, the difference between nouns, adjectives, and verbs has blurred somewhat: nouns take on the appearance of adjectives, verbs get used as nouns, and so on. The same is true of objects, properties, and methods—in some cases it isn't completely clear if a property should in fact be a method, or vice-versa. Only the most obsessive grammarian would deny this blurring in modern language. Only the most obsessive object modeler would deny the blurring in VBA/VBScript.

This can lead to a great deal of confusion. For example, in Outlook, Find is a method (verb); it's also a method in Excel, and this is the way most people would think of it. But in Word, Find is an object (noun). In Excel, Zoom is a property (adjective); in Word, Zoom is an object; and Outlook has no Zoom equivalent in any form.

Don't get too hung up on the terminology, and don't be overwhelmed by the huge number of objects, properties, and methods available in Outlook/VBScript and Office/VBA. The terminology ultimately comes to make some sense. And your work will commonly concentrate on a small subset of all the available objects, properties, and methods.

Application: The Fountainhead of All Objects

NOTE   Every object model has a root object. You can think of it as
              the starting point on a tree diagram, the root of a tree struc-
              ture, the apex of a branching diagram, whatever; it's the en-
              trance to the object model. Typically, this root object has
              the name Application.

Each Office host application's object model begins with the Application object. The Application object represents the entire application. Here's how to find help on the Application object. From inside the Script Editor, start the Microsoft Outlook Visual Basic help file (Help → Microsoft Outlook Object Library Help). Do a Find on "Application" or use the Index to go to the "Application Object" entry (see Figure 8-28).

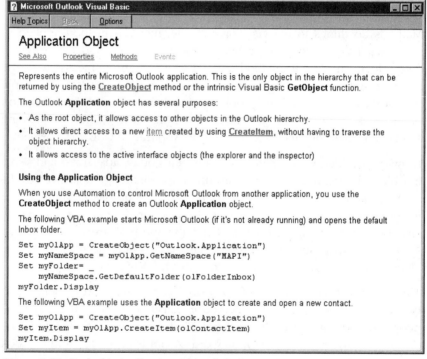

Figure 8-28: Outlook's Application Object help topic

Click on the Properties or Methods links to see a list of all this object's properties and methods, respectively, as shown in Figure 8-29.

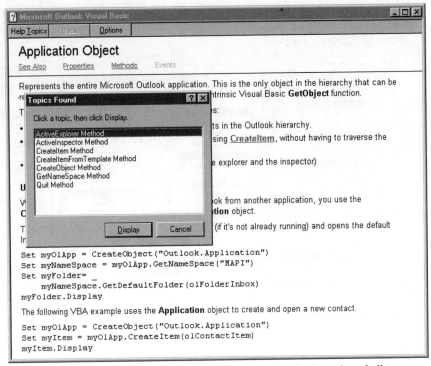

Figure 8-29: Using the Application Object's help topic to display a list of all its methods

To see a graphic of Outlook's entire object model, go to the help index item "Microsoft Outlook," then click on Display and choose "Microsoft Outlook Objects." This topic is in both the Microsoft Outlook Visual Basic and Microsoft Outlook Forms help files (see Figure 8-30).

The Office/VBA help files offer a nice feature not available for Outlook/ VBScript: each object's help topic begins with a simple chart of the current object, its parent object, and its child objects. These images are pop-ups, so when you click on them, you get a convenient list of topics to which you can jump (see Figure 8-31).

You can also use Office/VBA's Object Browser to navigate through and get help on Outlook's object library (more on the Object Browser shortly), or in Outlook 98 use the Outlook-only object browser (from the Script Editor select Script → Object Browser). Outlook 97 doesn't support any object browsers, so you'll have to do this from another Office application.

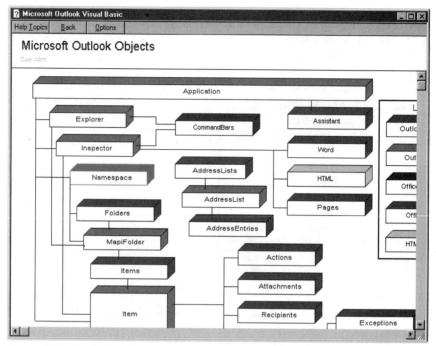

Figure 8-30: Outlook's object model in graphic form

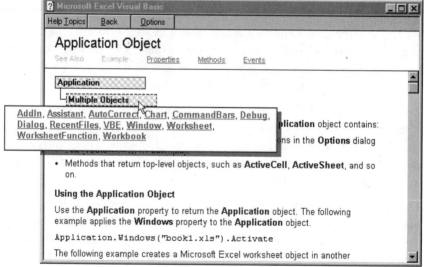

Figure 8-31: A quick look at the objects that belong to Excel's Application object

NOTE

Microsoft has posted detailed diagrams of all the Office 97 component object models on its Web site, along with indispensable information such as the name of the component's object library, help file, and additional notes (see Figure 8-32). We highly recommend you bookmark *www.microsoft.com/officedev/articles/omg/default.htm, http://objects.windx.com* (a Fawcette Technical Publications site), and *www.outlook.useast.com/outlook/OutlookObjectModel.htm.*

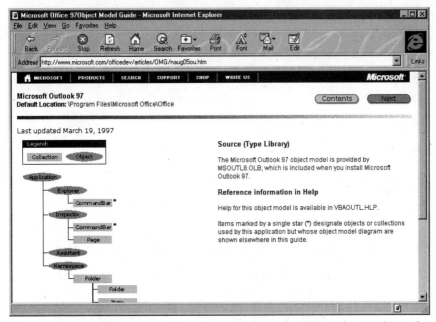

Figure 8-32: Microsoft Outlook 97's object model—on the Web and in sizzling color

Here are some code examples that involve the Application object. Type these examples into the Script Editor and run them one at a time, using the instructions in the section "Creating a New Program."

Example 8-11: Use the Application Object to Create a New Item

```
Option Explicit

Sub CommandButton1_Click
    Demo_CreateNewItem
End Sub

Sub Demo_CreateNewItem
    Dim objItem
    ' create a new standard item (2 = Contact item)
```

Example 8-11: Use the Application Object to Create a New Item (continued)

```
    Set objItem = Application.CreateItem(2)
    ' display it
    objItem.Display
End Sub
```

Example 8-12: Use the Application Object to Display the Active Outlook Window

```
Option Explicit

Sub CommandButton1_Click
    Demo_DisplayActiveWindow
End Sub

Sub Demo_DisplayActiveWindow
    Application.ActiveExplorer.Display
End Sub
```

Example 8-13: Use the Application Object to Shut Down Outlook

```
Option Explicit

Sub CommandButton1_Click
    Demo_QuitOutlook
End Sub

Sub Demo_QuitOutlook
    Application.Quit
End Sub
```

NOTE　　　The help file has this to say about the Quit method: "Closes all currently open windows. The associated Outlook session is closed completely: the user is logged out of MAPI
and any changes to items not already saved are discarded."
If you take the help file literally you might think Outlook
shuts down without warning you about unsaved changes
to open items. Thankfully, like its older Office siblings, it
does warn you for each open item that has pending changes. If you choose Cancel for any such open item, Outlook
continues running uninterrupted, again, just like its Office
siblings.

Office Object Model Anthology

Sooner or later almost every computer program has to interact with the
outside world. Very simple, old-fashioned DOS programs interacted with
the user by waiting for the user to type something and then acting on
whatever key was pressed. They interacted with a printer by writing lines,

one at a time, to the printer's port. They interacted with floppy disks by reading or writing one record of data at a time.

As they became more sophisticated, those old programs rarely interacted with the user directly. Instead, they took advantage of the programs built into DOS so they didn't have to muck around with nit-picking details: the location of a particular file on a hard drive; whether the user hit a backspace to delete the preceding character; or having to spool output to a print file so the program didn't have to constantly check whether the printer was busy. Gradually, programs shifted from working with the user over to working with the operating system. By and large, that was A Good Thing. Sure, the programmer had to learn how to call the operating system, but the additional hassle of figuring out operating system calling conventions far outweighed building your own print spooler from scratch.

Then came Windows, and all hell broke loose. By and large, Windows insulated programs from the user very effectively—so effectively that very few programs attempted to bypass Windows and interact directly with the user. Instead, programmers learned how to use Windows routines— learned how to "call the Windows Application Programming Interface" (or Windows API)—to get things done. The Windows API describes all the routines that can be called by Windows programs, along with a definition of variables to be passed to the routines, and the meaning of the values that should be returned. While it was, and still is, very difficult to write a solid Windows program, much of the complexity was tamed by setting the Windows API in concrete and forcing programmers to work through the Windows API.

Object models in general, and an application object model in particular, take this abstraction one step farther. Where an API defines the routines a program can use, along with their parameters and values, an object model defines the things (objects) a program can manipulate, along with valid operations on the objects. It's a subtle distinction, but one we've found useful for thinking about any Office application object model.

Hidden here is a fundamental secret behind an Office application object model: it makes virtually every nook and cranny of that application available to you for manipulation in your programs, and it does so in a very non-procedural (no, we won't say "object oriented") way. Microsoft has gone to great pains to ensure that the Office application object models describe all the things inside the host application (objects), along with characteristics of those things that you can change (properties), and activities you can perform on the things (methods). It's a significant step forward in the evolution of macro programming languages.

An Office application object model doesn't look like an API, like a set of procedures and their parameters. Instead, an object model's emphasis is strictly on objects, properties, and methods. Lots and lots and lots of objects, properties, and methods.

The Outlook Object Model

NOTE   Here it is, the mother lode...the Outlook object model.

We've already discussed the Application object located at the top of Outlook's object model (refer to Figure 8-30). Beneath it are several objects that contain all the lower objects in the model.

The Explorer and Inspector objects are Outlook's interface objects. The Explorer object is a window that displays a folder's contents. Think of it as your programmatic gateway to the Outlook object the user is working with. In the earlier section on the Application object, one of the code samples (Example 8-12) used the ActiveExplorer method, which returns an Explorer object representing the current explorer and forces it to be displayed. Next, in Example 8-14, we've added a statement to display the name of the active explorer's current folder. Beneath the Explorer object is the MAPIFolder object, which references individual folders; in this example, the CurrentFolder property returns a MAPIFolder object that represents the current folder displayed in the active explorer. To access folders and items without opening them you use the NameSpace object (more on this shortly).

Example 8-14: Working with the Explorer Object

```
Sub Demo_Explorer
    Dim objExplorer
    Set objExplorer = Application.ActiveExplorer
    objExplorer.Display
    MsgBox objExplorer.CurrentFolder.Name
End Sub
```

The Inspector object displays an item, such as a contact or task, and has Item and Pages objects beneath it. Here in Example 8-15 we use the ActiveInspector method to return the top-most inspector object. Then we use the CurrentItem property to return the current item displayed inside that inspector, and access a variety of properties common to all Outlook item types: Subject, MessageClass, and CreationTime.

Example 8-15: Working with the Inspector Object

```
Sub Demo_Inspector
    Dim objCurrentItem
    Dim objInspector
    Set objInspector = Application.ActiveInspector
    Set objCurrentItem = objInspector.CurrentItem
    MsgBox "Current item's subject is " & objCurrentItem.Subject
    MsgBox "Current item's message class is " & _
           objCurrentItem.MessageClass
    MsgBox "Current item's creation time is " & _
           objCurrentItem.CreationTime
End Sub
```

NOTE   If you run this procedure on an as-yet-unsaved mail mes-
         sage item, you'll get a creation time of 1/1/4501. This un-
         usual date is used by Outlook to indicate a date/time field
         that has yet to be assigned a value.

The other main Outlook object below the Application object is the
NameSpace object, referencing Outlook data stored in MAPI format
(currently the only format used by Outlook). NameSpace contains a
Folders collection which in turn contains an Items collection comprised
of individual Item objects. In Example 8-16, we show you how to use the
GetNameSpace method to return a NameSpace object. Next we use the
GetDefaultFolder method to get a MAPIFolder object that's the default
folder of the specified type (6 is the default Inbox mail folder). Then we
point to the item in the Items collection that has an index of 1 (this
happens to be the first item in the folder's list of items, meaning the first
item added to the folder). Notice that when you run this procedure, the
code returns information about the data you requested (the oldest
message in your Inbox) no matter what Outlook's user interface is doing
at the time.

Example 8-16: Working with the NameSpace Object

```
Sub Demo_NameSpace
    Dim objItem
    ' 6 = Inbox mail folder
    Set objItem = _
      Application.GetNameSpace("MAPI").GetDefaultFolder(6).Items(1)
    MsgBox "Item's message class is " & objItem.MessageClass & _
        ", and Item's subject is " & objItem.Subject
End Sub
```

There is a very extensive KnowledgeBase article on the odd implementation of CommandBars in Outlook's object model: "...unlike other

Microsoft Office applications, Outlook 97 command bars cannot be modified through the user interface. In addition, the Outlook object model does not support many of the options that are available through command bars in either the application or forms windows. However, you can access the CommandBars collection through the Outlook object model, allowing you to execute Outlook commands or display particular dialog boxes." For more information about this non-standard implementation, see *OL97: How to Use Command Bars in Outlook Solutions* (Q173604).

NOTE   For a list of the new components of the object model in Outlook 98, look in the "What's New?" topic of the Microsoft Outlook Forms Help file.

Other Office Object Models

NOTE   Since you'll probably be working with another Office application's object model from within Outlook, or using VBA and Automation from another Office application to control Outlook, you need an overview of all the other Office object models. Here goes.

Office 97 is rife with object models. To see them all (at least the ones currently available on your system), take a quick stroll among the dozens of available references from inside any Office/VBA project (you can't do this from inside Outlook). For example, from an Excel VBA project, select Tools → References, then scroll around to see the plethora of object and control libraries that are available to you, as shown in Figure 8-33. Table 8-5 provides a list of all the object models available to you in Office 97 Professional, along with the corresponding descriptive text that appears in the Visual Basic Editor's References dialog box.

It's annoying that the frame along the bottom of the References dialog box truncates the full path shown in the "Location" line. For a particularly long path and filename, you can't see all of it. (For example, it turns out that the default location of the Microsoft DAO 3.5 Object Library is *C:\Program Files\Common Files\Microsoft Shared\DAO\Dao350.dll,* but you'd never know this by looking at this dialog.)

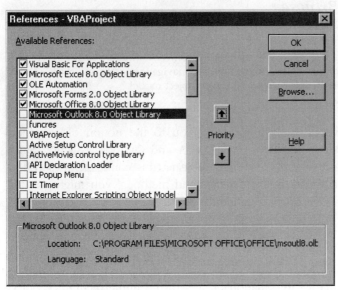

Figure 8-33: The References dialog from inside an Excel/VBA project

Table 8-5: Office object model names plus descriptions

Object Model's Application/Component Name	Description in the References Dialog Box
Access 97	Microsoft Access 8.0 Object Library
Excel 97	Microsoft Excel 8.0 Object Library
Outlook 97	Microsoft Outlook 8.0 Object Library
PowerPoint 97	Microsoft PowerPoint 8.0 Object Library
Shared components available to all Office 97 applications	
Office Assistant	Microsoft Office 8.0 Object Library
Office Binder	Microsoft Binder 8.0 Object Library
Office CommandBars	Microsoft Office 8.0 Object Library
Office FileSearch	Microsoft Office 8.0 Object Library
Other Office 97 components	
Data Access for ODBCDirect Workspaces	Microsoft DAO 3.5 Object Library
Data Access for Microsoft Jet Workspaces	Microsoft DAO 3.5 Object Library
Microsoft Forms (as in "User Forms," meaning dialog boxes)	Visual Basic for Applications
Microsoft Map 97	Microsoft Map
Visual Basic Editor	Microsoft Visual Basic for Applications Extensibility

The Object Browser

NOTE   The Object Browser included in Office/VBA and Visual Ba-
                sic is an indispensable tool for navigating, studying, and
                getting help on an application's object model.

We've spent several pages introducing you to the notion of an object
model and how one relates to Office/VBA and Outlook/VBScript. Since
the Outlook object model contains 29 objects (this count includes collec-
tions), along with numerous properties and methods, you might get the
impression that we've only scratched the surface.

You'd be right. And if you think Outlook's object model is rich, consider
that Excel's object model contains more than 150 objects, and that Office
in its entirety is comprised of more than 550 objects.

Your closest source of information on any of the numerous Office object
models is the Object Browser. It's a frequently-overlooked component of
the Visual Basic Editor. We find it indispensable.

OUTLOOK 98 Outlook 98 includes a rudimentary object browser that
                looks only at Outlook's type library, has no search capabili-
                ties, and—as of the time of this writing—has a dysfunction-
                al help feature. To run it, from the Script Editor select
                Script → Object Browser.

Given Outlook 97's omission of an Object Browser and the limitations of
Outlook 98's own object browser, you'll need to get in the habit of
starting one of the other Office applications, like Excel (see Figure 8-34).

The Office/VBA Object Browser displays all the valid objects, properties,
and methods accessible to your programs. It also has convenient hot links
from the objects, properties, and methods to the online help screens for
each of them (right-click an item in any of the browser's many panes and
choose Help). If you learn to use the Object Browser as your reference of
first resort, you'll stand a fighting chance of writing programs that actually
work.

To get into the Office/VBA Object Browser, go into the Visual Basic
Editor (or open an Access code module) and click View → Object
Browser (or simply hit F2). The interface is decidedly non-standard and a

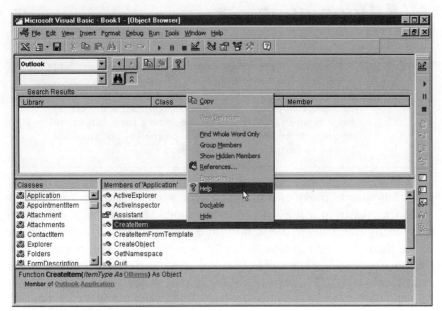

Figure 8-34: The Office/VBA Object Browser looking at the Outlook object model from inside Excel

bit obtuse, but stick with it and you'll have entire object models at your fingertips.

In summary, if you want to learn about the Outlook object model, follow these steps:

1. Manually locate the Application object in the Microsoft Outlook Visual Basic help file. You can also use the Object Browser to jump to a specific Office application's Application object. How fast it is to use the Office Assistant versus the Object Browser in such a case is merely a matter of which one is already running.

2. From the Visual Basic Editor in Excel or another VBA-enabled Office application, select Tools → References, then look for Outlook's type library in the References dialog's list (Microsoft Outlook 98 Object Model) and select it, then click on OK. Now use the Object Browser to focus in on that particular item's library in the Project/Library Box. For example, change it from "<All Libraries>" to "Outlook" and then browse the Classes and Members of... lists, right-clicking and choosing Help from the pop-up menu whenever you want more information on a specific item.

3. Fire up your Web browser and check out *www.microsoft.com/officedev/articles/omg/default.htm* or *http://objects.windx.com*.

OLE Automation

NOTE   OLE Automation is an amazing and powerful development technology for connecting applications. OLE Automation exposes an application's own object model to other OLE Automation applications. So when Excel (call it the *client*) connects up to Outlook (call it the *server*), Excel can examine and control Outlook's objects, properties, and methods through the magic of OLE Automation.

OLE Automation provides a framework for working with an application's object model from inside another application. Although Microsoft—in its perplexing campaign to avoid using the same name for a technology for more than six months—now officially uses the term "Automation," we'll stick with the original tried and true phrase.* In this section, we'll show you how to build a complete Office/VBA application that interacts with and controls Outlook to produce a table (in an Excel worksheet) of all first and second-level folders in the current profile. The table includes each folder's name, parent folder name, count of subfolders, count of items, count of unread items, description, default item type, default message class, entry ID, and store ID. Furthermore, this Office/VBA application can be run from Excel, PowerPoint, or Word with no changes to its code.

PrintFolderList: Use Excel to Interact with and Control Outlook

PrintFolderList is a utility you can run from any application that supports VBA. In a nutshell, it works its way through all of Outlook's primary folders (like Personal Folders), and reports on all its subfolders for each one. The results are put into a nicely formatted listing in a new Excel workbook. We're going to walk you through creating this utility, step by step. We'll do it in Excel so you'll have the opportunity to see what the Office/VBA development environment is like.†

---

* In the progress through Office versions, we had OLE clients, then containers, then controllers, and now back to clients again! OLE servers remained constant throughout, curiously.

† Due to space constraints, we won't be able to spend nearly the time on the Office/VBA development environment as we do in the other books in the series: *Excel 97 Annoyances*, *Office 97 Annoyances*, and *Word 97 Annoyances*.

Step 1: Create a new workbook

Create a workbook to host the VBA project and save it as *Outlook Annoyances.xls*.

Step 2: Create a new VBA project

1. Start the Visual Basic Editor: Tools → Macro → Visual Basic Editor.

2. Make sure the Project Explorer window is visible: View → Project Explorer.

3. In Project Explorer, left-click once on the project in the tree with the name VBAProject (Outlook Annoyances.xls) as shown in Figure 8-35, and choose Tools → VBA Project Properties. Type **OutlookAnnoyances** into the Project Name field, then click on OK. It should now read OutlookAnnoyances (Outlook Annoyances.xls) in the Project Explorer window, as shown in Figure 8-36.

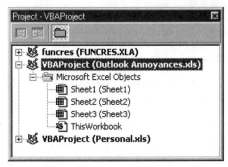

Figure 8-35: Excel's Project Explorer before renaming the project

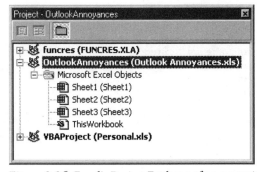

Figure 8-36: Excel's Project Explorer after renaming the project

4. Let's make sure your project (and any others you create from this point on) require explicit variable declaration. Select Tools → Options, and make sure the Require Variable Declaration box is checked, as shown in Figure 8-37, then click on OK.

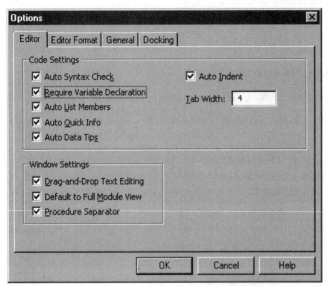

Figure 8-37: The Office Visual Basic Editor's Options dialog box (Editor tab)

Step 3: Create a new module and add code

1. Choose Insert → Module. A new module called Module1 is inserted into your project.

2. Establish a reference to the Outlook object model: Tools → References, check Microsoft Outlook 8.0 Object Library, then click on OK.

3. Type the declarations as shown in Example 8-17.

Example 8-17: Module-level Variables

```
Option Explicit

Declare Function FindWindow Lib "user32" Alias "FindWindowA" _
                (ByVal lpClassName As String, _
                ByVal lpWindowName As String) As Long
Dim blnHighestLevel As Boolean
Dim oxlTargetSheet As Excel.Worksheet
Dim lngRowIndex As Long
Dim strPrompt As String
Dim strTitle As String

' ----- Excel
Const EXCEL8_CLASS_NAME = "XLMain"
Const EXCEL8_OLEAUTO_NAME = "Excel.Application"
Const EXCEL8_SHELL_NAME = "EXCEL"

' ----- Outlook
Const OUTLOOK8_CLASS_NAME = "mspim_wnd32"
Const OUTLOOK8_OLEAUTO_NAME = "Outlook.Application"
Const OUTLOOK8_SHELL_NAME = "OUTLOOK"
```

There are four procedures in this utility:

fintOAAppLoad

> This function uses OLE Automation to load an application if it isn't already running, connect to it if it is already running, and returns an integer indicating final status either way.

PrintFolderList

> The main subroutine for this utility; this is the procedure you'll run to start the utility.

sGatherData

> This subroutine examines certain properties of the passed MAPI-Folder object and writes them to the Excel worksheet.

sOAShutDownApp

> This subroutine shuts down the requested OLE Automation server.

Let's build these procedures now.

1. In Module1's Code Window, select Insert → Procedure, type **fintOAAppLoad**, select the Function option button, leave the Public scope option button selected, then click on OK. Type the code shown in Example 8-18.

   This function uses the Win32 API function *FindWindow* in combination with the application's class name (Outlook's is "mspim_wnd32") as a sneak attack to see if the application is already running or not.[*] OLE Automation is notorious for starting a new instance of an application when you least expect (or want) it to, for unexpectedly closing previously running instances, and for not closing an instance that you *do* want closed. We've empirically studied the behavior of Office 97 applications being started and referenced via OLE Automation both when the application was already running and when it wasn't. We take the design approach of leaving the machine in the state it was in before we (meaning, the *PrintFolderList* utility) came along. This means using the running application if it's already running, and of course leaving it running when done; or if it wasn't already running, we go ahead and start it, interrogate it, then shut it down, all without the user's intervention.

---

[*] For a list of other Office applications' window class names, see the Microsoft KnowledgeBase article *Window Class Names for the Office Applications* (Q169240).

NOTE   The naming convention we use here is to identify function procedures with a lowercase "f" prefix and subroutine procedures with a lowercase "s." The next three letters—for functions only—indicate the return type, e.g., "int" for Integer or "str" for String. That's followed by the rest of its name. So "f" + "int" + "OAAppLoad" = "fintOAAppLoad."

Example 8-18: The fintOAAppLoad Function

```
' --------------------------------------------------------------
' Purpose:  Uses OLE Automation to load an application if it isn't
'           already running, connect to it if it is, and
'           returns an integer indicating final status either way.
'           NOTE: The particular syntax of GetObject() vs.
'           CreateObject() has been empirically tested to yield the
'           ideal expression for each application and version.
'
' Inputs:   objOAServer    - pointer to the server
'           strOAServerName - server's top-level class name, for
'                             example, "Excel.Application" for
'                             Excel 5, 95, 97...
'           strClassName   - the server's Class name, e.g.,
'                             "XLMain" for Excel
'
' Returns:  An integer where ...
'           0 = error
'           1 = was already loaded
'           2 = was *not* already loaded
'
' Updated:  12/04/94
'           11/19/97 (PCG) - switched to using FindWindow API
'           11/19/97 (PCG) - validated for Office 97
'           01/05/98 (PCG) - added Outlook and simplified
' --------------------------------------------------------------
Public Function fintOAAppLoad(objOAServer As Object, _
            strOAServerName As String, strClassName As String) _
                As Integer
    ' ----- Main body
    If strClassName = "" Then
        ' don't allow null to be processed
        fintOAAppLoad = 0
        Exit Function
    End If
    On Error Resume Next
    If FindWindow(strClassName, vbNullString) = 0 Then
        ' the Class name is not found (app is not already running)
        Select Case strOAServerName
            Case EXCEL8_OLEAUTO_NAME
                Set objOAServer = CreateObject(strOAServerName)
            Case OUTLOOK8_OLEAUTO_NAME
                Set objOAServer = CreateObject(strOAServerName)
            Case Else
```

Example 8-18: The fintOAAppLoad Function (continued)

```
                        ' reject any other server class name passed by
                        ' caller
                        fintOAAppLoad = 0
                        Exit Function
            End Select
            fintOAAppLoad = 2
    Else
        ' the Class name is found (app is already running)
        Select Case strOAServerName
            Case EXCEL8_OLEAUTO_NAME
                Set objOAServer = GetObject(, strOAServerName)
            Case OUTLOOK8_OLEAUTO_NAME
                Set objOAServer = CreateObject(strOAServerName)
            Case Else
                ' reject any other server class name passed by
                ' caller
                fintOAAppLoad = 0
                Exit Function
        End Select
        fintOAAppLoad = 1
    End If
    ' make sure there were no OLEAuto errors
    If Err <> 0 Then
        fintOAAppLoad = 0
    End If
End Function
```

2. Save your work (File → Save). As when creating any document or macro, you should always save your work whenever you type more than you'd care to retype. We won't include specific steps for saving your work from here on out.

3. Insert a new, public subroutine procedure named `PrintFolder-List`, and type the code shown in Example 8-19. This subroutine is the main subroutine for the utility and calls the other procedures as needed.

Example 8-19: The PrintFolderList Subroutine

```
' ----------------------------------------------------------------
' Purpose:   A utility you can run from any application supporting
'            VBA. PrintFolderList works its way through Outlook's
'            primary folders (like Personal Folders), and for
'            each one reports on all its subfolders. The results are
'            put into a nicely formatted listing, in a new Excel
'            workbook.
'
' Inputs:    None
'
' Updated:   12/05/97 (PCG)
' ----------------------------------------------------------------
Public Sub PrintFolderList()
```

Example 8-19: The PrintFolderList Subroutine (continued)

```
' ----- Declarations/initializations
Dim blnExcelHost As Boolean
Dim intExcelAppStatus As Integer
Dim intOutlookAppStatus As Integer
Dim oxlApp As Excel.Application
Dim rngHeadings As Excel.Range
Dim oxlWorkbook As Excel.Workbook
Dim oolInnerFolders As Outlook.Folders
Dim oolFolder As Outlook.MAPIFolder
Dim oolFolderLevel2 As Outlook.MAPIFolder
Dim oolNameSpace As Outlook.NameSpace
Dim oolApp As Outlook.Application
Dim strType As String
strTitle = "OutlookAnnoy Folder Lister"


' ----- Main body
' ----- Outlook (handle OLEAuto object references)
' determine Outlook's loaded status and react accordingly
intOutlookAppStatus = fintOAAppLoad(oolApp, _
    OUTLOOK8_OLEAUTO_NAME, OUTLOOK8_CLASS_NAME)
If intOutlookAppStatus = 0 Then
    strPrompt = "Could not connect to " & _
            OUTLOOK8_OLEAUTO_NAME & "."
    MsgBox Prompt:=strPrompt, Buttons:=vbInformation, _
        Title:=strTitle
    Exit Sub
End If
Set oolNameSpace = oolApp.GetNamespace("MAPI")
' test for 0 high-level folders in Outlook, abort gracefully
' if so
If oolNameSpace.Folders.Count = 0 Then
    strPrompt = "There are no folders in Outlook, " & _
        "so there's nothing to report."
    MsgBox Prompt:=strPrompt, _
            Buttons:=vbOKOnly + vbInformation, _
            Title:=strTitle
    ' shut down Outlook (if necessary)
    sOAShutDownApp oolApp, OUTLOOK8_SHELL_NAME, _
                intOutlookAppStatus
    Exit Sub
End If


' ----- Excel (handle OLEAuto object references)
If Application.Name = "Microsoft Excel" Then
    Set oxlApp = Application
    ' when Excel's the host, this is the equivalent of
    '    fintOAAppLoad() returning 1 ("was already loaded")
    intExcelAppStatus = 1
    blnExcelHost = True
Else
    ' determine Excel's loaded status and react accordingly
    intExcelAppStatus = fintOAAppLoad(oxlApp, _
        EXCEL8_OLEAUTO_NAME, EXCEL8_CLASS_NAME)
```

Example 8-19: The PrintFolderList Subroutine (continued)

```
    If intExcelAppStatus = 0 Then
        strPrompt = "Could not connect to " & _
                    EXCEL8_OLEAUTO_NAME & "."
        MsgBox Prompt:=strPrompt, Buttons:=vbInformation, _
            Title:=strTitle
            ' shut down Outlook first (if necessary)
        sOAShutDownApp oolApp, OUTLOOK8_SHELL_NAME, _
                        intOutlookAppStatus
        Exit Sub
    End If
    blnExcelHost = False
End If
' create a new workbook and set a reference to it
Set oxlWorkbook = oxlApp.Workbooks.Add
' set a reference to the new workbook's current sheet
Set oxlTargetSheet = oxlWorkbook.ActiveSheet

' ----- Do some initial formatting of the current sheet
With oxlTargetSheet
    ' put the current user's name in A1
    .Cells(1, 1) = "Outlook's current user name: " & _
        oolNameSpace.CurrentUser
    ' starting in A2, add the column headings
    lngRowIndex = 2
    Set rngHeadings = .Range(.Cells(lngRowIndex, 1), _
        .Cells(lngRowIndex, 10))
End With
rngHeadings.Value = Array("Name", "Parent.Name", _
    "Folders.Count", "Items.Count", _
    "UnReadItemCount", "Description", _
    "DefaultItemType", "DefaultMessageClass", _
    "EntryID", "StoreID")
rngHeadings.Font.Bold = True


' ----- Add the data (starting in A3)
lngRowIndex = lngRowIndex + 1
' walk through each highest-level Folder object in Outlook
'    and all subfolders (if any)
For Each oolFolder In oolNameSpace.Folders
    blnHighestLevel = True
    sGatherData oolFolder
    lngRowIndex = lngRowIndex + 1
    ' iterate through this high-level folder's subfolders,
    '    if there are any
    If oolFolder.Folders.Count > 0 Then
        blnHighestLevel = False
        Set oolInnerFolders = oolFolder.Folders
        For Each oolFolderLevel2 In oolInnerFolders
            sGatherData oolFolderLevel2
            lngRowIndex = lngRowIndex + 1
        Next
        Set oolInnerFolders = Nothing
    End If
```

Example 8-19: The PrintFolderList Subroutine (continued)

```
    Next

    ' ----- Do some additional formatting
    ' AutoFit the entire range we just entered
    oxlTargetSheet.Range("A1").CurrentRegion.Columns.AutoFit
    ' make just cols F, I, and J narrower for readability
    oxlTargetSheet.Range("F:F,I:I,J:J").Select
    ' Note: without the "oxlApp." prefix here, if this code is
    '     running outside Excel, and the host (like Word) has its
    '     own Selection keyword, then you'll get a compile error
    '     "Method or data member not found".
    oxlApp.Selection.ColumnWidth = 25
    oxlTargetSheet.Range("A1").Select

    ' ----- Cleanup
    ' make sure the new workbook is saved; release all Excel
    ' references
    If Not blnExcelHost Then
        ' make sure closing Excel via OLE Automation doesn't lose
        '     the new file
        MsgBox "You must save the new Excel workbook.", _
            vbOKOnly + vbInformation, strTitle
        oxlApp.Visible = True
        Do While oxlApp.Dialogs(xlDialogSaveAs).Show <> True
        Loop
        ' unreference any sub-Application objects before
        Set oxlTargetSheet = Nothing
        Set oxlWorkbook = Nothing
        ' shut down Excel (if necessary)
        sOAShutDownApp oxlApp, EXCEL8_SHELL_NAME, intExcelAppStatus
    Else
        ' all that's required is Set to Nothing to clean up
        Set oxlApp = Nothing
    End If
    ' shut down Outlook (if necessary)
    sOAShutDownApp oolApp, OUTLOOK8_SHELL_NAME, intOutlookAppStatus
End Sub
```

4. Insert a new, private subroutine procedure named **sGatherData**, and type the code shown in Example 8-20. This subroutine is called repeatedly. Its job is simply to gather up the data values of interest about the current folder object and write that data to the Excel worksheet.

Example 8-20: The sGatherData Subroutine

```
' ----------------------------------------------------------------
' Purpose:   Examine certain properties for the passed MAPIFolder
'            object and write them to the Excel worksheet.
'
' Inputs:    oolAnyFolder - a single MAPIFolder
'
' Updated:   12/05/97 (PCG)
```

Example 8-20: The sGatherData Subroutine (continued)

```
' ----------------------------------------------------------------
Private Sub sGatherData(oolAnyFolder As MAPIFolder)
    On Error Resume Next
    With oolAnyFolder
        oxlTargetSheet.Cells(lngRowIndex, 1) = .Name
        If blnHighestLevel Then
            oxlTargetSheet.Cells(lngRowIndex, 2) = _
                        "<<Highest level>>"
        Else
            oxlTargetSheet.Cells(lngRowIndex, 2) = .Parent.Name
        End If
        oxlTargetSheet.Cells(lngRowIndex, 3) = .Folders.Count
        oxlTargetSheet.Cells(lngRowIndex, 4) = .Items.Count
        oxlTargetSheet.Cells(lngRowIndex, 5) = .UnReadItemCount
        oxlTargetSheet.Cells(lngRowIndex, 6) = .Description
        oxlTargetSheet.Cells(lngRowIndex, 7) = .DefaultItemType
        oxlTargetSheet.Cells(lngRowIndex, 8) = .DefaultMessageClass
        oxlTargetSheet.Cells(lngRowIndex, 9) = .EntryID
        oxlTargetSheet.Cells(lngRowIndex, 10) = .StoreID
    End With
    On Error Goto 0
End Sub
```

5. Insert a new, public subroutine procedure named **sOAShutDownApp**, and type the code shown in Example 8-21. This subroutine handles shutting down the OLE Automation server application and de-referencing its associated object variable.

Example 8-21: The sOAShutDownApp() Subroutine

```
' ----------------------------------------------------------------
' Purpose:    Shut down the OLE Automation server.
'
'             NOTE: This proc Sets the server's object variable to
'             Nothing if the server application was already running.
'
' Inputs:     objOAServer  - pointer to the server
'             strShellName - server's shell name
'             intAppStatus - app's loaded status (see fintOAAppLoad)
'
' Updated:    12/05/94
'             11/19/97 (PCG) - validated for Office 97
'             01/05/98 (PCG) - added Outlook and simplified
' ----------------------------------------------------------------
Public Sub sOAShutDownApp(objOAServer As Object, strShellName As
String, _
                        intAppStatus As Integer)
    If intAppStatus = 1 Then
        ' was already loaded so leave it alone
        Set objOAServer = Nothing
        Exit Sub
    End If
    ' trap any error caused by the Quit method
```

Example 8-21: The sOAShutDownApp() Subroutine (continued)

```
    On Error GoTo ErrorTrap
    ' proceed differently depending on the OLEAuto server
    Select Case strShellName
        ' Case ... provide other Case statements as you see fit
        Case EXCEL8_SHELL_NAME
            objOAServer.Quit
        Case OUTLOOK8_SHELL_NAME
            objOAServer.Quit
        Case Else
    End Select
    Set objOAServer = Nothing
    Exit Sub
ErrorTrap:
    Select Case Err
        ' Case ... provide other Case statements as you see fit
        Case Else
            strPrompt = "sOAShutDownApp() encountered " & _
                "Error " & Err.Number & " - " & Err.Description
    End Select
    MsgBox Prompt:=strPrompt, Buttons:=vbExclamation, _
        Title:=strTitle
End Sub
```

Step 4: Take PrintFolderList for a spin

Now that you've finished developing *PrintFolderList*, let's test it:

1. Click your mouse anywhere inside the *PrintFolderList* procedure (between the **Public Sub** and **End Sub** statements) and select Run → Run Sub → UserForm (or press F5).

2. This will run the utility, and in a few seconds (a few more if Outlook wasn't already running) the Outlook folder list will appear (see Figure 8-38).

If you want to test *PrintFolderList* from another Office application, export Module1: right-click on Module1, then choose Export File, pick a location to store the file (it will be named *Module1.bas* by default), and then click on Save. Fire up the other host application, create a new VBA project, then from the Visual Basic Editor choose File → Import File and select *Module1.bas*. Make sure you set References to both the Excel 8.0 and Outlook 8.0 object libraries.

Outlook Calling Word

This macro, written by Helen Feddema, creates a new Word document from a template, and runs a Word/VBA macro which can encapsulate anything you want in the more flexible VBA language. Here are the steps to set up and run this macro:

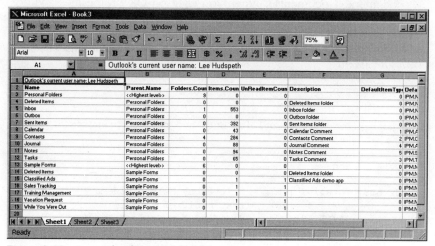

Figure 8-38: A sample of PrintFolderList's output

1. Create a new Outlook form with one command button, change its name to *cmdOutlookToWord,* and add the code shown in Example 8-22.

2. In Word, determine your user templates folder like this: select Tools → Options → File Locations, look at the folder listed for user templates, then click on Cancel when done.

3. In Word, create a new template and save it with the name *OutAnnoy Example.dot* in the same folder you determined in step 2.

4. From that template, select Tools → Macro → Visual Basic Editor. To turn on the Project Window, select View → Project Window.

5. Right-click on the item in the Project Window tree named *TemplateProject (OutAnnoy Example),* then select Insert and choose Module.

6. Type in the code shown in Example 8-23.

7. Select File → Close and Return to Microsoft Word to close the Visual Basic Editor.

8. Select File → Exit and save all changes to close Word.

9. Back in Outlook, publish the form to the forms library of your choice, then run it. You'll see a message box announcing, "This is just an example of how Outlook can remotely manipulate Word and even have it run a VBA macro..." followed by the name of the current

document (Document1). When you click on OK on the message box, Word is made active and visible.

Example 8-22: An Outlook/VBScript Procedure Calling Word and Running a Remote Word/VBA Macro

```
Option Explicit

' ------------------------------------------------------------------
' Purpose:  Demonstrate calling Word and remotely running a Word/
'           VBA macro.
'
' Inputs:   None
'
' Updated:  10/04/97 (HF)  - Written by Helen Feddema
'           01/13/98 (HF)  - Last modified
'           03/05/98 (PCG) - modified for Outlook Annoyances
' ------------------------------------------------------------------
Sub cmdOutlookToWord_Click
    ' ----- Declarations/initializations
    Dim objDocs
    Dim objWord
    Dim strLetter
    Dim strTemplateDir
    strLetter = "OutAnnoy Example.dot"

    ' ----- Main body
    ' ----- Open Word invisibly
    Set objWord = Item.Application.CreateObject("Word.Application")

    ' ----- Pick up Word user templates folder from Registry _
    strTemplateDir = objWord.System.PrivateProfileString("", _
                   "HKEY_CURRENT_USER\Software\Microsoft\Office\ _
                   8.0\Common\FileNew\LocalTemplates", "") & "\"
    strLetter = strTemplateDir & strLetter

    ' ----- Open a new letter based on the selected template
    Set objDocs = objWord.Documents
    objDocs.Add strLetter

    ' ----- Run Word macro
    objWord.Run "TestMacro"
    objWord.Visible = True
    objWord.Activate
    ' Note: this procedure leaves Word running, visible
End Sub

Function Item_Open()
    ' select the P.2 page
    GetInspector.SetCurrentFormPage("P.2")
End Function
```

Example 8-23: The Word/VBA Macro Called Remotely by Outlook in the cmdOutlookToWord_Click Procedure

```
Option Explicit

' --------------------------------------------------------------
' Purpose:   Put this procedure in any VBA module in
'            OutAnnoy Example.dot in Word's User templates folder.
'
' Inputs:    None
'
' Updated:   03/05/98 (PCG) - written for Outlook Annoyances
' --------------------------------------------------------------
Sub TestMacro()
    Dim strPrompt As String
    strPrompt = "This is just an example of how Outlook can " & _
        "remotely manipulate Word and even have it run a VBA" & _
        "macro..." & vbCrLf & vbCrLf
    strPrompt = strPrompt & "The active document's name is " & _
        ActiveDocument.FullName & "."
    MsgBox Prompt:=strPrompt, Buttons:=vbOKOnly + vbInformation, _
        Title:="OutAnnoy Example"
End Sub
```

9

Where and How to Get Help

Since Outlook is a relatively new product, Microsoft itself is often playing catch-up in an attempt to produce topical, current information about Outlook on its Web site. Since Outlook is, obviously, a Microsoft product, that's the place to start (*www.microsoft.com/outlook/*), but always check SlipStick's excellent Exchange/Outlook site next (*www.slipstick.com*), because this site often has even more current information (particularly about add-ins, utilities, and fixes) than Microsoft's site.

The Horse's Mouth

If you have an Outlook problem or question, you might try Microsoft's Product Support staff. In the U.S. the number to call is (425) 635-7145. Be prepared with your Product ID number (click Help → About), and if at all possible be sitting in front of your PC when you call. Keep in mind that, like all the major software companies, Microsoft has started outsourcing its support services, and you might be talking with someone who knows less about Outlook than you do. We've heard a lot of horror stories about PSS over the years; they're good at the basic stuff, but getting answers to complex questions can take forever. Assuming you get an answer at all.

Microsoft maintains several Outlook-related newsgroups on the Net at *msnews.microsoft.com*. The names of the groups change from time to time, but as we went to press the important ones related to Outlook started with *microsoft.public.outlook_beta* and continued for a total of 14 dedicated newsgroups. You can easily access these newsgroups using the

Internet Mail and News reader that comes with Internet Explorer 3.x (which is now melded into Outlook Express that comes with IE 4.x).

NOTE   Microsoft doesn't support these newsgroups. They're "peer to peer," which means the people who provide answers are acting out of the goodness of their hearts. Many of them are quite knowledgeable and have developed large-scale applications, written books of their own, or otherwise exhibited product knowledge of the highest caliber. These folks are typically—though not always—designated as Microsoft MVPs (Most Valued Professionals). Others come across as well-meaning but not terribly well-informed. Keep that in mind as you struggle through your problems.

Surfing the Web

Microsoft puts a lot of effort into its Web site, and as long as you don't mind looking for your own answers, the site can be very helpful. Microsoft's Outlook-related Web pages include the following:

- *www.microsoft.com/outlook/* contains the latest information on Outlook.

- *www.microsoft.com/officedev/* may occasionally have information about Outlook or VBScript (for example, visit *www.microsoft.com/ officedev/articles/omg/default.htm* to see diagrams of all the Office 97 object models).

- *support.microsoft.com/support/*, the Microsoft KnowledgeBase, remains an indispensable source of information, albeit with a pro-Microsoft spin. This is where you can find information on known bugs and problems, as well as tips and techniques for tackling them. Be prepared to deal with Microsoft's extremely annoying "Have you registered with Microsoft.com before?" nonsense. They force you to provide your email address (well, *an* email address anyway) and a Microsoft Product registration number, like the CD key from your copy of Office, before they'll let you see the support pages. It's all free (at least the last time we checked); the Redmond Rangers just want to keep tabs on what you're doing with those pages. Sheesh.

- *www.microsoft.com/vbscript* is the starting point for information about VBScript, including downloads, hot links, FAQs, documentation, and samples.

- *www.microsoft.com/OfficeFreeStuff/* lists the latest Office Assistant characters, Wizards, templates, workbooks, sounds, tools, and add-ons from Microsoft.

Non-Microsoft sites of interest include the following:

- *www.slipstick.com* is dedicated to maintaining an up-to-date list of tips, FAQs, and links on all things Exchange and Outlook.
- *www.outlook.useast.com/outlook/* is the USEast Outlook Developers Site, which according to its home page "is dedicated to providing information and resources to seasoned Outlook developers as well as to those who want to do simple modifications to Outlook."
- *www.activeie.com/oe/* is Eric Miller's site for user tips regarding Outlook Express. Very nice.
- *www.devx.com/* is Fawcette Technical Publications's "Development Exchange" site; these are the folks that publish *Visual Basic Programmer's Journal*.

Every serious Outlook user should have these pages on their browser's Favorites list.

NOTE   Also, as we discussed earlier in the book, make good use of Outlook's Help → Microsoft on the Web cascading menu.

ORK and CBT

In addition to these sources, Microsoft offers some advanced products that can be of use to the dedicated Office user. *The Microsoft Office Resource Kit* (ORK)—billed as "The Professional's Companion to Microsoft Office 97"—is a fair source of technical data on Office and its components, including Outlook. But it is written more for people who support Office in a network environment (Information Systems types) than for the "down in the trenches" users. You can order the ORK through Microsoft Press at (800) 677-7377.

For the developer who's not afraid of computer based training (CBT), there is *Mastering Microsoft Office 97 Development*, a CD-ROM based tutorial (er, "in depth, interactive training," according to the box) for developers. It's not bad for a good overview of the VBA object models, using DAO (data access objects), and the like.

Get *Mastering Microsoft Office 97 Development* from Microsoft's Internet Platform and Tools Division at (800) 621-7930. Ask for part number 087-00047-99.

TechNet

For a fee, Microsoft will send CD-ROMs full of information (some actually quite useful, too) right to your door via U.S. Snail Mail.

The TechNet program delivers two (sometimes more) CDs once a month for $299/year. You get resource kits for various Microsoft operating systems and products, technical notes, reviewers' guides, white papers, drivers, bug reports, and the latest patches. Also included is the Microsoft KnowledgeBase on CD-ROM, as well as numerous case studies from and by companies implementing Office solutions.

Magazines

All three of us write for *PC Computing* and its sister publication, *Office Computing*. We naturally recommend both of these publications for their in-depth coverage of Windows and Microsoft Office. In particular, if you're interested in creating custom solutions in Office with VBA, templates, workbooks, forms, or just about any other technique and appreciate a concise step-by-step approach, *Office Computing* can't be beat. Check *Office Computing*'s Web site at *www.zdnet.com/pccomp/oc/*.

Visual Basic Programmer's Journal provides outstanding monthly coverage of Visual Basic and related languages and development issues. We highly recommend this source. Call (303) 684-0365 (in the U.S.) for subscription information or visit their Web site at *www.devx.com/*.

Microsoft Office & Visual Basic for Applications Developer monthly magazine recently made its debut and focuses, not surprisingly, on developing custom Office applications. Call (916) 686-6610 (in the U.S.) for subscription information or check out *www.informant.com/mod/index.htm*.

Access-Office-VB Advisor is another monthly publication aimed at the Office developer. This magazine has an emphasis on database development using Access, but still covers VB, VBA, and non-Access Office applications. Call (800) 336-6060 (in the U.S.) to subscribe or visit their Web site at *www.advisor.com*.

The Office Annoyances Site

The Office Annoyances site (*www.primeconsulting.com/annoyances/*) is the place to go for the latest on the Office Annoyances books, downloads, updates, etc., covering all your Microsoft Office products. Here you'll find the Annoyances Update page that keeps you posted on the latest news affecting Office users. You can also post questions, comments, or your personal favorite annoyance on the Annoyance Board, our public Web-based bulletin board. Stop by and say "howdy!" We always like to hear from our readers.

WOW

We strongly urge all Annoyances readers to subscribe to WOW, *Woody's Office Watch,* our free weekly electronic bulletin with up-to-the-nanosecond news about Office. From the latest rumors to warnings about viruses, bugs, and patches; to contrarian opinions by Office's most devoted (and knowledgeable!) detractors; to the famous *ask.woody* column, WOW keeps you abreast of the good, the bad, and the ugly sides of Microsoft Office. And the price sure is right.

To subscribe, send email to *wow@wopr.com* or subscribe on the Web at *www.mcc.com.au/wow/index.htm.*

Microsoft Exchange Server

If you're using Outlook as your client software with Microsoft Exchange Server on the back end, you either have someone in your MIS department to turn to for help (lucky you) when dealing with public folders, private folders, offline folders, network security issues, *ad infinitum,* or you yourself may be that lucky individual. Should you find yourself in the latter position feeling dazed and confused, we recommend Sue Mosher's book *The Microsoft Exchange User's Handbook,* published by Duke Communications (ISBN 1-88241-952-9). As Sue describes it, this book "...is aimed at all users of Windows 95 and Windows NT 4.0, whether you're just learning to send mail on the Internet or you're the administrator of a 5,000-mailbox Exchange Server."

The same folks that publish *Windows NT Magazine* (Duke Communications International, Inc.) launched a technical newsletter for Exchange and Outlook administrators in March of 1998. Check it out at *http://www.winntmag.com/exchange.*

Index

F

facility, 146
FAQ
    Rules Wizard, 45
    VBScript, 363
Fast Find, after reinstalling Office, 117
Fatal Exception error during MSN
        session, 101
feedback, 296
fields, Contact, 194
file property, transferring to
        Journal, 122
file, inserting in Journal, 131
filtering
    email, 44
    view, 245
finding, 232
    advanced, 234
    meeting time, 154
    phone number, 239
    (see also filtering, searching)
fintOAAppLoad function, 352
firing events, 318
flagging message, 178
flags, on incoming messages, 264
folder
    hierarchy view, 251
    object, Outlook, 316
    opening on startup, 67
    public, 147
    restoring default, 67
    searching, 236
    size, 228
/folder switch, 67
follow-up alert (see reminder)
For...Next loop counter, 313
form
    commands, 303
    designing, 317
    editing, 298
    exporting, 290
    help, 304
    importing, 290
    managing, 316
    message, 299
    Outlook Forms, 306
    repository, 290
    sample, 302
    saving, 315
    updating, 315
Form Designer, Outlook, 321
Forms.pst, 302
Forward event, 328
FoxPro data, 186
free-form database, 169
From field, changing, 172

G

GetDefaultFolder method, 343
GetDriveType, 287
GetInspector property, 325
GetNameSpace method, 343
GoBack method, 335
GPF, when opening Outlook, 101
grouping, in a view, 247

H

header, message, 262
help, 362
    controls, 307
    forms, 304
    programming files, 290
help desk form, 303
hiding Outlook Bar, 67
hierarchy, of folders, 251
horizontal scroll bar, 253

I

IDE, 289
identifying version, 22
IMEP, 2
IMN, 5, 24
importing
    checklist, 184, 209
    data, 185
    database, 194
    forms, 290
    Outlook Express, 25
    Personal Address Book, 189
    phone numbers, 209
    VBA code modules, 290
Inbox Repair Tool, 4, 40
incoming messages, managing, 263
information service, 97

About the Authors

Woody Leonhard is the author of numerous books, including *Windows 3.1 Programming for Mere Mortals, The Underground Guide to Word for Windows, The Hacker's Guide to Word for Windows, The Mother of All PC Books, The Mother of All Windows Books, Word 97 Annoyances, Excel 97 Annoyances, Office 97 Annoyances,* and several others. He was series editor for Addison-Wesley's *Underground Guides* (11 books) and A-W's *Hacker's Guides* (4 books). He's a contributing editor at *PC Computing* (circulation 1,000,000+) and productivity editor for *Office Computing* (circulation 400,000). He also publishes a free weekly electronic news bulletin on Microsoft Office called WOW ("Woody's Office Watch"), available by sending email to *wow@wopr.com.* Woody's software company makes WOPR, Woody's Office POWER Pack, the Number-One Enhancement to Microsoft Office. A self-described "grizzled computer hack, frustrated novelist, and Office victim," by day he's a Tibetan human rights activist and co-founder of the Tibetan Children's Fund. Woody lives on top of a mountain in Coal Creek Canyon, Colorado.

Lee Hudspeth is co-author of six books on Office, the most recent being *Office 97 Annoyances, Excel 97 Annoyances,* and *Word 97 Annoyances* in the O'Reilly Annoyances series. He is co-founder of PRIME Consulting Group, Inc., of Hermosa Beach, CA (*www.primeconsulting.com*), a company that provides consulting, development, training, and add-ins for Microsoft Office and Windows, and hosts and develops Web sites. An inaugural member of Microsoft's Consultant Relations Program (which evolved into Microsoft's Solution Provider program, of which PRIME Consulting Group was an original member), Lee is a certified Microsoft trainer in Visual Basic and WordBasic. He routinely contributes to *PC Computing* magazine and *Woody's Office Watch,* co-authored the Microsoft Education Services course on Developing Applications in Word, and writes and delivers Office usage and development custom courses to interested parties the world over. Lee is a key architect of PRIME Consulting's Office add-ins PRIME for Excel and PRIME for Word, for which he has written innumerable lines of Visual Basic, VBA, and WordBasic code.

T.J. Lee is co-author of six books on Office, the most recent being *Office 97 Annoyances, Excel 97 Annoyances,* and *Word 97 Annoyances* in the O'Reilly Annoyances series. He is co-founder of PRIME Consulting Group, Inc., of Hermosa Beach, CA (*www.primeconsulting.com*), a company that provides consulting, development, training, and add-ins for Microsoft Office and Windows, and hosts and develops Web sites. T.J. was an inaugural member of Microsoft's Consultant Relations Program (which evolved into Microsoft's Solution Provider program, of which PRIME Consulting Group was an original member), and is a Microsoft Certified Product Specialist and certified Microsoft trainer. He routinely contributes to *PC Computing* magazine and *Woody's Office Watch,* co-authored the Microsoft Education Services course on Developing Applications in Word, has written countless courseware packages and manuals, and has taught and lectured for thousands of developers and end users. T.J. is also a key architect of PRIME Consulting's Office add-ins PRIME for Excel and PRIME for Word.

Colophon

The bird featured on the cover of *Outlook Annoyances* is a herring gull, one of 43 species of gulls. The herring gull is distributed across the Northern Hemisphere, primarily in temperate climates. These attractive gulls have white heads and breasts, blue-gray mantles, and bright yellow bills, with a single red spot on the lower mandible. They have been called vultures of the sea, because they will eat any piece of refuse, offal, or dead fish that comes their way. They rarely catch live fish, although they often catch shellfish and drop them on rocks or hard ground to crack the shells open.

Like all gulls, herring gulls are voracious eaters, and often eat so much that they cannot walk or fly. Sea storms can cause a dearth of food sources, so this gluttony is often necessary for survival for the gulls. Despite their unsavory eating habits, the relationship between herring gulls and humans has often been a beneficial one to the humans. The droppings of these gulls can fertilize soil. For this reason, in 1875, the herring gull colonies on the German islands of Borkum and Langeoog were protected. In Utah in 1848, the crops of Mormon settlers were nearly totally destroyed by a plague of crickets. The crops were saved by the arrival of a flock of gulls, probably herring gulls from California, who consumed all of the crickets. The grateful settlers erected a monument to the gulls, which still stands in Salt Lake City.

Edie Freedman designed the cover of this book, using a 19th-century engraving from the Dover Pictorial Archive. The cover layout was produced with Quark XPress 3.3 using the ITC Garamond font. Whenever possible, our books use RepKover, a durable and flexible lay-flat binding. If the page count exceeds RepKover's limit, perfect binding is used.

The inside layout was designed by Nancy Priest and implemented in FrameMaker by Mike Sierra. The text and heading fonts are ITC Garamond Light and Garamond Book. The illustrations that appear in the book were created in Macromedia Freehand 7.0 and screen shots were created in Adobe Photoshop 4.0 by Robert Romano. This colophon was written by Clairemarie Fisher OLeary.

More Titles from O'Reilly

Annoyances

Windows Annoyances

By David A. Karp
1st Edition June 1997
300 pages, ISBN 1-56592-266-2

Windows Annoyances is a comprehensive, detailed resource for all intermediate to advanced users of Windows 95 and NT version 4.0. This book shows step-by-step how to customize the Win95/NT operating systems through an extensive collection of tips, tricks, and workarounds. Covers **Registry**, **Plug and Play**, networking, security, multiple-user settings, and third-party software.

Word 97 Annoyances

By Woody Leonhard,
Lee Hudspeth & T.J. Lee
1st Edition August 1997
356 pages, ISBN 1-56592-308-1

Word 97 contains hundreds of annoying idiosyncrasies that can be either eliminated or worked around. *Word 97 Annoyances* takes an in-depth look at what makes Word 97 tick and shows you how to transform this software into a powerful, customized tool.

Excel 97 Annoyances

By Woody Leonhard,
Lee Hudspeth & T.J. Lee
1st Edition September 1997
336 pages, ISBN 1-56592-309-X

Excel 97 Annoyances uncovers Excel 97's hard-to-find features and tells how to eliminate the annoyances of data analysis. It shows how to easily retrieve data from the Web, details step-by-step construction of a perfect toolbar, includes tips for working around the most annoying gotchas of auditing, and shows how to use VBA to control Excel in powerful ways.

Office 97 Annoyances

By Woody Leonhard,
Lee Hudspeth & T.J. Lee
1st Edition October 1997
396 pages, ISBN 1-56592-310-3

Office 97 Annoyances illustrates step-by-step how to get control over the chaotic settings of Office 97 and shows how to turn the vast array of applications into a simplified list of customized tools. It focuses on the major components of Office 97, examines their integration or lack of it, and shows how to use this new Office suite in the most efficient way.

Internet for Everyone

The Whole Internet User's Guide & Catalog

By Ed Krol
2nd Edition April 1994
574 pages, ISBN 1-56592-063-5

Still the best book on the Internet. This is the second edition of our comprehensive introduction to the Internet. An international network that includes virtually every major computer site in the world, the Internet is a resource of almost unimaginable wealth. In addition to the World Wide Web, electronic mail, and news services, thousands of public archives, databases, and other special services are available. This book covers Internet basics—like email, file transfer, remote login, and network news. Useful to beginners and veterans alike, also includes a pull-out quick-reference card.

The Whole Internet for Windows 95

By Ed Krol & Paula Ferguson
1st Edition October 1995
650 pages, ISBN 1-56592-155-0

The Whole Internet for Windows 95, the most comprehensive introduction to the Internet available today, shows you how to take advantage of the vast resources of the Internet with Microsoft Internet Explorer, Netscape Navigator, Microsoft Exchange, and many of the best free software programs available from the Net. Also includes an introduction to multimedia for PCs and a catalog of interesting sites to explore.

AOL in a Nutshell

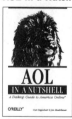

By Curt Degenhart & Jen Muehlbauer
1st Edition June 1998
536 pages, ISBN 1-56592-424-X

This definitive reference breaks through the hype and shows advanced AOL users and sophisticated beginners how to get the most out of AOL's tools and features. You'll learn how to customize AOL to meet your needs, work around annoying idiosyncrasies, avoid unwanted email and Instant Messages, understand Parental Controls, and turn off intrusive advertisements. It's an indispensable guide for users who aren't dummies.

Bandits on the Information Superhighway

By Daniel J. Barrett
1st Edition February 1996
246 pages, ISBN 1-56592-156-9

Most people on the Internet behave honestly, but there are always some troublemakers. Bandits provides a crash course in Internet "street smarts," describing practical risks that every user should know about. Filled with anecdotes, technical tips, and the advice of experts from diverse fields, Bandits helps you identify and avoid risks online, so you can have a more productive and enjoyable time on the Internet.

Smileys

By David W. Sanderson
1st Edition March 1993
93 pages, ISBN 1-56592-041-4

From the people who put an armadillo on the cover of a system administrator book comes this collection of the computer underground hieroglyphs called "smileys." Originally inserted into email messages to denote "said with a cynical smile" :-) , smileys now run rampant throughout the electronic mail culture. They include references to politics 7:^] (Ronald Reagan), entertainment C]:-= (Charlie Chaplin), history 4:-) (George Washington), and mythology @-) (cyclops). They can laugh out loud %-(I) wink ;-) yell :-(0) frown :-(and even drool :-)~

Internet in a Nutshell

By Valerie Quercia
1st Edition October 1997
450 pages, ISBN 1-56592-323-5

Internet in a Nutshell is a quick-moving guide that goes beyond the "hype" and right to the heart of the matter: how to get the Internet to work for you. This is a second-generation Internet book for readers who have already taken a spin around the Net and now want to learn the shortcuts.

How to stay in touch with O'Reilly

1. Visit Our Award-Winning Site

http://www.oreilly.com/

★ "Top 100 Sites on the Web" —*PC Magazine*
★ "Top 5% Web sites" —*Point Communications*
★ "3-Star site" —*The McKinley Group*

Our web site contains a library of comprehensive product information (including book excerpts and tables of contents), downloadable software, background articles, interviews with technology leaders, links to relevant sites, book cover art, and more. File us in your Bookmarks or Hotlist!

2. Join Our Email Mailing Lists

New Product Releases

To receive automatic email with brief descriptions of all new O'Reilly products as they are released, send email to:
listproc@online.oreilly.com
Put the following information in the first line of your message (*not* in the Subject field):
subscribe oreilly-news

O'Reilly Events

If you'd also like us to send information about trade show events, special promotions, and other O'Reilly events, send email to:
listproc@online.oreilly.com
Put the following information in the first line of your message (*not* in the Subject field):
subscribe oreilly-events

3. Get Examples from Our Books via FTP

There are two ways to access an archive of example files from our books:

Regular FTP

- ftp to:
  ftp.oreilly.com
  (login: anonymous
  password: your email address)
- Point your web browser to:
  ftp://ftp.oreilly.com/

FTPMAIL

- Send an email message to:
  ftpmail@online.oreilly.com
  (Write "help" in the message body)

4. Contact Us via Email

order@oreilly.com
To place a book or software order online. Good for North American and international customers.

subscriptions@oreilly.com
To place an order for any of our newsletters or periodicals.

books@oreilly.com
General questions about any of our books.

software@oreilly.com
For general questions and product information about our software. Check out O'Reilly Software Online at **http://software.oreilly.com/** for software and technical support information. Registered O'Reilly software users send your questions to:
website-support@oreilly.com

cs@oreilly.com
For answers to problems regarding your order or our products.

booktech@oreilly.com
For book content technical questions or corrections.

proposals@oreilly.com
To submit new book or software proposals to our editors and product managers.

international@oreilly.com
For information about our international distributors or translation queries. For a list of our distributors outside of North America check out:
http://www.oreilly.com/www/order/country.html

O'Reilly & Associates, Inc.
101 Morris Street, Sebastopol, CA 95472 USA
TEL   707-829-0515 or 800-998-9938
          (6am to 5pm PST)
FAX   707-829-0104

O'REILLY™

Titles from O'Reilly

WEB PROGRAMMING

Advanced Perl Programming
Apache: The Definitive Guide
Building Your Own
 Web Conferences
Building Your Own Website™
CGI Programming for the
 World Wide Web
Designing for the Web
Dynamic HTML:
 The Complete Reference
Frontier: The Definitive Guide
HTML: The Definitive Guide,
 2nd Edition
Information Architecture for the
 World Wide Web
JavaScript: The Definitive Guide,
 2nd Edition
Learning Perl, 2nd Edition
Learning Perl for Win32 Systems
Mastering Regular Expressions
Netscape IFC in a Nutshell
Perl5 Desktop Reference
Perl Cookbook
Perl in a Nutshell
Perl Resource Kit—UNIX Edition
Perl Resource Kit—Win32 Edition
Programming Perl, 2nd Edition
WebMaster in a Nutshell
WebMaster in a Nutshell,
 Deluxe Edition
Web Security & Commerce
Web Client Programming with Perl

GRAPHIC DESIGN

Director in a Nutshell
Photoshop in a Nutshell
QuarkXPress in a Nutshell

JAVA SERIES

Database Programming with
 JDBC and Java
Developing Java Beans
Exploring Java, 2nd Edition
Java AWT Reference
Java Cryptography
Java Distributed Computing
Java Examples in a Nutshell
Java Fundamental Classes
 Reference
Java in a Nutshell, 2nd Edition
Java in a Nutshell, Deluxe Edition
Java Language Reference,
 2nd Edition
Java Native Methods
Java Network Programming
Java Security
Java Threads
Java Virtual Machine

SONGLINE GUIDES

NetLaw   NetResearch
NetLearning   NetSuccess
NetLessons   NetTravel

SYSTEM ADMINISTRATION

Building Internet Firewalls
Computer Crime:
 A Crimefighter's Handbook
Computer Security Basics
DNS and BIND, 2nd Edition
Essential System Administration,
 2nd Edition
Essential WindowsNT
 System Administration
Getting Connected:
 The Internet at 56K and Up
Linux Network
 Administrator's Guide
Managing Internet Information
 Services, 2nd Edition
Managing IP Networks
 with Cisco Routers
Managing Mailing Lists
Managing NFS and NIS
Managing the WinNT Registry
Managing Usenet
MCSE: The Core Exams in a Nutshell
MCSE: The Electives in a Nutshell
Networking Personal Computers
 with TCP/IP
Palm Pilot: The Ultimate Guide
Practical UNIX & Internet Security,
 2nd Edition
PGP: Pretty Good Privacy
Protecting Networks with SATAN
sendmail, 2nd Edition
sendmail Desktop Reference
System Performance Tuning
TCP/IP Network Administration,
 2nd Edition
termcap & terminfo
Using & Managing PPP
Using & Managing UUCP
Virtual Private Networks
Volume 8: X Window System
 Administrator's Guide
Web Security & Commerce
WindowsNT Backup & Restore
WindowsNT Desktop Reference
WindowsNT in a Nutshell
WindowsNT Server 4.0 for
 Netware Administrators
WindowsNT SNMP
WindowsNT User Administration

WEB REVIEW STUDIO SERIES

Designing Sound for the Web
Designing with Animation
Designing with JavaScript
Gif Animation Studio
Photoshop for the Web
Shockwave Studio
Web Navigation:
 Designing the User Experience

UNIX

Exploring Expect
Learning VBScript
Learning GNU Emacs, 2nd Edition
Learning the bash Shell,
 2nd Edition
Learning the Korn Shell
Learning the UNIX Operating
 System, 4th Edition
Learning the vi Editor, 5th Edition
Linux Device Drivers
Linux in a Nutshell
Linux Multimedia Guide
Running Linux, 2nd Edition
SCO UNIX in a Nutshell
sed & awk, 2nd Edition
Tcl/Tk Tools
UNIX in a Nutshell, Deluxe Edition
UNIX in a Nutshell,
 System V Edition
UNIX Power Tools, 2nd Edition
Using csh & tsch
What You Need To Know:
 When You Can't Find Your UNIX
 System Administrator
Writing GNU Emacs Extensions

WINDOWS

Access Database Design
 and Programming
Developing Windows
 Error Messages
Excel97 Annoyances
Inside the Windows 95
 File System
Inside the Windows 95 Registry
Office97 Annoyances
VB/VBA in a Nutshell:
 The Languages
Win32 Multithreaded
 Programming
Windows95 in a Nutshell
Windows97 Annoyances
Windows NT File System Internals
Windows NT in a Nutshell
Word97 Annoyances

USING THE INTERNET

AOL in a Nutshell
Bandits on the Information
 Superhighway
Internet in a Nutshell
Smileys
The Whole Internet
 for Windows95
The Whole Internet:
 The Next Generation
The Whole Internet
 User's Guide & Catalog

PROGRAMMING

Advanced Oracle PL/SQL
 Programming with Packages
Applying RCS and SCCS
BE Developer's Guide
BE Advanced Topics
C++: The Core Language
Checking C Programs with lint
Encyclopedia of Graphics File
 Formats, 2nd Edition
Guide to Writing DCE Applications
lex & yacc, 2nd Edition
Managing Projects with make
Mastering Oracle Power Objects
Oracle8 Design Tips
Oracle Built-in Packages
Oracle Design
Oracle Performance Tuning,
 2nd Edition
Oracle PL/SQL Programming,
 2nd Edition
Oracle Scripts
Porting UNIX Software
POSIX Programmer's Guide
POSIX.4: Programming
 for the Real World
Power Programming with RPC
Practical C Programming,
 3rd Edition
Practical C++ Programming
Programming Python
Programming with curses
Programming with GNU Software
Pthreads Programming
Software Portability with imake,
 2nd Edition
Understanding DCE
UNIX Systems Programming
 for SVR4

X PROGRAMMING

Vol. 0: X Protocol Reference
 Manual
Vol. 1: Xlib Programming Manual
Vol. 2: Xlib Reference Manual
Vol. 3M: X Window System User's
 Guide, Motif Edition
Vol. 4M: X Toolkit Intrinsics
 Programming Manual,
 Motif Edition
Vol. 5: X Toolkit Intrinsics
 Reference Manual
Vol. 6A: Motif Programming
 Manual
Vol. 6B: Motif Reference Manual
Vol. 8 : X Window System
 Administrator's Guide

SOFTWARE

Building Your Own WebSite™
Building Your Own Web Conference
WebBoard™ 3.0
WebSite Professional™ 2.0
PolyForm™

O'REILLY™

TO ORDER: **800-998-9938** • **order@oreilly.com** • **http://www.oreilly.com/**

OUR PRODUCTS ARE AVAILABLE AT A BOOKSTORE OR SOFTWARE STORE NEAR YOU.

FOR INFORMATION: **800-998-9938** • **707-829-0515** • **info@oreilly.com**

International Distributors

UK, EUROPE, MIDDLE EAST AND NORTHERN AFRICA (except France, Germany, Switzerland, & Austria)

INQUIRIES

International Thomson Publishing Europe
Berkshire House
168-173 High Holborn
London WC1V 7AA, UK
Telephone: 44-171-497-1422
Fax: 44-171-497-1426
Email: itpint@itps.co.uk

ORDERS

International Thomson Publishing Services, Ltd.
Cheriton House, North Way
Andover, Hampshire SP10 5BE,
United Kingdom
Telephone: 44-264-342-832 (UK)
Telephone: 44-264-342-806 (outside UK)
Fax: 44-264-364418 (UK)
Fax: 44-264-342761 (outside UK)
UK & Eire orders: itpuk@itps.co.uk
International orders: itpint@itps.co.uk

FRANCE

Editions Eyrolles
61 bd Saint-Germain
75240 Paris Cedex 05
France
Fax: 33-01-44-41-11-44

FRENCH LANGUAGE BOOKS

All countries except Canada
Telephone: 33-01-44-41-46-16
Email: geodif@eyrolles.com

ENGLISH LANGUAGE BOOKS

Telephone: 33-01-44-41-11-87
Email: distribution@eyrolles.com

GERMANY, SWITZERLAND, AND AUSTRIA

INQUIRIES

O'Reilly Verlag
Balthasarstr. 81
D-50670 Köln
Germany
Telephone: 49-221-97-31-60-0
Fax: 49-221-97-31-60-8
Email: anfragen@oreilly.de

ORDERS

International Thomson Publishing
Königswinterer Straße 418
53227 Bonn, Germany
Telephone: 49-228-97024 0
Fax: 49-228-441342
Email: order@oreilly.de

JAPAN

O'Reilly Japan, Inc.
Kiyoshige Building 2F
12-Banchi, Sanei-cho
Shinjuku-ku
Tokyo 160 Japan
Tel: 81-3-3356-5227
Fax: 81-3-3356-5261
Email: kenji@oreilly.com

INDIA

Computer Bookshop (India) PVT. Ltd.
190 Dr. D.N. Road, Fort
Bombay 400 001 India
Tel: 91-22-207-0989
Fax: 91-22-262-3551
Email: cbsbom@giasbm01.vsnl.net.in

HONG KONG

City Discount Subscription Service Ltd.
Unit D, 3rd Floor, Yan's Tower
27 Wong Chuk Hang Road
Aberdeen, Hong Kong
Telephone: 852-2580-3539
Fax: 852-2580-6463
Email: citydis@ppn.com.hk

KOREA

Hanbit Publishing, Inc.
Sonyoung Bldg. 202
Yeksam-dong 736-36
Kangnam-ku
Seoul, Korea
Telephone: 822-554-9610
Fax: 822-556-0363
Email: hant93@chollian.dacom.co.kr

TAIWAN

ImageArt Publishing, Inc.
4/fl. No. 65 Shinyi Road Sec. 4
Taipei, Taiwan, R.O.C.
Telephone: 886-2708-5770
Fax: 886-2705-6690
Email: marie@ms1.hinet.net

SINGAPORE, MALAYSIA, AND THAILAND

Longman Singapore
25 First Lok Yan Road
Singapore 2262
Telephone: 65-268-2666
Fax: 65-268-7023
Email: daniel@longman.com.sg

PHILIPPINES

Mutual Books, Inc.
429-D Shaw Boulevard
Mandaluyong City, Metro
Manila, Philippines
Telephone: 632-725-7538
Fax: 632-721-3056
Email: mbikikog@mnl.sequel.net

CHINA

Ron's DataCom Co., Ltd.
79 Dongwu Avenue
Dongxihu District
Wuhan 430040
China
Telephone: 86-27-3892568
Fax: 86-27-3222108
Email: hongfeng@public.wh.hb.cn

AUSTRALIA

WoodsLane Pty. Ltd.
7/5 Vuko Place, Warriewood NSW 2102
P.O. Box 935,
Mona Vale NSW 2103
Australia
Telephone: 61-2-9970-5111
Fax: 61-2-9970-5002
Email: info@woodslane.com.au

ALL OTHER ASIA COUNTRIES

O'Reilly & Associates, Inc.
101 Morris Street
Sebastopol, CA 95472 USA
Telephone: 707-829-0515
Fax: 707-829-0104
Email: order@oreilly.com

THE AMERICAS

McGraw-Hill Interamericana Editores,
S.A. de C.V.
Cedro No. 512
Col. Atlampa 06450
Mexico, D.F.
Telephone: 52-5-541-3155
Fax: 52-5-541-4913
Email: mcgraw-hill@infosel.net.mx

SOUTHERN AFRICA

International Thomson Publishing Southern Africa
Building 18, Constantia Park
138 Sixteenth Road
P.O. Box 2459
Halfway House, 1685 South Africa
Tel: 27-11-805-4819
Fax: 27-11-805-3648

O'REILLY™

TO ORDER: **800-998-9938** • **order@oreilly.com** • **http://www.oreilly.com/**

OUR PRODUCTS ARE AVAILABLE AT A BOOKSTORE OR SOFTWARE STORE NEAR YOU.

FOR INFORMATION: **800-998-9938** • **707-829-0515** • **info@oreilly.com**

O'Reilly & Associates, Inc.
101 Morris Street
Sebastopol, CA 95472-9902
1-800-998-9938

Visit us online at:
http://www.ora.com/
orders@ora.com

O'REILLY WOULD LIKE TO HEAR FROM YOU

Which book did this card come from?

_____

Where did you buy this book?
❏ Bookstore   ❏ Computer Store
❏ Direct from O'Reilly   ❏ Class/seminar
❏ Bundled with hardware/software
❏ Other _____

What operating system do you use?
❏ UNIX   ❏ Macintosh
❏ Windows NT   ❏ PC(Windows/DOS)
❏ Other _____

What is your job description?
❏ System Administrator   ❏ Programmer
❏ Network Administrator   ❏ Educator/Teacher
❏ Web Developer
❏ Other _____

❏ Please send me O'Reilly's catalog, containing
a complete listing of O'Reilly books and
software.

Name _____ Company/Organization _____

Address _____

City _____ State _____ Zip/Postal Code _____ Country _____

Telephone _____ Internet or other email address (specify network) _____

Nineteenth century wood engraving
of a bear from the O'Reilly &
Associates Nutshell Handbook®
Using & Managing UUCP.

BUSINESS REPLY MAIL
FIRST CLASS MAIL   PERMIT NO. 80   SEBASTOPOL, CA

Postage will be paid by addressee

O'Reilly & Associates, Inc.
101 Morris Street
Sebastopol, CA 95472-9902